SPAIN

NATIONS OF
THE MODERN WORLD: EUROPE

edited by W. Rand Smith and Robin Remington

This series examines the nations of Europe as they adjust to a changing world order and move into the twenty-first century. Each volume is a detailed, analytical country case study of the political, economic, and social dynamics of a European state facing the challenges of the post–Cold War era. These challenges include the changing values and rising expectations, the search for new political identities and new avenues of participation as well as growing opportunities for economic and political cooperation in the new Europe. Emerging policy issues such as the environment, immigration, refugees, and reordered national security priorities are evolving in contexts still strongly influenced by history, geography, and culture.

The former East European nations must cope with the legacies of communism as they attempt to make the transition to multiparty democracy and market economies amid intensifying national ethnic, religious, and class divisions. West European nations confront the challenge of pursuing economic and political integration within the European Union while contending with problems of economic insecurity, budgetary stress, and voter alienation.

How European nations respond to these challenges individually and collectively will shape domestic and international politics in Europe for generations to come. By considering such common themes as political institutions, public policy, political movements, political economy, and domestic-foreign policy linkages, we believe the books in this series contribute to our understanding of the threads that bind this vital and rapidly evolving region.

SPAIN

Democracy Regained

SECOND EDITION

E. Ramón Arango

Westview Press

BOULDER • SAN FRANCISCO • OXFORD

Nations of the Modern World: Europe

All photos are courtesy of Office of Information, Spanish Embassy, Washington DC.

Published in 1995 in the United States of America by Westview Press, Inc., 5500 Central Avenue, Boulder, Colorado 80301-2877, and in the United Kingdom by Westview Press, 12 Hid's Copse Road, Cumnor Hill, Oxford OX2 9JJ

Library of Congress Cataloging-in-Publication Data
Arango, E. Ramón (Ergasto Ramón)
    Spain : democracy regained / E. Ramón Arango. — 2nd [rev.] ed.
        p.   cm. — (Nations of the modern world. Europe)
    Rev. ed. of: Spain, from repression to renewal. 1985.
    Includes bibliographical references (p.   ) and index.
    ISBN 0-8133-1465-8
    1. Spain—Politics and government—1975–   2. Spain—History.
I. Arango, E. Ramón (Ergasto Ramón). Spain, from repression to
renewal.   II. Title.   III. Series.
DP272.A7   1995
946.08—dc20   95-8694
                                                                                CIP

Printed and bound in the United States of America

        The paper used in this publication meets the requirements
    ∞   of the American National Standard for Permanence of Paper
        for Printed Library Materials Z39.48-1984.

10   9   8   7   6   5   4   3   2   1

For J. Taylor Rooks

Contents

Tables and Illustrations

Acknowledgments

I wish to thank Margaret Charlet Ganier for her professionalism and expertise and for the generosity with which she shared them. This book would not have been completed so expeditiously without her valuable assistance.

E. Ramón Arango

Acronyms

ACNP	Asociación Católica Nacional de Propagandistas; National Catholic Association of Propagandists
AIC	Agrupación Independiente Canaria; Canary Independence Association
AISS	Administración de Instituciones de Servicios Socio-Profesionales; Office of Institutions of Social-Professional Services
AMI	Acuerdo Marco Interconfederal; Interconfederal Outline Agreement
ANE	Acuerdo Nacional Sobre Empleo; National Agreement on Employment
AP	Alianza Popular; Popular Alliance
BIS	Brigada de Investigación Social; Social Investigation Brigade
CAMPSA	Compañía Arrendataria Monopolio de Petróleos; Regulatory Company of Petroleum Monopoly
CARS	Centro de Arte Reina Sofía; Queen Sofía Center of Art
CCOO	Comisiones Obreras; Workers' Commissions
CDS	Centro Democrático Social; Democratic and Social Center
CEDA	Confederaciones Españolas de Derechas Autónomas; Spanish Confederation of Rightist Autonomous Parties
CEOE	Confederación Española de Organizaciones Empresariales; Spanish Confederation of Business Organizations
CG	Coalición Gallega; Galician Coalition
CIS	Centro de Investigaciones Sociológicas; Center of Sociological Investigations
CiU	Convergencia i Unió; Convergence and Union

CP	Coalición Popular; Popular Coalition
CSIC	Consejo Superior de Investigaciones Científicas; High Council for Scientific Investigation
CT	Compensación Transitoria; interim compensation
DGPE	Dirección General del Patrimonio del Estado; General Directorate of State Assets
EA	Euzko Alkartasuna; Basque Solidarity
EC	European Community
EE	Euzkadiko Ezkerra
EEC	European Economic Community
ER	Esquerra Republicana; Republican Left
ERC	Esquerra Republicana de Catalunya; Republican Left of Catalonia
ETA	Euzkadi Ta Azkatasuna; Basque Fatherland and Freedom
ETA-militar	a Basque terrorist group
ETA-político-militar	a Basque terrorist group
FCI	Fondo de Compensación Interterritorial; Interterritorial Compensation Fund
FE de las JONS	Falange Española de las Juntas de Ofensiva Nacional-Sindicalista
FET y de las JONS	Falange Española Tradicionalista y de las Juntas de Ofensiva Nacional-Sindicalista
FGD	Fondo de Garantía de Depósitos; Deposit Guaranty Fund
FP	Federación Progresista; Progressive Federation
GAL	Grupo Anti-Terrorista de Liberación; Anti-Terrorist Liberation Group
GCJP	Consejo General del Poder Judicial; General Council of the Judiciary Power
GDP	gross domestic product
GRAPO	Grupo de Resistencia Antifascista Primero de Octubre; First of October Anti-Fascist Resistance Group
HB	Herri Batasuna; Popular Unity
INC	Instituto Nacional de Colonización; National Institute of Land Development
INH	Instituto Nacional de Hidrocarburos; National Institute for Hydrocarbons
INI	Instituto Nacional de Industria; National Institute of Industry
IRA	Instituto de Reforma Agraria; Institute of Agrarian Reform

IU	Izquierda Unida; United Left
JEMAD	Jefe del Estado Mayor de la Defensa; Chief of the Defense Staff
JUJEM	Junta de Jefes del Estado Mayor; Joint Chiefs of Staff
KAS	Koordinadora Abertzale Sozialista; Patriotic Socialist Front
LBE	Ley Básica de Empleo; Basic Employment Act
LOAPA	Ley Orgánica de Armonización del Proceso Autonómico; Organic Law for the Harmonization of the Process of Autonomy
LODE	Ley Orgánica del Derecho a la Educación; Organic Law on the Right to an Education
LOFCA	Ley Orgánica de Financiación de las Comunidades Autónomas; Organic Law on the Financing of the Autonomous Communities
LRU	Ley de Reforma Universitaria; Law of University Reform
MUC	Mesa para la Unidad Comunista; Round Table for Communist Unity
NATO	North Atlantic Treaty Organization
NI	Nueva Izquierda; New Left
OECD	Organization for Economic Cooperation and Development
OPEC	Organization of Petroleum Exporting Countries
PA	Partido Andaluz; Andalucian Party
PAD	Partido Acción Democrático; Democratic Action Party
PAR	Partido Aragonés Regionalista; Aragonese Regional Party
PASOC	Partido de Acción Socialista; Socialist Action Party
PC	Partido Carlista; Carlist Party
PC	Partido Comunista; Communist Party
PCE	Partido Comunista Español; Spanish Communist Party
PCERM	Partido Comunista de España Revolucionario Marxista; Revolutionary Marxist Communist Party of Spain
PCOE	Partido Comunista Obrero Español; Spanish Worker's Party
PCPE	Partido Comunista de los Pueblos de España; Communist Party of the Peoples of Spain

PDL	Partido Democrático Liberal; Liberal Democratic Party
PDP	Partido Democrático Popular; Popular Democratic Party
PEN I	Plan de Energía Nacional I
PL	Partido Liberal; Liberal Party
PNV	Partido Nacionalista Vasco; Basque Nationalist Party
PP	Partido Popular; Popular Party
PRI	Partido Revolucionario Institucional; Institutionalized Revolutionary Party
PSA	Partido Socialista de Andalucía; Socialist Party of Andalucia
PSOE	Partido Socialista de Obrero Español; Spanish Socialist Worker's Party
PSP	Partido Socialista Popular; Popular Socialist Party
PSUC	Partido Socialista Unificado de Cataluña; Unified Socialist Party of Catalonia
PTE	Partido de los Trabajadores de España; Workingmen's Party of Spain
RENFE	Red Nacional de Ferrocarriles Españoles; National Network of Spanish Railroads
RTVE	Spanish Radio-Television
SA	Sociedades Anónimas; Anonymous Societies
SA–AESA	Astilleros Españoles; Spanish Shipyards
SA–CAMSA	Compañía Arrendataria del Monopolio Petróleos; Leasing Company for the Petroleum Company
SA–ENDESA	Empresa Nacional de Eletricidad; National Electrical Enterprise
SA–ENP	Empresa Nacional de Petróleos; National Petroleum Enterprise
SA–ENSIDESA	Empresa Nacional Siderúrgica; National Steel Enterprise
SA–HUNOSA	Empresa Nacional Hulleras del Norte; National Northern Coal Mining Enterprise
SA–Iberia	Líneas Aéreas de España; Spanish Airlines
SA–Petroliber	Compañía Ibérica Refinadora de Petróleos; Iberian Petroleum Refining Company
SA–SEAT	Automóviles de Turismo; Spanish Society of Touring Cars
SCP	Servicio de Concentración Parcelaria; Land Parcel Consolidation Service
SEAT	Sociedad Española de Automóviles de Turismo

SMIG	Salario Mínimo Interprofesional Garantizado; guaranteed minimum wage
SNT	Servicio Nacional de Trigo; National Wheat Service
UC	Unidad Comunista; Communist Unity
UCD	Unión del Centro Democrático; Democratic Center Union
UGT	Unión General de Trabajadores; General Workers' Union
UMD	Unión Militar Democrática; Democratic Military Union
UN	Unión Nacional; National Union
UPC	Unión del Pueblo Canario; Union of the Canary People
UV	Unión Valenciana; Valencian Union
VAT	value-added tax

SPAIN

Introduction

"Spain is a miracle: one of the handful of countries that since World War I has escaped the economics, the politics, and the culture of poor capitalism."[1] Spain did escape—but only after suffering perils that might have destroyed a lesser nation and a lesser people: the dictatorship of Miguel Primo de Rivera; the disaster that was the Second Republic; the agony of the Civil War; and the seemingly interminable Franco regime that, for a time, brought down upon Spain (and by extension, upon Spaniards) condemnation and ostracism by all of the nations of the world save one, Argentina. But as Ray Alan has written: "Spaniards are one of the world's primary peoples, and their political and cultural eclipse under General Franco could only be temporary."[2]

Today, Spain has once again assumed an honorable place among the important nation-states of the world. True enough, it will never again be what it was in the sixteenth century—its *Siglo de Oro* ("Golden Century"). But then, France will never again be what it was in the eighteenth century, and Great Britain will never recapture the stature it had in the nineteenth. And Paul Kennedy says that the United States will never again be what it was only yesterday, in the middle of the twentieth century.[3] Spain is, today, a self-assured and integral part of the interdependent nations of Western Europe, an area that is a magnet for the countries of Eastern Europe and for Russia. For these countries only recently emerged from oppression, Spain is a paragon: a nation that has successfully made the transition from repression to renewal.[4]

The Spain that emerged from the transition is different from what it was before, different even from itself. The old, "different Spain" was an image projected by the tourist industry that sought to entice visitors and their currency to a land of castles and cathedrals, flamenco and guitars, bullfights, mantillas and carnations, picture-book villages seemingly untouched by time, and austere cities where life seemed to be locked away behind stone walls and iron gates. The image was not wholly inaccurate, but it was an image from the past that had somehow come little changed

1

into the present. This image-as-reality was a projection encouraged by Francisco Franco, who overlaid it with a militant religiosity and a sense of moral superiority untainted by the modern world. Spaniards both scoffed at and believed in their image—much as they approached their religion—because it was essentially the only Spain they were officially allowed to acknowledge. For a long time, the world was kept away—except to come, look, and leave—effectively insulating Spain and giving it a hermetic atmosphere that natives often found stifling but visitors found restorative, the anodyne to modernization.

That Spain no longer exists, or rather, the mentality of that Spain no longer exists. The externals of the old different Spain are still there, still enjoyed both by visitors (who often see little else) and by natives alike. But Spaniards enjoy the old different Spain much like adults enjoy Christmas. The new different Spain, the real Spain, is like the other 364 days of the year.

It is paradoxical that Franco himself unwittingly initiated the breakdown of old Spain when he allowed the transformation of the economy to begin in the late 1950s. He did not realize that the modernization he set in motion in the world of finance and economics would have a systemic effect that would eventually transform the rest of Spanish life and set Spain irreversibly in the direction of revolutionary change.

The new Spain can only be understood, however, by placing it within the context of eternal Spain, the land and the people that have remained constant.

ETERNAL SPAIN

THE LAND

Spain has a total land mass of 517,069 square kilometers, including two archipelagos—the Balearic Islands in the Mediterranean and the Canary Islands in the Atlantic—that are politically integral parts of the country. After Switzerland, Spain has the highest average elevation in Europe; its lowlands are limited to the valley of the Guadalquivir River, parts of the valley of the Ebro River, and a thin edge of coast along the Mediterranean and the Bay of Biscay. Approximately 20 percent of Spanish territory is 1,000 meters or more above sea level; 40 percent is between 500 and 1,000 meters; and 40 percent is under 500 meters. Ten percent of the land is bare rock; 35 percent is virtually unproductive due to high altitude, sparse rainfall, or poor soil. Forty-five percent is moderately productive, but even in those areas, water is scarce and topographical conditions are difficult. Only 10 percent of Spanish soil is of exceptionally good quality. By

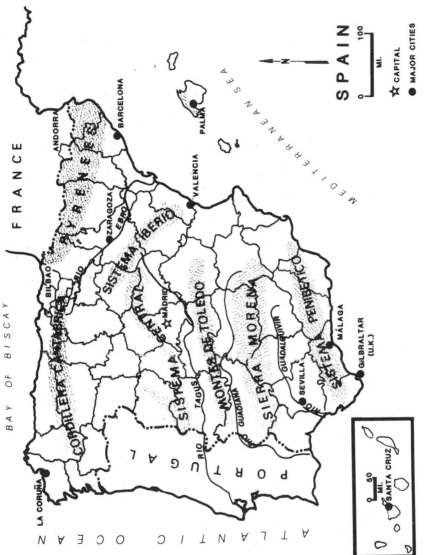

Rivers, Mountains, and Provinces

contrast, France, which is only slightly larger than Spain (including the archipelagos), has about double the amount of productive land.[5]

The Central Meseta

It is not the extreme height of the mountains, however, that gives Spain its topographical character. Its tallest peaks—the Mulacén in the Sierra Nevada, near Granada, and the Pico de Aneto in the Pyrenees—are only 3,480 meters and 3,390 meters, respectively, yet the elevation of the Iberian Peninsula is so high that the average altitude of Spain is 660 meters. The dominant topographic structure of Spain is, in fact, the high interior tableland, the *meseta,* which ranges from 518 to 823 meters above sea level. The central *meseta* occupies 210,000 square kilometers, a little less that 50 percent of the total area of peninsular Spain. The *meseta* is divided by the gaunt central sierras; the most prominent are the Sierra de Guadarrama and the Sierra de Gredos, which arch to an altitude of nearly 2,743 meters and run from the southwest to the northeast of Madrid. The northern, smaller portion of the *meseta* includes León and Old Castile; the vast southern portion encompasses New Castile, La Mancha, and Extremadura. This massive plateau dominates the country's geography and is responsible for the climate, rainfall, temperature, and vegetation that are the most characteristically Spanish. The *meseta* has also dominated Spanish history and politics, and it has influenced the national character sufficiently to make the "average" Spaniard more Castilian than Andalucian, Aragonese, Galician, Catalan, or Basque.

The *meseta* is a relentless and uninviting land, and life there has been, for the most part, an elemental struggle to survive. The *meseta* constitutes the major part of what is called "dry Spain," and most of the plateau receives no more than 51 centimeters of rainfall a year. The "continental" climate produces intensely hot summers and bitterly cold winters, with wide variations of temperature between day and night during both seasons. January lows average about 1.2°C; in the summer, temperatures often rise to 37.7°C at midday and then drop to 21.2°C during the night. Sparse and stunted *matorral* ("thicket") is the natural vegetation of the parched tableland. Where there is sufficient water, evergreen shrubs may grow as well, and stands of dwarf oak and conifers form modest woodlands in some areas. But where water is scarce, so is plant life. In dry Spain, the scarcity of water is compounded by its seasonal irregularity, for the heaviest rainfall does not coincide with the highest temperatures. In other words, in dry Spain, the growing season has the least amount of rainfall, making irrigation a necessity and an added expense. Wheat is the primary cultivated crop, and potatoes, barley, and rye are grown in certain areas. In La Mancha around Valdepeñas, extensive vineyards produce large quantities of undistinguished wine. Sheep, goats, and pigs are raised on the *meseta*, but the most exotic livestock are the fighting bulls, bred there, as in Andalucia, for the ring.

Andalucia and the Guadalquivir River Valley

The *meseta* ends in the south at the Sierra Morena. Between these mountains, which for centuries impeded movement to and from the *meseta*, and the Betic Cordillera, which defines the southern Mediterranean coast and includes the Sierra Nevada, lies the valley of the Guadalquivir River in the region of Andalucia. This is Arab Spain, today's tourist Spain. The color and vibrancy that the casual traveler mistakenly associates with all of the country is found here, and though the imagery of heat, sun, cool water, and shaded patios is inaccurate beyond Andalucia and parts of the Mediterranean coast, it does give evidence of the extreme variety and vivid contrasts to be found on the Iberian Peninsula. The climate of Andalucia is more benign than that of the *meseta*. The summers can be searingly hot, but the winters are mild, with January temperatures in the range of 10° to 15.6°C. Summer temperatures along both the Atlantic and the Mediterranean coasts may rise to 37.7°C. Away from the gentling influences of the ocean and the sea, the inland area between Seville and Córdoba—called by natives "the African frying pan"—has been subjected to temperatures higher than 43.3°C; it is heated by the Leveche, a hot, arid, and sometimes dust-filled wind blowing from North Africa.

Like the *meseta*, Andalucia is part of dry Spain, but the natural vegetation there is Mediterranean, not continental. Where water is sufficient, oak, pine, and even dwarf palms grow; where water is scarce, the natural vegetation is primarily scrub. Olives, which grow throughout most of dry Spain, are cultivated most extensively in Andalucia. In fact, Jaén, close to the eastern apex of the Guadalquivir Valley, is the center of the largest olive-producing region in the world. Grapes also thrive in Andalucia, but with the exception of Málaga wines and the extraordinary sherry produced around Jerez de la Frontera in the province of Cádiz, Andalucian wine is inferior.

The land along the Guadalquivir, tilled since a millennium before Christ, began to flourish after the Arabs arrived in 711 A.D. and developed the *huerta*. The *huerta* (Latin) or *vega* (Arabic) is irrigated, intensely cultivated land that still produces most of the same crops as were grown in Muslim times: onions, artichokes, asparagus, strawberries, pomegranates, figs, melons, oranges, lemons, sugar (cane and beet), rice, and tobacco (this last crop was unknown to the Arabs). The *huertas* may be found almost anywhere in dry Spain where good soil can be irrigated, and they still produce the highest agricultural yields in Spain.

The Maritime Zone

North of the central *meseta*, extending from the Pyrenees in the east through the Basque lands and Asturias to Galicia on the northwestern corner of the peninsula, is maritime Spain. The least known part of the country to the present-day traveler, this region should give the final lie to the image of Spain as all sun, heat, and aridity. This is "wet Spain," complete with a temperate climate, relatively mild winters, and comfortably warm summers. Winter temperatures on the coast range between 7.2° and 10°C; summer temperatures range between 18.3° and 21.2°C. It rains in this region every month of the year, with a regularity and dependability unknown throughout the rest of the country, and the sky is often overcast, softening the light and giving the region a mild and mellow atmosphere.

The outstanding topographic feature of maritime Spain is its mountains. In the east, the Pyrenees, which resemble the Alps, rise to 3,390 meters in the Pico de Aneto. The average height throughout most of the range is 1,525 meters. West of the Pyrenees and beyond the lower Basque Mountains lie the vast Cantabrian Mountains, which are almost as high as the Pyrenees. The Cantabrian *Picos de Europa* ("Peaks of Europe"), so named because they are supposedly the first European mountains one sees when approaching the continent from the ocean, rise to 2,648 meters. The Cantabrian chain slopes down in the west to the plateau of Galicia, which ends at the sea, forming a coastal landscape of rocky shore and pounding surf in many places.

The natural vegetation is like that of much of Atlantic Europe, with oak, chestnut, and beech trees and open grassland. Higher up, in the piedmont of the Cantabrian and Pyrenean chains, there are heathlands and peat bogs, and higher still are conifers. At the summit of the mountains, one finds true Alpine vegetation. Cultivated crops include corn, rye, potatoes, some wheat, apples (primarily used for cider in Asturias), and grapes (used in local wine). Pigs and cattle are the major livestock, and the largest dairy farms in Spain, supplying most of the nation's milk and cheese, are found here. The Galicians are also the fishers of Spain, and the waters off Galicia furnish the extraordinary variety of fish and shellfish that makes Spaniards the largest consumers of seafood in Europe.

The Ebro River Valley

Between the Pyrenees to the north and the massive and forbidding Iberian Mountains to the south lies the trough carved by the Ebro River, which drops from its source in the Cantabrian Mountains to empty into the Mediterranean south of Barcelona. In general, the climate of the valley is continental, like that of the central *meseta*, and the seasonal and unreliable rainfall is rarely heavier than 41 centimeters a year. The scanty natural vegetation is due to this aridity, and much of the landscape is badlands, with deeply furrowed and fantastically shaped hills cut by arroyos, which are dry except in flood times. With irrigation, however, certain areas of the valley are fertile, and the *huertas* of Zaragoza and Lérida, like those in the Guadalquivir Valley, are extremely productive. With proper protection against the cold, almost any crop that does well in Spain, including subtropicals, can be grown on these *huertas*. The Rioja Basin in the upper valley produces the finest table wine in Spain.

The Levant

The Levant is the purest Mediterranean region of Spain. It lies along the eastern coast from the mouth of the Ebro River to the Cabo de Gata below Almería. Like the *meseta* and Andalucia, the Levant is a part of dry Spain, with annual rainfall between 38 to 63.5 centimeters. But between Cabo de Nao (halfway between Valencia and Alicante) and Cabo de Gata, precipitation decreases so dramatically that dry terrain becomes semiarid, and the rainfall is no more than 10.2 to 12.7 centimeters, the lowest in Europe. The semiarid zone is like a small piece of North Africa in Europe. The climate and vegetation resemble that of Andalucia, but average temperatures drop as one moves north toward Catalonia, and in the semiarid zone, esparto grass replaces scrub as the most common natural plant. Cultivated vegetation grows close to streams or in irrigated *huertas* such as the ones found in the Guadalquivir and Ebro Valleys. Murcia, Lorca, and Alicante are major *huertas,* and the *huerta* of Valencia contains what is probably the richest soil in Spain. Crops include tobacco, cotton, noncitrus and citrus fruits, almonds, sugar, rice, cereals, olives, grapes, mulberries, and hemp. But dates are the special crop, grown in Elche in the oasislike *Huerta del Cura,* the largest grove of date palms on the European continent. Gazing at the *Huerta del Cura,* an unknowing visitor might well believe this land to be Arabia.

THE PEOPLE

The origins of the earliest inhabitants of Spain remain mysterious. No one is certain who the Iberians or the Basques are—or where they came from. Roger Collins asks, without providing definitive answers, whether the Basques are survivors or migrants. As the former, they would "constitute the sole survivors of the pre-Indo-European population of Europe [who] somehow succeeded in surviving the period of Indo-European migrations in the Bronze Age (c. 2500 B.C.–1000 B.C.) that otherwise swamped the material and linguistic culture of their late Stone Age relatives, leaving them a peculiar island of antiquity in a sea of newer people."[6]

As immigrants, the Basques might be the descendants of the Iberians, who some anthropologists believe came to Spain from North Africa through Andalucia; others contend they came from Georgia in the Caucasus Mountains and moved through central Europe to settle in Spain.[7] Whatever their origin, the Iberians dispossessed the Ligurians, the earliest people known to have lived on the Spanish peninsula.[8]

If the Basques are of Iberian origin, then, because of their physical isolation in the remote mountains of northern Spain, they maintained characteristics that became modified in the Iberians who settled the rest of Spain and formed a racial amalgam with the Celts (who came later), to form the Celtiberian. The difference between the Basques and the Celtiberians can be found, among other distinctions, in the blood of the Basques: It has a higher incidence of blood type O and a lower incidence of blood type B than that of any other European people, as well as the highest incidence of Rh-negative blood of any ethnic people in the world.[9] Most Basques consider themselves to be the oldest and purest race in Europe.[10]

The Phoenicians were the first people who can be accurately accounted for historically. They migrated in the eleventh century B.C. from what is today Syria and Lebanon, attracted by the copper, gold, mercury, and silver in the area now known as now Andalucia. The Phoenicians came primarily as traders, not as colonists, yet they lived along the southern Atlantic and Mediterranean coasts of Spain for almost six centuries. The Greeks arrived in the eighth century B.C. Like the Phoenicians before them, they came to trade and to exploit mineral wealth, but they also brought agricultural skills with them, and it is believed that they introduced the grape and the olive. The Greeks produced the first written accounts of Spain, based, in part, on Phoenician chronicles, and the earliest existing Spanish works of art have strong Hellenic characteristics.

The Celts came to Spain from their homeland along the Rhine while the Phoenicians and Greeks were moving into the south. The Celts, however, came to stay. They arrived in two waves—the first about 1000 B.C. and the second about 600 B.C.—and moved along the Cantabrian coast. They settled in Galicia, which even today remains the purest Celtic region in Spain. Eventually, the Celts spread into the center of the peninsula, where they encountered fierce opposition from the native Iberians. Over time, however, fighting gave way to marriage, and the union of these two peoples produced the first major ancestor of the modern Spaniard: the Celtiberian. But the creation of the Celtiberian "people" was only a racial union; there was no concomitant sociopolitical amalgamation. In any case, little about the Celts is known with historical accuracy. As Henri Hubert says in writing on the Celts throughout Europe, not just in Spain, "The political creations of the Celts are among the great failures of the ancient history of Europe." This is particularly significant given the extent of their conquests—over a third of the European continent, from the British Isles to the shores of the Elbe. Hubert aptly comments: "How little evidence the Celts have left of themselves, compared with what we know of the Egyptians, the Greeks, the Romans, even the Germans!"[11]

The Carthaginians arrived in Spain in 573 B.C. Invited by the Phoenicians to aid in the defense of Cádiz, the Carthaginians stayed to conquer their hosts and eventually absorbed them. Like the Phoenicians and the Greeks, the Carthaginians came primarily as traders, but they remained in Spain for almost four centuries until their civilization throughout the Mediterranean was destroyed by the Romans in the Punic Wars. Rafael Altamira notes that Rome brought political, social, linguistic, and juridical unification to Spain.[12] One could add that Rome also brought the beginnings of religious unification, following the conversion of Constantine in 312 A.D.. Rome subordinated and disciplined the peoples inhabiting Spain under a central authority sitting in Rome and built the roads that ended isolation and contributed to the formation of a uniform culture disseminated by Latin, the single official and common language.[13] Not all regions of the peninsula were romanized to the same degree or at the same pace, but in time, the socialization was so complete that it produced a new people—the Hispano-Romans, the second major ancestors of the modern Spaniard. The union of Romans and Celtiberians created the racial mainstream of Spain. Even if, because of geographic isolation, the Basques in their homeland have maintained a clearer racial identity than most other Spaniards, they must still be considered Spanish. In the same way, the Galicians are also Spanish in spite of the geographic isolation that has given the modern Galician a purer Celtic heritage than other Spaniards, for whom the Celts make up only a part of their ancestry.

The Visigoths, who invaded and conquered Spain in 414 A.D. following the collapse of the Roman Empire, were soon absorbed by an overwhelmingly Hispano-Roman society, and it would be virtually impossible to isolate their descendants today. Moreover, the northern European physical characteristics that might identify them—height and skin and hair coloring, primarily—were already present in the Spaniards because of the Celts.

The Moors, who ended Visigothic rule in Spain, are a different story. They lived in Spain from 711 to 1492 A.D., not just in the south, where their civilization flourished, but throughout most of the peninsula at various times during nearly 800 years. Intermarriage among Christians and Muslims was not uncommon, and it would be difficult to find many Spaniards today (with the possible exception of the Galicians and the Basques) who do not have Moorish ancestors.

During the century that followed the end of the Reconquest in 1492, Muslims who would not renounce their religion were expelled from Spain. Those who rejected Islam and stayed were absorbed into the Spanish mainstream and lost both their racial and religious identity. The Jews, who had constituted a major ethnic minority in both Muslim and Christian Spain and whose erudition and talent had contributed incalculably to both cultures, had already been ordered out of the country by an edict issued by Ferdinand and Isabella in 1492.

Since the end of the Reconquest, Spain's racial and religious composition has remained virtually unchanged. In modern times, the country has not attracted immigrants in sufficient numbers to alter the ethnic makeup. After 1609, when most Muslims left the peninsula, Spain had no religious subcultures. The Reformation never came to Spain (the Jesuits saw to that), and Protestantism has never taken root. Even today, when more and more Spaniards no longer practice their faith, those who lapse do not embrace other religions; there are only roughly 100,000 Protestants and 12,000 Jews in Spain.[14] In fact, most of those Spaniards who no longer attend mass were married in the church, will probably be buried by the church, and allow their children to be baptized in the church.

The decline in the practice of Catholicism in post-Franco Spain can be attributed, in large part, to the Spanish church's history of support for autocratic or authoritarian regimes. The failure to embrace other religions can be explained, in part, by the cultural identity that links being Spanish to being Catholic. The failure can also be attributed to the secularization that has taken place in all Western societies during the past century. As Spain moves into the European mainstream, it should not be surprising to witness the erosion of religious faith among the people. The exodus from the farms, the rejection of the rural and small-town life in which the priest loomed so large, and the growth of cities have all contributed to secularization. Furthermore, the demands of the burgeoning middle class for instant gratification fly in the face of the asceticism and forbearance taught for centuries in Spanish classrooms and pulpits. Moreover, modern capitalism is so far removed from its links to Protestantism—in the way Max Weber and R. H. Tawney explain it—that there will likely be no growth in Protestantism to rationalize neocapitalism's economic posture. Spain is becoming *athée* in the way the French use the term—not atheistic but unconcerned with God.

NEW SPAIN

The economic transformation of Spain since the 1960s has produced profound changes among Spaniards. Although the nation's population density is among the lowest in Europe—74.66 inhabitants per square kilometer (compared to 107 in Portugal, 97 in France, 185 in Italy, 230 in Great Britain, and 341 in the Netherlands)—the distribution produces a significantly higher human concentration in the areas of recent intensive growth: the coastal areas and the big cities. Spain's most eminent economist, Ramón Tamames, writes,

> According to 1981 figures, we find that only 33.1 percent of the total population reside in the Spanish interior (representing 66.9 percent of the peninsular territory); whereas 66.9 percent of the peninsular population lives on the Spanish periphery (representing only 33.1 percent of the country's surface area). The interior has an average density of 52.34 inhabitants per square kilometer, characteristic of a weak consumer market, while the periphery has 140 inhabitants per square kilometer, a density much closer to the average European-type consumer market.[15]

Madrid, the largest city in Spain, located at the very center of the interior *meseta*, is an exception to this demographic profile, as are the smaller but still major interior cities like Zaragoza and Valladolid.

The Spanish workforce has migrated to the big cities both in the interior and along the coasts, causing major economic and political problems. The small-town and rural interior is becoming (or, more accurately, has already become) seriously depopulated, and the burgeoning cities and the overcrowded coasts suffer from the usual catalog of ills brought on by accelerated, unplanned growth: inadequate public services such as housing, education, health, and recreation; rising crime; drug addiction; air and water pollution; and other environmental threats.

Perhaps more basic than any other problem, the cities and coastal areas, irrespective of their spectacular economic growth, are simply unable to offer employment to the tens of thousands who annually migrate there. Unemployment in Spain is the highest in Western Europe. As Tamames notes, "According to the 1981 census, of Spain's 8,022 municipalities, 4,771 (58.2 percent) have fewer than 1,000 inhabitants, accounting for less than 5 percent of the population. This means that almost half of the country's territory contains a minimum percentage of the population. In contrast to these marked 'municipal minifundia,' the largest municipalities with over 50,000 inhabitants represent more than 18 million inhabitants, or 50 percent of the total population."[16] Towns and villages in interior Spain look like their counterparts in the rust belt of the United States, and they, too, have yet to discover new sources of economic growth. The rising incomes in urban Spain have yet to trickle down into the depopulated countryside. Spain is only beginning to see its picturesque but deserted interior villages and towns rediscovered (as is happening in France, for example) by affluent Spanish urbanites looking for second homes, or by tourists seeking beauty and history beyond the beaten paths. Cottage industries, of growing significance in other European countries, are still relatively underdeveloped in Spain.

Spain's population is the youngest in Europe. The nation also has the lowest growth rate in Europe, with less than ten births per thousand annually. (Twenty per thousand is the world average.) The availability of contraceptives, the legality of abortion, and the increasing secularization of the Spaniard (who listens less and less attentively to the teachings of the Catholic Church) have contributed to the declining birthrate. Changing migratory patterns have also altered birthrates. Urban people need fewer children to survive economically; in fact, large families are, in general, detrimental to personal advancement in the cities. Just the opposite situation existed in the countryside, where large numbers of children contributed to the family income by working the farms, dairies, ranches, and orchards. Now, however, the exodus from the countryside has undermined the family farm, and agriculture in modern Spain is becoming increasingly mechanized. Children in large numbers are simply unwanted in both urban and rural modern Spain (Table I.1).

This study of the new Spain in its eternal setting is part of a series of studies devoted to the countries of Europe, entitled Nations of the Modern World: Europe. As the end of the twentieth century approaches, the great alternatives to democracy have, at least for now, been repudiated. Yet it was on Spanish soil where the battle among the contending ideologies—fascism, communism, democracy—was first fought, giving Spain a very special and poignant place in the history of this century. What if the conflict had all been resolved in the Spanish Civil War? What if the Spanish tragedy could have obviated the international tragedy that was soon to follow?

Although fascism in its virulent, pandemic form was eradicated by World War II, recent outbreaks of the pathogen within Europe are again causing alarm. Hatred of foreigners is the common theme among the neofascists, but there appears to be no transnational infrastructure linking them. Indeed, by its very nature, xenophobia is usually contained within national borders. But the continent is on alert.

By contrast, communism in Eastern Europe and in the Soviet Union was not destroyed from the outside: It imploded at the end of the 1980s, its great theories tumbled by reality. It is ironic that in those countries left bereft of Marxist ideology, xenophobia—the hallmark of fascism—should become the new faith of disgruntled neoconservatives, yesterday's communists. (Ah, the simple clarifications of European politics!)

Democracy alone remains standing. It is perhaps the only viable political form for the postindustrial age, now in its infancy in parts of Europe (such as Spain) but already well advanced in others (such as Germany and

TABLE I.1   Regions and Provinces, Mid-decennial Census of April 1, 1986

1. Andalucia
Population: 6,875,628
Area: 87,268 sq. km.
Provinces: Almería, Cádiz, Córdoba, Granada, Huelva, Jaén, Málaga, Seville

2. Aragon
Population: 1,214,729
Area: 47,669 sq. km.
Provinces: Huesca, Teruel, Zaragoza

3. Asturias
Population: 1,114,115
Area: 10,565 sq. km.

4. Balearic Islands
Population: 754,777
Area: 5,014 sq. km.

5. Basque Country
Population: 2,133,002
Area: 7,261 sq. km.
Provinces: Alava, Guipúzcoa, Vizcaya

6. Canary Islands
Population: 1,614,882
Area: 7,273 sq. km.
Provinces: Las Palmas, Santa Cruz de Tenerife

7. Cantabria
Population: 524,670
Area: 5,289 sq. km.

8. Castile-La Mancha
Population: 1,665,029
Area: 79,226 sq. km.
Provinces: Albacete, Cuidad Real, Cuenca, Guadalajara, Toledo

9. Valencia
Population: 3,772,002
Area: 23,305 sq. km.
Provinces: Alicante, Castellón, Valencia

10. Castile-León
Population: 2,600,330
Area: 84,147 sq. km.
Provinces: Avila, Burgos, León, Palencia, Salamanca, Segovia, Soria, Valladolid, Zamora

11. Catalonia
Population: 5,977,008
Area: 31,970 sq. km.
Provinces: Barcelona, Gerona Lérida, Tarragona

12. Extremadura
Population: 1,088,543
Area: 41,602 sq. km.
Provinces: Badajoz, Cáceres

13. Galicia
Population: 2,785,394
Area: 29,434 sq. km.
Provinces: La Coruña, Lugo, Orense, Pontevedra

14. Madrid
Population: 4,854,616
Area: 7,995 sq. km.

15. Murcia
Population: 1,014,285
Area: 11,317 sq. km.

16. Navarre
Population: 512,676
Area: 10,421 sq. km.

17. La Rioja
Population: 262,611
Area: 5,034 sq. km.

18. Ceuta and Melilla
Area: 32 sq. km.

Source: Based on information from John Paxton, ed., The Statesman's Year Book, 1989–1990 (New York: St. Martin's Press, 1989), pp. 1114–1115.

Sweden). Democracy is the thread that today draws the European nation-states together.

In *Spain: Democracy Regained,* I will address the topics common to all the country studies that make up the series—land, people, and society; historical influences; political institutions; political forces; public policy; political economy; and foreign relations. In Part One, the historical forces that shaped Spain will be examined, beginning with the Reconquest, the phenomenon that created the nation-state and that more than any other molded Spain as we know it. Spain offers the earliest example of religion used as a agglutinative force in building the modern nation-state. The use was cynical and calculated, given the fact that the Catholic Kings—Isabella and Ferdinand—felt little animus toward Muslims and Jews, particularly the latter. Indeed, some of the most valuable and trusted advisers and public stewards to the king and queen and their predecessors were Jews. The Spanish experience is of particular relevance today when secular ideology—fascism and communism, primarily—has lost its hold on the imagination. Religion in its political guise has emerged once again to fill the lacuna. Spain perhaps can be used not as a model but as an example of the terrible price that is paid for such perversion. There, religion continued to be the recurrent theme of all subsequent Spanish history until the post-Franco era, and Catholicism was perhaps more militant in Spain than in any other part of Christendom.

The rule of the Hapsburgs, who assumed the throne after the Catholic Kings, will be contrasted to that of the Bourbons, who came to the throne in 1700—setting forth the struggle between the center and the periphery that has plagued Spanish politics throughout its history.

During the Second Republic, conflict evolved over all the unresolved issues of Spanish society and politics that could not be settled by the democratic process and that ultimately led to the Civil War. I will analyze the crosscutting cleavages of religion, economics, and regime that ultimately paralyzed the Second Republic. This disastrous democratic experiment, like that of the Weimar Republic in Germany, offers a classic example of the perils of introducing democracy in a nation-state unready for its implementation. The pertinence of such analysis is of particular importance today when all of Europe east of the Oder-Neisse, similarly unprepared for democracy, is struggling to make democracy work despite similar cleavages.

In 1939, victory in the Civil War went to the forces of the Right—the political expression of the old Spain discussed earlier. Rightists ruled without interruption from 1939 to 1975 under General Franco. His regime is analyzed in terms of the four phases into which it can be divided, with special attention given to the role played by the military during the Franco dictatorship. The modernization of Spain and its subsequent unplanned consequences began in phase four of the Franco's regime, from 1959 to 1975. This unwittingly set the stage for the extraordinary accomplishments that Spain would later make, examined in Part Two.

The transition to democracy took place peacefully between 1975 and 1979; not a single law of the Franco regime was broken (although Franco's legacy was designed to have been the uninterrupted continuation of the dictatorship through the person of the king). Spain's extraordinary achievements in this period are carefully examined. Time alone will tell if the Spanish experience can be used for comparative analysis or if Spain's experience was unique.

An analysis of the policy decisions made by the political party that brought about the transition—the Democratic Center Union (Unión del Centro Democrático—UCD)—is highlighted. In a country where, for nearly forty years, no major issue had been open either to public discussion or to public participation in problem resolutions, all issues—political, social, and economic—suddenly became public property. Yet solutions in any one of these categories could have easily jeopardized solutions in the other two. The UCD opted for the primacy of political over social and economic issues, deferring the latter two until the new, democratic infrastructure was in place. The pacts that addressed the social and economic issues but delayed them for future solution were made in elitist, closed-door bargaining that flew in the face of notions of popular participation. Yet given the public's total lack of practical political experience, elitist bargaining was perhaps the only alternative. The relevance of this problem-solving technique is of profound comparative importance as we look at Spain in relation to the Eastern European countries, Russia, and the other component parts of the former Soviet Union. There, the public today, like that in Spain yesterday, has no skills in participatory democracy, but unlike the Spanish situation, political, social, and economic issues have been confronted simultaneously, often with disastrous results.

The UCD made fundamental foreign policy decisions affecting Spain's place in the world. The Soviet Union posed no direct threat to Spain at the time of the transition or, for that matter, at any time, despite Franco's relentless harangue against "Godless communism." But the UCD sought and finally attained Spain's membership in the North Atlantic Treaty Organization (NATO), not as a means of defending the country from a nonexistent Soviet threat but as a means of establishing Spain's presence in Europe. For similar reasons, the UCD sought membership in the European Community (EC), although this was not accomplished until after the Socialists came to power in 1982. The UCD believed that membership in the two most powerful and democratic international institutions in the West would help secure democracy in Spain and, in particular, constrain the still-feared Spanish military by making it a part of a larger, democratic military establishment. Although it has long had a special relationship with other Spanish-speaking countries and with the Islamic nations of the Middle East (because of the lengthy Muslim presence on Spanish soil), Spain under the UCD chose to make its future in Europe, just as it would under the Spanish Socialist Worker's Party (Partido Socialista de Obrero Español—PSOE).

The demise of the UCD is of equal importance to a comparative study because it shows that an elitist party devoid of grassroots organization cannot survive in a modern, mass-democratic polity. Yet without the existence of such a party at the beginning of the transition, democracy might not have been established in Spain. The same paradox is visible in the former communist nations now undergoing a similar transition.

Part Two concludes with an analysis of the political institutions that the constitution of 1978 established. Of special comparative interest are the constitutional provisions for autonomy for the regions of Spain that might serve as models for other nations. How to incorporate historically restive regions and ethnic groups into newly formed democracies while allowing for self-determination is an unresolved problem throughout much of Eastern Europe and the former USSR. The problem also confronts established nation-states such as Canada, where separatism has become a potent issue.

In Part Three, I describe and analyze the parties that played the political game in Spain since 1975. Of special significance for the viability of democratic politics is the disappearance of the extreme Right and the restructuring of what was the extreme Left—the Communists—into the more moderate Unified Left, a political grouping led by the Communists but with a broader appeal than that of the former Communist party. The United Left seeks to attract not only the classic Communist voter but also those who would normally vote Socialist but who are unhappy with the PSOE's transformation into essentially a social democratic party. To broaden its appeal, the Communist party has moved to the right. It is interesting to observe that national parties to the left of the Communists have not sprung up in Spain, as they have in France, for example. And most surprising of all is the virtual disappearance of the anarchists, the most powerful group on the left during the Second Republic.

The most significant aspect of political party development in democratic Spain has been the movement of the PSOE and the Popular Party (Partido Popular—PP), the largest and most important parties on the left and right, respectively, toward the center of the political spectrum. This has effectively made each the political alternative of the other in what has become, for all practical purposes, a two-party-dominant system at the national level. (If Spain had Great Britain's electoral system, it would be an unqualified two-party-dominant system at the national level, but then, if Great Britain had Spain's electoral system, it would be a limited multi-party system, much like Germany.) The moderation of the two major political parties stems from the growing consensus among Spaniards, who no longer seem to need a vast array of party offerings in order to participate meaningfully in the political process.

In addition to the national parties, several regional parties play roles in the politics of Autonomous Communities such as Euzkadi and Catalonia, and they have sufficient strength to place deputies in the national legislature.

In Part Three, I also examine political violence, which has plagued Spanish democracy since its birth. (Only since the late 1980s has such violence begun to be brought under control; perhaps it will cease in the not-too-distant future.) This section illustrates, among other things, the extreme difficulty that democracy, particularly a fledgling one like that in Spain, faces in combating political violence. Draconian techniques available to the order-keepers of a nondemocratic system are foreclosed to their counterparts in a democratic one. And in democracies recently emerged from dictatorship, the public is particularly sensitive to the behavior of law enforcement agencies; citizens are on the alert for evidence of potential abuse that would recall the times of repression when any overt action against the regime was labeled political violence and ruthlessly suppressed.

ETA (Euzkadi Ta Azkatasuna), the major perpetrator of political violence in Spain in the years just before Franco's death, was looked upon as heroic not only by the Basque population, whose rights ETA championed, but also by many other Spaniards: ETA was willing to fight and die for freedom from Francoist oppression. After Franco's death, however, and after the transition to democracy had begun, ETA's violence did not abate. Its actions were now directed not against the hated Franco regime but against the hated Spanish state. It became clear that all along, ETA violence had had two thrusts—one against Franco, the other against the state, regardless of who governed it. Therefore, to the ETA, a democratic Spanish state was as illegitimate as an authoritarian one if that state refused to honor the Basque rights to self-determination embodied in the ancient *fueros* ("laws"). Thus, history was used to rationalize and legitimize any antistatist activity, including violence. This is particularly relevant to comparative study today. In vast parts of the world, ethnic and religious separatism has laid claim to historical rights of self-determination—rights that are deemed retrievable by any means (including violence), even against democratic regimes that seek to both defend national sovereignty and respect subnational rights. The Spanish experience is exemplary.

The transformation of the Spanish economy to capitalism, discussed in Part Four, has special importance for those countries that are currently attempting to move from one economic system to another. Until the economic changes initiated by Franco in the late 1950s, Spain's economy had been autarkic and heavily regulated by the state, with a large percentage of the means of production under total or partial state ownership. Autarky, embraced when the world ostracized Spain after the end of World War II, matched Franco's political policy of keeping the despised modern world at bay. But by the 1950s, autarky had led Spain to economic despair: There simply were not enough raw materials, goods, and services produced within the country to maintain even a Third World level of existence in Spain. Franco's pragmatism (and his fear of massive popular uprising) led him to seek out technocrats committed to capitalism in order to rescue Spain from economic ruin. Their success in the 1960s led to Spain's version of the economic "miracle" that had occurred earlier in Germany and Italy.

Problems began in the mid-1970s, catalyzed by the actions of the Organization of Petroleum Exporting Countries (OPEC), and they remained unsolved as the country moved from dictatorship to democracy between 1975 and 1979. It was not until the Socialists came to power in 1982 that the problems of the economy were faced. Ironically, the Socialists under Felipe González adopted a policy of economic rigor that was not too different from that of Ronald Reagan or Margaret Thatcher. González's fellow Socialist, François Mitterrand, had already adopted a similar policy after a more orthodox Socialist program had proved unworkable in France. Thus, Spain's economic policy fit comfortably within the economic environment of Western Europe and prepared the country for its admission to the European Community in 1985.

In Part Five, I will look at the Socialists now in power. Under their guidance, Spain became ensconced in Europe, adjusted to the tough demands of EC membership, signed the treaty at Maastricht to extend European unity, and was active in NATO. (The PSOE had rallied to the idea of joining NATO after coming into office, reversing its earlier stance. That stance was dictated by a socialist ideology that was subsequently repudiated.) Spain was given a role in the Middle East peace talks, and it supported the United States in the Gulf War.

The Spanish Socialists' foreign policy was more widely supported by the citizenry than was its domestic policy. In office, the Socialists had to make tough domestic decisions on issues that had been in limbo since the UCD administration signed pacts deferring socioeconomic change until democracy was established. Attention was long overdue in a number of areas: education, health, housing, the courts and the legal system, the armed forces, inflation, employment, and explosive moral issues such as abortion. The PSOE renounced orthodox socialist doctrine in 1979. It had correctly and pragmatically understood that success at the polls would elude the party until it had done so. Thus, classic socialist correctives to socioeconomic problems were no longer available. But once in office, the PSOE moved even further away from socialist fraternity and solidarity as the government was forced to balance economic rigor against the electoral commitment to extend socioeconomic democracy to the masses. Spain joined its fellow European Community members in facing this dilemma. The economy of the late 1980s and early 1990s simply could not provide sufficient funding to extend social welfare programs or even to maintain what had previously been provided. In Spain, however, the reduction in socioeconomic democracy seemed to be taking place even before extension (comparable to that of its fellow EC members) had taken place. The debate on how to resolve this dilemma opened a major fissure within the PSOE, dividing those who believed the party had veered too far from its socialist roots (even if they accepted the doctrinal decisions made in 1979) and those who championed technocratic pragmatism. The fissure remains open.

NOTES

1. Adam Przeworski, *Democracy and the Market: Political and Economic Reforms in Eastern Europe and Latin America* (Cambridge: Cambridge University Press, 1991), p. 8.

2. "The New Spain: A Survey," *The Economist,* April 2, 1977, p. 6.

3. Paul Kennedy, *The Rise and Fall of the Great Powers* (New York: Random House, 1987).

4. E. Ramón Arango, *Spain: From Repression to Renewal* (Boulder: Westview Press, 1985).

5. See W. B. Fisher and H. Bowen-Jones, *Spain: An Introductory Geography* (New York: Praeger, 1966).

6. Roger Collins, *The Basques* (New York: Basil Blackwell, 1987), pp. 13–16.

7. Rodney Gallop, *A Book of the Basques* (Reno: University of Nevada Press, 1970), pp. 6–9.

8. Pierson Dixon, *The Iberians of Spain* (London: Oxford University Press, Humphrey Milford, 1940), pp. 1–6.

9. William M. Douglas, *Death in Murelaga* (Seattle and London: University of Washington Press, 1969), p. XI.

10. Marianne Heiberg, *The Making of the Basque Nation* (Cambridge: Cambridge University Press, 1989), p. 13. See also Carleton Stevens Caon, *The Races of Europe* (New York: Macmillan, 1939), pp. 501–504. There is a fairly extensive literature on the Basques, given the rather esoteric nature of this topic. A center for Basque studies at the University of Nevada publishes widely in English through the university's press. Among the best works in Spanish are B. E. Lasa, *Orígenes de los Vascos*, vol. 4 (Zaráuz: Editorial Icharopena, 1959), and Julio Caro Baroja, *Los Vascos* (Madrid: Ediciones Minotauro, 1958).

11. Henri Hubert, *The Greatness and Decline of the Celts* (London: Kegan Paul, Trench, Trubner and Co., 1934), quotes are from pp. 273 and 75–81, respectively. See also T.G.E. Powell, *The Celts* (London: Thames and Hudson, 1980).

12. Rafael Altamira, *A History of Spain* (New York: Van Nostrand Company, 1949), chapter 3.

13. Eventually, popular speech corrupted the official language, and out of that corruption grew the three Romance languages of modern Spain: Castilian (what is today called Spanish), Galician, and Catalan. The origins of the fourth language in Spain, Basque (*Euzkera*, in the Basque language), are as mysterious as the origins of the Basques themselves.

14. John Paxton, ed., *Statesman's Year-Book* (New York: St. Martin's Press, 1983). See Carmen Irizarry, *The Thirty Thousand: Modern Spain and Protestantism* (New York: Harcourt, Brace & World, 1966), and Américo Castro, *The Structure of Spanish History* (Princeton: Princeton University Press, 1954), chapter 15.

15. Ramón Tamames, *The Spanish Economy* (New York: St. Martin's Press, 1986), p. 10.

16. Ibid., p. 11.

Part One

Roman Colony to Dictatorship

1

Conquest and Reconquest

The Iberian Peninsula became part of the Roman Empire in 26 B.C. after two centuries of war. Rome fought first against the Carthaginians in the First and Second Punic Wars (264–241 B.C. and 218–201 B.C., respectively, the latter waged primarily in Spain) and then against the local peninsular peoples. Spain was unified for the first time under Rome, which created a political and bureaucratic structure in the new colony that endured for almost 400 years. Rome ruled through governors set up in the seven provinces into which the peninsula was eventually divided. New cities were created, and existing ones were expanded as centers for romanization in which the various indigenous peoples were amalgamated into a single society.

Two devices were used to keep the Spaniards loyal. First, citizenship in a municipality, with its small-scale imitation of imperial life in Rome, was promoted through various inducements: reductions in tribute, grants of land, and more efficient justice. Second, for those with ambition and ability, the ultimate prize was resettlement in Rome itself.[1] Among the talented Spaniards who added glory to Rome were philosophers Marcus Seneca and his son Lucius; the poet Lucan; the epigramist Martial; the geographer Pomponius Mela; the orator, critic, and teacher Quintilian; and the emperors Trajan, Hadrian, Marcus Aurelius, and Theodosius. Theodosius, the last emperor of the undivided empire, was a convert to Christianity. He decreed what might be called the last legacy of Rome, one that established particularly strong roots in Spain: religious orthodoxy. When Constantine converted from paganism to Christianity, he did so as an individual and did not compel the conversion of his subjects. Theodosius, by contrast, used religion as a weapon of politics, and upon his conversion, he decreed Christianity the official religion of the empire, thereby wedding church to state and equating heresy and treason.

As Theodosius had decreed, the empire was divided when he died. After 395 A.D., the eastern half was ruled from Constantinople and the western half still governed from Rome. The reasons for the decision to divide the empire and for the decadence of the empire as a whole, which had begun almost a century earlier, are not germane to this study. What is important is that the weakness and corruption of Rome left all the component parts of the empire vulnerable, and by 409 A.D., the empire had collapsed in Spain.

INVASION FROM THE NORTH

Filling the vacuum left by the Romans, the Suevians, Vandals, and Alans poured into the peninsula from northern Europe and quickly overpowered the natives. The cultural heritage of Rome withstood the barbarian onslaught in Spain, but the sociopolitical unity crumbled, leaving the Spaniards exposed to conquest. The centralism maintained by the emperors had seemingly never taken deep root in Spain, perhaps indicating the Spaniards' quarrelsome reluctance to be governed at all and their preference, if being ruled were inevitable, for a government as close to the people as possible. The first Germanic invaders were not successful in establishing their hegemony, however. Fighting among themselves over the division of their conquests, they were conquered by the Visigoths, who moved into Spain in 414 A.D. By 585 A.D., the year in which Galicia was conquered, the Visigoths had established total sovereignty over all of Spain, with the exception of the impenetrable Basque lands, which maintained their independence.

For almost 300 years, the Visigoths ruled Spain from their capital in Toledo.[2] The influence of the Visigoths was less lasting than that of the Romans, yet they left major legacies, which lay dormant for almost eight centuries after the Moorish conquest. The first was religion. The Visigoths who came to Spain were Arians, but savage opposition from the natives who had become Catholic under the empire persuaded the Visigothic king, Reccared, to convert to Catholicism in 587 A.D.[3] Reccared declared his new faith to be the official religion of Spain, and for the second time, church and state were fused. As Stanley Payne observes, "After conversion of the Arian Visigothic dynasty in 587 there developed a greater degree of interpenetration between Church and state than in any other European kingdom of that era."[4] The law, created by recasting diverse Visigothic and Hispano-Roman laws into a single code promulgated in 654 A.D., was the second legacy of the Visigoths, and it fostered the reunification of Spanish society. The recasting, begun during the reign of King Chindasuinth (642–653 A.D.), was completed during the reign of his son, King Reccesuinth (649–672 A.D.), who also began administrative reforms that his successor completed.[5] The third legacy was the institution of the monarchy. The Roman unity of Spain had been based upon the sovereignty of the emperor in Rome, whose will was made manifest through his agents, the governors. The Visigothic kings were the first to govern a unified Spain from *within* the country.

Succession to the Visigothic throne was not hereditary. It was the custom for the nobles to choose their king, yet this seemingly reasonable and democratic practice was enmeshed in treason, intrigue, and often civil war.[6] The elected kingship contributed significantly but inadvertently to the Muslim conquest of Spain, for the moment a king died and the throne passed to his elected successor, the nobles who had been overlooked set out to subvert the election. In 711 A.D., the authority and power of King Roderick, who would be the last Visigothic king of Spain, was so undermined by insurrection that he was unable to rally sufficient loyal forces to withstand the Moorish invaders from North Africa. In fact, the bishop of Seville, a member of a rival clan seeking to unseat Roderick, persuaded his followers not to resist the Islamic invaders, thinking that the Muslims could later be repulsed under a new Visigothic sovereign. It is ironic that a prince of the church helped to expose Spain to the "infidel," who put an end to three centuries of Visigothic rule within six years.

THE MUSLIM CONQUEST

The invaders, who remained on the Iberian Peninsula for almost eight centuries, were not a single people. They are commonly called Arabs or Moors, but they also included Syrians, Berbers, and members of other races from North Africa and the Middle East. What unified all these Semitic peoples was the Islamic faith they carried into Spain in 711 A.D. They crossed at Gibraltar and spread throughout the peninsula until they were stopped in 718 A.D. and pushed back by Christian forces led by the Visigothic nobleman Pelayo at Covadonga, in the mountains of Asturias. Theoretically, the Reconquest of Spain from the Moors began in that year, moving out of the isolated redoubts of Christianity left untouched by the Muslims in the cold and inhospitable north. However, the Reconquest did not begin in earnest until the eleventh century.

The Muslim conquests on the Iberian Peninsula were unified into a single, dependent emirate of the caliphate in Damascus until the ruling dynasty in Syria was overthrown in 750 A.D. Abd ar-Rahman I, a prince of the deposed Umayad family, fled to Spain and defeated the emir of Córdoba, who was governing in the name of the new caliph. Abd ar-Rahman I then proclaimed himself the monarch of the independent emirate of Al-Andalus, with its capital at Córdoba, and cut all ties with Damascus. It took almost two more centuries to consolidate the kingdom, however. The preeminence of Abd ar-Rahman and his descendants was challenged by local Muslim chieftains, who established small, independent kingdoms throughout the peninsula after 750 A.D. It was not until the reign of Abd ar-Rahman III (912–961 A.D.) that the last vestiges of resistance to Cordoban rule were quashed and the independent emirate was converted into a caliphate equal in grandeur to that in Damascus.

The Cordoban emirate and particularly the later caliphate became the center of what many scholars consider to be one of the most brilliant civilizations (and undeniably the most exotic) ever to exist in Western Europe. Following the division of the Roman Empire and the subsequent devastation of the Western Empire by the barbarians, scholarship and learning went into a deep decline in Christian Europe, but it was kept alive by Islamic scholars in the Middle East. Learning returned to Europe through Spain with the Arab invaders, who brought not only the knowledge of Greece and Rome but also that of the Orient. The wonders of Muslim Spain attracted scholars and traders from throughout the Western world. Abd ar-Rahman III's private library is said to have contained 600,000 volumes, and he established over fifty public libraries throughout Al-Andalus. In Spain, the study of jurisprudence, philosophy, grammar, mathematics, geometry, physics, astronomy, botany, music, architecture, medicine, and alchemy (the forerunner of chemistry) reached heights unprecedented in Europe. The decorative arts and landscape gardening were dazzling. Glass was invented in Córdoba in the ninth century, and paper (invented in Asia) was first brought into Europe through Spain. Moorish textiles, leather goods, and articles of precious metal were considered to be among the finest in the world. And in agriculture, the Moors developed irrigation and perfected the *huerta*—which is still an integral part of Spanish farming—and they are credited with introducing cotton, silk, sugar, rice, apricots, peaches, pomegranates, and oranges into Europe.

In 1011, after fifty years of misrule by the inept heirs of Abd ar-Rahman III, who died in 961, civil war broke out among the Muslim aristocracy of Al-Andalus. Twenty years later, the once powerful caliphate collapsed, and independent Islamic kingdoms called *taifas* emerged from its ruins: Granada, Córdoba, Seville, Murcia, Lérida, Zaragoza, Valencia, Badajoz, Algeciras, Toledo, Málaga, and Almería—the last two little more than small port cities and their immediate hinterlands whose independence was protected by the difficulty of overland access.[7] Political division was not compensated by a unifying religious orthodoxy. All the Muslims in Spain were Sunnite without, as Bernard Reilly phrases it, "even a tincture of Shias," but the faith was "relaxed and did not bother itself overmuch with the absence of a caliph," that is, without a spiritual centerpiece.[8] Islam in Muslim Spain contrasted dramatically with Catholicism in Christian Spain, with its appetite for zealots and martyrs obsessed with the Reconquest. At that time in Spain, Islam was at a fateful disadvantage.

THE RECONQUEST

In the 250 years following the battle at Covadonga, the Christians were able to push the Muslims no further back than a line along the Douro River that runs through the middle of the northwest quadrant of the Iberian peninsula. Below the Douro, the Muslims were entrenched, and the Christian advance was stalled until Al-Andalus disintegrated in 1031, giving the Christians an advantage that they pursued relentlessly. The demise of Al-Andalus left Muslim Spain divided for conquest at a time when Christian Spain was sufficiently consolidated to pursue the religious crusade. By 1031, there were five Christian realms in Spain—León, Castile, Navarre, Aragon, and Catalonia, ruled by descendants of the warriors who had turned back the Muslims in 718 A.D. While slowly expanding Christian hegemony over the north of Spain, they contended among themselves, through battle and marriage, for political preeminence.

The Reconquest of Muslim Spain began in earnest in 1085, when Alfonso VI of Castile took Toledo from the Moors, leading an army made up of Castilians, Leonese, Galicians, Asturians, Basques, Navarrese, and Aragonese. Although these peoples were not yet united politically as Spaniards, they were already united spiritually as Catholics in their common hatred of Islam. For the next 200 years, Christians and Muslims fought for the soul of Spain. In 1195, the Muslims crushed the Christians at the Battle of Alarcos and appeared to be in the ascendancy, but in 1212, the Christians defeated the Muslims in the single most important battle of the Reconquest, at Las Navas de Tolosa. This marked the turning point in the Christian campaign against Islam: Never again were the Moors able to stop the Christians more than temporarily. Between 1236 and 1248, Córdoba, Jaén, Seville, and Murcia fell to the Castilians. In 1238, Valencia was taken by the Aragonese, and by the end of the thirteenth century, all of Spain was in the hands of Christian sovereigns, with the exception of the *taifa* kingdom of Granada.

By this time, the Christian kingdoms had been reduced to three: Navarre, Aragon, and Castile. Catalonia became a part of Aragon through the first of the three great nuptial mergers that led to the unified Spanish nation-state. In 1137, the heir to the throne of Aragon married the sovereign of Catalonia, and their descendants ruled over the expanded kingdom of Aragon. In 1230, Castile and León were permanently united to form the kingdom of Castile, and in 1469, the last merger took place when Isabella, heir to the throne of Castile, married Ferdinand, heir to the throne of Aragon. By 1479, after Isabella and Ferdinand had ascended to their separate and independent thrones, only the kingdoms of Granada and Navarre kept the royal couple from ruling the entirety of Spain.[9] In 1481, the battle for Granada began. Eleven years later, on January 2,

1492—the single most important date in Spanish history—Ferdinand and Isabella victoriously accepted the keys to the city and its kingdom and expelled the last Muslim sovereign from Spain. After nearly 800 years, Spain was once again Catholic, and for their role in the final struggle between Christianity and Islam, Isabella and Ferdinand were thereafter referred to as the Catholic Kings. When Ferdinand conquered Navarre in 1512, eight years after the death of Isabella, Spain became both Christian and united.

The unity of Spain obsessed the Catholic Kings, particularly Isabella, the Castilian, who saw her kingdom in the center of the country as the undisputed master of the peninsula. Even before Spain was united, Isabella and Ferdinand had begun to consolidate their authority by weakening the power of the great nobles who might have acted as a counterforce to centralization. They enticed the grandees away from their estates to a life rich in favors and perquisites at the royal court. But the Catholic Kings did not touch the *fueros* or the *cortes* (parliament) that continued to exist in the kingdoms that had been conjoined into the single nation-state.[10] They sought to weaken these institutions, but they dared not dismantle them. Throughout the eight centuries of the Reconquest, the rulers of the Christian kingdoms had granted *fueros* to entice and reward those warriors and their families willing to remain and colonize the isolated borderlands between Muslim and Christian domains. Once the battles had been won, the Christian kings returned to their headquarters to pursue dynastic ambitions against fellow Christian sovereigns, often not returning to the Reconquest for many years. Without permanent settlement and defenses, newly won Christian territories were therefore vulnerable to reconquest by the Moors. The *fueros* granted political, commercial, and legal rights to those Christian pioneers willing to hazard the dangers of the frontier.

These *fueros* were cherished as immutable and perpetual, and they became an integral part of the sociopolitical fabric of Spanish life. A *cortes* was already functioning in both Castile and Aragon by the twelfth century, and others were formed later in León, Catalonia, and Navarre. These bodies, made up of representatives from the nobility, the clergy, and the bourgeoisie, were summoned at the monarch's command when he or she needed more money than the royal coffers contained. The *cortes* would agree either to grant or withhold funds, always stressing its own right to exist. The prerogative of having a voice in their own governance, whether through the *fueros* or the *cortes*, was a sacred sentiment to Spaniards centuries before the emergence of modern democracy; indeed, present-day separatism in post-Franco Spain has its origins in this tradition. These individual regional *cortes* continued to exist until the arrival of the Bourbons at the beginning of the eighteenth century, and remnants of the *fueros* persisted into the twentieth century. It was not so much Spain but rather, in

Jaime Vicens Vives's words, "the Spanish in their pluralistic unity"[11] that came into being in 1492. A single *cortes* representing the whole nation did not appear until the nineteenth century.

In the pursuit of unity, the Catholic Kings turned Catholicism to the service of the state. The separateness that was maintained through the *fueros* and the *cortes* would be overcome by religious solidarity and orthodoxy. The peoples of Spain, the vast majority of whom identified not with the new nation-state but with their own regions, would become Spaniards through Catholicism, just as their ancestors had become reconquerors through the same faith. The single-minded pursuit of the Reconquest became the single-minded maintenance of the state. For the third time (the first was under the Romans, the second under the Visigoths), church and state were wed, and treason and heresy once again became synonymous. With Isabella and Ferdinand, however, the fusion was accompanied by an intolerance that branded Spaniards as fanatics. Ten years following the fall of Granada, the Catholic Kings reversed the terms of the treaty of surrender that had guaranteed freedom of religion to the Muslims in the defeated kingdom—a freedom that had reflected the tolerance characteristic of life in both Christian and Muslim Spain for centuries.

From the beginning of the Reconquest until after the battle at Las Navas de Tolosa, Christians had lived in Muslim lands, Muslims had lived in Christian lands, and Jews had lived in both. As the frontiers between Muslim and Christian territories moved back and forth during the Reconquest, members of the three religions had often found themselves governed by men of other beliefs. If not with great love, they had at least lived together with mutual respect and forbearance.

> In medieval times it was a society of uneasy coexistence (*convivencia*), increasingly threatened by the advancing Christian reconquest of lands that had been Muslim since the Moorish invasions of the eighth century. For long periods, close contact between communities had led to a mutual tolerance among the three faiths of the peninsula: Christian, Muslim, and Jews. Even where Christians went to war against the Moors, it was (as a thirteenth-century writer argued) "neither of the law [of Mohammed] nor because of the sect that they hold to" but solely because of conflict over land. Christians lived under Moorish rule (as *Mozárabes*) and Muslims under Christian rule (as *Mudéjares*). The different communities shared a broad culture that blurred racial prejudices, and military alliances were made regardless of religion. St. Ferdinand, King of Castile from 1230 to 1252, called himself "King of the Three Religions," a singular claim in an increasingly intolerant age.[12]

Poul Borchsenius expresses similar ideas, albeit more poetically:

Most European countries were imprisoned in the spiritual gloom of the
Middle Ages; ignorance, superstition and fanaticism laid their heavy burden
on people's minds.

There was only one country where things were different. Far down in the
south-west corner of our part of the world, where the Spanish peninsula
forms a bridge between Europe proper and Africa, the torch was about to be
lit.

By one of the strange freaks of history, it so happened that the three great
religions, Islam, Christendom, and Judaism, met one another in Spain, each
accompanied by its people, its culture, and its special message. Spain was
the setting for their clash and the resultant drama. They were on friendly
terms with each other, even close friendly terms. ...

And it was this interplay of ideas that together brought the three peoples
of the Iberian peninsula to a flowering whose like the world has not seen.
For this reason we look on the Spanish Middle Ages as a mythical golden
age in which the protagonists were either Mohammedans, Christians, or
Jews.[13]

After the battle at Las Navas de Tolosa, the tide turned permanently
against Islam, and ultimate victory for the Christian forces became inevitable. With this new reality, Christian forbearance toward the other two
religions began to erode. The prejudices of the Christian masses and the
policies of the Christian monarchs, undergirded by the policy of the
church as manifested in the papal Inquisition established throughout
Christendom in 1227, interacted in Spain to nourish the increasingly cruel
repression of Muslims and Jews. When Spain became a nation-state under
Isabella and Ferdinand, this orthodoxy was given political dimension as
the preeminent means of maintaining the nation-state. On February 11,
1502, the final blow to tolerance came when the Catholic Kings decreed
that all Muslims who would not convert to Catholicism would be expelled. Several years earlier, on March 31, 1492 (less than two months after
the fall of Granada), Jews had been ordered either to be baptized as Catholics or to leave Spain within four months. And even earlier, in 1477, the
new and official religious intolerance, with its political goal of national
unity, had been established when the Catholic Kings decreed what became known as the New Inquisition. This was created primarily to examine *conversos*—Jews who, out of fear, had converted to Catholicism but
whose fidelity to their new faith was suspect. The linkage between treachery and heresy had become fixed.

In an attempt to put the Inquisition into perspective, Jean Mariéjol
writes:

Restoration of order was not the only great problem facing the government
[of Ferdinand and Isabella]. A graver problem demanded its attention: the

assimilation of foreign peoples, Jews and Muslims, whom a succession of conquests and that of Granada finally brought under the crowns of Aragon and Castile. What should be done with these people? The Jews aroused disquiet by their wealth and proselytizism, the Moslems by their numbers. Should they be permitted to live and multiply as they pleased? Should they be driven out? Tolerance, so honored in our time, was alien to the spirit of the age. Although religious prejudice was very intense, expulsion appeared a very barbarous proceeding, and men were not blind to the economic dangers of such a measure. Yet religion was so intimately linked to the idea of the state that it seemed unthinkable for a prince to allow adherents of Moses and Mohammed to live side by side with Christian folk.[14]

Mariéjol goes on to note that

in Spain heresy was more than a religious question; it was also a political and national issue. Rome displayed more tolerance towards the *Mariscos* [converted Muslims] and *Marranos* [converted Jews] because, even in case of relapse, to her they were nothing more than hardened sinners. The Spaniards regarded them as both apostates and aliens. The clergy shared the passions of the multitude; the multitude breathed the fanaticism of the clergy. That is why the Holy Office, which left a deservedly odious memory in other nations, enjoyed a great popularity in Spain. It was not from fear alone that nobles and commoners became familiars of the Inquisition. These corrections gratified that jealous, exclusary and somber patriotism which found satisfaction of ancient hates in a pitiless severity.[15]

THE HAPSBURG DYNASTY:
GLORY AND DECADENCE

With the death of the Catholic Kings, the German Hapsburgs came to rule Spain. They were the descendants of the union between Juana, the daughter of Ferdinand and Isabella, and Philip, the son of Maximilian I, emperor of the Holy Roman Empire. When Isabella died in 1504, Juana inherited the crown of Castile, but when Ferdinand died in 1516, he left the crown of Aragon not to his daughter but to her son, Charles, for Juana, had in the meantime, been declared insane and locked away in a convent. After the death of his mother—who remained queen of Castile despite her madness and imprisonment—Charles became the first monarch since the time of the Visigoths to rule all of Spain from a single throne. Three years after he became King Charles I of Spain at the age of sixteen, he was elected Emperor Charles V of the Holy Roman Empire.[16]

The reign of Charles V belongs more to the history of Europe than to the history of Spain. His realms included the Germanies and Austria (and parts of what would later be Czechoslovakia, Yugoslavia, and Poland); the Low Countries; parts of France (Franche-Comté and Rousillon); over half of Italy; all of Spain; and all of the New World except Brazil (including a large part of what is today the United States). Charles was a visionary who dreamed on a global scale of a Europe politically united through his crown and spiritually united through Catholicism. He envisioned Christian soldiers and missionaries under his banner extending this unity to the New World.

As emperor, Charles had many enemies: Henry VIII of England, Francis I of France, Suleiman I of the Ottoman Empire, Pope Clement VII (in his temporal capacity as sovereign of central Italy), and Martin Luther among them. He fought Francis and Henry for political supremacy and sacked Rome, taking Clement prisoner for failing to break an alliance with Francis. Charles fought the Turks who were menacing the very gates of Vienna in the name of Muhammad, and he struggled to crush Luther's ideas, which threatened the spiritual unity essential to his universalist scheme.

Charles's role as emperor transcended Spain, but his background and his role as king is important for this overview. When Charles came to Spain to claim his throne in 1517, he had never before set foot in his own country. He had been born and reared in the Low Countries and was Flemish in language and culture. He spoke no Spanish and was ignorant of Spanish mores, and he soon made a serious error in judgment, appointing a Fleming to act as regent when he left the country in 1520 to electioneer for the imperial crown. The people rose up in arms, not against the right of the king to rule but against his effrontery in ruling through a non-Spaniard. This was known as the revolt of the *comuneros* (citizens of the local communities in Castile). Charles rectified his mistake and henceforth governed Spain by keeping the *fueros* intact and honoring the existence of the regional *cortes*. Unfortunately, he made incessant demands upon the legislatures to fund the pursuit of his worldwide ambitions, and he can be blamed for inflicting economic harm on Spain from which it suffered for generations. Yet he also thrust greatness on Spain, inaugurating its Golden Age; Charles took Spain with him, so to speak, into the enormous theater of the Holy Roman Empire. He forced upon Spaniards a cosmopolitanism that has ever since waged war in their souls against the provincialism that had its roots in the singular obsession of the Reconquest.

By 1555, Charles was exhausted, his dream of universal brotherhood and security unrealized. He was ahead of his time—an internationalist among nationalists, a believer in spiritual orthodoxy at a time when heterodoxy was rampant. He was also a restless man whose dominions spanned continents but who had no home. Charles finally decided to give up his power, abdicating in Belgium in 1555. He retired to Yuste, a remote village in Extremadura in western Spain, the country that he had grown to love but that he had not visited for thirteen years prior to his return. When he abandoned his thrones, he divided his domains and gave the Hapsburg Empire to his brother Ferdinand. To his son Philip, he gave Spain, the New World, the Italian possessions, and the Low Countries. Charles died in 1558. As J. H. Elliott writes, "His retreat to Yuste and the accession of his Spanish-born son fittingly symbolized the hispanization of the dynasty."[17]

Philip II was the first *Spaniard* on the throne; he was not a Fleming like Charles nor a Castilian like Isabella nor an Aragonese like Ferdinand. He also possessed characteristics and values that Spaniards came to honor: an almost mystical devotion to Spain and to Spanish unity, a dedication to the work of being king, and a profound religious faith. Philip ruled with the *fueros* and the regional *cortes* relatively untouched, as had his father, but he acted to centralize the state administratively and symbolically by creating a permanent capital in 1561. Until Philip II chose Madrid, an obscure Castilian village in the geographic center of the peninsula, as the capital, the government had been located wherever the monarchs happened to be as they crisscrossed their realms in constant travel.

Philip relentlessly pursued political unity through religious orthodoxy. The cruel alternatives presented to the Moors by the Catholic Kings—renounce Islam or leave Spain—had produced converts in name only, and they resisted absorption into Christian life. Sixty years later, they were still steeped in Islamic culture and faith; moreover, they were thought to be in close contact with Turkish coreligionists whose control of the Mediterranean Charles V had been unable to break and who continued to threaten the Christian hegemony of Europe. In 1568, the Muslim converts in Alpujarra, a village in the province of Granada, revolted against the king. Philip put his troops under the command of his half brother Don Juan of Austria; and after two years of savage fighting, with atrocities committed by both Christians and Muslims, the revolt was put down, and the Granadan Arabs were scattered like so much debris throughout Spain. The following year, Don Juan crushed the Turkish sea power in the naval battle of Lepanto, off the coast of Greece, accomplishing for the rest of the continent what his great-grandparents had accomplished for Spain: the eradication of what Christians in that militant religious age saw as the scourge of Islam.

Philip II did not achieve a comparable triumph over Protestantism, which he considered no less heinous than Islam. In the Low Countries (particularly in the United Provinces, later called the Netherlands), Protestantism had made deep inroads not only as a religious force undermining the papacy but also as a political force undermining Spain. For the Dutch, to be Protestant was to be anti-Spanish, and to be anti-Spanish was to support independence. In 1579, the Netherlands declared its independence with the help of England. Protestantism linked the two nations spiritually, but England was inspired by more than religion. In the struggle for political supremacy in Europe and in the colonies, Spain was England's most formidable opponent. Anything that weakened Spain strengthened England, and the revolt of the Dutch undermined Spanish power. Elizabeth I of England relished Spain's predicament and did everything possible to exacerbate it. Taking up the challenge for Spain and for Catholicism, Philip launched the Spanish Armada in 1588 to humble England, crush its sea power, and cut its lifelines. His defeat was psychologically devastating. Although Spain emerged from the disaster still a great nation, hindsight now tells us that 1588 represented the zenith of Spanish power in the world.

My account of Spanish political history accelerates significantly after the death of Philip II in 1598, in part because the main themes of politics had already been established by that date: unity and separatism; regional rights (the *fueros* and the *cortes*); religious orthodoxy; and the unity of church and state, with its equation of heresy and treason. These themes endured for generations, even centuries, and most of them are still present in modern Spain.

The concept of a perennial struggle between two Spains is perhaps too frequently invoked as an explanation of the tensions in Spanish history, but this does not necessarily mean that the concept lacks all value in relation to specific periods. If it is unwise to search too closely for a continuity extending over several centuries, it is still possible to see a recurrence of certain types of divisions that are common to all societies but that have been particularly sharp at certain moments in the history of Spain. The peninsula's geographic position and historical experience periodically tend to make it divide, especially over the question of its relationship—whether political or cultural—with the other parts of Europe. One such moment of division occurred in the middle decades of the sixteenth century. At a time of great religious and intellectual ferment throughout Western Europe, many naturally felt that Spain would only be safe if it remained true to its own secluded past. But it was no less natural for others to react with enthusiasm to new ideas from abroad and see in them fresh hope for the regeneration of society. Since there was no obvious compromise between these two points of view at a time when the European situation itself discouraged compromise, the struggle was likely to be long and arduous. It was, indeed, intermittently fought from the 1520s to the 1560s, and it ended in victory for the traditionalists; by the end of the 1560s, the "open" Spain of the Renaissance had been transformed into the partially "closed" Spain of the Counter Reformation.[18]

Philip II was followed by successors unworthy of their heritage, and during the reigns of the last Hapsburgs—Philip III, Philip IV, and Charles

II—the degeneration of Spain paralleled the degeneration of the sovereigns themselves. Internationally, the final humiliation came in 1643 at the Battle of Rocroi, in the rebellious Low Countries, when French troops routed Spain's most celebrated soldiers, the *Tercios*. Spain thus suffered defeat by both England and France, the two nations that eclipsed it to become the major European powers for the next 250 years.

Spain continued to be an integral part of the European scene, but it played only a secondary role after the 1600s. Domestically, it continued its self-mutilation. In 1609, the Spanish expelled all Moors from the national territory, casting out a people who had lived on the peninsula for nearly 900 years. With the Jews gone since 1492 and the Moors banished, Spain had crippled itself. The Moors and the Jews had been among the most creative people in Spanish history, and when they were driven out, their genius went unreplaced.

NOTES

1. See C.H.V. Sutherland, *The Romans in Spain, 217 B.C.–A.D. 117* (London: Methuen & Co, 1939). Sutherland analyzes Roman citizenship in Spain as it was interpreted by Caesar, Augustus, the Julio-Claudians, and Trajan.

2. A. E. Thompson, *The Goths in Spain* (Oxford: Clarendon Press, 1969), p. 156.

3. Ibid., 105–109.

4. Stanley G. Payne, *Spanish Catholicism* (Madison: University of Wisconsin Press, 1984), p. 4.

5. Thompson, *The Goths in Spain*, pp. 190–217.

6. Aloysius K. Ziegler, *Church and State in Visigothic Spain* (Washington, D.C.: Catholic University of America, 1930), pp. 16–17.

7. Bernard F. Reilly, *The Contest of Christian and Muslim Spain, 1031–1157* (Cambridge, Mass., and Oxford: Blackwell, 1992), p. 12.

8. Ibid. See also Stanley Lane-Poole, *The Moors in Spain* (Baltimore: Black Classic Press, 1990), chapter 12.

9. The royal motto of Isabella and Ferdinand symbolized their separateness within their unity or more precisely, the separate entity of each sovereign's realm within the unity of Spain created by their marriage. The motto has almost become symbolic of the separateness within unity of the peoples of Spain even today. That motto—*Tanto Monta Monta Tanto Isabel Como Fernando*—is difficult to translate smoothly and succinctly. Awkwardly but accurately translated, it says: "Isabella mounts the throne with sovereignty equal to that of Ferdinand, who mounts the throne with sovereignty equal to that of Isabella."

10. The word *cortes* is both singular and plural.

11. Jaime Vicens Vives, *Approach to the History of Spain* (Berkeley: University of California Press, 1970), p. 32.

12. Henry Kamen, *Inquisition and Society in Spain* (London: Weidenfeld and Nicholson, 1985), p. 1.

13. Poul Borchsenius, *The History of the Jews,* vol. 3, *The Three Rings* (New York: Simon and Schuster, 1965), pp. 9–10.

14. Jean Hippolyte Mariéjol, *The Spain of Ferdinand and Isabella* (New Brunswick, NJ: Rutgers University Press, 1961), pp. 38–39.

15. Ibid., 57–58.

16. Intricacies of the inheritance of the Spanish throne and election as emperor of the Holy Roman Empire are beyond the scope of this study, but they make fascinating reading to those so interested. Among the best accounts is A. W. Lovett, *Early Hapsburg Spain, 1517–1598* (Oxford: Oxford University Press, 1986), chapters 3 and 4.

17. J. H. Elliott, *Imperial Spain, 1469–1716* (London: Edward Arnold Publishers, 1963), p. 202.

18. Ibid., p. 208.

2

Spain Under the Bourbons

Charles II produced no heirs, and when he died, his throne went to the French duke of Anjou, Philip, grandson of Louis XIV and Maria Theresa, Charles's sister. The legacy was challenged by the English, who feared that France would become the master of Europe if there were Bourbon kings on both sides of the Pyrenees. Never was it more clear that Spain had ceased to be a major nation and become the pawn of more powerful ones. Ultimately, the choice of Spain's next sovereign was decided by the War of the Spanish Succession, in which England allied with Portugal, the Netherlands, and the Holy Roman Empire to support the Hapsburg archduke, Charles, against France and a hapless Spain. France was victorious, and in 1700, the French duke became Philip V, the first Bourbon on the Spanish throne.

Like the Hapsburgs before them, the Spanish Bourbons involved Spain in European dynastic intrigues and wars that continued to drain the country's dwindling resources, with little benefit accruing to Spain. In fact, Spain lost colonies bartered away in treaties that secured only temporary peace. Spain fought wars with France, England, and the Holy Roman Empire in 1719; with England in 1739; with the Holy Roman Empire in 1740; with England again in 1762; with Portugal (in Brazil) in 1776; and, for a fourth time, with England (the American Revolution) in 1779.

Domestically, the Spanish Bourbons reversed the policies of the Hapsburgs and their predecessors, enforcing political unity by destroying almost all the *fueros* and the regional *cortes*—traditional institutions that meant nothing to the newly arrived Bourbons. They patterned their centralist policies after those of Louis XIV, who allowed no political institutions to stand between the sovereign and his subjects. Philip V, for example, stripped Catalonia, Aragon, and Valencia of their historical rights and representative bodies. He was particularly vengeful against these provinces because they had supported the Hapsburg pretender in the War of the Spanish Succession, but he was only slightly less severe with the Basque provinces and Navarre, which had used better judgment. Philip

37

made it clear that the Bourbons would tolerate no infringement on the absolutism of the king or on the authority of the center. His policy seriously undermined the legitimacy of the Bourbon house among its new subjects, and not until the reign of Charles III (1759–1788), one of Spain's few good rulers, were the Bourbons accepted as legitimate sovereigns and legitimate Spaniards, despite their French origin and their flouting of Spanish traditions.[1]

THE NAPOLEONIC INTERLUDE

The people's loyalty was tested during the reign of the two kings who succeeded Charles III—Charles IV and Ferdinand VII, the two worst sovereigns in Spanish history. (Ferdinand was perhaps the worst of all.) Their reigns are important because they are part of the Napoleonic history of Spain. In 1808, Charles IV was deposed by Napoleon and replaced by the latter's brother, Joseph Bonaparte. The people of Madrid responded to this usurpation by revolting against the French occupiers on May 2, 1808, and the uprising soon spread throughout the country. The War of Independence—as Spaniards call this guerrilla war—lasted from 1808 to 1814, when the Spanish finally ousted the French. The Peninsular War—as it is called by non-Spaniards—was part of the larger European campaign against Napoleon, and victory over the French was achieved primarily because of British intervention in Spain. The valor of the Spanish people cannot be denied, however. Ironically, they fought in the name of Ferdinand VII: His father had been far more despotic (and corrupt and inefficient) than Joseph Bonaparte, who had brought a constitution that, in many ways, was quite progressive. The Spaniards fought for what they considered to be the legitimate Spanish royal house, and they mythologized Ferdinand VII, the heir of the deposed Charles IV, as *el deseado*—the desired one, who would bring honor back to Spain.

During the hiatus of authority that lasted while the Bourbons were out of Spain and the Napoleonic rulers were fighting to maintain their control, self-governing juntas sprang up throughout the country. These juntas elected representatives to an assembly that met from 1809 to 1813 in Cádiz on the South Atlantic coast, out of French reach. This was the first *cortes* in Spanish history representing all of the country in a single legislative body. From this *cortes* came the celebrated liberal constitution of 1812 that established the terms of the Bourbon restoration: a limited monarchy with separation of powers, full guarantee of civil and human rights, land reform for uncultivated acreage, abolition of all existing seignorial rights, local self-government, abolition of slavery, public education, and tax reform. The constitution recognized Catholicism as the state religion, but it abolished the Inquisition, restricted the number of monasteries and convents, and required the clergy to pay taxes.

The constitution of 1812 reflected only one interpretation of the meaning of the War of Independence. Both liberals and conservatives fought to oust the French, but each had a different rationale for doing so.

> Was the war, as liberal patriots maintained, a revolution to regenerate Spain by new laws? Had the social contract been broken and the nation "which had done all" in the way of resistance to the intruder resumed its constituent powers? Were, as conservatives replied, the old laws which they continued to administer, and the old institutions which they still manned, the only valid constitution? Were, therefore, the deputies of the *Cortes* to limit themselves to the study of the "means and methods of expelling the French army," or was their sacred task to endow Spain with a constitution that would limit the despotism which had ended in French invasion?[2]

Ferdinand VII repudiated the entire constitution the moment he ascended the throne in 1814, and he reestablished a regime more absolutist than that of Charles IV. Ferdinand's repression became so severe that the people revolted in 1820, reinstalled a constitutional monarchy, and, in an action that defies logic, requested the same Ferdinand to return as king. Ferdinand swore fidelity to the constitution, but after his reactionary French cousin Charles X sent troops to restore absolutism to Spain, he once again showed his true colors, reverting to the despotism that had characterized his earlier behavior.

POLITICAL DEVELOPMENTS

The reaction to the constitution of 1812 and to the reign of Ferdinand VII shaped political alignments for the remainder of the nineteenth century. Yet just as in the War of Independence, when long-suffering patriots fought in the name of the despotic Bourbon house, the philosophical positions after 1814 were not neat. The liberals accepted the constitution, the limited government, and the guarantees of civil rights, but they rejected the historical regional rights that antedated the constitution. They would tolerate no restrictions on the absolute sovereignty of the central government and were determined to weaken the power of the church by confiscating its property. The conservatives, on the other hand, rejected the constitution, supported an autocratic monarchy and a militant church, and repudiated the guarantees of civil and political rights set forth in the document, but championed the ancient democratic *fueros* that the Bourbons had all but destroyed.[3]

When Ferdinand died in 1833 without a male heir, his throne passed to his daughter, Isabella, who was still a child. Under the Bourbon Salic law, a female could not inherit the crown; under the tradition of the Hapsburgs and earlier precedents, a woman *could* inherit. The liberals supported Isabella. The conservatives initially opposed her but came to accept the Isabelline succession, becoming the liberals' primary opponent in the struggle to gain control of the political system. But a deeply disgruntled conservative faction rejected Isabella, and in the name of Ferdinand's brother Charles—from whom they took their name, Carlists—they began a civil war fought primarily in the Basque country, Navarre, and Catalonia. The war continued until 1839. Carlist wars would break out twice in the late 1840s and for a third time from 1870 to 1876. The question of dynastic legitimacy was obviously a part of the Carlist cause, yet, as Martin Blinkhorn argues, such controversy in other European countries finally petered out.

> Where Jacobitism, its closest British equivalent, quickly passed from the defeat of 1745 to become a hobby for eccentrics, and French legitimism was reduced after 1880 to being the obsession of a diminishing number of dreary aristocrats, Carlism continued as an important minority force in Spanish politics down to the twentieth century, thanks to its consistent ability to mobilize a mass following which, if never sufficient to bring victory, nevertheless prevented it from dying.[4]

What gave Spanish Carlism its wider, deeper appeal? The preservation of regional rights—the ancient *fueros*—contributed to the Carlist mystique. As José Luis Clemente contends, the goal of the liberal constitution of 1812 was to restructure Spain into a unitary nation-state divided into equal and uniform provinces, imitating French departments, that were to be governed from the *Cortes* at Madrid.[5] Whatever *fueros* still existed from earlier times, that is, those not already swept away by the Bourbons between 1700 and 1808, would disappear, leaving the Basque lands and Catalonia without their political distinctiveness.

But beyond the dynastic and foral controversies, Carlism spoke to an even deeper animosity. Again Blinkhorn explains:

> Around the often undeserving persons of the Carlist pretenders to the Spanish throne, there grew up a cause which attracted a substantial minority of mostly rural Spaniards to a crusade against the dominant developments of the age: urbanism and industrialism in the socioeconomic sphere; tolerance, skepticism and atheism in that of religion; centralization of administration; and in the world of politics, liberalism and socialism. To counter these horrors, Carlism slowly formulated a programme calling for the "installation" of a "traditional" but not absolute monarchy; administrative devolution in

the home of the historic *fueros* (rights, laws and privileges) of the Spanish religion; a corporative social and political system guaranteeing universal well-being and harmony; and, infusing everything, "Catholic Unity" involving uniformity of belief, expression, and behaviour.[6]

In the meantime, Spain was ruled by the regents of Isabella, first her mother and then, following the mother's exile, General Baldomero Espartero. After 1843, the queen herself ascended the throne, but her reign became so corrupt and morally scandalous (her amorous life was the talk of Europe) that she was forced to abdicate after a revolution in 1868.

In light of future Spanish politics, perhaps the most far-reaching event of Isabella's reign was the confiscation of church property, which took place during the administration of liberal prime minister Juan Alvarez Mendizábal.[7] The church lost most of its independence of action when it lost its sources of revenue. Henceforth, the state paid the salaries of the clergymen under the terms of the concordat negotiated with the Vatican in 1851. Dependence on the state turned the Spanish church into the state's apologist, a posture that reached its ultimate development during the Franco regime. True enough, there had been an intimate relationship between church and state since the Reconquest, but it had been a relationship between equals, not between subventioner and supplicant. Gerald Lovett writes:

> As new social forces and new political doctrines entered the stage, what had originally been reformist [liberal] was bound to become conservative. Only the Spanish Church remained in the position it had taken at the end of the War of Independence. In 1812–1813 it joined one of the two political groups emerging in the Cortes and evolved from what had been one of the foundations of the State into the ally of the conservatives. For the past 150 years it has allied itself fairly consistently with the conservative elements in the nation. The anticlericalism created among liberals by its support of Fernando VII and its continued alliance with the forces that could guarantee it best against liberal assaults on its position has continued to be a hallmark of a large sector of Spanish intellectuals and professionals.[8]

Stanley Payne adds:

> The introduction of modern liberalism early in the nineteenth century produced the first major break in the history and institutional relationships of Spanish Catholicism since the eighth century, more than a millennium before. Though that break was by no means a complete one, it altered fundamentally the character of Church-state relations, the economic basis of the Church, the relation between religion and society, and even certain aspects of religiosity in general.[9]

After the revolution in 1868, the military again ruled Spain, until a new king was chosen in 1870. The selection of Amadeo, the brother of King Victor Emmanuel II of Italy, prompted the Carlists to rise again, and another civil war ensued. This time the Republicans, a new force in Spanish politics, joined the Carlists in opposing the king, and in 1873, Amadeo abdicated. A republic was established that lasted less than a year, during which time there were four presidents and constant war with the Carlists. Finally, the insurgents were subdued, and as punishment for the Carlists' challenge to national unity, Madrid abolished all remaining *fueros* except a few minor ones in Navarre.

The republicanism that inspired the unfortunate First Republic was a romantic, elitist phenomenon that had little popular support. It emerged from European sources that believed that political turmoil, particularly international disorder, sprang from dynastic competition and intrigue. Thus, if dynasties disappeared, so, too, would the conflict they spurred. Republicanism was seen as the antidote to monarchism, and federalism, part of the republican canon, would keep republicanism from being abusive: "By restoring political sovereignty to 'natural groups' such as the towns, federalism would prevent the abuse of power by Madrid politicians."[10] Irrespective of its lack of popular support, however, nineteenth-century republicanism—and its accompanying federalism—was one more of the unresolved political ideas (like liberalism, conservatism, Carlism, and socialism) that kept Spain disquieted. The Bourbons were restored in 1875 in the person of King Alfonso XII, Isabella's son, who ruled with extensive power under a new constitution created in 1876. The cabinet was responsible to the king and not to the bicameral legislature that could be summoned, prorogued, and dismissed by the monarch. The monarch's only restriction was that the legislature be replaced within three months of dismissal. Alfonso had the makings of a good sovereign, but unfortunately, he died young. He was succeeded by his queen, Maria Cristina, who was pregnant with the heir, born King Alfonso XIII in 1886. The queen acted as regent until 1902, when the king reached the age of sixteen and ascended the throne with full power.

THE SECOND RESTORATION

Several issues of major importance for later Spanish politics originated during the decades of misrule between the Bourbon restoration in 1814 and the second restoration of 1875—a period that included thirty-five military uprisings, or *pronunciamientos*, eleven of which were considered successful.[11] First, the military entered the political arena, where it would remain a formidable presence until the end of the Franco regime and even into the post-Franco era. Second, regionalism took on a new dimension as Catalonia and the Basque country (the two centers of dissidence before the restoration in 1875) became the country's most prosperous regions. The people of both areas believed that the government in Madrid drained them financially through taxation without granting them commensurate political power in return. Catalonia was particularly incensed, for it had become the manufacturing center of the nation and wanted tariffs to protect its new industries. Along with the Basque provinces, Catalonia demanded the return of regional rights, the *fueros*, that would give them a degree of political and economic freedom and flexibility. Third, socialism gave an increasingly strident voice to the growing proletariat of Catalonia, the Basque provinces, and Asturias, the coal-mining center of Spain. Equally shrill was the anarchist voice of discontent, heard both in rural Andalucia and in urban Catalonia.

During the regency of Maria Cristina, these issues fermented while Spain enjoyed a rare period of relatively stable government. Once the third uprising of the Carlists had been put down in 1875, the oligarchy (although divided politically into the Liberal and Conservative parties respectively) realized that only solidarity against the increasingly urgent demands of the masses could preserve the kind of Spain enjoyed by the gentry. Antonio Cánovas del Castillo and Praxedes Sagasta, leaders of the Conservative and Liberal parties, arrived at a tacit agreement to put aside past differences and govern Spain in rotation. They secured the necessary electoral majorities by rigging national elections, which under the constitution of 1876, guaranteed universal male suffrage. Their arrangement became known as the "peaceful rotation" (*turno pacífico*).[12] The two major party chiefs then worked to forestall further revolt among the Carlists by offering to make the movement's defeated military commanders officers in the armed forces of the restored monarchy. Given the pandemonium of Spanish politics between the first restoration of the Bourbons in 1814 and the second in 1875, some believe that the peace and order achieved by the Liberal-Conservative collusion was worth the price of constitutional corruption. An additional price was paid, however, that boded ill for long-term peace and order. The trade-off between the two elite parties froze a socioeconomic status quo that excluded both the growing urban proletariat of Catalonia and the Basque lands, whose frustration was mounting, and the Andalucian peasantry, whose requests for land reform were rapidly becoming demands. Forced out of meaningful politics and deprived of effective electoral expression, the lower classes turned to socialism and anarchism. Eventually, they also turned to direct action: strikes, violence, and assassination.

The death of Cánovas in 1897, the assassination of Sagasta in 1903, and the accession of the boy-king Alfonso XIII in 1902 put an end to the artificial stability. The two major parties fractionalized as they searched for new leadership, and the growing social and regional unrest generated a proliferation of new parties. The lack of clear legislative majorities played into the hands of the new king, who manipulated unstable coalitions to his advantage. But Alfonso lacked both political intelligence and scruples, and he had grandiose notions of kingly rights that, regardless of their constitutionality, were out of step with the political realities of the twentieth century. Moreover, he took his title of commander in chief of the armed forces literally, giving the military his tacit approval to act without informing the *Cortes*.

During Alfonso's reign, proletarian unrest continued to mount, particularly in Catalonia. In 1909, during what was later called *la semana trágica* ("the tragic week"), the masses took to the streets in Barcelona in an outburst of class hatred hitherto unknown in Spain, unleashed against all the forces of oppression—military, political, and economic. Gerald Brenan describes the event as "five days of mob rule in which union leaders lost all control of their men, and twenty-two churches and thirty-four convents were burned. Monks were killed, tombstones were desecrated and strange and macabre scenes took place as when workers danced in the streets with the disinterred mummies of nuns."[13]

Frightened as never before, the oligarchy retaliated by organizing private police forces, often made up of men who were little more than paid killers. The violence between these toughs and the ruffians of the socialist labor union—the General Workers' Union (Unión General de Trabajadores)—and the anarchist trade union—the National Workers' Confederation (Confederación Nacional de Trabajadores)—accelerated year by year. Between 1917 and 1921, 1,472 political crimes were committed in the major cities of Spain, 809 in Barcelona alone.[14] Unfortunately for the solidarity of the workers, the violence between socialists and anarchists was often as bloody as that between the labor groups and the hired gunmen of the oligarchy.

The intensification of proletarian fury led to a change in the political orientation of the Basque and Catalan socioeconomic elites, particularly the latter. The "stalemate society" achieved by Cánovas and Sagasta had maintained the preindustrial and precapitalist values favored by the majority of the Spanish gentry—the landowners, ranchers, citrus and olive growers, and mine owners and operators. But the burgeoning capitalist entrepreneurial class of Catalonia and the Basque territories suffered from discrimination by the political decisionmakers in Madrid, who maintained a policy of free trade that benefited producers of raw materials and foodstuffs meant for export. The Catalans and Basques wanted protection for infant industries, and they chafed under Madrid's restrictions. Their demands for autonomy were as much economic in origin as cultural or historical. The desire to escape what was considered centrist suffocation grew stronger, yet the behavior of the workers eventually caused the regional oligarchy to fear the proletariat more than it hated the government in Madrid, which commanded the forces of law and order needed to crush labor violence. Catalonia therefore muted its clamor for autonomy in exchange for protection from Madrid, and by royal decree, Alfonso rewarded the region with a partial restoration of the *fueros* in the form of a highly symbolic but almost powerless legislative body called the Mancomunidad.

THE ROLE OF THE MILITARY

Catalonia's new political posture played into the hands of the armed forces, whose arrogance had been growing since the turn of the century. Indeed, the military had come to consider itself indispensable to public order and immune to civilian political control. It excoriated any individual or group whose behavior was deemed to undermine national unity—not only the socialist and the anarchist lower classes but the regionalist upper classes as well.

The military first entered domestic politics when most of the overseas army returned to Spain after the Latin American colonies (with the exception of Cuba and Puerto Rico) declared themselves independent during the reign of Joseph Bonaparte. The remaining colonial forces returned after their humiliating defeat in the Spanish-American War of 1898. Back for good, the military sought a place to redeem its honor, and decided upon Morocco. The cities of Ceuta and Melilla on the Moroccan coast had been Spanish for centuries—Melilla since 1497, Ceuta since 1581. After the turn of the twentieth century, when the European powers were jockeying to occupy what still remained native on the African continent, the Spanish military set out to annex the hinterland of the two Spanish cities, with the sanction of Alfonso XIII. The resistance put up by the local Berber tribes was as fierce as it was unexpected, and the Spanish soldiers—mostly recruits from the poorer classes whose families could not afford to buy off the military service of their sons—were literally slaughtered; 10,000 were lost in one battle alone at Anual.

The reaction at home was volcanic. The *Cortes* began an investigation of the army and of the king's alleged collusion, but before its report could be made, General Miguel Primo de Rivera executed a coup d'état in 1923 that abolished the constitution. Primo proclaimed himself dictator, but Alfonso XIII remained as the state's figurehead, an arrangement that suited both the king and the caudillo. Without Primo, the king would probably have lost his throne; without Alfonso, the dictator would have lacked legitimacy.

The proximate causes of the coup d'état, or what James Rial calls "the revolution from above," were the consequences of the war in Morocco. But the deeper causes were rooted in the constitution of 1812 and the subsequent politics of the nineteenth century. The conflict between liberals and conservatives was never reconciled within a properly working parliamentary process. After years of upheaval and frequent violence, the cynical arrangement made by Cánovas and Sagasta after the second restoration produced stability and peace, but it was little more than a division of the spoils between two major political players who continued to find each other's ideas and policies repugnant. To use an analogy taken from the field of addiction therapy, the two politicians were the enablers of a deeply dysfunctional political system, providing palliatives that further corrupted an already decaying polity.

The liberal-conservative irresolution within the political system was compounded by the Carlists' unregenerate opposition to both these forces. After three civil wars, the Carlist military leaders were absorbed into the armed forces loyal to the heirs of the Isabelline monarchy, but they were, in many ways, like the *conversos* in earlier centuries who converted to Christianity to save their skins but never lost their original faith. (The Carlists would also be among the most jubilant celebrants at the fall of Alfonso XIII in 1931.)

The republicans added to the political quagmire by opposing the liberals, conservatives, and Carlists alike, all of whom supported some form of monarchy. But as we have already seen, the republicans lacked popular support. They were idealistic, romantic elites who saw a republic as a kind of shining city on the hill, intrinsically providing a corrective to all political ills. They failed to comprehend the turbulence that can exist within republican systems. (The Civil War in the United States, one of the few republics in the world at the time, should have given Spanish republicans some pause; that war had been over for only nine years when the ill-fated Spanish republic came into being.)

Two political forces, both of them opposed to liberalism, conservatism, Carlism, and republicanism, would mobilize the masses: socialism (Marxism) and anarchism. These were, however, in deadly opposition to each other. In the international arena, socialism had won the battle for the minds of the working masses following the Second International in 1898, but in Spain (as in Russia), anarchism remained a potent force. Both socialism and anarchism gave choice to the workers and peasants of Spain, but the mutual hatred felt by adherents to the two ideologies undermined Spanish working-class solidarity.

All these unresolved conflicts had brought Spain near political hysteria by the time Primo de Rivera appeared on the scene.

THE LAST DECADE OF BOURBON RULE

In its early stages, the dictatorship was far from universally condemned. The working class, the small middle class, and the intelligentsia suffered from Primo's rigid censorship and his abolition of free trade unions and political parties. The classes that ran Spain, however—primarily the landowners but also the new industrialists—were satisfied with the general's accomplishments and welcomed the protection that the army afforded against domestic violence and strikes. To Primo's credit, he initiated economic improvements such as highway and railway construction and hydroelectric and irrigation projects. Believing as he did in the almost redemptive quality of rural and small-town life, he also sought to invigorate local government through the Municipal Statute (Estatuto Municipal), which would encourage local self-government and break the imposed uniformity that treated all local units, regardless of size, in the same manner. At the national level, he created the Patriotic Union (Unión Patriótica), a kind of citizens's rally for good government—as defined by Primo, of course. He also had a new constitution created, but it ended up a mishmash of political *isms* and notions; one such concept—corporatism—was reflected in an upper house filled by various interest groups.

Unfortunately, his ambitions overreached Spain's human and natural resources, and when the post–World War I boom slid toward the depression of the late 1920s, Spain found itself seriously overextended economically and politically exhausted. Spectacular events such as the world fairs held in Seville and Barcelona were insufficient to stimulate the lagging economy or regenerate a destitute part of the country like Andalucia. Primo's failure to solve the economic crisis dampened the support of earlier enthusiasts, and his bad judgment in other areas contributed to his waning popularity. He also courted the church, but his strategy backfired. Primo failed in his attempt to extend to both a private Jesuit and a private Augustinian college the right to grant official university degrees, a privilege traditionally enjoyed exclusively by the state universities. Moreover, his orders to revoke the Mancomunidad granted by Alfonso alienated most of the Catalan elite who had earlier been his champions.

As long as the army stayed loyal, there was little that anyone could do to remove Primo, though the king was also becoming increasingly restive in his figurehead role. But Primo then made a fatal mistake. In his rush to reform Spain and to cut expenses, he decided to reduce the gargantuan officer corps; at the time, the ratio of officers to soldiers in the Spanish military was the highest in Europe. The army elite immediately appealed to Alfonso to countermand Primo's orders, switching their allegiance from the dictator to the king. With the army on his side and eager to cleanse himself of the caudillo's contamination, Alfonso demanded that

Primo resign. The general, in no position to bargain, complied. In January 1930, he left for France, where he died a few months later. James H. Rial appraises the Primo years:

> As dictator, Primo intended more than serving as the military's avenging angel. His goal was nothing less than national regeneration. He brought to government qualities that had been largely absent during the last years of the constitutional regime—energy, confidence, and an intense if somewhat ill-focused ambition for his country's future. Nonetheless, he too failed. His economic policies produced only a short-lived, unevenly distributed spurt. He expanded on the constitutional regime's social reforms but left office with class rifts as deep as before. His greatest failures, however, were political, where he tried and needed most to succeed. The Patriotic Union attracted more place seekers than patriots, and the National Assembly generated more divisions than it healed. The regime's constitutional proposal was so unworkable that Primo could not even use it to withdraw from power.[15]

By the time the proposal was ready, the balance of power between Primo and Alfonso XIII had changed so drastically that the king refused either to sign it into law or to submit it to referendum.

Primo's resignation came too late to save either the monarch or the monarchy. Opposition to the crown had developed even within impeccably conservative groups for whom republicanism had previously been synonymous with revolution. Alfonso tried to hold on, appointing a civilian government to replace Primo, but he would not call elections. The king was faced with a dilemma. If it were judged that the dictatorship had merely interrupted constitutional continuity, then the 1876 constitution was still in force and elections had to be called. If the dictatorship had destroyed the constitution, then a new one had to be created by an elected constituent assembly, either to restore the monarchy or to establish a republic. If elections were not called and Alfonso chose to remain, he would become a dictator and thereby destroy the honor of the Bourbon royal house.

Alfonso opted for three successive elections: municipal, provincial, and parliamentary. He hoped that antimonarchical sentiments would cool by the time the parliamentary elections were held, but the results of the municipal elections were so overwhelmingly prorepublican in the big cities and in all the provincial capitals except Cádiz that the king decided upon voluntary exile. His move was perhaps prompted by the action of the city councils of Oviedo, Seville, and Valencia in proclaiming the Republic of Spain and by the action of the Catalan separatists, who deliriously (and prematurely) announced the Republic of Catalonia. Republicanism had ceased to be merely a romantic notion supported by a small number of idealistic elites, as it had been in the late nineteenth century; it was now supported by the masses as the only alternative to monarchism. Even the commander of the Civil Guard, General José Sanjurjo, declared for the republic, and the army had already disassociated itself from the king, who was left alone and powerless. On April 14, 1931, Alfonso left Spain, never to return. He did not abdicate, however; he simply went into exile in Rome, where he died in 1949.

NOTES

1. For a good, concise history of the rule of the Bourbons from their accession in 1700 through the reign of Carlos III, see W. N. Hargreaves-Mawdsley, *Eighteenth-Century Spain, 1700–1788* (Totowa, N.J.: Rowman and Littlefield, 1979).

2. Raymond Carr, *Spain 1808–1975* (Oxford: Clarendon Press, 1982), p. 93.

3. For an excellent summary of this convoluted plot, see Gerald H. Lovett, *Napoleon and the Birth of Modern Spain* (New York: New York University Press, 1965), pp. 843–850.

4. Martin Blinkhorn, *Carlism and Crisis in Spain, 1931–1939* (Cambridge: Cambridge University Press, 1975), p. 12.

5. José Luis Clemente, *Bases documentatles del Carlismo y de las guerras civiles de los siglos XIX y XX*, vol. 1 (Madrid: Servicio Militar, 1985), pp. 15–16.

6. Blinkhorn, *Carlism and Crisis in Spain*, p. 3.

7. The liberal state did not give the lands of the church to the poor. Liberalism in Spain was much like liberalism throughout the rest of Europe—a bourgeois phenomenon supported by a class that hated and feared the poor and the dispossessed as much as conservatives did. The liberals sought to eliminate not the conservatives as a class but only their antique, precapitalist political and economic privileges. Consequently, the church lands were sold to those who could afford to pay for them, not only the new liberal bourgeoisie but also the old conservative aristocracy. Greed to acquire more land led the traditional elites (although they were devout Catholics) to swallow their repugnance for the liberals who had so generously provided their windfall and to embrace the hated liberal state. Liberals and conservatives would cooperate again after the second Bourbon restoration in 1875.

8. Lovett, *Napoleon and the Birth of Modern Spain*, p. 849.

9. Stanley G. Payne, *Spanish Catholicism* (Madison: University of Wisconsin Press, 1984), p. 71.

10. C.A.M. Hennessy, *The Federal Republic in Spain* (Westport, Conn.: Greenwood Press, 1962), p. xiii. Hennessy believes that nineteenth-century republicanism in Spain was not the progenitor of twentieth-century Spanish republicanism, with its widespread popular support.

11. The historian Vicens Vives defines *pronunciamiento* as a military uprising that usually involves merely subverting all or part of the army and sometimes the police force, thereby depriving the government of the means to defend itself. See Jaime Vicens Vives, *Approaches to the History of Spain* (Berkeley: University of California Press, 1970).

Raymond Carr, *Spain 1808–1975*, p. 124, offers a more elaborate and precise definition: "The *pronunciamiento* was the instrument of liberal revolution in the nineteenth century. It was an officer revolt, justified by a crude political theory which made the officer corps the ultimate repository of a general will. When that will was vitiated either by the monarch's evil counsellors or, as the later theoreticians of military indiscipline were to maintain, by the corrupt operation of Parliamentary institutions run by a clique of 'anti-national' politicians, then it could be salvaged by the heroic gesture of a general or the conspiracy of an officers' mess. The origins of military intervention in politics lay perhaps in the role of generals in the eighteenth-century administration, and in the conflicts of politicians and soldiers during the War of Independence, but it was in Ferdinand's reign that this intervention developed the rigid form of classical drama. First came the preliminary soundings (the *trabajos*) and the winning over of officers and sergeants by a small activist group in touch with civilian conspirators; then the *compromisos* by which accomplices were bound to action; finally the chosen leaders set off the last stage by the cry—the *grito*. It was here, in the traditional speech to the drawn-up troops, that revolutionary formalism was most apparent."

12. For a provocative, favorable rationale of the process, see Carr, *Spain 1808–1975*, pp. 355–366.

13. Gerald Brenan, *The Spanish Labyrinth* (New York: Macmillan, 1944), p. 34.

14. Stanley G. Payne, *The Spanish Revolution* (New York: W. W. Norton, 1970), p. 60.

15. James H. Rial, *Revolution from Above* (Fairfax, Va.: George Mason University Press, 1986), p. 230.

3

Democracy and Civil War

THE SECOND REPUBLIC

By 1931, the republic was perhaps an idea whose time had come.[1] The monarchy had ended ignominiously after the collapse of the dictatorship, and the prestige of the army, which had propped up both institutions, had fallen precipitously after both its masters were repudiated. When the time for the republic finally arrived, however, the great majority of Spaniards were unable to perform the difficult and self-disciplined task of making democracy work. Much like Germany prior to the Weimar Republic, Spain prior to the Second Republic lacked democratic experience. The democracy of republican politics existed in isolation within a nondemocratic society. The family, the church, the schools, the bureaucracy, the workplace, the trade unions, and the political parties (including those on the left) were autocratic organizations that afforded the Spaniard little opportunity to learn how to play the democratic game. In short, the political system was incongruent with the socioeconomic system, to use Harry Eckstein's analysis.[2]

The electoral system devised for the Second Republic exacerbated problems in an already unrealistic political system. Designed to produce stability and to reward the strongest parties, the electoral system gave an exaggerated majority to the victors at the polls. The party or coalition of parties that won a majority, no matter how slight (as modest as 51 to 49 percent), received a disproportionately large number of legislative seats. For example, the winning party or coalition in Madrid would receive 13 of the city's 17 seats in the *Cortes*; in Barcelona, the winner would take 16 of the 20 seats.

The first artificial legislative majority went to the Left, inaugurating what is now referred to as the Red Biennium (December 9, 1931, to December 31, 1933). In fact, the domination of the Left began with the elections to the constituent assembly that became the first legislature of the new republic after the *Cortes* approved the constitution. The leftists in power included the Liberals, who, in accordance with the European liberal tradi-

51

tion, were liberal on civil and political issues but conservative on economic ones. Only a part of the Left was Marxist, but on questions of church and state, the Liberals matched the Marxists in their deep anti-Catholic prejudice, and this position was clearly spelled out in the controversial constitution approved by the *Cortes* in 1931.

THE CONSTITUTION OF 1931

Instead of a balanced, objective instrument designed to accommodate the nation as a whole, the constitution of 1931 can best be described as a weapon to humble the Right. "The new constitution of 1931, while codifying important principles, followed in the mold of all preceding modern Spanish constitutions in being the creation of one significant sector of political society to be imposed on that portion which did not share its values. In certain key respects it was no more the product of broad consensus and national agreement than its nineteenth-century predecessors."[3] This is particularly true of the articles regarding religion. The church had, indeed, become a corrupt institution, pandering to the wealthy classes since the middle of the nineteenth century, and it probably deserved its constitutional comeuppance. Realistically, however, the emotionally charged articles on religion could only enflame what was still a strongly Catholic nation. Devout Catholics could not fail to condemn a constitution whose articles declared freedom of religion; abolished the state clerical budget; closed all Catholic schools except seminaries (in a country in which over half of all schools were Catholic); forbade all clergy to teach in state schools; outlawed the Jesuits and confiscated their property; legalized divorce; and abolished religious burial unless specifically provided for by the deceased. None of the economic provisions—on land reform, for example—inspired nearly the anti-Republican sentiment that the gratuitously anticlerical and antireligious articles did. Furthermore, most of Spain's very large and influential clerical population was far from wealthy; the average parish priest, for instance, lived on an income little different from his parishioners. The church's wealth, which had gradually been rebuilt since the confiscations of the mid-1800s, was enjoyed only by the ecclesiastical elite. To cut off a humble priest's meager pay and then prevent him from earning a living in the state schools was to create a body of anti-Republican zealots. These opponents could have been supporters of the socioeconomic reforms of the Left had they been handled more logically and less emotionally by the framers of the constitution.

The Right was determined to undo the entire document, and it got the chance to do so with the elections that ushered in the Black Biennium (December 31, 1933, to February 16, 1936). Leftists claimed that the victory of the Right was due, in part, to the support of the newly enfranchised women voting on instruction from their priests. The Right also won because the anarchists deprived the Left of enormous electoral support by refusing to go to the polls, which would have compromised their antistatist ideology. Like the leftist government that preceded it, the rightist government reflected an artificial majority in the *Cortes,* and it behaved as blindly and as unintelligently, politically speaking, as had the Left from 1931 to 1933.

THE STRUGGLE BETWEEN LEFT AND RIGHT

When the Right began to reverse the laws passed by the Left and to amend the constitution, the Left in the *Cortes*—represented by Manuel Azaña, the prime minister during the Red Biennium and the motive force during the constituent assembly—announced that it was breaking all association with the existing institutions of the country. Nothing could be more indicative of the Spaniards' absolute incomprehension of the spirit of democratic politics than this outburst from Azaña: He was effectively saying that if the institutions of the state were used to produce legislation that he and his followers disliked, then the institutions would be ignored. Yet Azaña had helped create these very institutions and had used them in precisely the same way during the preceding two years. The rightist government then matched the political ignorance of the Left by pardoning General José Sanjurjo, who had attempted a coup d'état during the Red Biennium. The Right was, in essence, taking the position that a conspiracy to overthrow the government was acceptable as long as that government was leftist.

By the autumn of 1934, tensions between the Right and the Left outside the parliament exceeded those inside the parliament, and they finally erupted in violence when the working classes rose up in Madrid, Barcelona, and Oviedo. The spark that ignited the revolts was the rightist government's perfectly legitimate, if perhaps ill-advised, decision to bring into its coalition the Spanish Confederation of Rightist Autonomous Parties (Confederaciones Españolas de Derechas Autónomas—CEDA). This party was so abhorred by the Left that the leftists would not even countenance its access to government power: They had announced that the inclusion of CEDA would bring on violence. The revolts in Madrid and Barcelona were quickly put down, but the rebellion in Asturias, which involved over 30,000 workers, raged for almost two weeks before being crushed by the army. U.S. historian Stanley Payne, a man not given to exaggeration, has called this uprising the most intensive, destructive proletarian insurrection in the history of Western Europe to that date.[4] And as Spanish historian Salvador de Madariaga, a moderate conservative, has written: "With the rebellion of 1934 the Left lost every shred of moral authority to condemn the rebellion of 1936."[5]

However one views the events of 1934, it was clear from that time forward that there would be no peaceful solution to Spain's Left-Right conflict. City streets and country roads became battlefields for paramilitary organizations reflecting the entire political spectrum, and the official forces of order—the army, the Civil Guard, the Frontier Customs Guards, and the newly created Assault Guards—were themselves divided ideologically. Most supported the Right; some supported the Left. The elections held in February 1936 returned political control to the Left, but once again, the electoral system produced an artificial majority as inconclusive as that of 1931 or 1933, thus failing to resolve the dilemma politically.

The new government, called the Popular Front, was a fragile alliance of leftist parties, including the Communists. Its program, less extreme than that of 1931, could be considered more social democratic than socialist, and the anticlerical obsession had abated. Yet deep divisions among the leftist parties prevented the government from implementing its reforms and doomed the Second Republic to a precipitous sweep to the Left inside the *Cortes* and insurgence by the Right outside. Blame must fall particularly hard on the Socialist party, the largest party in the Popular Front, which was rent by conflict between the increasingly revolutionary and rigidly orthodox Francisco Largo Caballero and the more moderate Indalecio Prieto. As de Madariaga has stated flatly: "What made the Spanish Civil War inevitable was the Civil War within the Socialist party."[6] Stanley Payne places blame on the CEDA as well. The party had the potential for mobilizing a majority of Spanish conservatives into allegiant republicans but would not itself forthrightly embrace republicanism. "Though the CEDA was much more reluctant than the Socialists to enlarge its political volume, it remained ambiguous about ultimate goals, which for some members clearly were to replace the Republic with a corporative and more authoritarian system."[7]

What ultimately triggered the Spanish Civil War was the government's pardon of the insurgents in 1934: The government had obviously learned nothing from Sanjurjo's pardon two years earlier. The paramilitary forces of the Right reacted to the government's flagrantly provocative behavior with street violence, which was matched by violence from the paramilitary forces of the Left. On July 12, right-wing parliamentary leader José Calvo Sotelo was taken from his home and murdered by the prorepublican Assault Guards, in retaliation for the killing of one of the guard's officers by three anti-republican Falangists that same day. On July 17, 1936, the military finally rose up against the government from its camps in Morocco, and the rebellion spread to Spain the next morning.

Within days, that rebellion turned into a civil war that was to last three years.

THE SECOND REPUBLIC: AN APPRAISAL

If the Spanish political system at the beginning of the Primo dictatorship was already overloaded almost to the point of collapse, then the system at the end of the Second Republic was infinitely more burdened.[8] With the coming of the Republic, groups and parties suppressed by Primo, all on the left, reemerged, and new leftist groups came into being. On the right, classic conservative groups and parties coexisted with newly born authoritarian organizations. Moreover, the ideas that most of these groups and parties espoused were so passionately and often blindly held that compromise among them was foreclosed. The rational consensus on the rules of the game that is the essence of democratic decisionmaking simply could not take hold in the Second Republic.

Ramón Tamames gives a schematic of the parties and groups in the Second Republic, whose confrontation finally paralyzed the fragile democratic political process. On the left, there were three republican parties, four regional autonomy parties, and six workers' parties and groups. On the right, there were five republican parties, one regional autonomy party, three monarchist parties, and four authoritarian parties.[9]

Stanley Payne elaborates on the schematic with what he describes as a minimal list of the leftist and liberal revolutionary or reform projects, without even counting the variety of counterrevolutionary proposals: moderate liberal democracy, regional nationalism and autonomy, the moderate republican left, democratic evolutionary socialism, advanced social democracy, semirevolutionary socialism, Leninism, Trotskyism, Stalinism, syndicalism, and anarchosyndicalism.[10]

Consider the explosive encounter of these forces in light of observations I made in an earlier study:

> The Second Republic collapsed because the Spanish people were not prepared to make it work. The statement is not an indictment; it is not a condescendence. The Spaniards were not ready because they were ignorant not just of the nuances of the art of democratic living, they were ignorant of the fundamentals as well. The society remained deeply conflictual; no political consensus was ever reached either about ends or about means. The system was neither legitimate nor efficient to a large enough majority of the people for a long enough period of time to fulfill the criteria of stability, if by stability we mean, with Harry Eckstein "persistence of pattern, decisional effectiveness, and authenticity." In fact, it can perhaps safely be said that the Second Republic was counter or antipolitical when politics is defined by Bernard Crick as "the activity by which differing interests within a given

unit of rule are conciliated by giving them a share in power in proportion to their importance to the welfare and the survival of the whole community." On the contrary, the contending groups in Spain were not conciliated; they opposed one another in the *a outrance* sense spoken of by Alfred Grosser who distinguished *Opposition* from *opposition.* "The first implied a rather precise role in the pluralistic political system clearly defined by constitution and custom. The second suggests a variety of attitudes and behavior of which the only common characteristic is hostility to power."[11]

CIVIL WAR

The Civil War in Spain was first and foremost Spanish, irrespective of the involvement of other nations that either aided the republicans (called the Loyalists) or the insurgents or rebels (called the Nationalists) or refused to aid either. The democracies, especially Great Britain, France, and the United States, refused to help their kindred democracy, though Spain deserved assistance under the rules of international law. Germany and Italy supported the rebels with arms, munitions, personnel, and money, and after the democracies turned their backs on Spain, the Soviet Union provided aid to the republic, which cost it very dearly. The story of the interplay of international forces has been told and retold, yet the recounting often seems to diminish the "Spanishness" of the war. This is particularly true when the war is seen as a prelude to World War II, which broke out five months after the end of the war in Spain. In World War II, Germany and Italy again fought the Soviet Union, just as they had in Spain, but this time, the democracies fought in league with the Communists. All these international convolutions notwithstanding, the war in Spain was Spanish in origin, pursuit, and outcome. And though the ending might have been different if the foreign involvement had been different, the Spanish Civil War would have occurred even if the rest of the world had done nothing but watch.

THE REPUBLICAN CAMP

The uprising of the generals in Morocco precipitated not only the Civil War between the Loyalists and the Nationalists but also a civil war among the Loyalists, who were deeply divided into what de Madariaga called "a true revolutionary hydra with a Syndicalist, an Anarchist, two Communist, and three Socialist heads, furiously biting at each other."[12] The major Socialist party, the Spanish Socialist Worker's Party, was split into two factions, the moderate half led by Prieto, the extreme by Largo Caballero. The third Socialist head was the Unified Socialist Party of Catalonia. The Communists were divided between the main national party and its Catalan counterpart. There was yet another head not mentioned by de Madariaga—the dissident Marxist, anti-Stalinist, Trotskyite party known as the Workers' Party of Marxist Unification. Much of the energy the Loyalists should have directed against the insurgents was spent instead against fellow republicans, seeking to remake Spain in the image of each group's ideology. At issue in this civil war within the Loyalist camp was the question of priorities. Which should be pursued first—the larger or the smaller civil war? Should all efforts be exerted to defeat the insurgents, delaying the revolution until that war was won, or should the revolution be carried on simultaneously within the larger war and given precedence if necessary?

The extremists, particularly the syndicalists and the anarchists, fervently believed that the revolution should be pursued while the larger war raged. The less radical elements, the liberals and the moderate Socialists, felt equally strongly that the larger war should be won first; socioeconomic reform would then come in its wake. The Communist party joined the more moderate voices, and as a result, it was branded as counterrevolutionary by the militant Socialists and anarchists. During the early months of the Civil War, the Communist party appeared to represent stability and caution. Raymond Carr writes: "The Jacobin paradox—that a party whose revolutionary credentials and ultimate revolutionary intentions are above reproach is best equipped to risk a policy of temporary social conservation—brought the Communist party a flood of recruits. Its membership rose from perhaps 40,000 in July, 1936, to 250,000 by March, 1937, and in the process it almost ceased to be a workers' party."[13]

The Spanish Communists had suddenly muted their revolutionary voice, following directions from the leaders in Moscow who reasoned that the defeat of the Republic would turn Spain if not into an ally of Germany and Italy then at least into a supporter of their anti-Communist policy. A Republican victory, on the other hand, would have come about primarily because of Soviet aid. Postwar Spain could then be communized automatically without need for the revolution, and the Soviet Union should thereby gain a totally dependent ally in Western Europe.

In the immediate aftermath of the insurrection, Republican Spain fragmented into self-governing juntas, defended by militias primarily loyal to their own ideologies—whether communist, socialist, anarchist, or syndicalist. There were few governmental orders from Madrid, which was under siege and cut off from much of the country. And for all practical purposes, there was no Republican army, for the overwhelming majority of the national armed forces had defected to the insurgents. The Republic was bravely defended by the various militias, but each fought as it saw fit in the name of its own belief. There was no overall Republican command or direction.

The advisers from the USSR, who accompanied Soviet aid, moved quickly to unify political authority in Madrid and to whip a Republican army into shape, if necessary by crushing resistance from unsympathetic juntas and their militias (particularly the hated anarchists and Trotsky-ites). The Soviets pressured the Republican legislature to make Largo Caballero prime minister, not because he was a Communist (he was not) but because he was the most vocal and the most charismatic Marxist leader in Spain. The Soviets thought that he would be steadfastly pro-Soviet, and they openly courted him, calling him the Spanish Lenin. It was at this juncture that many foreign observers began to label the Republic communist, but the Republic in war was very different from what it had been in peace. The Communist party had won no seats in the 484-member legislature in 1931 and garnered only 1 in 1933 and 17 in 1936. Communism had been a weak political force in prewar Spain, and it came to dominate the Republic only after the war began, when the USSR coupled political influence to military assistance. Moreover, Largo Caballero soon proved to be a Spaniard first and a Marxist second. He resisted further Soviet infiltration of Spanish politics. He wanted Soviet aid for Spain, not the sovietization of Spain: Although a Marxist ideologue, Largo Caballero was unwilling to be a part of the Comintern's political strategy for Europe. He was replaced by a collaborator more willing to play the puppet, Juan Negrín, but the Soviets soon lost interest in Spain. They began a steady withdrawal when their involvement, which had never been wholehearted, failed to produce the desired goal. Hugh Thomas comments: "With crablike caution ... Stalin seems to have reached one conclusion, and one conclusion only, about Spain; he would not permit the Republic to lose even though he would not help it to win. The mere continuance of the war would keep him free to act in any way. It might even make possible a world war in which France, Britain, Germany, and Italy would destroy themselves with Russia, the arbiter, staying outside."[14]

When it became obvious to the Soviet leaders that the war was not going to be fought in the way they had hoped, their aid to Spain was drastically reduced. Then, after the agreement in Munich in September 1938, international events drew Soviet attention away from Spain and toward a reappraisal of the USSR's relationship with Nazi Germany. Signatories to the agreement at Munich yielded to Hitler's demand for the Sudetenland, thus effectively acquiescing in the destruction of the Czechoslovak nation-state, itself almost on the border of the Soviet Union. Spain was no longer useful, and the Republic was abandoned. From that moment on, a Nationalist victory became inevitable.

THE REBEL CAMP

The rebels were also politically divided, but they were united in their conviction that the Republic had to be destroyed. The shape that Spain would take after the overthrow would be decided later; the immediate goal was to win the war—a war the conspirators had not foreseen. They had rebelled in the tradition of the *pronunciamiento*, characteristically a quick blow to the state that brought in a new regime with little bloodshed; it was a kind of game among soldiers who knew when to surrender. The Republicans did not play the soldiers' game, however, and their resistance turned the military uprising into a full-fledged civil war. Supporting the insurgents were the classic forces of the Spanish Right: the majority of the military leadership; the monarchists (both Alfonsine and Carlist); the hierarchy of the Catholic Church; the great landowners; the powerful business interests; the aristocracy; the Falange; and all those who, without specific group identification, championed a united Spain in a tradition that dated back to the Catholic Kings.

The ongoing tension between the center against the periphery caused the paradoxical realignment of some of the Catholic forces at the outbreak of the Civil War. The Catalans had been granted home rule in the form of the Generalitat in 1931, during the Red Biennium of the Second Republic. But a similar demand for local self-government by the Basques had been rejected. The Basque region was then (and is today) the most devoutly Catholic area in Spain, and during the first biennium, leftist leaders feared the creation of what Indalecio Prieto called a "Vatican Gibraltar" in Spain—a deeply Catholic autonomous enclave whose first loyalty would be to the church and not to the Republic. It was not until after the Civil War had broken out that Basque home rule was finally granted, on October 13, 1936. In exchange for this reward from the Republic, the provinces of Alava, Guipúzcoa, and Vizcaya fought on the side of the Loyalists, even though the Republic remained profoundly anti-Catholic. (A similar demand for home rule by Galicia, made in the waning prewar days of the Republic, was estopped by the outbreak of hostilities.)* The fourth Basque province, Navarre, fought alongside the Nationalists, who championed Catholicism but condemned regionalism. Navarre became the home base of the Carlists, and the paladins of autonomy and of the ancient *fueros* leagued themselves, ironically, with the rebels, who would eventually remake Spain into a rigid, unitary state.

---

*Demands for autonomy by Catalonia, the Basque region, and Galicia made *under the Republic* would have enormous significance during the transition when Autonomous Communities were established within Spain as a new constitution was created in 1978.

Commitment to Catholic values was perhaps the only characteristic that *all* the insurgents had in common (although it would probably be safe to say that, almost to the man, the military elite was made up of monarchists who sought the immediate restoration of the throne once the Republic was crushed). The dedication to Catholicism was, however, little more than an unstructured spirit. Only one group taking part in the uprising was committed to what might be called an ideology, using that word somewhat loosely. The Spanish Phalanx of the Juntas of the National-Syndicalist Offensive (Falange Española de las Juntas de Ofensiva Nacional-Sindicalista—FE de las JONS) was a party pieced together by José Antonio Primo de Rivera (the son of General Primo) from two already existing Fascist groups—José Antonio's own Falange Española and the Juntas de Ofensiva Nacional-Sindicalista, itself the result of a merger of two earlier groups. It is almost impossible to make this hybrid rational. Hugh Thomas has written of José Antonio that "his speeches and writings leave the impression of a talented undergraduate who has read but not quite digested an overlong course of political theory."[15] José Antonio and his political movement were romantic (meaning fanciful, impractical, unrealistic, adventuresome, idealistic, passionate, ardent, chivalrous) and poetic. He dreamed of a unified, Catholic Spain; condemned class warfare; proselytized for an authentic national syndicalism; and anathematized liberalism, socialism, capitalism, and traditional conservatism. Yet he called for revolutionary economic reform in language usually associated with the Left, not the Right, all the while extolling violence, bloodshed, and death.

Even though José Antonio was a handsome, charismatic, swashbuckling *señorito*—the kind of indulged young gentleman often admired by the Spanish gentry—his ideas held little appeal for the elite until the months immediately preceding the outbreak of the Civil War. In fact, his party did not win even a single seat in the national elections of 1936. The FE de las JONS had not hidden its distrust of the military (José Antonio had not forgotten the army's abandonment of his father in 1929), which alienated that powerful body on the right. The party's antimonarchical sentiments, an aspect of its anticonservative bias, had estranged both the Alfonsine and the Carlist supporters, and its call for profound socioeconomic reform had struck fear into all of the propertied classes. Nonetheless, after the elections in February 1936, the FE de las JONS became the most militant and virulent antigovernmental force in Spain, and its ranks swelled with those horrified by the Left.

It would be interesting (if futile) to speculate about how Spain would have emerged from the Civil War if José Antonio had not been jailed by the republic in March 1936, four months before the uprising, and secretly executed on November 20, 1936. What kind of struggle for dominance would have taken place between Franco, who became the absolute military and political chief of the rebels soon after the war broke out, and the man who could have become the spiritual voice of the new Spain? As I will show in the next chapter, Franco ingeniously took the FE de las JONS, leaderless without José Antonio, and wed its amorphous and pliable beliefs to the passionate but narrow traditionalism nurtured by the Traditionalist Communion (Comunión Tradicionalista) of the Carlists to create the even more formless and pliant (and internally contradictory) Falange Española Tradicionalista y de las Juntas de Ofensiva Nacional-Sindicalista—FET y de las JONS.

THE TWO IDEOLOGIES

It is impossible to know with certainty why the Loyalists lost and the Nationalists won. We may conjecture, however. Many of the ideologies that swirled within Loyalist Spain were either alien to Spanish tradition or divisive to the state and society. The Soviet communism introduced while the Republic was at war, for example, was an international movement indistinguishable from the Soviet Union. Anarchism, though not indigenous, had taken deep root in Spain but was itself a fissiparous force that was counterproductive to a consolidated Republican war effort. Regionalism also acted at cross-purposes to the center, and the newly autonomous regions of Catalonia and the three Basque provinces were unable to maintain a tranquil relationship with Madrid. Most of the elements within the Republic at war acted centrifugally, pulling the state apart. By contrast, the Nationalists plumbed wellsprings that were indigenously Spanish: unity, order, hierarchy, nationalism, Catholicism. The insurgents used the historical Spanish contempt—even hatred—for all things foreign as an instrument of unity. Foreign intervention did not seem to compromise these sentiments. There was no Nazi or fascist counterpart to the Comintern, and the rebel leaders allowed no direct political control to be tied to Italian or German aid. The rebels made a strong case that Nationalist Spain never sold the Spanish soul. Franco remained forever noncommittal toward his benefactors and never appeared to show them gratitude. Thus, the forces fighting for the Nationalists represented indigenous, centripetal elements in Spanish society. The strongest centrifugal forces—the intensely regionalist Carlists from Navarre—had chosen between their religion and their autonomy and were committed, albeit reluctantly, to national unity.

NOTES

1. There are only a few studies about the Second Republic. The best and the latest in English is Stanley G. Payne, *Spain's First Democracy: The Second Republic, 1931–1936* (Madison: University of Wisconsin Press, 1993). Also in English is Gabriel Jackson, *The Spanish Republic and the Civil War: 1931–1939* (Princeton:

Princeton University Press, 1965). In Spanish, the best is probably Julio Gil Pecharromán, *La Segunda República* (Madrid: Historia 16, 1989).

2. Harry Eckstein, *Division and Cohesion in Democracy* (Princeton: Princeton University Press, 1966), p. 265.

3. Payne, *Spain's First Democracy*, pp. 375–376.

4. Stanley Payne, *The Spanish Revolution* (New York: W. W. Norton, 1970), p. 155.

5. Salvador de Madariaga, *Spain: A Modern History* (New York: Praeger, 1958), p. 435.

6. Ibid., p. 455.

7. Payne, *Spain's First Democracy*, p. 379.

8. For the Primo dictatorship, see Chapter 2, this volume. For a more extensive appraisal of the Second Republic, see E. Ramón Arango, *The Spanish Political System: Franco's Legacy* (Boulder: Westview Press, 1978), pp. 77–84, and Payne, *Spain's First Democracy*, pp. 371–384.

9. Arango, *The Spanish Political System*, pp. 85–86.

10. Payne, *Spain's First Democracy*, p. 373.

11. Arango, *The Spanish Political System*, pp. 77–78. The Eckstein quote is from his *Division and Cohesion in Democracy* (Princeton: Princeton University Press, 1966), p. 229; the Crick quote is from his *In Defense of Politics* (Baltimore: Penguin Books, 1964), p. 21; and the Grosser quote is from his "France: Nothing but Opposition," in Robert Dahl, ed., *Political Oppositions in Western Democracies* (New Haven: Yale University Press, 1966), p. 284.

12. de Madariaga, *Spain: A Modern History*, pp. 524–525.

13. Raymond Carr, *Spain, 1808–1975*, 2d ed. (Oxford: Clarendon Press, 1982), p. 661.

14. Hugh Thomas, *The Spanish Civil War* (New York: Harper & Row, 1963), p. 216.

15. Ibid., p. 70.

4

The Franco Regime

The political evolution of the Franco regime can be roughly divided into four phases, each identified by basic systemic change. The first phase, 1936–1941, is almost coterminous with the Civil War; the second extends from 1942 to 1952; the third from 1953 to 1958; and the fourth from 1959 to the death of Franco on November 20, 1975.[1]

THE FIRST PHASE: 1936–1941

The image that the regime would project to the world for nearly forty years was established during Franco's first three years in power. The changes that took place during the subsequent life of the regime would scarcely alter that image for those who were convinced that the regime was fascist at the beginning and throughout his tenure. What was said and done in Spain from 1936 to 1939 clearly justified the initial appraisal.

The insurgents had planned a coup d'état that would be successful within a few days, following the classic pattern of Spanish *pronunciamientos*. When the Republic withstood the first attacks and girded itself for prolonged resistance, the rebellion turned into civil war. Franco was made supreme military commander—generalisimo—by his fellow generals on October 1, 1936, after a series of events—death in battle, capture and execution, and an airplane accident—had eliminated all but one of the major Nationalist commanding officers in the early days of the uprising. The remaining general, Emilio Mola, who might have challenged Franco's newly acquired power, was forced by battlefield defeats to acquiesce to the generalismo, whose troops—the first-rate Moroccan forces, including the fearless Spanish Foreign Legion—had been victorious in their initial encounters with the Loyalists. Franco's unassailable military preeminence, coupled with his pre–Civil War prestige as Europe's youngest general, made him the inevitable choice of his fellow conspirators. They also gave him supreme political power when it became apparent that the territories captured from the Republicans would have to be governed until the

General Francisco Franco

war was over. Franco was officially made "head of government of the Spanish State" on October 1, 1936.

The insurgents had already outlawed political parties on September 13. In their place, Franco created the FET y de las JONS to be Nationalist Spain's only legal political organ, and he became its leader. Thus, by April 1937, Franco was commander-in-chief of the armed forces, head of state, head of government, and head of the single party. He became chief and sole legislator on January 30, 1938, when he was given the exclusive power to make law. His power spread as Republican territory fell to the rebels and became consolidated throughout the country with the Nationalist victory in 1939. Franco's amassment of total power is stunning given the fact that he was not part of the original cabal that had plotted the overthrow of the Republic: He had come late to the conspiracy. Until his death in 1975, Franco kept all his power intact, declaring himself to be "responsible only to God and History."

Franco invalidated all laws of the Republic that ran counter to his political, moral, and ethical beliefs. On March 9, 1938, strikes were forbidden by the Labor Charter (which was converted retroactively into the first Fundamental Law on July 26, 1947). Late in March 1938, civil marriage was banned; all marriages would henceforth be performed in the Roman Catholic Church under its requirements, provisions, and prohibitions. Divorce was made illegal, retroactive to 1932, and religious education became compulsory in all schools. In April 1938, the National Service of Economic and Social Reform was established to return to the original owners most of the land that had been nationalized in the Republic's agrarian reform. On April 12, 1938, Franco decreed that every publication in Spain had to be censored before release, a draconian measure that remained unchanged until 1966; only publications of the Catholic Church and its hierarchy in Spain were exempt. On July 20, 1938, Franco also ordered that, with the exception of Catholic and state ceremonies, no public meetings could take place without official permission. Perhaps the most overtly totalitarian law of the new state was promulgated on February 9, 1939. The retroactive Law of Political Responsibilities made criminally liable all those who had contributed to the "red subversion" since 1934 (the year of the uprising in Asturias) and all who had actively opposed the Nationalist movement. On March 1, 1940 (eleven months after the Civil War had ended), Franco outlawed all Masonic, Communist, and anarchist organizations as alien, ungodly intrusions in Spanish life, and on January 25, 1941, he extended the prohibition to all groups and associations not approved by the government. Again, only organizations of the Catholic Church were exempt.

It was during this period of wholesale repression that the accusations of totalitarianism were hurled at Franco, who did nothing to dispute their charges. "Our state will be the totalitarian instrument in the service of national unity,"[2] Franco announced. "Spain will be organized within a fully totalitarian concept through those national institutions that assure her totality, her unity, and her continuity."[3] In his message to the Spanish people on the second anniversary of the rebellion, Franco proclaimed that "in the place of a neutered state with no ideals will be substituted a totalitarian state with the mission to give direction to the people."[4]

Domestically and internationally, Franco also supported others with totalitarian leanings. His first (and perhaps only) confidant was his brother-in-law, Ramón Serrano Súñer—a militant pro-Nazi whom Franco appointed minister of the interior in charge of internal security from 1938 to 1942. Franco joined the Anti-Comintern Pact on March 21, 1939, a week before the end of the Civil War, and signed a secret treaty of friendship with Hitler. When Germany invaded Poland in September 1936, Spain declared itself neutral but left its seaports and airports open to the Germans and Italians. As the war swept spectacularly to the advantage of the Axis powers between 1939 and 1941, Franco moved from neutrality to the more activist policy of nonbelligerency, and in June 1941, Spain sent a voluntary air unit, the Blue Division (División Azul), to fight with the Germans against the Soviet Union.

THE SECOND PHASE: 1942–1952

After the ill-fated Nazi invasion of the Soviet Union in June 1941, it became apparent that the Axis powers, which had assisted Franco and helped make his victory possible, would be defeated in World War II. Consequently, the caudillo began to retreat from the totalitarianism that would be unacceptable to the victorious Allies. Spain after 1942 was no longer a totalitarian system, and it should not be compared to the Nazi system in Germany, nor even to the more benign fascist system in Italy. Although some students of politics today consider the distinctions between totalitarian and authoritarian systems to be semantic, the differences at that time were fundamental—distinct in the degrees of penetration and mobilization and in the role played by ideology. Authoritarian states, regardless of how cruel they were, were considered to be far less heinous than totalitarian ones.

Franco had always maintained that the Spanish model of any system would be made from Spanish cloth cut to Spanish measure; even when declaring his totalitarian convictions during the Civil War, he stressed that Spain was unlike any other system because of its Catholicism. This was a valid point, for no thoroughly totalitarian system would have tolerated a force that it could not control. The Catholic doctrines upon which Franco claimed his regime was grounded were not determined by Franco in Madrid but by the pope in the Vatican. Moreover, according to Franco's belief, the primary purpose of human existence was through the salvation of the soul through the church, not service to the state—the basic tenet of totalitarianism. Nor did Franco govern through charisma and terror as did most totalitarian leaders. True enough, Franco's power remained absolute until the moment of his death. But after the first phase of his regime, when brute force was commonplace, he used his power not so much to bludgeon but to balance those groups and institutions without whose support he would have been unable to rule: the army, the hierarchy of the Catholic Church in Spain, the FET y de las JONS (later the National Movement), the monarchists (Alfonsine, Carlist, and later Juan Carlist), the economic oligarchy, the aristocracy, and the Opus Dei (a semisecret Catholic lay organization).[5] These groups, which became known as Franco's political "families," set the limits of the Spanish political game. Outside those limits were the groups forbidden to take part in the balance, primarily the working class and the regionalists, and any of the organizations, either political parties or pressure groups, that had articulated their demands before the Civil War. At the beginning of the regime, these groups were suppressed, often violently, and throughout most of the remaining years of the regime, they remained cowed and quiescent. Toward the end of the regime, however, they once again began to stir.

Within the limits of the political game, Franco skillfully used his power to keep any group from achieving permanent ascendancy, maintaining that his own superior power was indispensable to the stability of the regime. Franco would discipline an overly ambitious family by dropping it from the balance; if two families were vying for preeminence or favor, he would drop both from the balance. The rejection usually brought them quickly back into line. As Stanley Payne says: "Rather than relying on any one force, Franco drew them together in an eclectic hodge-podge, with himself as arbiter."[6] For almost forty years, he juggled a kind of political pluralism that belonged neither in a democracy nor in a totalitarian regime. The significance of his maintenance of these authoritarian coalitions will be discussed later in conjunction with the transition following Franco's death.

During the second phase of his regime, Franco shifted away from his pro-Axis policy. Serrano Súñer was convinced to go into permanent political retirement, and in June 1942, Franco appointed the pro-British count of Jordana as foreign minister. In October 1943, the generalisimo also moved from nonbelligerency back to neutrality and withdrew the Blue Division from Germany. It must be conceded, however, that throughout his courtship of the Germans, Franco made few concessions to Hitler, particularly concerning Operation Felix—the Axis plan to seal the western Mediterranean by capturing Gibraltar and controlling North Africa. This operation, which could have changed the outcome of World War II, would have necessitated a march across Spain, a plan that Franco refused to consider. When Hitler and Franco met at Hendaye on the Spanish-French border on October 23, 1940, the stubbornness of the always proper and unflappable generalisimo prompted Hitler to remark that he would prefer to have several teeth pulled than to go through another session with Franco.

On the domestic front, Franco began to formulate the Fundamental Laws that, when completed, would make up his "constitution." The Labor Charter, the first Fundamental Law, had already been created in 1938, in part to forbid strikes and to outlaw unions. It also guaranteed job security, regulated salaries, and controlled the relationship between employer and employee. Labor and management were compelled to join the official state syndicates, designed to coordinate all economic activity, and end the conflictual relationship that Franco claimed had corrupted the economic process in capitalist societies.[7] In theory, the Labor Charter treated employers and employees evenhandedly; in practice, it greatly favored employers. As an example, most professional and commercial organizations were allowed to operate, although labor unions had been banned.

The second Fundamental Law (July 17, 1942) set up the *Cortes,* or legislature, but representation in this body was severely limited. The *procuradores* (an antique, predemocratic term for legislators) were indirectly elected from municipal councils, syndicates, and official state organizations (such as professional associations and universities), but the great majority of the members of those groups were appointed by Franco. Moreover, the generalisimo remained chief (if no longer sole) legislator, with the power to annul any law that the *Cortes* might have the temerity to pass against his will (this never occurred, however). On July 17, 1945, Franco proclaimed the third Fundamental Law, the Charter of the Spanish People, which was the Spanish equivalent of a bill of rights. Before this decree, there had been no constitutional guarantees to protect citizens from the dictates of the FET y de las JONS, which policed all civil rights. The guarantees in the charter were still limited, for these rights could be suspended if their enjoyment threatened or undermined the "national, spiritual, or social unity of Spain"—all of which was interpreted by Franco alone.

To give the people some role in the political process, Franco proclaimed the fourth Fundamental Law on October 22, 1945. The Referendum Law allowed the Spaniards to approve or disapprove political matters of transcendental importance. A referendum could only be presented by Franco, however, and there was no guarantee that the verdict of the people would be carried out if it were contrary to Franco's purpose. The fifth Fundamental Law was promulgated on July 6, 1947. The Law of Succession in the Headship of State (Ley de Sucesión en la Jefatura del Estado) declared Spain to be a monarchy, with the monarch to be designated by Franco alone at a date of his choosing. The law was approved in referendum by 73 percent of the electorate.

Despite the transparency of the Fundamental Laws, the referendum approving the Law of Succession was the first manifestation of popular support for the regime and the first step toward establishing an identifiable and measurable rational-legal legitimacy. The referendum not only approved the restoration of the monarchy and the succession to Franco but also retroactively ratified all the previous Fundamental Laws. But if the Fundamental Laws were designed, in part, to win approval for the Franco regime from the democracies of the world, they were created in vain. Spain remained a pariah nation: It was denied a seat in the United Nations and in all of its subsidiary organizations and, with the exception of Argentina, deprived of diplomatic relations with the major nations of the world, which refused to exchange ambassadors. Spain was alone and destitute. Shattered by the Civil War, the Spanish economy was still in ruins in 1947.

THE THIRD PHASE: 1953–1958

Franco's wife, Carmen Polo de Franco, always said that God's hand had guided the fortuitous events that resulted in her husband's ascent from one of many conspirators to the supreme ruler of Spain. But it was the United States, not God, that gave Franco's regime new life when the Americans came courting in the early 1950s. The Cold War—and the Korean War, in particular—had seemingly vindicated Franco's ceaseless warnings that communism was humanity's most dangerous scourge. From the time he took control of Nationalist forces in 1936 and all of Spain in 1939, Franco had proclaimed that the Civil War was a crusade against communism and that it deserved the free world's gratitude, not its condemnation. To Franco the self-proclaimed anti-Communist warrior, the Americans were coming as expiators. To Franco the pragmatic politician, the Americans were coming as saviors. This is important to recognize because the anti-Americanism that spread through Spain after Franco's death and that still lies just beneath the surface has its origins in 1953. In the minds of many of those who hated the dictatorship, U.S. aid saved Franco when his regime was near economic collapse and allowed him to stay in power for twenty-two more years.

By the late 1940s, the Spanish economy was in shambles.[8] Spain's isolation from the family of nations had forced it into autarky, or economic self-sufficiency. For a nation rich in resources, this policy might have worked for a longer time, but Spain was poor in resources, devastated by war, and unable to attract the foreign investment it needed to rebuild its economy. Autarky soon ran its course, and the nation was in extremis. Before the situation deteriorated into nationwide penury and hunger, however, the United States unwittingly came to the rescue.

In the early 1950s, the United States, following the policy of containment, was seeking air and naval bases from which to encircle the Soviet Union and secure U.S. defense. Spain—with its strategic geopolitical location almost astride two continents, lying at the confluence of the Atlantic and the Mediterranean and behind the barrier of the Pyrenees that even in the age of missiles remain a formidable obstacle to conventional ground forces—was considered indispensable for U.S. security. The United States went shopping with enormous resources in hand, and Franco welcomed its overtures. He made extraordinary demands for money and arms in exchange for air bases at Morón, Torrejón, and Zaragoza and a naval base at Rota. But whatever his demands, the United States needed Franco, and though he pretended otherwise, Franco needed the United States. Washington paid $225 million for starters ($141 million for military and $84 million for nonmilitary purposes).[9]

There were those at that time in Spain who felt that Franco had given away too much for too little, that Spanish sovereignty had been encroached upon. But it must be understood that, from Franco's view, the deal was not strictly economic, even though Spain's immediate economic needs were the driving force behind the negotiations. The proximate benefits for Franco were political. U.S. money allocated for nonmilitary purposes shored up and primed the Spanish economy at a time when continued deprivation among the people could have led to open revolt. The money earmarked for military purposes was used to begin the modernization of the armed forces, primarily the army, which had no foreign enemies: Its sole purpose was to maintain domestic law and order.

The agreement with the United States was signed on September 26, 1953, just a month after Franco had signed a new concordat with the Vatican to replace the one concluded in 1851. Through these negotiations, Franco's Spain was recognized as a legitimate political system by the world's most powerful democratic nation and by the world's most powerful spiritual institution. The symbolism of this dual endorsement was not lost on the rest of the world. On December 15, 1955, Spain was admitted to the United Nations. Its ostracism had come to an end.

Franco accepted the largesse with little apparent gratitude and did not immediately alter the regime to make it more appealing to either his material or his spiritual benefactor. But profound systemic change was about to take place, whether he wanted it or not. Franco could not have foreseen the transformations that would occur in Catholicism as a result of the Second Vatican Council opened by Pope John XXIII on December 7, 1965, but the doctrinal liberalization that came out of Rome would undermine the philosophical underpinnings of the Spanish regime. Concerning his material benefactor, however, Franco should have realized that the impact of the United States with its aggressive society and economy, could not have been withstood by even a strong and self-confident nation, much less by a destitute and crippled Spain that was still suffering from the wounds of the Civil War and innocent to the ways of the modern world. Franco's provincialism and his refusal to learn from what he considered alien sources (i.e., any source outside Spain and any source inside Spain of which he disapproved) made it impossible for him to understand that the magnitude of U.S. assistance and the U.S. presence in Spain would have ineluctable repercussions. U.S. money, tourists, and military and civilian personnel poured into Spain, followed by money and tourists from around the world. The shock of modernization set changes in motion that totally altered Spanish life.

THE FOURTH PHASE: 1959–1975

Franco's anti-communist propaganda, which ended only with his death, had been matched at the beginning of his regime by anticapitalist propaganda. "Bourgeois capitalists," he said,"spill blood while making fabulous profit from Spanish lives."[10] Franco had proclaimed that the Nationalist victory in the Civil War would lead to "the triumph of economic principles in conflict with old liberal theories by whose myths colonialism had been established in many sovereign states."[11] His anticapitalist animus had been enthusiastically shared by the men who had helped him organize the FET y de las JONS in 1936. After 1953, when Spain finally had the funds to begin restructuring the economy, the old guard of the Falange prepared to put its ideology into practice. Franco declared otherwise and decreed, reluctantly but resolutely, that the Spanish economy would be rebuilt on a capitalist foundation, not on the corporativist base borrowed from Italy that Franco had originally planned to copy. The ideologues of the FET y de las JONS were manipulated into compliance. Franco's balancing act was once again skillfully used, but the ideologues remained faithful to the beliefs they had embraced in the 1930s—even though in Italy, those beliefs had been buried along with the Fascist regime as a result of World War II. To ease the blow to the economic principles of the National Movement (the new name for the FET y de las JONS), Franco underscored the party's political preeminence in the sixth Fundamental Law, the Principles of the National Movement, which he declared permanent and unalterable on May 17, 1958. By his embrace of capitalism, Franco precipitated the first major fracture among the supporters of the regime. The corporativist diehards of the FET y de las JONS were officially silenced. But they became bitter enemies of those whom Franco anointed to carry out Spain's economic restructuring, the most important step in the life of the regime since its birth in 1939.

Franco placed the economic direction of Spain in the hands of a group of technocrats most of whom belonged to the Opus Dei (Latin for "God's work"), a semisecret Catholic lay organization that recruited primarily from Spain's upper middle and upper classes.[12] Many of these men had been educated in graduate schools specializing in finance, business administration, and economics in the United States, France, and Great Britain, and they shared philosophical convictions that reconciled modern capitalism with Catholicism. Placing their expertise at the service of the Spanish state, these technocrats performed the miracle that brought Spain economically into the postwar world. Their accomplishments are discussed in Chapter 10.

While the economic and social changes of the 1960s were taking place, Franco moved to undergird his regime politically and, at the same time, to loosen the restraints under which the Spanish people had long chafed. By this time, they were beginning to express their discontent. On December 14, 1966, Franco presented the seventh and final Fundamental Law for approval through referendum. Of the 21,803,397 eligible voters, 19,466,709 voted yes. In effect, the Organic Law of the State (Ley Orgánica del Estado) closed the door on the past and actualized the political system whose structure Franco had begun to build in the midst of the Civil War. The law reconciled the inconsistencies that existed among the earlier Fundamental Laws, reworded the few vestiges of terminology that could be called totalitarian, and continued liberalization (or perhaps more accurately, the retreat from authoritarianism). It provided for the direct election of representatives to the *Cortes* (by heads of families—male or female, not through universal suffrage) and separated the role of head of state from that of head of government (although Franco continued to act as both until 1973). As of January 10, 1967, the day the Organic Law went into operation, the political system was ready for posterity in a form Franco considered to be essentially and permanently fixed. On July 22, 1969, he announced that his successor would be Juan Carlos, bypassing the prince's father, Don Juan de Borbón. The choice further consolidated the power of the Opus Dei technocrats who had supported the prince over his father. Don Juan was also the choice of the leadership of the National Movement, whose authority Franco had once again diminished.

Retreat from Authoritarianism

Even before the Organic Law was approved, Franco had begun to ease the reins held tight on the people since the early years of the Civil War. The press law of April 29, 1938, was at last replaced by the new Press and Publishing Law of March 18, 1966, which abolished censorship prior to publication. On June 28, 1967, the *Cortes* approved the Law on Religious Freedom, which declared that Spaniards with non-Catholic religious beliefs could no longer be discriminated against by law. Under its terms, civil marriage would be allowed for non-Catholics; participation in religious ceremonies, in the army, and in the schools would no longer be obligatory; and members of non-Catholic religious associations could organize and publicly practice their faith. Whatever the degree of liberalization embodied in this and other new laws, however, Franco could reverse at any time by decree: The dictatorship remained as absolute as it had been at the beginning.

The liberalization did not undercut opposition to the regime. On the contrary, opposition grew in proportion to the success of the economic miracle. The earliest opposition to the Franco regime had virtually been eradicated in the years immediately following the Civil War. When the defeated Loyalists, especially the Communists, sought to destroy the regime through guerrilla warfare, the enemies of the new state were ruthlessly hunted down and exterminated. An airless peace was finally achieved in Spain. But after the hermetic seal was broken in the 1950s, Spaniards became haltingly but increasingly restless. Economic well-being, which spread to a larger and larger number of people during the next two decades, did not stifle demands for freedom. Franco had thought that the newly affluent middle class and the increasingly prosperous working class could be bought off by the liberalization represented in the new laws. The new middle class would not be assuaged, however, and the working class was dissatisfied with its economic progress. Although their standard of living had undeniably improved since the days of autarky, Spanish workers had not yet caught up with laborers in the rest of Western Europe, and many aspired to rise to the middle class. Moreover, workers could not bargain collectively (except in a limited way in individual firms), could not strike, could not organize into unions, and could not vote except as heads of households.

Thus, opposition persisted, even after the guerrillas were destroyed and the system became entrenched in the mid-1940s. There was, first of all, what Juan Linz called the "semiopposition"—"those groups that are not dominant or represented in the governing group but are willing to participate in power without fundamentally challenging the regime."[13] For example, the Falange became part of the semiopposition when Franco rejected its approach to economic rejuvenation and instead embraced the theories of the Opus Dei. Any of the major supporting groups of the regime (army, church, Falange) temporarily out of Franco's favor became part of the semiopposition. Beyond the semiopposition was the "alegal opposition," made up of those working to change the system peacefully. They were too estranged from the regime to be brought into the ruling elite (though they often maintained personal friendships with its members), and they would not have accepted the invitation had they been asked to join. Yet these dissidents were able to pursue their careers only because of the regime's forbearance; they were vulnerable not only to the whims of Franco but also to accusations that they were opportunists who wanted the best of two mutually exclusive worlds. University professors such as Enrique Tierno Galván, Antonio Tóvar, and José Luis Aranguren and journalists such as Joaquín Ruiz Giménez are examples of the alegal opposition. Ruiz Giménez had been minister of education from 1951 to 1956 but broke with the regime after 1956. He joined the alegal opposition and later founded *Cuadernos para el diálogo* (*Workbooks for Dialogue*), probably the most influential popular magazine in Spain critical of the regime. Finally, beyond the alegal opposition, there was the illegal opposition of underground political parties and the secret Workers' Commissions (Comisiones Obreras—CCOO).

Opposition to the regime in the 1950s and 1960s oscillated between the alegal and the illegal. It came primarily from three sources: university students, labor, and the church. Students in the late 1950s and early 1960s had begun to reel under the heady impact of foreign ideas and foreign peoples pouring into Spain after Franco opened the country to the world in 1953. In their quest for independence and intellectual freedom, these young men and women increasingly resisted compulsory membership in the government-sponsored university syndicates, which were apologists for the regime. Franco was compelled to treat the students gingerly—an approach he did not find appealing—and he grudgingly granted them limited freedom to create their own university organizations. His dilemma was that the vast majority of Spanish university students at that time came from the upper middle and upper classes: Clamping down too harshly on student restiveness might harm the children of Franco's own supporters.

Franco's approach to labor demands was less tolerant. The working classes and their representatives—the Communist, Socialist, and Anarchist parties and the trade unions—had been Franco's most dogged enemies during the Civil War. His first Fundamental Law, the Labor Charter, had been created, in large measure, to break labor's back by forbidding strikes, outlawing all free trade unions, and forcing the workers into the official state syndicates. In time, however, particularly after the mid-1950s, labor began to organize clandestinely; Communists and radical Catholics created the secret Workers' Commissions (Comisiones Obreras) that eventually infiltrated the Jurados de Empresa, the quasi-representative bodies created in 1953 within the syndicates to give labor a somewhat stronger voice.[14] The regime even tolerated certain nonpolitical strikes. Franco remained adamant, however, in refusing the workers' fundamental demand: the right to organize free trade unions openly. At the time of his death, he was no closer to accepting this demand than he had been in 1938, when he took his first stand against the working class.

The Dilemma of Vatican II

The liberalization within the Catholic church in Spain presented Franco with his most painful dilemma. His regime had been based upon traditional, conservative Catholic doctrines and had been supported by the church hierarchy in Spain, which had remained silent in the face of political and economic repression. In fact, Franco had claimed that because of the church, his regime had never been totalitarian. In exchange for giving its support, the church was allowed to shape and control the ethics, morality, and education of the country. As long as the Vatican did not fundamentally restructure its own thinking on politics and economics, the Spanish regime was philosophically secure. But if the church were to change, then the Spanish system would also have to change to remain loyal to the teachings of the church.

The Second Vatican Council forced the universal church to recognize the reality of urban, secular, industrial life. The individual's political and economic rights, claims for a share of the good things of this world, and demands for political and economic freedom became the rallying cry of the progressives, whose voices shook the Vatican assembly and shaped its decrees. The cry was taken up by the younger, liberal clergy within the Spanish church, and the fundamental elements of Francoism came under public scrutiny and attack. How could Franco silence their voices without challenging the institution whose teachings were the basis of his regime? He could not keep out the new doctrines and directives and still proclaim himself a son of the "Holy Mother Church." This was a conflict Franco never reconciled.

By the early 1960s, the regionalists—a fourth source of opposition— had grown increasingly insistent. Against them, Franco unleashed repression so severe that many Spaniards feared the regime was returning to the mood and tactics of the early 1940s. The voices of the regionalists—the Basques, Catalans, and Galicians—had been raised in vain at Franco. Angered by his refusal to entertain their pleas for permission to speak their own language and to honor their own culture and heritage, they turned to violence.

In what could be labeled his most shortsighted policy, Franco, in the name of national unity, forbade any native language other than Spanish to be written or spoken anywhere in Spain, even in the privacy of one's home. National unity was perhaps Franco's most relentless obsession, and although one may sympathize with his desire to hold Spaniards together, his actions were intolerable. As history teaches, a suppressed people will eventually explode, but Franco refused to acknowledge history (though he had declared himself "responsible only to God and History"). The historical *fueros* in whose name the regionalists made their demands were rejected by Franco as an anachronism in modern Spain.

The most notorious and brutal of the regionalist groups was the Basque Fatherland and Freedom (Euzkadi Ta Azkatasuna—ETA). This and other clandestine organizations are discussed in Chapter 9. ETA had been created in 1952 as a propaganda organ of the outlawed Basque Nationalist Party, the PNV. In 1958, ETA broke away from the PNV and became avowedly Marxist and revolutionary. Because its members spoke for the freedom desired by most of their fellow Basques, they were tolerated and often admired despite their reign of terror and assassination that still goes on today. The most daring operation carried out while Franco was alive was the assassination of Admiral Luis Carrero Blanco on December 20, 1973, only six months following his appointment as Franco's first prime minister.

In the 1960s, there were spectacular trials involving members of ETA and other groups accused of killing police officers, soldiers, and civil guards. The trials were held before military tribunals, and for all practical purposes, the verdicts were determined before the opening statements of the defense were made. The world was shocked at the blatant disregard of justice, but world opinion notwithstanding, three men were executed in 1963. The next trials, probably the ones that received the most publicity, took place in Burgos in 1970. Franco commuted the sentences of the convicted terrorists, probably in response to world opinion. Yet in March 1974, he allowed a young convicted member of another terrorist group, the Iberian Liberation Movement, to be executed by garrote, an ancient instrument of execution by strangulation formerly used for those guilty of certain violent crimes. (In this method of execution—of Spanish origin—the victim is secured in a chair that has an iron collar with a screw at the back. The collar is placed around his or her neck and tightened by the screw until death comes either by asphyxiation or by cracking the spinal column.)

In August 1975, a new antiterrorist law made the death penalty obligatory for those convicted of terrorist acts that caused the death of a member of the police, the security, or the armed forces or that resulted in the death or mutilation of a kidnap victim. The law also stipulated that all political groups of communist, anarchist, or separatist tendencies and any other group that recommended or used violence as an instrument of social and political action would be subject to maximum penalties. Moreover, it was made a crime to condone or defend acts of terrorism, to criticize a sentence passed on a convicted terrorist, or to call for solidarity with a convicted terrorist. Punishment could include imprisonment for up to two years, a fine of 50,000 to 500,000 pesetas, or both.

That same month, four trials of terrorists resulted in the conviction of eleven men and women. Five were executed (all men), and six were reprieved by Franco's order. Three months later, in November 1975, the generalisimo was dead. He left his fellow Spaniards apprehensive and fearful, with memories of the Civil War recalled by the caudillo's last official message—an ironic epitaph for the man who, in 1964, had celebrated the quarter-century anniversary of the end of the war under a banner extolling "25 Years of Peace."

FRANCO AND THE MILITARY THROUGHOUT
THE FOUR PHASES OF THE REGIME

The rekindled memories of the Civil War brought with them renewed fear of the military—above all, the army. During the dictatorship, the armed forces had become domesticated, totally loyal to Franco personally; fidelity was purchased by the caudillo, who calculatedly doled out positions and perquisites in exchange for blind devotion. But the military, though soft and outdated, could still be deadly if released against its primary target, the Spanish people.

With Franco's death, the center of the military's universe was gone, and the transference of loyalty to his successor was problematic. The description and analysis of the trauma involved in the transference, given in Chapter 5, will be better understood after the following analysis.

For the entirety of his regime, Franco had a curious symbiotic relationship with the military. Symbiosis is defined as "the living together of two dissimilar organisms, especially when this association is mutually beneficial."[15] Franco—a soldier, a general—became dissimilar from his peers when, in late September 1936, his fellow conspirators lifted him from their ranks and made him supreme general, generalisimo, and soon afterward supreme leader, caudillo. Franco became the centerpiece of *caudillaje*, the concept that one man personifies total power in all its guises—military, political, and spiritual.[16] Franco's *caudillaje* became immutable throughout Spain with the Nationalist victory in March 1939; that victory, in turn, imbued the caudillo with charisma that endured until his death.

But the military, without which he could not have maintained his power, was only one of the families that Franco manipulated in order to remain supreme. After the Civil War, to ensure that the military would have no single, coordinated voice, Franco did not revive the ministry of defense that he had created in his first wartime cabinet in January 1938. Rather, in August 1939, he restructured the defense ministry into three separate ministries—army, navy, and air—and gave each a seat in the cabinet. The ministers he appointed would be responsible solely to the prime minister, who was, of course, Franco until 1973. But these ministers were not the commanding officers of their respective branches. Each branch of the military also had chiefs of staff, who together made up the Joint Chiefs of Staff (Alto Estado Mayor), responsible solely to the prime minister, Franco. However, these chiefs also were not the commanding officers of their respective branches. Who, then, *was* in charge? Was it the ministers or the chiefs of staff? Was it the commanders? Actually, Francisco Franco was in charge. John Hooper writes: "Following one route the chain of command passed through the *Alto Estado Mayor*, a joint staff body usually

commanded by an army general, which came under the direct control of
the prime minister's office. Following another route, it passed through the
ministers in charge of the three armed services ministries who were responsible to the prime minister in their capacity as members of the cabinet."[17] The lines of authority were joined in Franco alone. By deliberately
diffusing military power, he had made it virtually impossible for the
armed forces to present any sort of fait accompli to the head of state-head
of government. Franco thus juggled and balanced the various families
that supported his regime, and within the most potentially threatening of
the families—the military, which controlled the regime's firepower—he
also manipulated its three branches, calculatedly keeping each branch
separate from the others. Moreover, within the cabinet, the three armed
forces ministers took part in the broader consensual political process involving all the other ministers. Each military minister was compelled,
therefore, to dilute whatever corporate mentality he brought with him in
order to arrive at political decisions that embraced the entire political system.

Once the Civil War was over, Franco had planned to reduce the military more or less to its size in the Second Republic. Franco was a military
dictator in that he, a soldier, was the ultimate power in Spain, supported
primarily by the military. But militarism was not his guiding principle.
Militarism is defined as "the tendency to regard military efficiency as the
supreme ideal of the state and to subordinate all other interests to those of
the military."[18] Stanley Payne puts it in more academic terms: "the intense
development or hypertrophy of military institutions for strictly military
purposes."[19] In any event, Franco's decision to reduce the military's size
immediately following the Civil War was delayed by the outbreak of
World War II, which might have involved Spain militarily in some way
despite its declaration of neutrality. Toward the end of World War II and
for several years beyond, insurgency broke out in Spain—led by those
who were convinced that the victorious Allies would not tolerate a dictator who had collaborated with the Axis and was still considered to be fascist. But the Allies were quite prepared to leave Spain alone and had no in-
tention of invading it to oust the dictator. Franco was, therefore, "safe."

Once the feared Allied invasion failed to materialize, the Franco regime had no external enemies; the only possible exception was Morocco,
which could have moved to retake Ceuta and Melilla—two small cities on
the Mediterranean coast of Africa that have belonged to Spain for over 400
years and that Spain considers to be integral parts of the nation-state. Furthermore, Franco himself had no imperialist designs and posed no threat
beyond Spain's borders. Therefore, he could proceed with his plans to reduce the size of the armed forces once he had hunted down and had either
destroyed or driven out the insurgents.

But how does a leader keep even modest-sized armed forces occupied if it lacks the two fundamental military purposes: either to defend the nation-state from external enemies or to prepare the nation-state for aggressive war? The primary—almost sole—purpose of the military (especially the army) during the Franco regime was to maintain internal security and, where necessary, to carry out political repression. In addition, military personnel became the commanders of the major police forces: the General Police Corps (Cuerpo General de Policía), later renamed the Superior Police Corps (Cuerpo Superior de Policía); the plainclothes detectives; the Armed Police (Policía Armada), later renamed the National Police (Policía Nacional), created by Franco to monitor potentially subversive political activity in the cities and to mobilize, if necessary, into riot squads; the Social Investigation Brigade (Brigada de Investigación Social—BIS), a secret police unit created by Franco, whose sole purpose was to track down dissidents and stamp out opposition; and the Civil Guard (Guardia Civil), created in 1844 to keep the peace in the countryside. Moreover, throughout the Franco regime, the ministry of the interior (Gobernación), which was in charge of internal security in Spain (as it is in all European systems), was headed by a military man.

Franco's military comrades in the Civil War were given special treatment during his long reign, and like Franco, many of them lived to be old men and retired late. Their special treatment gave them a vested interest in the longevity of the regime and helped to keep them from even considering allegiances other than to Franco. Furthermore, Franco bestowed on them gifts of *pluriempleo* ("multiemployment"). Thus, generals and admirals on active duty drew full military salaries and enjoyed all the military perquisites—housing or housing allowances, medical care, purchasing privileges at military commissaries, educational provisions for their children, retirement programs, medals and badges, and even titles of nobility—and were also given positions in the civilian world in what José Antonio Olmeda Gómez refers to as "public administration as war booty."[20] The proportion of military men in all the Francoist cabinets amounted to 32.4 percent. In the *Cortes*, military men occupied seats as corporatist representatives; that is, military men represented the army, navy, and air force as bodies integral to the system in the same way that clerics represented the church or professors represented the academy. Indeed, 28.21 percent of the legislators were military men.[21] Beyond this, there were enormously lucrative appointments to the state-controlled economic entities—public sector enterprises created by Franco to maintain (albeit unsuccessfully), Spain's economic self-sufficiency after the world ostracized the regime following World War II. The officers were appointed strictly as individuals; they were in no way the army, navy, or air force voice in the

private sector. The appointments were designed strictly to keep potentially restive men happy.

The most powerful positions within the military and the most lucrative positions given as rewards within the private sector went first and
foremost to the men of Franco's generation. These were the Africanists,
professional soldiers who had gone through the military academies and
come to prominence during the Moroccan wars in the second decade of
the 1900s and in the early 1920s. But the Civil War produced another
group of military men who had no professional background but who had
become an integral part of the armed forces nonetheless. When the war
broke out, not all the officers in the armed forces joined the rebellion. In
fact, a very high percentage—some say the majority—of senior officers remained loyal to the Republic. But as the rebellion turned into a long and
brutal civil war, the rebel forces needed more lower-ranking officers to fill
the void left by the professionals who had fallen in battle. The openings
were filled by battlefield promotions, provisional second lieutenants
(*alféreces provisionales*), and second lieutenants made from ordinary, non-
professional soldiers. After the Civil War was over, most of the *alféreces* remained in the army: The war and Franco's appointments gave them careers they could not possibly have attained if war had not broken out and
had not ended with the Nationalist victory. These men then became a part
of the regular army, going up for promotion with the professionals already in uniform and the new professionals that the military academies
once again began to turn out after the war was over. As Paul Preston
notes: "After a period of eight months study in the specially created
Transformation Academies (*Acadêmias de Transformación*), 10,709 were incorporated into the regular army as lieutenants between 1939 and 1946.
That was the equivalent of 50 years of graduates from the military academies."[22] Since promotion in the Spanish military was strictly by seniority,
the provisional lieutenants rose in rank above even the most outstanding
post–Civil War military academy graduates.

The *alféreces provisionales* were a very special breed, however. They
were not Franco's peers, as were his fellow conspirators in the war.
Rather, they were his creations, inferior even when they eventually rose to
high rank within the military and within the private sector as a result of
pluriempleo. The distinction between the provisional lieutenants and the
professional military men involved differences of class, breeding (military
breeding), and comradeship. Even after integration into the regular army,
the provisional lieutenants were a group apart, but they had a special relationship to Franco, who was the sole source of their security. Without him,
they would never have been made officers; without him, they would
never have been allowed to stay in the army after the war; without him,
they would not have progressed up the ranks through promotion; and

without him they would not have been rewarded with appointments to the private sector. Their devotion to Franco and to his regime was fanatical. They were like one-owner guard dogs, loyal to the death and fierce in their protection of the regime—whose protection was their own protection. Toward the end of the regime, as the foundation of Francoism began to shift and, in some instances, to crumble, the *alféreces provisionales* remained tenaciously committed to Franco personally and to his regime and its unaltered continuity after his death. They formed an organization called the Brotherhood of Provisional Lieutenants (Hermandad de Alféreces Provisionales), which bore an eerie resemblance to the brotherhoods of Catholic laymen dedicated to a patron saint. These Christian confraternities still parade barefoot through the streets during Holy Week, costumed as penitents and carrying on their shoulders enormous platforms featuring their respective saints, usually portrayed in agony. The analogy to religious fanaticism is not misplaced. The *alféreces provisionales* were living embodiments of the amalgam of militarism and Catholicism that José Antonio Primo de Rivera, the father of the Falange, said was the bedrock of Spanish values. "Doubtlessly there are but two valid ways for people to conduct their lives: one religious and the other military, or, if you wish, only one since there is no religion which is not military, nor any army which is not welded together with religious sentiment. It is high time for us to understand that the key to Spain's revival is this religious and military sense of life."[23] The Hermandad later became the core of the "bunker"—the diehards of the Franco regime who played so ominous a role during the transition, as discussed in Chapter 5. (The term *bunker* refers to Hitler's bunker, with its colony of to-the-death disciples.)

But as the years passed following the Civil War, the officer corps of the armed forces came to be made up neither of the old guard close to Franco nor of the *alféreces provisionales*. The new generation of officers came from the military academies, committed to the regime but aware of their status as military professionals. They were an inbred group, for the most part sons and nephews of military men and future husbands of the daughters of military men. They were imbued with the religiomilitary asceticism that was part of their indoctrination, particularly at the General Military Academy (Academia General Militar), the army academy at Zaragoza. But increasingly, the more independent-minded of the graduates from all three academies—army, navy, and air—became aware of unfortunate realities of the military in Francoist Spain. The younger officers knew that the armed forces had become isolated and alienated from Spanish civilians, who considered the military the repressive arm of the regime. They also were aware that from a professional point of view, the Spanish military was woefully inferior to the armed forces of most modern nations. A Spanish officer could take little pride in himself as a professional when compared to his counterparts internationally.

I do not mean to suggest that the Spanish army was a comic opera organization. It could, in fact, be very effective in repressing Spanish civilians, but it had not been tested in international combat since the Spanish-American War in 1898, in which it went down to defeat. And in colonial wars in Morocco in the second decade of this century, the army had been mauled by what the Spaniards considered an inferior people. The professional deficiency of the Spanish armed forces during the Franco regime can be blamed primarily on the fact that the largest part of the military budget went to salaries for the inflated officer corps; only the meager amount left over went toward modernization. (It should be mentioned here that the Spanish military was "rescued" by the enormous funds that poured into Spain following the defense pacts signed with the United States in 1953. Under the terms of the agreements, the United States paid the bill for the modernization of the Spanish armed forces. But its modernization can be evaluated only in comparative terms. The newly "modernized" Spanish military was furnished primarily with U.S. weapons and equipment left over from World War II and the Korean War.)

The decay of military professionalism in Spain, coupled with the politicization of the military and the militarization of politics, is profoundly important to an understanding of the longevity of the Franco dictatorship (particularly its last years), as well as the transition from Francoism to democracy. The politicization of the military and the militarization of politics are the obverse and reverse of the same coin. The military was politicized, as we have just seen, by having its officers placed in the cabinet, the *Cortes*, and the public sector enterprises, corrupted by favoritism. The military's primary function throughout the Franco regime was to keep the dictatorship in power. Even as late as 1968, twenty-nine years after the Civil War, that function was reiterated by Admiral Luis Carrero Blanco, who would become prime minister in 1973. In a speech, he made it unequivocally clear that, in Paul Preston's words, "national defense took a back seat to political repression."[24] Politics was militarized in the sense that the military was called upon to do the dirty work of Franco's government. It was the military that crushed the opponents of the regime, not only in the streets and countryside but also in the courts, where military tribunals replaced civilian courts and were given jurisdiction over anyone accused of insurrection (a term applied to any action the regime considered threatening). Thus, the military's professionalism was perverted to a task that was contrary to its nature. It became the enemy of the people rather than their protector, the occupying force of its own land.

The skeins of the preceding analysis now come together. As Franco aged and sickened toward the end of the 1960s, it became evident that the regime under the caudillo's personal rule would soon be coming to an end. The Franco regime was most assuredly not crumbling, but the families that constituted the regime were examining their options for the future. Some Francoist families, or, more precisely, some elements within some Francoist families, had already begun to distance themselves from the regime but not necessarily from some form of Francoism without Franco: the Church, the economic elite, the monarchists. Nowhere was the conflict within a family over its post-Franco role more bitter than within the military. On one side were the diehards who, along with members from other families, were determined to carry Francoism unmodified into the future. The diehards, or *ultras*, included the old guard and the *alféreces provisionales*. To them, Francoism was a divine creation that was destined to live beyond Franco; to forsake Francoism would be not only treachery but also apostasy. "Francoism can never disappear, because God does not want it to come to an end in Spain and, after Franco, Francoism will continue and there will be Francoism for centuries because Spain which is eternal and which had an eternal destiny in the universal scheme needs Francoism."[25] Of course, there was also a powerful, pragmatic rationale to their fanaticism: They would be out of work once Franco was dead if unmodified Francoism did not continue into the future.

The diehards represented one aspect of the multifaceted response to Franco and Francoism within the military. Other groups were not so clearly defined, but what gave them common sentiment, if not common cause, was the commitment to a professional military—one that stood outside politics, not within it as active participant or above it as protector and savior in the manner set forth by Franco in the Organic Law of the State, his last Fundamental Law. The law assigned to the military the task of guaranteeing "the unity and independence of the fatherland and the integrity of its territories and national security and the defense of the institutional order." Their commitment to professionalism would fly in the face of such a charge. The majority of the non-diehards simply wanted a professional military, and they sought to distance themselves from political involvement in whatever regime followed Franco's death. Beyond these men, there was a group that wanted not just a professional military but a professional military within a democratic political system. I had first thought to begin the previous sentence with "to the left of these men," but I changed my mind to avoid "poisoning the wells." To many readers, left conjures up visions of Marxism, and, indeed, the military men seeking democracy in Spain were accused of sympathy and collusion with the Portuguese military insurgents, who *were* Marxists. But left can also characterize those who take a stand against the status quo and who support fundamental political change. In this sense, the military men in Spain who sought a democracy after Franco were to the left.

The conversion of many of these younger officers to democratic values came, in part, as a result of their contacts with the civilian world, which they had entered in order to supplement their military pay. The great perquisites that fell to the old guard and to the *alféreces provisionales* were not available to young officers, who had little or no connection to the Civil War. *Pluriempleo* of the sort described earlier was furnished by Franco only to the selected few, but multiemployment was not forbidden to the rest of the officer corps if a man could find extra work for himself in the civilian sector. This contact with the civilian world—which even in regimented Francoist Spain was wide open when compared to the hermetic, isolated military world—sparked the development of a new mentality within the younger moonlighting officers. Aware of how unprofessional they were in their own calling when compared to the military elsewhere in the world, they now also saw how unprofessional they were in comparison to their peers in the civilian sector. In other words, a Spanish economist was a better economist than a Spanish soldier was a soldier. And position to position, a Spanish economist was as good as a German economist, for example, but a Spanish military officer was inferior to his German counterpart. In August 1972, a group of these younger enlightened officers formed a secret society that later would become the Democratic Military Union (Unión Militar Democrática—UMD). They were committed not to overthrowing the Franco regime or its possible Francoist successor but to preventing the diehards from blocking Spain's transition to democracy if democracy was the people's choice. The Burgos trial in 1970 was the catalyst that set into motion the various persuasions within the armed forces. On trial before a military tribunal were eighteen men (two of them priests) accused of belonging to ETA, the underground Basque separatist group. Six of the accused were sentenced to death, but their sentences were later commuted by Franco, who bowed to intense international pressure, including that from the Vatican. Perhaps it was the commutation that galvanized the diehards, now revealing themselves to be more royal than the king and urging Franco to proceed with the death sentences. Some of the diehards even urged that the executions be carried out by the garrote, rather than the customary firing squad; the garrote was last used in 1963 to execute the communist militant Julián Grimau. Death administered in this particularly grotesque way would send a message to the "enemies of Spain," both inside and outside the country: Francoism would tolerate no challenge, nor would it deviate one centimeter from the predestined path laid out for Spain by the rebels at the beginning of the Civil War in 1936.

It was this unyielding, defiant posture taken by the diehards that convinced the younger, progressive military men in the Democratic Military Union that, unchallenged, the *ultras* would take Spain into a future of reaction and repression for decades to come. Given the network of intelligence organizations that informed the regime, the existence of the Union could not have been unknown to the government, but not until late 1973 and early 1974 was serious note taken of the UMD's potential threat. The catalysts for the eventual confrontation that would take place in mid-1975 was the assassination of prime minister Carrero Blanco in December 1973 and the military rebellion in Portugal against the Salazar-Caetano dictatorship in April 1974.

Never, perhaps, had the Franco regime seemed more vulnerable than when ETA killed Carrero Blanco with a car bomb. The terrorist organization had struck at the very top—the penultimate figure in the Franco regime and the man handpicked by Franco to lead Spain, along with Juan Carlos, into post-Franco Francoism. The transition as foreseen by Franco, would be sustained by the power of the military, just as the regime itself had been sustained. But the military was no longer a monolith, and the UMD appeared to be a powerful subversive element within it. It was later discovered that there were never more than 250 to 300 militants within the organization, but the number of sympathizers was never known. Whatever its size, the UMD had, by December 1974, made contact with the leaders of the major oppositional political organizations in Spain—the communists, socialists, and Christian democrats.

In April 1974, the Portuguese army led the successful uprising against the Salazar-Caetano regime, and even though the circumstances in Portugal were totally different from those in Spain, it was the disaffected officers within the army who led the revolution. In Portugal, military men radicalized in the colonial wars in Angola and Mozambique and converted to Marxism rose up against the reactionary leadership in the land to which they had returned after the collapse of the Portuguese empire in Africa. In Spain, although the members of the UMD were neither radical nor Marxist, they *were* disaffected, and in the eyes of the diehards, they were potentially subversive. The diehards were uncompromisingly opposed even to the slightly modified Francoism that it appeared Carrero Blanco, with Franco's approval, had been planning for Spain. The *ultras* were even more opposed to the cautious reforms gingerly put forth by Carrero's successor, Carlos Arias Navarro. But even tentative reforms could receive the support of disaffected groups such as the UMD.

During the uncertain time that followed Carrero's death, the unity of the armed forces as the bulwark against any reform was paramount in the minds of the *ultras*. To rid the armed forces of what could be a debilitating source of democratic subversion within their ranks, the military diehards struck. Taking advantage of Arias Navarro's absence from Spain (he was attending the Helsinki Conference called to establish norms of international human rights), the *ultra* generals carried out a plan carefully conceived by General Jaime Milans del Bosch. In what resembled a blitzkrieg attack on terrorist hideaways, the police, in collusion with the military, swept down on the dwellings of seven UMD leaders in Madrid and arrested them in the early dawn of July 29, 1975. Two more leaders were arrested later in the week. The nine officers were court-martialed in March 1976, expelled from the armed forces, and sentenced to prison for terms ranging up to eight years.*

THE FRANCO REGIME: AN EVALUATION

It is incontrovertible that at the time of Franco's death, Spaniards were better off economically; better fed, housed, and clothed; healthier; better educated; more open to opportunity; more equal (or, at least, less unequal); safer; more at peace, and in many ways, happier than they were when Franco came into power or perhaps at any time in their history. It is also incontrovertible that Spaniards were then living under a dictatorship as personal and as total as it was when Franco first was given absolute power early in the Civil War.

How does one evaluate a repressive regime out of which good emerges?[26] For what must Franco be given credit, or should he be given any credit at all? Must only opprobrium be heaped upon the regime because it came into existence through violence and eschewed democracy from the very beginning to the very end? Were all good things fortuitous and all the bad things carefully planned and executed? Perhaps the German political scientist Walthe L. Bernecker lifts us off the horns of the dilemma by providing a dispassionate evaluation schema that places all Francoist outcomes into three categories: those planned and engineered by the regime, those not directly designed but simply taken advantage of once they began to develop, and those that were unforeseen and potentially counterproductive to the regime.[27] This formula allows us to look at the nearly forty years of the dictatorship without making value judgments.

Because the Franco regime was so caught up in the great passions of the twentieth century, any evaluation of it cries for absolutes. But for the observer of the Franco regime, there is no easy resolution of moral ambiguity, as there is, for example, in evaluations of the Hitlerian and Stalinist regimes. In those two cases, the means were so bestial that no positive

---

*They were subsequently granted amnesty but were not permitted to reenter the armed forces. In 1986, the PSOE government reinstated the nine men and allowed them to reenter their respective armed service, if they so chose, at the rank they occupied when they were arrested. Most chose to enter the interim reserve (*reserva transitoria,*) which paid an appropriate military salary while allowing them to pursue their civilian careers.

ends could possibly justify their use. In the Franco regime, however, the dimensions of the positive achievements force an uneasy reappraisal of the means by which they were produced. The Franco regime was not a colossal monstrosity like that of Hitler or Stalin. It was human-sized, and like a human, it was filled with an ambiguity that defies simple moral judgment. The dispassionate evaluator is therefore left torn and disquieted.

Those of us who spiritually and intellectually identify with the Second Republic may wish to reinvent history, imagining that if the Loyalists had been victorious in the Civil War, Spain would have seen the Republic restored and democracy triumphant. But Stanley Payne awakens us to reality:

> It is idle to insist, as do many of Franco's critics on the left, that a utopian progressive democracy would have produced better government for Spain. That goes without saying, but substitutes a strictly theoretical value judgment for an empirical comparison. Historical analysis and utopian desires are two different things. No such democratic utopia was at hand in Spain in 1939, which in fact had produced quite the opposite. Electoral democracy had resulted in absolute polarization between left and right, eliminating virtually all centrist liberal influence and thus creating a latent authoritarian situation before Franco appears on the scene. His regime must thus be judged not by utopian invocations which have no contact with reality but in terms of historical alternatives that actually existed. These were few and in no case idyllic. Had the Nationalists lost the Civil War, it is difficult to conclude that the result would have been political democracy. The revolutionary wartime People's Republic was not a liberal democracy, but was driven by powerful revolutionary forces determined to proscribe the other side altogether. Its mass political executions were as extensive as those by Franco's supporters. The effect of the Civil War, irrespective of the victor, was to temporarily banish democracy from Spain. Franco's solution was very far from optimal—indeed at first one of the worst feasible responses. ... Nevertheless, the strength of the subsequent dictatorship was not derived from its rigorous repression alone, however important that was, but also from the knowledge in much of Spanish society that the alternative had not been very different. An evolutionary authoritarianism was in a certain sense about as much as the Spanish could expect from the impasse into which they had maneuvered themselves.[28]

Payne then quotes Julián Marías:

> Spaniards were deprived of many freedoms, something I always found intolerable; but there were not too many who missed them; on the other hand, they did have other freedoms, affecting private life in particular, and were afraid of losing them. The deprivation arose from the outcome of the Civil

War; but most people were convinced that if the other side had won instead, the status of freedom would have been no better, for both sides had promised its destruction, and indeed did destroy it during the war itself. It was not likely that Spaniards' interest would be mobilized toward a reversal of the war's result; and since those who actually proposed this were the most politicized fragments of the country, it meant that the majority remained relatively indifferent. It could be said that a large number of Spaniards waited without haste for the end of the regime.[29]

NOTES

1. See E. Ramón Arango, *The Spanish Political System: Franco's Legacy* (Boulder: Westview Press, 1978).

2. Jorge Solé-Tura, *Introducción al régimen político Español* (Barcelona: Ediciones Ariel, Espulgues de Llobregat, 1971), pp. 23–24.

3. *Palabras de Franco* (Bilbao: Editora Nacional, 1937), p. 15.

4. *Palabras del caudillo* (Madrid: Ediciones de la Vicesecretariá de Educación Popular, 1953), p. 315.

5. The proper name of the Opus Dei is Societas Sacerdotalis Sanctae Crucis (Priestly Society of the Holy Cross). It is a secular institute of the Catholic Church, headquartered in Rome, with a worldwide membership. It was founded by a Spaniard, José Mariá Escrivá de Balaguer y Albás, in order to pursue "God's work" not by withdrawing from the world into convents and monasteries but by remaining in the world pursuing a secular occupation while personally leading a dedicated Christian life and influencing others by work and deed. It is not a religious order; there are no canonically binding vows. However, most of its highest-ranking members—unmarried, university educated, with no physical handicaps, and from good social backgrounds—do take noncanonical vows of poverty, chastity, and obedience, and they most often live together in special but anonymous residences. Its detractors called the society the "white Freemasonry" or the "Holy Mafia."

6. Stanley Payne, *Franco's Spain* (New York: Crowell, 1967), pp. 24–25.

7. The syndicates were created to be one of the three basic units of society in which Spaniards would share common experiences and values. The other two were the family and the local community. These three groups reflected Franco's organic concept of society as being made up of interlocking, mutually supportive, noncompetitive parts. The syndicates were designed to provide employers and employees with a forum in which to meet and solve problems, not as opponents or antagonists but as the obverse and reverse faces of a single organization; the organization's unity of purpose should totally outweigh whatever differences might exist within it. All employers and employees in a particular economic activity were members of a single syndicate organized in two sections, one for employers and one for employees. There were twenty-nine syndicates, representing all economic activities except the professions (which had their own organizations), civil servants, and domestics. The syndicates were formed at the community, provincial, and national levels in a kind of democratic centralism, with the higher level indi-

rectly chosen from the lower. The national syndicates were not autonomous entitites, however; they were completely under the control of the state. Moreover, in the operation of the syndicates at all levels, the great advantage lay with the employers and not with the employees, whom Franco deeply mistrusted as a group.

8. See Chapter 10 for an extensive evaluation of the Spanish economy.

9. In the first ten years, the United States poured into Spain more than $1.5 billion in economic assistance and more than $500 million in military aid. The pact was renewed in 1963 and 1970, and in 1976, its status was raised from executive agreement to treaty. On January 24, 1976, the United States and Spain signed a Treaty of Friendship and Cooperation.

10. *Palabras del Caudillo,* pp. 26–27.

11. Ibid., p. 118.

12. See Note 6.

13. Juan Linz, "Opposition To and Under an Authoritarian Regime: The Case of Spain," in Robert A. Dahl, ed., *Regimes and Opposition* (New Haven: Yale University Press, 1973), p. 191.

14. The Jurados de Empresa were created in 1953 and established in every firm employing more than fifty workers. They operated within a single firm (in contrast to the syndicates, which represented all firms of a similar nature in a particular geographic area). Initially, their role was primarily to communicate workers' viewpoints and complaints to management. But this role expanded after 1957, when the Franco regime allowed limited collective bargaining to take place at the level of the individual firm.

15. Jess Stein, ed., *The Random House Dictionary of the English Language* unabridged ed. (New York: Random House, 1966), p. 1440.

16. José Antonio Almeda Gómez, "The Armed Forces in the Francoist Political System," in Rafael Bañón Martínez and Thomas M. Barker, eds., *Armed Forces and Society in Spain, Past and Present* (Boulder: Social Science Monographs, distributed by Columbia University Press, New York, 1988), pp. 257–259.

17. John Hooper, *The Spaniards, A Portrait of the New Spain* (New York: Viking, 1986), p. 73.

18. Stein, ed., *The Random House Dictionary of the English Language,* p. 905.

19. Stanley Payne, "The Role of the Armed Forces in the Spanish Transition," in Robert P. Clark and Michael H. Haltzel, eds., *Spain in the 1980s: The Democratic Transition and a New International Role* (Cambridge, Mass.: Ballinger Publishing, 1987), p. 80.

20. Bañón Martínez and Barker, eds., *Armed Forces and Society in Spain,* p. 263.

21. Ibid., p. 296.

22. Paul Preston, "Decay, Division, and the Defense of Dictatorship: The Military in Politics, 1939–1975," in Frances Lannon and Paul Preston, eds., *Elites and Powers in Twentieth-Century Spain* (Oxford: Clarendon Press, 1990), p. 210.

23. Bañón Martínez and Barker, eds., *Armed Forces and Society in Spain,* p. 261.

24. Paul Preston, *Elites and Powers in Twentieth-Century Spain,* p. 214.

25. Ibid., p. 220.

26. The most objective and balanced biography of Franco is Stanley G. Payne's *The Franco Regime, 1936–1975* (Madison: University of Wisconsin Press, 1987). The most severely critical is Paul Preston's *Franco: A Biography* (London: Harper Collins, 1993). Brian Crozier's *Franco: A Biographical History* (London: Eyre & Spottiswoode, 1967), although certainly not panegyrical, sees Franco more favorably, judging him solely by Spanish standards. Crozier speculates that Spain (and the West) would have been far worse off had Franco not come into history. J.W.D. Trythall's *The Caudillo: A Political Biography of Franco* (New York: McGraw-Hill, 1970) has somewhat the same tone as Crozier's work. George Hill, in *Franco: The Man and His Nation* (London: Robert Hale Limited, 1967), like Crozier, strives to evaluate Franco by Spanish standards, placing him within the Spanish historical context. It should be noted, however, that Trythall's study was published five years before and Crozier's and Hill's were published eight years before Franco's death and the rehardening of the regime that began with the Burgos trials in 1970.

27. Payne, *The Franco Regime*, p. 636.

28. Ibid., p. 637.

29. Julián Marías, *Understanding Spain*, Frances M. López-Morillas, trans. (Ann Arbor: University of Michigan Press, and San Juan: Editorial de la Universidad de Puerto Rico, 1990), p. 406.

Part Two

Return to Democracy

5

The Transition (1975–1978)

Franco knew that the most perilous time for a regime under the rule of an autocrat was the moment of the autocrat's death. This would be particularly true where the ruler founded the regime and had been in absolute power for decades. Such was the situation in Spain on November 20, 1975, when Franco died peacefully in his bed. He was as powerful at the end of his rule as he was the day he was given absolute dominion over Spain, "responsible only to God and History." Franco had governed personally, keeping on a short leash both ideologies (such as those that inspired the Falangists or the Carlists) and organizations (such as the syndicates, the *Cortes*, the military, or the National Movement) that could develop institutionalized lives of their own. Only the Catholic Church was exempt from the law that controlled all other institutions. Yet under the terms of the Concordat of 1953, Franco even had a role in the selection of the bishops appointed in Spain by the pope: He submitted a short list from which the pope could remove unwanted nominees and add some of his own. Franco then made the final choice from this revised list.

Franco's techniques of governing made the transition from autocrat to successor even more precarious. The political families whose support was essential for Franco's existence were themselves dependent upon him for their *own* existence. Without their support, the regime would have collapsed, but without his presence, the families would have torn at one another, opening gaps through which the masses could enter and destroy. This circularity was maintained by Franco's political genius at balancing, in ever-shifting coalitions, the families that supported him, never allowing any one of them to reach preeminence. He foreclosed a "palace" conspiracy by giving each family only enough power to make any threat to the system a threat to itself. One key to his plan for a successful transition was to grant or deny access to political power in post-Franco Spain to the same groups that had been granted or denied such access during the dictatorship. The same balance of forces would then produce the same stability after his death that had existed during his lifetime.

But the plan was flawed from its conception. Franco could not or would not see that those groups to be included or excluded from the post-Franco political game had changed profoundly since the early 1960s: They had grown more heterogeneous, more pluralistic, more restless. Consequently, they would be more difficult to balance after Franco in the way that he had done, even had they been willing to continue to play that game. From the industrial and financial elites that were part of the bedrock of Francoism, new elements had appeared—progressive young entrepreneurs, financiers, managers, directors, economists, lawyers—and an entirely new stratum of elites came from within the rapidly growing service sector. Many of these men and women had taken postgraduate degrees in the heady academic centers of democratic capitalism in the United States, Great Britain, France, and West Germany. Taking their places within the burgeoning Spanish society and economy, they were resistent to accepting roles as pawns of a manipulative political system. True enough, they had been privileged pawns and were permitted to be active politically late in Franco's regime, but their activity had been constrained within his autocracy.

Moreover, all but a few unregenerate members of one of the families in the Franco balance had withdrawn from the political game. The Spanish church, following directives set forth at Vatican II, had begun to distance itself from the regime; eschewing partisan politics, it was thereby executing a complete about-face from the legitimizing posture it had assumed since the days of the Civil War. As José María Maravall and Julian Santamaría comment: "The action become publicly explicit when it published a document in 1971 acknowledging its error taking sides in the Civil War."[1]

According to the plan for post-Franco Spain, the laboring classes would continue to be excluded from politics, a role they had already shown they would no longer accept. Again, Maravall and Santamaría discuss this:

> If we take the numbers of working hours lost through strikes as an indication of working-class pressure, these rose from 1.5 million hours in 1966 to 8.7 million in 1970 and then to 14.5 million in 1975. This conflict was widely discussed by the recently liberalized press and it had serious political impact. But at the same time, and in a more specific way, the working-class movement took on a political dimension. From 1963 to 1967 political demands had made up only 4 per cent of all strike demands; after 1967 they escalated to 45 per cent.[2]

For the sake of this analysis, let us accept that Franco's ability to balance could have encompassed even these restive, muscular forces. But his plan for the future after his death had one irremediable flaw: The great balancer himself would be absent, and the plan did not call for one individual who alone would inherit all his roles. Franco jealously guarded his power and authority; the notion of training a successor to the *totality* of his power would have been unthinkable. He chose, instead, to create two political heirs: a king as head of state and a prime minister as head of government.

Franco trained Prince Juan Carlos to be king, having set forth the monarch's power in the 1967 Organic Law of the State, the last of his "constitutional" Fundamental Laws. The king's power would be vast but not limitless, like Franco's. Unlike Franco, he would be bound by the Fundamental Laws in their totality and constrained in his appointive powers by the Council of the Realm. The council was created on July 6, 1947, in the Law of Succession in the Headship of State, another Fundamental Law, that declared Spain to be a kingdom.

No member of the Spanish royal family had been allowed in Spain since Alfonso XIII had left the country in 1931; all members of the Spanish Bourbon house had lived in exile since that time. But in 1946, when Juan Carlos was eight years old, Franco proposed to Don Juan de Borbón—Juan Carlos's father, who as the son of Alfonso XIII was the immediate heir to the Bourbon throne—that he allow his son to come to Spain for his education and training as a *possible* heir to the throne. At that time, Franco had yet to chose his political successor. There were several possible choices: Don Juan himself; his son, Juan Carlos; and another grandson of Alfonso XIII—Juan Carlos's cousin, Alfonso de Borbón Dampierre (who later married Franco's granddaughter, giving rise to speculation that a Bourbon-Franco dynasty might be in the making). There was also the Carlist pretender, Carlos Hugo. Out of this confusion of pretenders, Franco chose Juan Carlos to be groomed, thus giving him an advantage that none of the others had. Don Juan, anxious to reinstate the dynasty through his progeny even if the reinstatement might pass him by, agreed to Franco's terms. On November 7, 1948, Juan Carlos arrived in Spain, accompanied by his younger brother, also named Alfonso, who would be his companion. During the next several years, the brothers were educated in Madrid and San Sebastián in a special school created at the insistence of Don Juan, who was permitted by Franco to choose the teachers and the curriculum. The school was made up of a dozen or so carefully selected boys invited to study with the princes.[3] Juan Carlos received his *bachillerato* ("high school diploma") in 1954, and in 1955, he began four years of military training—two years at the army college, and one year each at the naval and air colleges. In 1960, again at the insistence of Don Juan, Juan Carlos began, in private, an intense, specially designed, two-year program of university-level study under the guidance of six distinguished professors. Following his studies, he did brief internships in several ministries. In 1962, Carlos married Princess Sofía, the daughter of King Paul and Queen Frederica of Greece.[4]

On the edges of the spotlight, always in Franco's shadow, Juan Carlos waited. Finally, on July 22, 1969, Franco proclaimed that at his death, Juan Carlos would become the king of Spain. Before the *Cortes* on the following day, the prince swore allegiance to Franco, to the principles of the National Movement, and to the Fundamental Laws of the state. Juan Carlos had turned thirty-one in January; he took the oath as a man, thereby engaging the solemn Spanish concept of honor: What you swear, you will fulfill. As we will see, this was highly significant for the manner in which the alteration of the regime would take place after Franco's death. As I wrote in my study of the Franco regime:

> The designation of Juan Carlos as his successor assured for Franco the continued legitimacy of the political system he had created. Had Franco chosen Don Juan—the son of Alfonso XIII, the last reigning king of Spain, who had gone voluntarily into exile in 1931 but *who did not abdicate*—the entire legitimacy of the Franco era could have been challenged after Franco's death. The Civil War had brought an end to the Second Republic; there were no remaining rational-legal elements of Republican legitimacy. But the monarchy preceding the Republic had never given up its claim to sovereignty. Don Juan was the direct link to that sovereignty, and his selection by Franco would have carried not only the new rational-legal legitimacy which emerged from the Fundamental Laws created by Franco but also would have carried the direct traditional legitimacy of the Bourbon dynasty. In fact, many of the supporters of Don Juan claimed that he would be head of state not by the workings of Franco's constitution but by the heredity that predated the Franco regime and that in reality made his regime, like the Republic before it, an interlude and not a recommencement.[5]

In 1938, Franco created the position of prime minister but left it vacant, assuming the positions of head of state and head of government himself. In 1962, he created the position of deputy prime minister, giving the office to Admiral Luis Carrero Blanco, the caudillo's closest associate since the days of the Civil War—a man who was almost his alter ego. Then, in January 1973, in failing health and with his succession clearly in mind, Franco made Carrero Blanco prime minister. It must be reiterated that the Fundamental Laws did not apply to Franco. The choice of prime minister was his alone, and the choice could be revoked at any time. Furthermore, the prime minister was responsible not to the *Cortes* but to Franco. Carrero Blanco was, above all, unswervingly loyal to Franco. A resolute authoritarian, disdainful of democracy, passionately anticommunist, and devoutly Catholic, he was closely associated with, if not a member of, the Opus Dei, whose accomplishments he championed. By this statement, I

His Majesty King Juan Carlos I and Her Majesty Queen
Sofía

mean that Carrero supported the neocapitalism introduced into Spain by
the Opus Dei (thereby repudiating the corporativism still kept alive by Falangists, who held out hope that their socioeconomic "revolution" could
perhaps still take place after Franco's death). Thus, Carrero would bring
Francoism *as it had evolved from 1936 to 1975* into the post-Franco era. He
would be the steadying force behind Juan Carlos, who would incarnate
Francoist legitimacy. Thus, Carrero Blanco was the key player in Franco's
meticulously conceived scheme. Juan Carlos was an untested political
player, but it was assumed that after twenty-five years of careful groom-
ing and a close personal relationship with Franco and his wife (both of
whom had true affection for the prince, which was reciprocated), Juan
Carlos could be trusted to be what he had been created to be: a faithful dis-
ciple of Francoism.

The players were now in place to begin the post-Franco era—Juan
Carlos as head of state and Carrero Blanco as head of government. The decision made in January 1973 did not set in motion a rehearsal for

Francoism without Franco, however. The ruler remained fully in control, but the plan for his succession could now be seen. As Franco said, in what has become a legendary statement, "Everything is tied down and well tied down" ("Todo está atado y bien atado").

Thus far, I have discussed Juan Carlos and Luis Carrero Blanco as individuals; I have not discussed the monarchy and the prime ministership as institutions.[6] Individuals live and die; institutions have lives of their own. In healthy political systems, it is institutions, not individuals, that provide the enduring foundations of stability. But Franco distrusted institutions for the very fact that they *did* have lives of their own, and he would tolerate no life (at least no political life) that he could not immediately control. None of the political positions manipulated by Franco was ever able to be institutionalized fully. Yet the paradox is stunning. If it had not been for weak institutionalization and for the primacy of personalities over institutions, Spain would probably not be a democracy today: Entrenched institutions would have been resistent to any but cosmetic changes.

Franco's best made plans were blown away with the body of Luis Carrero Blanco, who was assassinated on December 20, 1973, by a car bomb planted by ETA. There were no replacements for Carrero in Franco's scenario. His unique characteristics could not be duplicated. Moreover, Franco had committed an enormous act of faith in choosing him, and there was no one else he fully trusted. The ruler could have reassumed the office himself, but that would have been contrary to his master plan, for which there was no alternate. And time was growing short. He was eighty-one years old, and his health, which had been robust for so long, had finally begun to deteriorate. In reality, he had waited far too long to begin to prepare for his succession, but that is clear only in hindsight.

Franco chose Carlos Arias Navarro to assume the prime ministership. Arias was a surprising appointment. Most insiders had expected the position to go to Admiral Pedro Nieto Antúnez; like Carrero, he was an intimate contemporary of Franco, but his advanced age and political inflexibility militated against him.[7] Arias had been a professional police administrator, a tough former mayor of Madrid, and a minister of the interior (in charge of domestic security) in Carerro Blanco's cabinet. He had few connections with the political families that Franco juggled, so he could, in theory, act as an arbiter in the Franco manner. But he did not have Carerro's unique characteristics and appeared uneasy and temperamentally unsuited for his new position. A dedicated Francoist, Arias nevertheless realized that for the regime's future stability, a broad-based legitimacy was imperative. He thus began his administration with hesitant reformist steps (with Franco's tacit approval or, perhaps more accurately, without Franco's vigorous disapproval). In his address to the *Cortes* on

February 12, 1974, Arias proposed a new law of associations (avoiding the forbidden word *party*) that would, in the convoluted language of the regime, "promote the orderly concurrence of criteria" (in other words, contrastive political opinions) within the limits established by the National Movement. He appointed liberals (at least as judged by Franco's standards) to be minister of information and minister of the presidency (the prime minister's office)—Pio Cabanillas and Antonio Carro, respectively. This period of openness came to be called the "spirit of February 12," yet even during this temperate hiatus, the regime showed its heavy hand. In February, the bishop of Bilbao, Antonio Añoveros, was put under house arrest to await expulsion from the country for having authorized a sermon to be read in every church in his diocese upholding the Basque people's right to use the forbidden Basque language. (It took pressure from an incensed Vatican to put the bishop back where he belonged.) In March, the regime executed a young Catalan terrorist amid cries for clemency from throughout Spain and from the rest of Europe. He was put to death by the horribly excruciating garrote. Nothing could have more potently dispelled the "spirit of February 12" than this grisly execution. The old image of Spain as cruel and reactionary was once more projected around the world.

During the "spirit of February 12," the media were as free as they had been since the fall of the Republic in 1939, but this openness and the proposed legislation to allow political associations were opposed both by the reformers, who wanted more change, and the diehards, who wanted no change whatsoever. Arias was caught between the two, vacillating as he did throughout his premiership between encouragingly progressive rhetoric and repressive action. Moreover, at this time, he could not turn to Franco for resolution, for the caudillo had become seriously ill and incapacitated in June. By decree, Juan Carlos became acting head of state from July 19 to September 2, 1974, but had no decisionmaking power. Thus, political action lay in limbo. The unreconstructed hard-liners, derisively called "the bunker" by the reformers and made up primarily of military men and Falangists, used this period of ominous uncertainty to oppose any alteration of the Francoist system. A weakened and convalescent Franco reassumed power on September 2, 1974, under the influence of the hard-liners and members of his private household, who would increasingly insulate him from all outside influence until his death. Within that household were Franco's wife, Carmen Polo; his son-in-law, playboy surgeon Cristóbal Martínez Bordiu, the marquess of Villaverde; his adjutant, naval Captain Antonio Urcelay; his head of military household, General José Ramón Gavilán; and his personal physician, Vicente Gil, who would be replaced after Franco's first serious illness because of bitter friction between Gil and the marquess over medical procedures related to Franco's treatment. The regime was clearly in crisis, but it was not about to collapse from within or be overthrown from without. *Crisis* has a very precise definition, which perfectly describes Spain between September 2, 1974, and November 20, 1975: "a stage in a sequence of events at which the trend of all future events, especially for better or for worse, is determined."[8] The political crisis within the regime was paralleled by turmoil in the streets, reflecting the deep uncertainty of repressed people facing an unknown future.

The associations bill finally became law in January 1975, rubber-stamped by the *Cortes,* but it bore little resemblance to Arias's initial project. Promulgated by decree by Franco on December 21, 1974, the bill had been approved by the unregenerate National Council of the Movement. Whatever slack the caudillo may have been cutting with Arias's reformist initiatives was unceremoniously pulled tight; the reins remained taut thereafter. The new law provided for political participation only through associations whose legality would be judged by the National Movement itself. Moreover, the law made it extremely difficult to create associations. Organizations had to have at least 25,000 members distributed among at least fifteen provinces, and the movement would help finance the associations, thereby further compromising whatever independence they might have. There would also be no "contrasts of opinions"; the associations would, instead, resemble chapels within a single church. Even before the statute became law, however, opposition to the regime had begun to swell. In July 1974, the Democratic Junta was created in Paris, made up of Communists, a branch of the Socialist party, the Carlists (who were still claiming the throne for their pretender, not only against Juan Carlos but against his father, Don Juan, as well), and representatives of the outlawed Workers' Commissions. Its platform called for a *ruptura* ("total break")— one of the great catchwords of the transition)—and the immediate dismantling of the National Movement and the syndicates, the legalization of all political parties and trade unions, and the election of a constituent assembly whose first task would be to decide whether the new regime would be a constitutional monarchy or a republic. In Spain, terrorist activity exploded with such virulence that in April 1975, the Basque region was placed under martial law, an action that inflamed even those Basques who condemned violence (the great majority of the population). In August 1975, the new antiterrorist law made the death penalty mandatory for convicted terrorists and specified that all terrorists would be tried in military courts. In the following month, five alleged terrorists were executed with Franco's approval; once again, he ignored the impassioned appeals to commute their sentences. He seemed to be resurrecting the violent, repressive days that followed the Civil War.

By mid-1975, members of the nonviolent political opposition were organizing within Spain. The Platform of Democratic Convergence linked in common cause the Socialist party (PSOE); the Social Democrats of Dionisio Ridruejo, a former Falangist who had broken with the regime in 1942; the Democratic Left, headed by Joaquín Ruiz Giménez; the Carlists (who had abandoned the Democratic Junta); the PNV (the moderate Basque nationalist party); and other small regionalist parties. The rightist Christian Democrats and the Liberals did not affiliate with the Democratic Convergence but remained sympathetic. Within the political elite itself, several highly placed men, cabinet ministers among them, began writing a column under the pseudonym Tácito. Published in the newspaper *Ya,* the column supported *reforma,* another of the great catchwords. Among the Tácitos were Federico Silva Muñóz (minister of public works from 1966 to 1970), Pio Cabanillas (appointed minister of information and tourism in 1974), and José María de Areílza (an early Falangist who was Franco's ambassador to Argentina, France, and the United States at various times and minister of foreign affairs from December 1975 to July 1976). It was Areílza who coined the widely repeated expression the *civilized right* to describe his brand of conservatism. In June 1975, the Unión del Pueblo Español (Union of the Spanish People) was created, initially under the chairmanship of Adolfo Suárez, to become the voice of *continuismo*—still another catchword, which meant the continuation of the Franco regime. This group stressed that meaningful liberalization—a kind of democratization without democracy—could take place while maintaining the basic system intact after Franco's death.

In retrospect, it can be reasonably conjectured that Franco's serious illness in the summer of 1974 had been the beginning of the deterioration that would lead to his death the following year. His sickness began on July 6 with an attack of thrombophlebitis—a blood clot in the vein—complicated by already existing Parkinson's disease. He was taken to the hospital in Madrid, where he underwent every manner of internal examination; every orifice of his body was probed in an effort to discover the possible causes of his problems. His condition seemed to improve until a relapse on July 18–19, accompanied by hemorrhaging of the stomach, made his intimates fear for his life. But he recovered sufficiently by July 30 to return home, weak and voiceless, under the care of his new personal physician, Vicente Pozuelo Escudero, whose additional task was to fight the depression that complicated Franco's recovery. The generalismo improved considerably during the fall of 1974, but in January 1975, he suffered infections in the gall bladder and prostate. By this time, the reality of his mortality had been brought home to the entire nation.

After having resumed a fairly normal life since the spring of 1975, Franco again took sick on October 12, 1975, and had the first of three heart attacks that led to cardiac arrest on October 23. Following that, he developed water in the lungs and in the digestive tract, the latter caused by an intestinal blockage and complicated by a stomach hemorrhage that was brought on by the treatment for Parkinson's disease. On October 30, Franco, for the second time, decreed that Juan Carlos would become acting head of state. On November 3, he underwent the first of three operations; between the first and second surgeries, he had to be put on dialysis because of kidney malfunction. Between the second and third operations, Franco had another massive hemorrhage, followed by peritonitis, and after the third operation, he suffered further hemorrhage and blood poisoning. By then he had also developed pneumonia and endotoxic shock. On November 20, 1975, at 5:25 A.M., his heart stopped for good. Even Franco, ever the stoic, was heard to say shortly before the end, "My God, how hard it is to die."[9]

On November 22, 1975, Juan Carlos took the oath as king of Spain, and on the next day, Franco was laid to rest within the massive funerary monument-cathedral he had built in the Valley of the Fallen (Valle de los Caídos) to honor the Nationalists who died in the Civil War. At this moment, the transition began. On December 2, 1975, Juan Carlos appointed Torcuato Fernández Miranda to be president (presiding chief) of the Cortes, which position also made him president (presiding chief) of the Council of the Realm. Fernández Miranda, a distinguished lawyer, legal scholar, and, earlier on, Falangist intellectual, had been tutor to Juan Carlos during the prince's formative years and had remained an intimate friend and adviser. Fernández Miranda had also been a strong supporter of Juan Carlos's accession to the throne against the other contenders. Juan Carlos reappointed Arias as prime minister, thereby giving the appearance that transition would be synonymous with *continuismo*. Once again, Arias promised a new statute of associations, but his address to the *Cortes* in January 1976 sounded more like homage to the past than hope for the future. No mention was made of regional reform, the repeal of the hated antiterrorist statute, or change in the syndicalist structure, and even before legislative action could begin on the legalization of political parties, Arias informed the country that neither the Communist nor separatist parties would ever be tolerated.

Violence continued unabated, particularly in the Basque provinces, and political opposition to the new regime was consolidated in the Democratic Coordination, which confederated the Democratic Junta and the Platform of Democratic Convergence. This time, even those Christian Democrats who had earlier been aloof joined the forces that opposed not only the government but also the members of the "bunker"; the "bunker" members meanwhile pledged resistance to any change whatsoever and championed a return to the "regime of July 18" (the day the Civil War broke out in 1936). On June 9, 1976, the new Law of Political Associations was passed by the *Cortes*. It provided that the legality of associations (Communist and separatist excluded) would no longer be determined by the National Movement but by the ministry of the interior. Yet in an astonishingly illogical—even perverse—omission, the *Cortes* failed to amend those articles of the penal code that forbade all political activity. *Continuismo* seemed dead.

HISTORIC RENDEZVOUS: THE ENCOUNTER
OF JUAN CARLOS AND ADOLFO SUÁREZ

On July 1, 1976, King Juan Carlos demanded and received Arias Navarro's resignation, and two days later, he replaced him with Adolfo Suárez. Breaking through the dangerous indecision that was keeping the country floundering, Juan Carlos led Spain into treacherous, uncharted democratic territory. It was surely one of the most exciting political adventures of our time, and its result was one of the most unusual in history: the peaceful transition from dictatorship to democracy. Let me state unequivocally that without Juan Carlos, Spain would not be a democracy today. But Spaniards and the rest of the world knew little about the king that would prepare them for his bold initiative. During the years of his apprenticeship, there had been little sympathy in Spain either for him or for the monarchy. In fact, he was often taunted by youthful demonstrators when he appeared in public with the refrain, "España mañana sera republicana," which rhymes in Spanish and translates as "Tomorrow Spain will be republican." Santiago Carrillo, the Communist chief, said early on (though he would change his mind) that history would nickname the monarch "Juan Carlos the Brief." In the past, the monarch had shown no spark that would indicate passion beneath the surface. His carefully crafted and monitored speeches either said nothing or praised Franco, in whose shadow he always stood. One observer said that the prince often appeared *gormless*—a wonderfully evocative British word that means witless, senseless, or stupid.[10] But it was no gormless man who took direction of Spain in mid-1976. It was as if he suddenly threw off the disguise, showing his compatriots the true man that had been forced to dissimulate in order to survive. He now showed himself to be a modern, progressive, intelligent man with a modern, progressive, intelligent wife, devoted to democracy and willing to make the ultimate sacrifice to bring it about: the relinquishment of his own power.

We do not yet know (perhaps we never will) what shaped the man. We do not know all that went on first in the special school and later in the university-level tutorials of his formative years. We do not know what life crises shaped or reshaped him. And we do not know what influence his father, Don Juan, a man of liberal sentiments, may have had on him. During his early years in Spain, Juan Carlos was always in contact with his parents, who lived in exile in Estoril, Portugal, and he saw them often.[11] The relationship between Franco and the royal family had always been ambiguous. The Nationalist rebellion had taken place in order to destroy the Second Republic, and early in the Civil War, Franco had declared that, after victory, the monarchy would be restored in Spain. The Spanish Bourbons were, therefore, early supporters of the uprising because without it, they would have been unable to regain the throne. Don Juan had even offered to join the Nationalist forces, but Franco refused his proposal. In 1947, Franco declared in the Law of Succession in the Headship of State that Spain was a monarchy, with the monarch to be designated by him at some unspecified future date. Before then, in March 1945, Don Juan had proclaimed his Lausanne Manifesto in which he declared his own commitment to democracy, excoriated the Franco regime, and denounced the caudillo's totalitarian concepts of the state and his retrograde political and economic behavior. Don Juan called for Franco to step down and allow a peaceful transition to begin. The reason for his condemnation of Franco is clear: Franco was the obstacle to the normal operation of the Bourbon dynastic succession, which would have made Don Juan the king of Spain. The reasons for his conversion to democracy are more vague, but perhaps his exile showed him the bankruptcy of dictatorship. After Alfonso XIII left Spain in 1931, the royal family lived for ten years in Rome under Mussolini's fascist dictatorship. After the death of Alfonso in 1941, Don Juan, now married and with children, moved first to Switzerland and then, after the end of World War II, to Portugal under Antonio de Oliveira Salazar's dictatorship.

The Lausanne Manifesto effectively foreclosed any possibility that Don Juan would be named Franco's heir; his only hope was if Franco died suddenly without a successor having been declared. The generalisimo's designation in 1969 of Juan Carlos as his heir and future king of Spain must have been a blow to Don Juan, but it would fly in the face of logic to assume that he expected a different outcome. After all, Juan Carlos had spent twenty-one years in what obviously had been preparation for Franco's decision. Perhaps what was more of a blow to Don Juan was Juan Carlos's acceptance of the designation without first consulting him. Don Juan had to trust that his son's preparation, which he himself had carefully overseen, would produce the kind of king Don Juan would have been.

We do know, however, that Juan Carlos was aware of and in contact with groups within the Spanish political elite that sought profound systemic change. The most influential of these groups was the Tácitos, whose members named themselves after the Roman historian Tacitus, author of works on political transition in imperial Rome. The group came into being in May 1973, partly in reaction to the appointment of Carerro Blanco, whom the group considered to be the personification of stubborn Francoism. Many of the Tácitos came from the higher ranks of the Francoist regime, among them career diplomats and members of the elite corps of the Spanish civil service. The group was secret in that it did not publicize itself, and its members were known primarily inter alia. But it certainly was not clandestine. Moreover, given the extensiveness of the Franco intelligence system, it would be fanciful to think that the regime was unaware of its existence. Charles Powell writes:

> Indeed, Alejandro Royo Villanova, one of the younger members of the group, has evidence that the Admiral was "quite sympathetic towards 'Tácito,' because he believed there should be a degree of opposition, but a respectable one, and one which was not Marxist." Seen in this light "Tácito" seemed "a minor, necessary evil." It is unlikely that this paternalistic benevolence would have continued for long had Carrero Blanco witnessed the group's later development, but it is nevertheless a surprising example of toleration of internal dissent.[12]

The Tácitos began under the auspices of the National Catholic Association of Propagandists (Asociación Católica Nacional de Propagandistas— ACNP), a prestigious lay organization founded in 1908 to propagate the Catholic faith. With time, the Tácitos became independent of the ACNP and encouraged non-ACNP members to join. The Tácitos met in private to discuss politics and circulate position papers among themselves.

The group gradually became committed to the idea that the only viable future for Spain was as a democracy, more precisely as a constitutional monarchy. The qualifying adverb *gradually* is used because the Tácitos's ideas evolved with the regime. Had Carerro Blanco lived, the changes sought by the Tácitos would, of necessity, have been subtle and incremental. To have pushed for profound and immediate change would have risked suppression. With Carerro's death and the appointment of Arias, the Tácitos were encouraged by the changes that the new prime minister initially supported, and they accepted appointments in both his first and second cabinets. However, Arias's failure to reform eventually led the Tácitos to champion the ideas discussed here. They realized that in order to transform Spanish politics successfully, those groups in Spain that had thrived economically and politically under Franco would have to be convinced that they could maintain and even improve their status better in a democracy than in a continued dictatorship after Franco was dead. The free world's economic and political elites, whose continued support was vital for Spain, had come to terms with the Franco regime, knowing that

one day he would, of course, die. But the Tácitos realized that an unreformed dictatorship continuing beyond Franco's death would most likely
meet with renewed international ostracism.

> By the early 1970s, the Franco regime's legitimacy rested largely on the "or-
> der" it had restored to Spanish life and on the socioeconomic progress over
> which it had presided. In "Tácito's" view, an excessively high price was be-
> ing paid for the former, and the regime was no longer necessary for—and
> was possibly a hindrance to—the consolidation of the latter. The very nature
> of the regime had prevented it from achieving an effective national reconcili-
> ation after the Civil War, and had fostered anachronistic antagonisms.
> "Tácito" believed the Francoist state had failed to assert the supremacy of
> civil over military authority, and held it responsible for institutionalizing an
> anomalous relationship with the Church. Furthermore, the regime's twin
> policies of political centralization and cultural repression had only served to
> exacerbate the regional question. In the sphere of labour relations, official
> legislation and institutions were questioned by workers and employers
> alike. Finally, "Tácito" resented the fact that the regime's origins had pre-
> vented Spain's integration into Europe and her full acceptance by the inter-
> national community.[13]

The analysis in the preceding paragraph and quotation does not imply that the Tácitos were devoid of idealistic commitment to democracy
for democracy's sake alone, but it does make clear that they were also
pragmatic men who knew that without a practical vested interest in
democracy on the part of a large percentage of the socioeconomic elite,
democracy in Spain would fail. They also knew that democracy could
only be created by the elites of the Franco system from the top down. At
this time, the nonelite forces on the left seeking democracy from the bottom up were advocating *ruptura,* which the Tácitos knew would bring an
immediate response from the military and end, for the foreseeable future,
any chance of democracy coming to Spain either from the top down or
from the bottom up.

The Tácito pragmatism can be seen in the group's enthusiastic support for Arias's first government and in the fact that several Tácitos accepted appointments in his cabinet. But the failure (or the unwillingness)
of the first Arias government caused division among the Tácitos, some
fearing that continued association with an unenthusiastic and unsuccessful reformer would tarnish their group's legitimacy. Still, some Tácitos
once again accepted appointments in Arias's second government, perhaps
believing that with Franco now dead, the prime minister could more successfully push his programs through the *Cortes.* It was the failure of
Arias's second attempt at reform that persuaded the Tácitos to look to the
king.

Juan Carlos was indispensable for the reforms now envisaged by the Tácitos—reforms that would convert the authoritarian Franco legacy into a constitutional monarchy. To be successful, the conversion had to take place without contravening any Francoist law, so that there would be no break in political legitimacy. In other words, Francoist law would be used to change the regime established by Francoist law. It was in this manner that the military would be finessed. The armed forces had been loyal to Franco, whose legitimacy had been passed by Francoist law to the new king. Juan Carlos himself was legitimized in two ways: by Franco, who had established Juan Carlos's reign, and by the king's royal heritage, which made him the heir of the last monarch to rule Spain, Alfonso XIII. The military had also been loyal to Alfonso and had fought for his restoration through the Civil War. Alfonso XIII had not abdicated in 1931 but had simply left the throne, and the legitimacy of the Second Republic had been destroyed by the Civil War and by subsequent Fundamental Laws legitimized by the people in the referendum that approved the succession. Thus, Juan Carlos's position was as secure as logic and emotion could make it. For the military to refuse to support the decision of the king would, therefore, be a form of treason; to rise up against him would be overt treason not only against the legitimate ruler but against the legitimate heir to Franco.

On July 3, 1976, Juan Carlos appointed Adolfo Suárez to replace Arias as prime minister. Those outside the inner circle of the king were stunned by the appointment, which did, from the outside looking in, seem completely ill advised. Suárez has spent his entire professional life serving the Franco regime and was not known by those surrounding him to have liberal persuasions. He had most recently been vice secretary-general of the National Movement, appointed in February 1975. Before that, he had been civil governor of Segovia and later director-general of Spanish Radio-Television—RTVE. The only indications of his underlying liberal orientation could perhaps be seen when Suárez resigned the leadership of the National Movement to become chairman of the Union of the Spanish People, an association of political elites who had served Franco but who were convinced that reform was necessary if the regime were to survive Franco's death.[14]

Juan Carlos had come to know the liberal side of Adolfo Suárez. They had become friends years earlier when the prince began to acquaint himself not only with the younger members of the Franco elite but also with individuals who were in the active clandestine opposition, including young socialists. Juan Carlos's contacts had been facilitated, in great part, by his personal secretary, Jacobo Cano. Cano was the former headmaster of the ACNP's preparatory school for boys, the University College of San Pablo, where Juan Carlos frequently visited. Intimately associated with the ACNP and with the Tácitos who originated within it, Cano was a major bridge between Juan Carlos and the liberalizing elites in Spain.[15]

Suárez was among those liberalizing elites. John Hooper writes: "During the last months of Franco's life, Juan Carlos had asked a number of politicians and officials for their opinions on how the country could best be transformed. One of the most detailed and realistic appraisals came from Suárez."[16] Arias's resignation following his failure to push through his program of reform set the stage for the drama (the word is apt) that would finally bring democracy to Spain—"democracy without adjectives," as the Spaniards who brought it forth would say, democracy without restrictions or reservations. To carry out the total transformation of the Francoist regime without breaking a single Francoist law, two political actors working in perfect harmony would be needed. One actor, King Juan Carlos, was already in place and committed to change. He needed a prime minister who was similarly committed. But according to the laws that came into operation after Franco's death, the king was not free to choose whomever he wanted as prime minister. True enough, the prime minister would be responsible only to the king and not to the *Cortes*, but the king could only choose one of three candidates presented by the Council of the Realm, the most conservative body created by Franco for post-Franco Spain. It is at this time that the connections between Juan Carlos, Adolfo Suárez, and Torcuato Fernández Miranda become visible. When Juan Carlos appointed Fernández Miranda as the president of the *Cortes* in December 1975, he knew that Fernández Miranda would also become ex officio the president of the Council of the Realm. It was now the task of Fernández Miranda to have Suárez's name included among the three presented to the king. Given Fernández Miranda's impeccable political past and his intimacy with Juan Carlos, it was not too difficult to accomplish this. Moreover, Suárez's own political past was as orthodox as any devout Francoist could wish. Even his chairmanship of the Union of the Spanish People could be rationalized: The Union advocated change *within* the existing political system, the kind of change Arias attempted but failed to achieve. It was only one step beyond changing the existing political system to creating a new political system using the laws of the existing system to bring about that change.

The accomplishments of Juan Carlos and Adolfo Suárez were nothing short of revolutionary and miraculous given the odds against them. Together they embraced democracy and set out on a course that rejected any attempt to revive *continuismo*. The reforms they adopted emerged out of the existing Fundamental Laws of the Franco regime. And while following the laws to the letter, they were eventually able to legally dismantle both the laws and the regime and create a democratic, constitutional monarchy.[17]

Both the *immobilistas* ("immobilists") of the old regime and the *rupturistas* ("fracturers") attacked the program—the former because, for them, all change was anathema (they had equally opposed *continuismo*); the latter because they believed change had to emerge from the ashes of Francoism, not from its living laws and institutions. The *rupturistas* also demanded that the people have the option to choose between monarchism and republicanism. However, the *rupturistas* had no alternative but to accept the Juan Carlos–Suárez formula. They had no power base for resistance, and rejecting the plan would play into the hands of the immobilists. To call for a republic, as some continued to do (particularly the Communists and the Socialists), would provoke the military beyond forbearance. The only thing that kept the armed forces contained during this hazardous period was their devotion and loyalty to Juan Carlos, who was not only the king but also Franco's heir. (Recall the solemn oath taken by Juan Carlos when Franco designated the prince his heir.) The nature of the monarchy—absolutist or constitutional—was of secondary importance to the military; the existence of a monarchy was beyond question. And a peaceful transition from dictatorship to democracy could take place only if the throne continued to command the allegiance of the armed forces, without whose support the immobilists were powerless to prevent reform.

As they pursued their democratic goal, Juan Carlos and Suárez maneuvered to keep the opposition from both the Right and the Left either off balance or assuaged. The king replaced some military leaders known to be unsympathetic to liberalization and continued to issue amnesty decrees for political prisoners, a policy he had initiated while Arias Navarro was premier. This was particularly designed to calm the Basques, who along with the Catalans were granted (again, by royal decree) the right to use their own language for the first time since 1939. In the same month (December 1976), the king abolished the Court of Public Order in a decree stipulating that all future judicial actions involving terrorism would take place in regular courts, not in military tribunals.

THE ELECTIONS OF 1977

The greatest accomplishment of the first six months of collaboration between Juan Carlos and Suárez was the Law of Political Reform, which the prime minister announced on September 10, 1976, and which the *Cortes* passed on November 16, 1976. In effect, the law ended the dictatorship and called for the creation of a new bicameral legislature, elected by universal suffrage, that would act as a constituent assembly.

In accordance with the Francoist Fundamental Laws, the statute was submitted to the Spanish people in a referendum held on December 16,

1976. Of the 78 percent of the electorate that took part, 94.2 percent gave their approval.

The overwhelming vote of the people in favor of reform was not surprising. What was surprising was the overwhelming vote of the *Cortes* that put the democratization into motion. In the *Cortes*, 425 *procuradores* were in favor of the move, 59 were against, and 13 abstained—in a legislature that less than six months earlier had thwarted *continuismo* by refusing to depenalize political activity. In November, the *procuradores* voted the *Cortes* out of existence; it would continue to function only until the election of the constituent assembly took place. In the politics of persuasion that achieved this phenomenal about-face, the roles of the king and the prime minister were preeminent. Suárez openly courted the opposition and created an atmosphere of trust and cooperation. In an unprecedented fraternal gesture shortly after he took office, he met with Socialist leader Felipe González, whose party was still officially committed to republicanism. In September, Suárez conferred with the senior officers of the military, and he later consulted with most of the other leaders of the opposition. Once again, these forces had consolidated and expanded in October 1976 to form the Platform of Democratic Organizations, presenting to the government the most united front the opposition had yet assembled. Suárez acceded to most of the platform's demands but agreed to implement them only before the general election, not before the referendum as the dissident leaders had wanted.

During the first six months of 1977, Suárez and the king prepared the country for the first free elections since 1939, set for June 15. They began to remove the restraints of the Franco regime, fulfilling their promises to the opposition. In February 1977, the first group of political parties, including the Socialist party, was legalized. On March 16, the right to strike was established, and on March 30, the *Cortes* approved a law permitting the organization of free trade unions. Less than a month later, three major unions submitted their statutes and began operation. The legalization of trade unions was preceded by the dissolution of the entire syndicalist structure of the Franco regime, with its mammoth bureaucracy and vast holdings of real estate, newspapers, and welfare institutions, now all suddenly redundant. A special body had to be created—the Office for Institutions of Social-Professional Services (Administración de Instituciones de Servicios Socio-Profesionales—AISS)—to relocate within the bureaucracy more than 32,000 regular employees of the syndicates.

On April 1, the National Movement was abolished; on April 11, the Communist party was legalized, perhaps the most dangerous action of the entire transition. The military had been schooled to see the Communists as the greatest evil in modern society, and their annihilation had been the primary rationale for the Civil War. Legalizing the Communist party might have sparked the military elite to overthrow the fledgling regime, but not legalizing the party would have placed restrictions on the democratic process even before it began, resulting in what the phrasemakers called "democracy with adjectives." This issue was preeminent even for those democratic reformers who abhorred Marxism, and it became symbolic of the open society emerging in Spain that, it was hoped, would be strong enough to accommodate and survive any ideology. As it turned out, the military did not rise up, primarily because Juan Carlos held it firmly in his grip, compelling the armed forces by the sheer force of his will to swallow this dose of democracy like the brave and obedient men they had sworn to be. But Spain was not to be spared preelectoral violence. Terrorists struck between May 12 and 14, and six people were killed in the ongoing campaign to undermine the Juan Carlos–Suárez collaboration, provoke the army to revolt (thus fulfilling the prophecy that the military would not tolerate free elections), and, if elections nevertheless took place as scheduled, to strike enough fear into the voters to keep them away from the polls.

On June 15, 1977, the Spaniards voted—18,447,714 of them, or over 79 percent of the electorate. No party won the absolute majority of either votes or seats in the new 350-member lower house, the Congress. (The upper house was named the Senate, and the two bodies together constituted the *Cortes*.) A voting system of proportional representation gave the centrist coalition, the Democratic Center Union (Unión del Centro Democrático—UCD), 34.8 percent of the votes and 165 seats; the Spanish Socialist Worker's Party (Partido Socialista de Obrero Español—PSOE) 29.4 percent and 118 seats; the Spanish Communist Party (Partido Comunista Español—PCE) 9.3 percent and 20 seats; the Conservative Coalition, the Popular Alliance (Alianza Popular—AP), 8.4 percent and 16 seats; the Catalan party, Convergence and Union (Convergencia i Unió—CiU), 3.7 percent and 11 seats; and the Basque Nationalist Party (Partido Nacionalista Vasco—PNV) 1.7 percent and 8 seats. At the beginning of the campaign, 161 parties had been legalized, and more were legalized between the opening of the campaign and the elections. By election time, however, the number of parties had shrunk. Some had disappeared for lack of support. Some had been so small that Spanish wags said their membership could fit into two taxicabs. Some had joined federations, hoping to increase their chances of success. The UCD, for example, was a federation of about a dozen parties whose members were social democrats, Christian democrats, and liberals of various hues. The union was dominated by Suárez, who had held the nation in suspense about his own candidacy until early May. The AP, on the other hand, was a conservative federation created by Manuel Fraga Iribarne from half a dozen right-wing (but not reactionary) political groups.

What did the elections reveal about Spanish politics and society eighteen months after Franco's death? The biggest surprise was the poor showing of the Communist party. Perhaps the enthusiasm for its legalization had been misread as enthusiasm for the party that had so carefully cultivated its mystique as the bravest and strongest opponent of Francoism. Possible reasons for the Communists' electoral weakness are discussed in Chapter 8. A second surprise was the total annihilation of those Christian Democrats who had chosen not to affiliate with the UCD and had opted instead to present themselves at the polls as a single party. In a Latin nation so overwhelmingly Catholic, in whose history the church had played so dominant a role, a confessional party would be expected to fare well, yet the election results indicated that unalloyed confessionalism was dead. (The Christian Democrats within the larger federation had a relatively healthy political future, however.[18]) The extreme Right seemed equally dead electorally; its federation, the National Union (Unión Nacional—UN), won but a single seat in Congress. The plight of the Communists, the Christian Democrats, and the extreme Right confirms the relative moderation of the Spanish people, who voted, instead, for the UCD and the PSOE. I would call the Socialists moderate even at that juncture: The party was still officially republican and Marxist (an adjective it would drop in less than two years), but its leader, Felipe González, had already demonstrated the commitment to consensus that would soon characterize the party as well.

The moderation of the Spaniards should have come as little surprise to those who had been following the various poll results published with great regularity since shortly before Franco's death. Pollsters asked the Spanish people about their politics, religion, jobs, income, and political philosophy; about their concerns and their contentment; and about their opinions on domestic and international affairs and the personalities involved in them. Much of this information may be found in the massive study *Informe sociológico sobre el cambio político en España, 1975–1981*, published by the Fundación Foessa. The 1975 surveys revealed a reform-minded but far from desperate or radical people. Turning statistics into prose, the report states:

> Although the image of a society divided into classes continues to be predominant, we do not find a society in conflict or suffering social tension. Only 17 percent perceive society to be composed of classes in confrontation. Reformist aspirations and social demands have been produced in a climate of opinion moderated by the following factors: a) private economic conditions that have reached levels of well-being no one expects to be lowered in the future; b) an acceptance by the majority of the sanctity of personal, private property and its use by the family, although not necessarily its full use

by the owners of the means of production; c) preservation of the conventional familial roles of authority; d) an acceptance of the principle of equality of opportunity, and not of the principle of absolute equality, operating in an environment of social mobility which militates against conflictual tensions.[19]

In 1981, the research team of Peter McDonough, Antonio López-Piña, and Samuel H. Barnes corroborated the Foessa finding, and four of their subsequent publications have shown, through survey research, that Spanish political moderation not only endures but has become more pervasive.[20]

In perhaps the most perceptive of the four articles, published in 1988, the authors show that the diverse forces in Spanish history—region, religion, and class—have lost most of their potency. Although these forces still play a significant part in present-day Spanish politics, their intensity has abated, contributing to the consolidation of Spanish democracy.[21]

About class, the authors write:

In present-day Spain, class antagonism, or more properly, issues involving the distribution of economic costs and benefits, tend toward the bottom of the conflict scale. While they are far from conflict-free, and while they may in fact influence support for and opposition to specific governments more than presumably touchier factors, such as religion, the modernization of Spanish society—in particular, the passage toward a more complex occupational system of stratification—has reduced the regime-threatening undercurrent of economic controversies. They are usually framed as questions of more or-less instead of either-or, militantly revolutionary versus archreactionary alternatives.[22]

About regionalism, they comment:

At least two factors mitigate the explosiveness of center-periphery resentments. One is geographic mobility. Growing proportions of Spaniards resident in the Basque country, for example, trace their origins elsewhere in Spain, and their regional identities, such as they are, tend not to be rooted in hostility to the country as a whole. In addition, the decentralized reforms of the post-Francoist regime—in particular, the creation of an *estado de las autonomías* (a federative regime)—have modified many regional demands.[23]

The religion-irreligion division, though no longer a destructive force, remains the most politically volatile, and, as the authors have found, it "still retain[s] a capacity to galvanize public opinion. … For all the apparent secularization of past decades, 'religion' versus 'irreligion' carries connotations of ideological polarities, between the left and the right generally, in a way that class and regionalism usually do not."[24]

Nonetheless, McDonough, López-Piña and Barnes go on to observe, "it is also likely that, in recent years (unlike during the days of the Second Republic, with the expulsion of religious orders, the confiscation of Church properties, and the like), secularization has come to be associated in Spain more with pluralistic tolerance than with ideological aggression and revolutionary nationalism."[25]

Of singular importance for the stability of the democratic political process in post-Franco Spain is the absence of any inflexible attachment of a particular political cleavage—region, religion, class—to a particular political party. Although the Left-Right (or more accurately, the Center-Left/Center-Right) division is certainly visible, the distinction between the two alternatives is more often than not soft- rather than hard-edged. "The cleavage around which the party system is most directly organized is neither region, nor religion, nor class but instead 'ideology' or more accurately left-right *tendance*."[26] In Spain the match between social cleavages and political partisanship is oblique.[27] As a consequence, competitive parties can face one another with room for maneuver, making policy output possible. In other words, each competitive political party represents a variety of groups, with no single group fully represented by a single political party. The party system thus contains *crosscutting cleavages*, the term coined by Seymour Martin Lipset, who observed over three decades ago that "the choices for stable democracy are embraced to the extent that groups and individuals have a number of crosscutting, politically relevant affiliatons."[28]

José Pedro Pérez-Llorca, one of the founding fathers of the 1978 constitution, believes that Spaniards were ready for democracy because the majority of them shared a consensus about the kind of political system and society they wanted. As we shall see, the consensus for democracy, though powerful, was vague about details, and the people were more divided than they may have realized in the way they wanted democracy to be carried out. But the majority were united in their conviction that the foundation upon which diversity would rest would be democratic. Most profound was the popular opinion that Spain must never again repeat the horrors of the Civil War. This historical memory shaped the Spaniards' view of the future, and the most exhilarating consensus in this area was the wish to be like other Western Europeans, all of whom, in 1977, were democratic. (Even the Portuguese had thrown off dictatorship with the revolution that began in April 1974.) Most Spaniards shared the fervent desire for membership in the Common Market and in other Western European forums.

Because democracy was found throughout Western Europe, Pérez-Llorca believed that Spain now had the best chance in its history to embrace democracy successfully. The international European environment was propitious and supportive. "Contrary to the 1930s, Western Europe at the time of the transition was unanimously democratic. The new social structure and the passage of time itself made the previous regime, which in its day had had enthusiastic support in many areas, increasingly irrelevant to Spain, with no true contact with or deep support from civilian society."[29] Finally, in Pérez-Llorca's opinion, Spain was ready to wed political reality to socioeconomic reality. Even though the nation was far from democratic in 1977, the socioeconomic system was already poised for democracy as a result of the profound change that had swept through Spain beginning in the late 1950s. Political democracy would synchronize the entire system.

The election produced a modified Left-Right split, with the Right dominated by the Center-Right UCD, flanked by more extreme parties to its right, and the Left dominated by the Center-Left PSOE, flanked by more extreme parties to its left. Together, the two major parties gathered almost two-thirds of the popular vote. The UCD became the largest party in the Congress, but it did not have an absolute majority. It formed a minority government, rejecting the grand coalition proposed by Santiago Carrillo. The PSOE, as the second largest party, could thwart any program the UCD put forth if the Socialists allied themselves in opposition with other "out" parties. Some form of consensus—another of the catchwords of the transition—was necessary if the constitution writers were to succeed, and the congressional committee set up to draft the constitution was a compromise group, reflecting the fundamental moderation discussed earlier. It included members of the UCD, the PSOE, the PCE, the PNV, and the AP.

It was to the enormous benefit of Spain that no party was sufficiently strong to hand down a constitution reflecting exclusively one political philosophy. Had the elections given one party or a group of like parties an absolute mandate or had a bare electoral majority given the victors an exaggerated sense of mission, Spain might have suffered again as it did in 1931. At that time, a constitution created by a zealous Left, itself representing a minority of the population, ignored the wishes of another minority of the population on the right, which eventually rebelled in 1936. The transition to democracy between 1975 and 1978 was perhaps successful because, as one Spanish observer puts it, "The right was willing to accept change, and the left was willing to refrain from pushing it too far."[30]

COMPROMISE AND CONSENSUS

The Moncloa Pacts

One must not forget that while the government and the *Cortes* were working to create the constitution for a new political order, they also had to operate the existing Francoist system until that new order came into being. The problems of state and society would not wait, yet long-range solutions could not be attempted until after the new constitution was approved. In the meantime, Spain's severe economic difficulties had to be faced. Rampant inflation and spiraling unemployment had the working classes reeling, and the energy crisis was siphoning countless millions of pesetas to the OPEC nations. The legislature created in 1977, therefore, had two herculean tasks to perform: the creation of a new constitution and the more prosaic but no less daunting day-to-day job of running Spain. The two tasks, though related, could be mutually destructive, for they required two distinct ways of representing the people—one constitutive, the other legislative. Constitutively, the deputies from both the Left and the Right represented the national democratic consensus to remake Spain politically. There was a kind of harmony among the deputies that came from the knowledge that they were working toward the same political goals, irrespective of how elusive those goals might be. Legislatively, however, the same consensus did not exist about solutions to day-to-day economic problems; rather, such problems were approached from more narrowly ideological perspectives. If these potentially divisive perspectives were projected into the arena in which the constitution was being created, the existing political harmony could be torn apart.[31]

Juan Carlos and Suárez agreed that the two tasks should be handled separately but by the same players, and they called for a series of meetings to address the potentially divisive economic problems. The meetings resulted in the Moncloa Pacts, named for the residence and office of the prime minister, the Moncloa Palace, where the meetings took place over the weekend of October 8–9, 1977. The conference, attended by representatives of the political parties in the *Cortes*, focused initially on the Fuentes Report, a 100-page document prepared by deputy prime minister for economic affairs, Enrique Fuentes Quintana. The discussions went far beyond the written report, however, and covered almost the entire range of socioeconomic problems facing Spain. The consensus reached by the participants on Sunday, October 9, was elaborated in special commissions from October 10 to October 25. The pacts were signed by the negotiators on October 25, 1977, and approved by the *Cortes* two days later, on October 27. The pacts were essentially trade-offs among the parliamentary party leaders of the Left, Center, and Right. The parties at the Center and on the Right pledged to continue and expand socioeconomic reforms at an unspecified future date after the constitution was created and ratified. The parties on the Left agreed that essential socioeconomic reforms would be brought about within the existing market economy, distributing the burdens of adjustment among the various societal groups. The deputies from the Left also agreed to convince the trade unions affiliated with their parties not to make excessive demands, which the enemies of the transition to democracy (primarily the military diehards) could use as a pretext to overthrow the transitional government and legislature.[32] The participants at Moncloa agreed to face some problems at once and to postpone consideration of others until after the constitution was created and ratified.

Steps were taken immediately to stabilize the economy. Wage ceilings were set for 1978 at a maximum of 22 percent above wages of the previous year (even though inflation was running about 29 percent higher); wages would be pegged to prices. The money supply, credit, and state and social security expenditures were tightened, except for pensions. Guidelines were distributed to allow for part-time employment, avoiding some of the regulations that come into effect for permanent employment. To promote both reemployment for those out of work and first-time employment, the state agreed to pay 50 percent of social security contributions. The pacts committed the state to continue intervention in the economy, to continue central bank financing of large public deficits, and to continue governmental protection of established economic interests. In short, the state would continue to play a managing or directive role in the Spanish economy very similar to the one it played during the Franco regime—a role enthusiastically supported by Spanish entrepreneurs.[33]

Urgent energy problems were addressed in two ways in the Moncloa Pacts: the first extended the energy plan initially drawn up in 1975—Plan de Energía Nacional I (PEN I)—which called for the establishment of realistic pricing for all types of energy; the expansion of technological energy resources; and the diversification of the energy supply. The second went beyond PEN I and called for the reduction of petroleum consumption from 15 to 10 percent of Spain's total energy consumption; special consideration of environmental problems related to energy and its production and consumption; and the development of new sources of energy, particularly nuclear energy.[34]

In the Moncloa Pacts, the government agreed to reforms in the highly regressive tax structure inherited from the Franco regime. For the countryside, agricultural policy was redefined in regard to land leasing; cooperative farming enterprises; agrarian reform and development; community woodlands; crop management; land savings banks; and farm council elections.[35] For the cities, agreements were reached to control urban land speculations.

The conferees at Moncloa also agreed to reform the military and the police[36] and to return to the trade unions, which the army and police considered enemies of the state, all property confiscated by Franco after the Civil War: buildings, newspapers and publishing houses, and union funds. The pacts included the commitment to set up a governing body responsible for guaranteeing the objectivity of Radiotelevisión Española

(RTVE) and scrutinizing its finances.[37] And under the terms of the pacts, the newspaper publishing company would receive one peseta from the state for each newspaper sold. Since newspaper prices were officially controlled, this subvention aided new and struggling publications and rewarded the most popular newspapers.[38]

In addition, the pacts pledged the government to reform the judicial system, the bureaucracy, and the educational system, making it affordable and accessible. They opened the way for divorce legislation, circumventing those who favored constitutional language that would have prevented its legalization. Finally, the conferees at Moncloa implicitly agreed to hold to the status quo in foreign policy. The parties on the left pledged not to campaign against the continuation of U.S. bases in Spain, and the parties of the center and right concurred not to push the issue of NATO membership for Spain.

Forging the Constitution

In their efforts to conciliate the legitimate grievances of those provinces that had suffered so long under Madrid's heavy hand and to make the national environment as congenial as possible for the gestation and birth of the constitution, Suárez and the king began to recognize regional demands. In September 1977, a preautonomy decree was issued for Catalonia, reestablishing the Generalitat, the local regional legislature first created during the Second Republic. Three months later, a preautonomy decree was issued for the Basque provinces of Alava, Guipúzcoa, and Vizcaya. Navarre, the fourth Basque province, which chose not to be in league with the other three, was given separate treatment. Autonomy would have to wait until the provisions of the new constitution went into effect, but these early actions ensured that when the constitution was ratified, the three Basque provinces and Catalonia—the regions that had endured the harshest repression under Franco—would be the first to enjoy autonomy. The Navarrese had fought with Franco during the Civil War and thus earned his devotion, not his enmity.

The preautonomy decrees did not stop there. Once autonomy had been accepted as legitimate for Catalonia and the Basque lands, other regions of Spain quickly voiced their own demands. Galicia had a claim almost as that of special as Catalonia and the Basque territories, based primarily on a separate language and culture. A preautonomy decree went out to Galicia in March 1978. Similar decrees went to Valencia, Aragon, and the Canary Islands in March; to Andalucia, the Balearic Islands, Extremadura, and Old Castile-León in April; to Murcia and Asturias in August; and to New Castile-La Mancha in September.

In the Congress, the constitution was drafted by a 7-member sub-committee of the 36-member Committee on Constitutional Affairs. On the main committee were 17 members of the UCD, 13 Socialists, 2 Communists, 2 members of the AP, 1 Catalan, and 1 Basque. The subcommittee had 3 members of the UCD, 1 Socialist, 1 Communist, 1 member of the AP, and 1 Catalan. Had the members of the main committee foreseen the problems that the Basques within the Congress would cause later, perhaps they would have substituted a Basque for a Catalan on the subcommittee or included both.[39]

The consensus that produced the main committee and subcommittee memberships prevailed, more or less, during the first drafting of the document, finished by mid-November 1977. But both this consensus and the strict secrecy that surrounded the research and writing of the articles were dealt a blow when part of the first draft was leaked to a magazine and published. A few days later, the entire first draft was published without authorization in a Madrid newspaper. A second draft was presented to the main committee for full debate in mid-December, following the unplanned public airing that resulted from the leaks. By early January, over 1,000 amendments had been proposed to the second draft, which then went back to the subcommittee for additional work. By then, consensus was under severe strain: Even moderate individuals may fall out when sensitive issues are discussed in public, and not all members of the main committee or subcommittee were moderates or representatives of moderates. The Basques and some Catalans, for example, remained obdurate to the bitter end. Moreover, many issues were undeniably explosive: regional autonomy, the place of the Catholic Church in the new system, state aid to private schools (almost all of them Catholic), abortion, divorce, and the right of employers to use the lockout.

More significant than the inflexibility of the Basques and a few Catalans were the confrontations between the two major parties, the UCD and the PSOE, which were approaching an impasse. The solution that broke the impending deadlock demonstrated the reality of power and how it was used at this stage of the transition. Prime Minister Suárez and Felipe González, the most powerful politician in Spain after Suárez, instructed their seconds-in-command to find a solution to the stalemate out of the glare of publicity. In typical Spanish fashion, they did so sitting over a table in a Madrid restaurant. They worked through the night of May 28, 1978, reaching agreement about dawn the next day. From that point on, the full committee's approval of the draft was assured, even though there would be more debate and the representatives of the minor parties would protest furiously at what they saw as railroading by the two major parties.

Debate on the floors of the Congress and the Senate took place on July 4 and 5, 1978, and after a joint committee reconciled the differences between the drafts as they emerged from the two houses of the *Cortes*, the final vote was taken on October 31. The long and detailed finished document contained 169 articles and 15,000 words. Of the 350 members of the Congress, 345 were present for the vote: 325 representatives, including all but one of the Catalans, voted yes; the no votes came primarily from the Basques and 5 members of the AP. Of the 248 members of the Senate, 239 voted yes, the no votes coming from the Basques and the Catalans.

The constitution was ratified by the Spanish people in the referendum held on December 6, 1978. The response of the electorate was not overwhelming, but there was approval by an absolute majority. The percentage of the electorate that voted in the constitutional referendum of 1978 was far smaller than that voting for the 1976 referendum approving the Law of Political Reform, initiating the systemic restructuring of Spain. In the 1976 referendum, 16,573,180 of the 17,599,662 citizens who went to the polls voted yes, in a total electorate of 22,644,290. In other words, 73.2 percent of the eligible voters cast yes ballots. In the referendum of 1978, by contrast, of the 17,873,301 votes cast, 15,706,078 were yes votes, and only 1,400,505 people voted no, but there were 8,755,879 abstentions. The yes vote was 87.87 percent of all those voting, but only 59.87 percent of the total electorate went to the polls. John Coverdale offered the following analysis: "The degree of approval was, however, impressive for three reasons: this was the third time Spaniards had been called to the polls in two years; it was widely believed that the constitution would be easily approved and that, therefore, there was little need to vote; and a detailed text was bound to alienate more people than a general proposal for democratic reform like that presented two years earlier."[40]

The constitution was sanctioned by King Juan Carlos I in the presence of the *Cortes* on December 27, 1978, and published in the Official Bulletin of the State (*Boletín oficial del estado*) on December 29, 1978, entering in force as of that date.

NOTES

1. José María Maravall and Julian Santamaría, "Political Change in Spain and the Prospects for Democracy," in Guillermo O'Donnell, Philippe Schmitter, and Laurence Whitehead, eds., *Transition from Authoritarian Rule: Southern Europe* (Baltimore: Johns Hopkins Press, 1986), p. 78. This volume and its three companions by the same editors and publisher—*Transitions from Authoritarian Rule: Comparative Perspectives, Transitions from Authoritarian Rule: Latin America,* and *Transitions from Authoritarian Rule: Tentative Conclusions About Uncertain Democracies*—make up an indispensable quartet for an understanding of transitions from authoritarian rule to democracy.

2. Maravall and Santamaría, "Political Change in Spain," p. 77.

3. T. D. Allman, "The King Who Saved His Country," *Vanity Fair*, vol. 55, no. 8 (August 1992), p. 168.

4. See John Hooper, *The Spaniards: A Portrait of the New Spain* (Middlesex, England: Viking, 1986), chapter 3.

5. E. Ramón Arango, *The Spanish Political System: Franco's Legacy* (Boulder: Westview Press, 1987), p. 147.

6. See Donald Share, "The Francoist Regime and the Dilemma of Succession," *Review of Politics*, vol. 48, no. 4 (Fall 1986), p. 563.

7. For commentary about this appointment, see Antonio Carro Martínez's contribution in Angel Bayod, ed., *Franco visto por sus Ministros* (Barcelona: Editorial Planeta, 1981), pp. 347–359.

8. Jess Stein, ed., *Random House Dictionary of the English Language*, unabridged ed. (New York: Random House, 1967), p. 344.

9. In Spanish, the word for the process of dying is *agonía* ("agony"), irrespective of whether great suffering is involved. *Agonía* also means "agony" in the more conventional sense. Franco's hideous death made both definitions real.

10. Hooper, *The Spaniards*, p. 36.

11. Allman, "The King Who Saved His Country," pp. 166–167.

12. Charles T. Powell, "The 'Tácito' Group and the Transition to Democracy, 1973–1977," in Frances Lannon and Paul Preston, eds., *Elites and Parties in Twentieth-Century Spain* (Oxford: Clarendon Press, 1990), pp. 258–259. See also Paul Preston, *The Triumph of Democracy in Spain* (London and New York: Methuen, 1986), and Donald Share, *The Making of Spanish Democracy* (New York: Praeger, 1986).

13. Powell, "The 'Tácito' Group," p. 253.

14. Students of the transition continue to speculate about Suárez's somewhat late conversion to democracy. I say "somewhat late conversion" because showing a wholehearted commitment to democracy earlier in his career would have made loyalty to Franco a risky sham. Few politicians could sustain such a precarious existence, much less rise to eminence within a regime they secretly abhorred. Yet conversion did take place, be it pragmatic or idealistic; some sort of political learning occurred. The study of political learning is in its infancy and faces the same hurdles as does the general study of learning, of which political learning is a subcategory. The problems are massively compounded when the learning process involves not the mastery of motor or physical skills but the embracing of abstract concepts or the forging of emotional bonds. No one knows with scientific precision how people fall in love or why. No one can tell us empirically how one loses faith in God or gains it. Most individuals are not St. Paul, stricken by a thunderbolt on the road to Damascus. But difficulty in measuring how learning takes place must not dissuade us from attempting to understand this. Focusing on political learning, Nancy Bermeo takes small, tentative steps in "Democracy and the Lessons of Dictatorship" *Comparative Politics*, vol. 24, no. 3 (April, 1992), pp. 273–299. She does not attempt to explain *how* political learning takes place but does tell us *what* must take place if a transition to democracy among the elites is to succeed: "At the most basic level, critical elites must change their assessments of the relative effectiveness of democratic institutions for the fulfillment of group goals. In order for

this to happen, at least one of four subsidiary changes must take place. Elites must change their evaluations of the alternatives to democratic rule; they must change their reevaluation of democracy itself; they must change the ordering or nature of group goals; or they must change their perceptions of one another" (p. 274).

15. Powell, "The 'Tácito' Group," p. 256.

16. Hooper, The Spaniards, p. 29.

17. For a fulsome panegyric that corroborates my evaluation, see Rafael López Pintor, "Transition Toward Democracy in Spain: Spanish Mood and Elite Behavior," Working Papers #80 (Washington, D.C.: Woodrow Wilson International Center for Scholars, 1980).

18. There are several explanations for the failure of the Christian Democrats at the polls, a surprising performance when compared to that of their counterparts in postwar Italy, Germany, and France (where the party carried another name). It cannot be forgotten that in Western Europe before World War II, parties identified with the Catholic Church were on the right and their commitment to democracy was, at best, suspect. The wartime experience in France and Italy, in particular, established the democratic bona fides of the Christian Democrats who fought valiantly (along with Communist and Socialists) in the anti-Fascist, anti-Right underground. After the war, the public rewarded their change of heart and their heroism with success at the polls.

In Spain, by contrast, Christian Democrats were linked by their confessionalism to Franco, whose major supporters included the Catholic Church. True enough, Christian democrats during the dictatorship had been divided in their loyalty to Franco, but in the public's mind, the linkage between Francoism and Christian democracy was palpable. Thus, the repudiation of Francoism called for the repudiation of confessionalism. The Christian Democrats who joined the UCD were "protected" or "disguised" by the other parties in the union, but the Christian Democrats who went alone to the polls in their eponymous party took the full brunt of the anticonfessionalist animus. In addition, the hierarchy of the Catholic Church in Spain after 1975 was not supportive of the Christian Democrats. The transition to democracy took place during the stewardship of Cardinal Primate Vicente Enrique y Tarancón (raised to the rank in 1969), a strong advocate of the policies established at Vatican II that discouraged active partisan church involvement in politics—a total volte-face from the past. The Spanish church under Enrique y Tarancón took what has been called an active neutrality stand in the political process and thus refused to endorse any political party—even the Christian Democrats.

For an excellent work on the Catholic Church in Spanish history, see Stanley S. Payne, Spanish Catholicism: An Historical Overview (Madison: The University of Wisconsin Press, 1984).

19. Fundación Foessa, Informe sociológico sobre el cambio político en España, 1975–1981 (Madrid: Editorial Euramérica, S.A., 1981), pp. 8–9.

20. See four works by Peter McDonoush, Antonio López-Piña, and Samuel Barnes: "The Spanish Public in Political Transition," British Journal of Political Science, 11 (1981), pp. 49–79; "Authority and Association: Spanish Democracy in Comparative Perspective," The Journal of Politics, vol. 46, no. 3 (August 1984), pp.

652–688; "The Growth of Democratic Legitimacy in Spain," *American Political Science Review*, vol. 80, no. 3 (September 1986), pp. 735–760; and "Social Identity and Mass Politics in Spain," *Comparative Political Studies*, vol. 21, no. 2 (July 1988), pp. 200–229.

21. McDonough, López-Piña, and Barnes, "Social Identity and Mass Politics," p. 210.

22. Ibid., p. 203.

23. Ibid.

24. Ibid., p. 204

25. Ibid., p. 208.

26. Ibid., p. 218.

27. Ibid., p. 220.

28. Seymour Martin Lipset, *Political Man: The Social Bases of Politics* (Garden City, N.Y.: 1960), pp. 88-89.

29. José Pedro Pérez-Llora, "The Beginning of the Transition Process," in Robert P. Clark and Michael H. Haltzel, eds., *Spain in the 1980s: The Democratic Transition and a New International Role* (Cambridge, Mass.: Ballinger Publishing, 1987), p. 16.

30. Clark and Haltzel, eds., *Spain in the 1980s*, p. xiii.

31. Pérez-Llorca, "The Beginning of the Transition Process," p. 21.

32. Richard Gunther, "Democratization and Party Building: The Role of Party Elites in the Spanish Transition," in Clark and Haltzel, eds., *Spain in the 1980s*, p. 53. See also Robert Graham, *Spain: A Nation Comes of Age* (New York: St. Martin's Press, 1984), pp. 270–271.

33. Thomas D. Lancaster and Gary Prevost, eds., *Politics and Change in Spain* (New York: Praeger, 1975), pp. 54–55.

34. Ramón Tamames, *The Spanish Economy: An Introduction* (New York: St. Martin's Press, 1986), p. 103. See also Lancaster and Prevost, eds., *Politics and Change in Spain*, pp. 172–173, and Thomas D. Lancaster, *Policy Stability and Democratic Change: Energy in Spain's Transition* (University Park and London: Pennsylvania State University Press, 1989), pp. 68–69.

35. Tamames, *The Spanish Economy*, p. 45.

36. Lancaster and Prevost, eds., *Politics and Change in Spain*, pp. 104–107.

37. Hooper, *The Spaniards*, p. 137.

38. Graham, *Spain: A Nation Comes of Age*, p. 137.

39. For an expositon and analysis of the politics involved in creating the constitution, see Andrea Bonime-Blanc, *Spain's Transition to Democracy* (Boulder: Westview Press, 1987).

40. John Coverdale, *The Political Transformation of Spain After Franco* (New York: Praeger, 1979), p. 119.

6

Collapse of the Center (1979–1982)

The Spaniards went to the polls for the first time under the new constitution on March 1, 1979, the fourth electoral venture since Franco's death in 1975. (The first three were the referendum of 1976, the 1977 elections, and the referendum of 1978.) Turnout was poor. Perhaps this was due to the citizens' weariness from having just voted three months previously, or perhaps it was a premature manifestation of the cynicism that seeps into any working democracy. Perhaps the abstention rate was an indication that Spanish democracy was becoming healthier; citizens apparently felt that they could ignore their newly acquired electoral duty with impunity. Whatever the explanation, political participation had been falling steadily since the first balloting in 1976 and 1977, when the abstention rate was 22.6 percent and 21.6 percent, respectively. The rate rose to 32.3 percent in 1978 and 33.6 percent one year later. In 1979, although the electorate had been expanded by almost 3.5 million by lowering the voting age to eighteen, the number of votes cast dropped by almost 317,000.

The basic power structure at the national level remained more or less the same as a result of the elections, however. The UCD picked up 2 seats in the 350-seat Congress, once again giving it a plurality with 167 seats (165 in 1977); the PSOE won 121 seats (118 in 1977); the PCE, 23 (20 in 1977); and the AP (under a temporary new name, Democratic Coalition) received 9, down from 16 in 1977. Juan Carlos once again nominated Adolfo Suárez to be prime minister, and Suárez was confirmed on March 30, 1979. But if the power structure remained about the same, there was evidence that political change was in the making. For the first time, extremist parties won seats in the *Cortes*. Popular Unity (Herri Batasuna—HB), the political counterpart of the most violent Basque terrorist group, ETA-militar, won 3 seats in the Congress. (To show contempt for the political system, however, its deputies refused to attend parliamentary sessions.) Basque Left (Euzkadiko Ezkerra—EE), the political wing of the more moderate but still violent Basque terrorist group ETA político-militar, got 1 seat, as did the National Union (Unión Nacional), a federation of neofascist groups. The Socialist Party of Andalucia (Partido Socialista de Andalucía—PSA), a nonextremist, regionalist affiliate of the PSOE, won 5 seats, joining the nonextremist Catalan and Basque regionalist parties, the CiU and the PNV. The AP lost almost half its representation in the Congress.

Even more significant than these phenomena was the altered appearance of the UCD. The party had begun to move to the right, a shift that eventually would lead to Adolfo Suárez's resignation from the premiership and departure from the party, although he himself had helped to initiate the shift during the 1979 campaign. The electorate had always perceived the UCD to be more to the right than the party acknowledged. In fact, the party sought to project a centrist image and to occupy a political space that enclosed the "civilized Right" and the non-Marxist, social democratic Left. It sought the Catholic vote but eschewed any suggestion of confessionalism, a tactic made possible, in part, by the attitude of the hierarchy of the Spanish Catholic Church, which maintained a low political profile in the earlier electoral outings. Speaking through the Catholic Episcopal Conference, the church was not so quiet in the 1979 campaign, and though it did not endorse the UCD (or the AP, for that matter), it did warn against those parties whose "commitments affect religious values or fundamental rights." The bishops' pronouncement went on to say: "We are especially concerned about proposals for the legalization of abortion, for divorce, and for educational reform that might limit the right of parents to choose the proper kind of education for their children."[1] The bishops' targets were, of course, the PSOE and the PCE, and Suárez found common ground with the church in his televised speech on the final day of campaigning. He declared that his party offered the alternative of "Christian humanism" to "Marxist socialist materialism."[2]

Perhaps Suárez felt he could politically afford this overtly rightist, pro-Catholic appeal because the Socialist party had not yet made its momentous decision to eliminate the adjective *Marxist* from its self-definition. That action would not take place until the Extraordinary Congress of the PSOE in September 1979. The Communist party went to the polls in 1979 with Leninism already excised from its definition, but it remained Marxist. Thus, Suárez tarred both parties in his plea for the support of good Christians. His strategy was successful: The UCD stayed in power, the PSOE remained in second place, the PCE merely held its own, and the AP (from which Catholic voters switched to the UCD) appeared moribund.

Although officially still Marxist, the Socialist party succeeded in the local elections that took place on April 3, 1979, the first nationwide municipal elections since April 12, 1931. At stake were 69,613 town and parish council seats in 8,041 municipalities. The UCD put up candidates in almost all the constituencies; the PSOE did so in fewer than half of them. The UCD won 29,614 of the seats, the PSOE 12,220, and the PCE 3,608. The remaining seats were divided among nine other parties and 14,817 independent representatives.

The PSOE received fewer than half the seats taken by the UCD, but the location of these seats gave the Socialists an enormous boost. Madrid, Málaga, Barcelona, Valencia, Zaragoza, and Gerona elected Socialist majorities, and Seville voted Socialist as well, its votes going primarily to the Socialist Party of Andalucia. In short, the majority of the great population centers (except Bilbao in the Basque provinces) voted for the PSOE. These victories were the first in a series that would take the PSOE to both national and local power in 1982 and 1983, and they were won primarily at the expense of the party's major rival, the UCD.

THE UCD IN TROUBLE

Between 1979 and 1982, the Socialists and their increasingly popular leader, Felipe González, gained stature and strength after ridding themselves of what González considered to be an outdated Marxist identity that was a major impediment to electoral success. But the PSOE grew in importance not so much because it continued to best the UCD in electoral competition but because the UCD's position was gradually weakened either by the action of other parties—regionalist parties primarily—or by the UCD's own self-inflicted wounds.

By the spring of 1980, the steps prescribed in article 151 of the constitution for the rapid achievement of autonomy had been taken in the three Basque provinces—Vizcaya, Guipúzcoa, and Alava (Navarre chose to become an autonomous region unto itself)—and in all four of the Catalan provinces. On March 9, 1980, elections were held for the legislature of Euzkadi (the Basque name for the new Basque region), and similar elections were held in Catalonia on March 20. In Euzkadi, regionalist parties won first, second, and fourth places in the elections. The PSOE came in third with 14 percent of the votes, but the UCD received only 8.4 percent. In Catalonia, the regionalist CiU won the plurality with 28 percent of the vote, followed by the PSOE with 23 percent. The UCD (with its Catalan affiliate) was fourth with only 11 percent. The elections to the legislature in newly autonomous Galicia took place eighteen months later, on October 20, 1981. The AP won the plurality with 34 percent of the vote, followed closely by the UCD with 31 percent. The most devastating blow to the position and pride of the UCD was delivered by the PSOE in the elections to the legislature of autonomous Andalucia, held on May 23, 1982. The PSOE overwhelmed all the other parties, winning 52 percent of the vote and 66 seats out of 109. The nearest competitor, the AP, won 17 percent and 17 seats. The UCD received a little over 11 percent and 14 seats. Only the PCE performed worse, with 8 percent and 8 seats. The defeat of the UCD in Andalucia came when the party was struggling in Madrid to keep itself from flying apart. Andalucia and Galicia are among the poorest, least literate, most backward parts of Spain, in many ways almost Third World in their plight. Euzkadi and Catalonia, by contrast, are the richest, most progressive, most educated regions of Spain, comparable in income and lifestyle to the most advanced parts of Western Europe. The rejection of the UCD by regions as dissimilar as these reflects the fragmented image that the party was projecting by the spring of 1982.

The first signs of disintegration had appeared in 1979, when the UCD's constituent elements began to chafe. Some believe the UCD was a cynical, opportunistic creature of those political elites who had served Franco but were ready to accommodate themselves to democracy in order to maintain power. Others believe that the UCD was the expression of truly progressive men and women who wanted Spain to make the transition to democracy as peacefully and painlessly as possible. Whatever the case, the UCD was truly the party of the transition. But once the constitution of 1978 came into force and members of the first *Cortes* were elected in 1979, the centripetal force that had kept the pieces of the UCD together dissolved. The goals that had magnetized the diverse parts—liberals, social democrats and Christian democrats primarily—between 1977 and 1979 had been reached, and the natural incompatibilities among the members now emerged.

The UCD had been created from the top down by those already in power. For these men (and a few women), the UCD and the state were synonymous. Most of the UCD philosophy had come out of Francoism, under which the state and the caudillo were one. Indeed, the automatic identification of the incumbent with uncontested power had become almost second nature to UCD members. The notion that the apparatus of the state could some day be controlled by another party was not fully comprehensible to the UCD elites, who never fully learned how to fight politically because they never believed that they would need to. The "center" with which the party identified appeared sacred and seemingly eternal, verified for the party by the results of the 1979 elections. In some ways, the "barons" of the UCD were like the hidalgos of the sixteenth century, for whom work was beneath contempt. To the political hidalgos of the UCD, work—in the form of grubby, sweaty electioneering—was alien, and the tailored suits and silk ties of the UCD elite contrasted tellingly with the corduroy pants and pullover sweater of a tieless Felipe González. The UCD had not built an effective, bureaucratized, and institutionalized grassroots party structure. It went to the hustings primarily through personalities, as did the PSOE and the PCE. But the parties on the left had been created from the bottom up by men and women outside the halls of power, and their grassroots infrastructures had been carefully built and tended. When those at the top of the UCD began to fight and fall out among themselves, the party fragmented, for it had almost no existence apart from its founding fathers.

THE POLITICAL DEMISE OF ADOLFO SUÁREZ

Adolfo Suárez will deservedly rank as one of the great political actors in post-Franco Spanish history. But his reputation would have remained more secure had he left the political stage after the elections of 1979 while his star was ascendant. He, of course, could not have foreseen the trajectory of his eminence, but hindsight tells us that what he and the king saw as a single drama was, in reality, two separate plays, with the same actors but with radically different plots and direction: Play number one might have been entitled *Dismantling the Franco Regime and Creating a New Constitution;* play number two, *Governing the New Regime.*

In play number one, Suárez was, without exaggeration, extraordinary. His personal political attributes met the circumstances of the day as, along with the king, he brought about the peaceful transition from Francoist authoritarianism and oversaw the creation of the democratic constitution and its approval by the people. Play number two opened with the elections of 1979 that brought a plurality victory to Suárez and his party, the UCD, and kept him as prime minister. The play ended for Suárez when he resigned on January 29, 1981, no longer able to govern an increasingly intractable Congress and an increasingly disillusioned electorate. The play itself ended its run in the 1982 elections, when the people not only brought down Suárez's replacement in the premiership but also destroyed forever the UCD.

The dismantling of the Franco regime and the creation of the constitution were achieved by elites who were committed to the transformation and willing to compromise among themselves to achieve it. *Among themselves* are key words because here they imply the consociational technique of intergroup consensus accomplished behind closed doors, away from scrutiny by the media or by constituents.[3] When consociational democracy is at work, no one among the elites comes away completely satisfied with the end product, but no one comes away so alienated that he or she refuses to accept the compromise. Everyone gets something of value. The product or compromise is then presented to the public as an accomplished fact to be accepted or rejected, as if it had been created with no conflict. No inputs come from the elites' constituencies except those that have been filtered through the elites. Furthermore, no publicity is sought or revealed by the elites, for that would shed light on the process of compromise whereby one elite defers to another for a higher good (as interpreted by the elite, of course). In the light of full publicity, intraelite bargaining would look to nonelite observers like trafficking with ideological ortho-doxy, showing the elites to be unworthy of popular trust. Nonetheless, the consociational process is democratic to the extent that the elites represent the full spectrum of popular sentiments—or as much of the spectrum as is amenable to compromise. (Extremes at either end may never be brought into consociationalism.) The process is also democratic because the prod-uct is offered to the public for final approval through the ballot.

Spanish consociationalism, as the term is used to describe the political process in the early period of the transition, had to be modified only slightly to fit the classic model set forth by Arendt Lijphart. Moreover, the Spanish political process closely resembled consociationalism as it oper-ates in the Benelux countries, where the technique seems to exist in its purest form. Lijphart has written:

> Successful consociational democracy requires: (1) That the elites have the ability to accommodate the divergent interests and demands of the subcul-tures. (2) This requires that they have the ability to transcend cleavages and to join in a common effort with the elites of rival subcultures. (3) This in turn depends on their commitment to the maintenance of the system and to the improvement of its cohesion and stability. (4) Finally, all of the above re-quirements are based on the assumption that the elites understand the perils of political fragmentation.[4]

Additionally, Lijphart has said that three factors appear to be strongly conducive to the establishment or maintenance of cooperation among elites in a fragmented system—external threats to the country, the multiple balance of power among the subcultures, and a relatively low total load on the decisionmaking apparatus.[5]

Let us compare Lijphart's model to its Spanish variant, beginning with the four requirements. The Spanish elites who took part in the transi-tion to democracy were all committed to the same goal: the transforma-tion of the Franco system. They knew full well the perils of fragmentation. The historical memory of the politics of the Second Republic remained vivid forty years after its demise: a deadly, zero-sum game between Right and Left that exploded into civil war and ended in dictatorship. Thus, the elites had a powerful incentive to overcome the hostility that historical memory could have rekindled. No one party was hegemonic among the dozens that proliferated at the beginning of the transition. Moreover, most were parties of notables, and by their very natures, they facilitated accommodation by the elites. Further, the Spanish people had been so successfully depoliticized by the Franco regime that they offered little resistance to elitist manipulation at this early stage of the transition. Spanish elites could behave as they had always behaved—this time, however, they were committed to democracy.

Let us now turn to the three factors that appear strongly conducive to cooperation among elites. There was, of course, no external threat to Spain in the mid-1970s, but the fear of internal upheaval—coup d'état or counterrevolution (the enemies of the transition within Spain believed democracy to be revolutionary)—most assuredly focused the elites' attention. As mentioned earlier, no one subculture—whether regional, religious, or class-based—was dominant; there was, instead, a movable balance among the subcultures that kept power tenuous and those pursuing it amenable to cooperation. Lastly, the total load to be carried by the elites was low, at least in terms of the *number* of loads to be borne simultaneously. (The *size* of the load that was to be borne—the transition to democracy and the creation of a democratic constitution—was, of course, immense.) The Moncloa Pacts were near-perfect examples of consociational agreement: the reduction of the number of loads that would otherwise have had to be carried all at the same time. Energy used to solve socioeconomic and finely nuanced political problems would have sapped the supply of energy needed to accomplish the political task of bringing about the successful transition to democracy. The Moncloa Pacts articulated these problems and then put them aside, to be handled after the primary task had been accomplished.

Adolfo Suárez's skills were perfectly adapted to this kind of elite compromise, having been honed in the Francoist world where elites were constantly maneuvering around the ruler's "fixed sun." Although Franco could not be moved unless he chose to be, he nevertheless could be influenced by those skillful in persuasion—like the Opus Deists, who convinced him to embrace neocapitalism in the 1960s. Franco's world was, in many ways, consociational but not democratic. The world of the transition remained consociational but removed the "fixed sun" of Francoism and gave the process democratic goals.

Suárez had prospered politically in the Franco regime. (He had been the civil governor of Segovia, later director-general of Spanish Radio-Television, and then secretary-general of the National Movement.) He had learned well the delicate game of survival among contending Francoist "families." His late conversion to democracy (whether spiritual or pragmatic we shall probably never fully know) was apparently wholehearted, but a change of political heart or mind is rarely automatically accompanied by a change in political skills or techniques. Prior to his appointment by Juan Carlos in July 1976, there was never an opportunity for

Suárez to learn to play the open, conflictual, electorally responsible game of democratic politics. He used the only skills he had, all learned under Franco. And during the early years of the transition before the elections of 1979, they proved eminently successful.

Partial credit for Suárez's success must be given to his fellow right-of-center players, who, like himself, had come out of Francoism and were skilled in consociational bargaining. They made it easier for Suárez, even when some in the UCD—the Christian Democrats and Liberals—felt he was too far to the left, and others in the party—the Social Democrats—felt he was too far to the right. Even the most extreme voice on the democratic right, Manuel Fraga Iribarne, head of the AP, was willing to play by consociational rules and became a great defender of the constitution.

Part of the credit must also be given to those to the left of center who had returned from exile or emerged from clandestinity within Spain to take part in the transition. These men and women had no consociational skills and were expected to be deeply conflictual, but the most extreme on the left (or rather, those who had been *expected* to be the most extreme) accepted the consociational rules of the game. The Communists—or more precisely, Santiago Carrillo—agreed that the good of Spain should prevail over doctrinal orthodoxy. The Socialists were still, in theory, unregenerate Marxists during the early transition. They talked more aggressively than they acted, however, and they, too, took part in consociationalism (pragmatically adapting their Marxist rhetoric to democratic reality after their electoral failure in 1979). On the left, it was the Communists who could have derailed the transition, but their leader chose not to do so. Two quotations give evidence of Carrillo's commitment. He called the Moncloa Pacts "an act of national responsibility in order to restore democracy." He also spoke about the necessity to reach concord on the place of the Catholic Church in democratic Spain:

> I believe that the religious question has been surmounted in its essentials in this country; we should all do everything to overcome it once and for all. Particularly the forces of progress, the democratic forces, the forces who want socialism, have a special interest in not clashing with the Catholic Church and in not contributing to maintain any obstacle which could confront these forces, which, let us not forget, gave an ideological basis to the [Francoist] rebellion and "the crusade," and which could still give an ideological basis to a resistance that would be very dangerous for the advance of democracy and socialism.[6]

Both the Left, particularly Carrillo, and the Right, particularly Fraga, helped make it possible for Suárez to negotiate the creation of the constitution: Some observers even call both Carrillo and Fraga unsung heroes of the constitution. They also helped make it possible for Suárez to negotiate the Moncloa Pacts, which essentially were agreements to postpone socioeconomic reform until some time after the constitution was ratified and the first constitutional government had come into existence. The reforms were so urgent and so potentially divisive that had debate on them intruded into the debate on the constitution, both the constitution and the pacts would have been aborted. Ironically, consociationalism was used at Moncloa to bring about the agreement to delay the solution of problems that were too explosive to be accommodated by consociationalism. Moreover, the agreements at Moncloa also postponed the elaboration of issues that were to be alluded to in the document—among them, divorce and abortion—but whose full exposition in the constitution would have pushed the negotiators into irreconcilable camps. (It is particularly significant that the Communists and especially Carrillo agreed to postpone the solution of socioeconomic issues that went to the very core of Marxist doctrine. If political issues (the creation of the constitution) took precedence over economic issues (the postponement of Moncloa), then the essence of Marxism—that economics determines politics—is turned on its head and fundamentally denatured. A heavy price was paid by the Communist party and the Communist cause by Carrillo's commitment to democracy, but his commitment contributed enormously to Suárez's success and thus to Suárez's reputation.)

Perhaps the successful creation of the constitution and of the pacts at Moncloa gave Suárez a false sense of his talents for democracy, although it cannot be stressed enough that the achievement of those two extraordinary goals would have assured him an honored place in Spanish history. Once the constitution was ratified, however, and the first elections under the constitution took place, the task of governing Spain on a day-to-day basis began, and from that point until his resignation in 1981, Suárez appeared to be less and less in control of events that became increasingly ominous. The techniques used to accomplish the two earlier tasks were insufficient or, more precisely, were inappropriate to the new task at hand. The consociational negotiations that characterized the early transition took place behind closed doors, away from public scrutiny. Moreover, constitution-making is a rarified function, remote from the experience of ordinary men and women. The problems facing the new government—unemployment, inflation, terrorism, military subversion, and demands for regional autonomy—were, by contrast, a part of the everyday experience of average men and women, and they were too vital for the citizens' well-being to be negotiated without direct public input. Not only did each problem itself require immediate remedy, several of these also became interconnected in such a way that the solution of one exacerbated the other. Moreover, these public problems were urgently in need of solutions at the very time when the public affected by them was becoming increasingly disillusioned with the democratic process.

The disenchantment (*desencanto*), as it was called in Spain, did not cause people to look back nostalgically at authoritarianism, although some wags did say, "We had it better against Franco" (*"Vivíamos mejor contra Franco"*)—a play on the pro-Franco slogan, "We had it better with Franco" (*"Vivíamos mejor con Franco"*). The disenchanted felt that they had been more politically alive (or emotionally engaged) while *against* Franco than they were now when they saw democracy daunted by present-day tasks. Their disillusionment can be understood. The Spanish people had been oppressed for so long and had nourished democratic aspirations for so long that democracy's performance could not possibly have matched the peoples' expectations. Those who live in a democracy know full well that the system often involves little more than treading water, but those new to democracy want a more spectacular exhibition. But the *desencanto* went further than that. The people were disappointed with democracy's limitations, and their attitude toward democracy's practitioners had begun to sour. The governing elites of the UCD, although democratically elected, continued to treat the electorate disdainfully, in a manner reminiscent of that embraced by Francoist elites, seemingly ignoring their voices. The disdain may have been tolerable during the early transition when the constitution was being created, but now the people were beginning to gain confidence, and they resented the condescension.

The problems facing the elites were daunting, indeed. Spain's democracy was born into a harsh economic environment. True, the democracy that arrived in 1978 came into a healthier economic climate than had the ill-fated democracy born in 1931, in depths of the world depression. Nevertheless, the post-Francoist democracy was deeply troubled economically and forced to operate in an interdependent economic world that even leaders of the powerful economies (like those of the United States, Germany, and Japan) could not bend to their wills. The oil crises set off by the OPEC decisions in 1973 were particularly severe on Spain, a country that was overwhelmingly dependent on oil and where oil was almost totally imported. The crises caused by the astonishing increase in petroleum prices reverberated throughout the Spanish economy during the ensuing years and pushed countless businesses into bankruptcy, particularly those fragile businesses that had survived until then only because of Francoist paternalism. Business collapse triggered business collapse until unemployment became severe. Moreover, economic rationality was demanding a reduction in the highly featherbedded public sector of Francoist Spain, further contributing to unemployment. And as high prices for oil were passed on to the consumer, inflation soared. Yet the Suárez government could not or would not implement redistributive economic programs that had been agreed upon at Moncloa and that could possibly have brought about economic alleviation to the working class. The laboring class felt that it continued to bear the brunt of elitist decisions beyond its control. Although the new regime was perhaps democratic politically, it was little different from the Franco regime economically to many workers. It seemed that economic democracy would not follow political democracy.

Suárez personified this disillusionment, and his handling of problems beyond the economic ones contributed to the people's growing disgruntlement and lack of faith. The demands for regional autonomy, terrorism, and military subversion interlocked to form a seemingly inescapable web, which eventually entrapped Suárez.

The Web

The military was the "gray eminence" of the early years of the transition; in fact, it was not until the abortive coup on February 23, 1981, that the political presence of the military began to recede and the military leaders came to accept the position subordinate to civilian control that characterizes the posture of armed forces in all democracies. The military was not an actual player in the consociational process that produced the constitution and the Moncloa Pacts. The actual players were political party elites. But the military elites, especially the diehards (or *ultras*) in the army, appeared to set the boundaries of the arena in which the process would take place. I say "appeared to" because neither the actual negotiators of democracy nor the military leaders made clear what they would and would not do or what they would or would not tolerate. There was no announced game plan; there were no rules of the game. What existed was a vision in the minds of Juan Carlos and Adolfo Suárez of the kind of Spain they wanted to create. In a new democratic Spain, the role of the military would be different from that in the Franco regime, but in the seemingly experimental world of the early transition, that new role had yet to take shape. In the meantime, the military lived in limbo—unfamiliar territory for an organization that had guaranteed the status quo for nearly forty years. But unlike any of the other actors in the transition, the military had the physical means to bring the entire project to an end.

As a result, a perilous contest ensued in which the political elite, particularly Suárez, maneuvered a dangerous, refractory military to accept the first steps of the transition. Suárez had the full support of Juan Carlos, without whom negotiations with the military would have been unsuccessful. It was he who commanded the loyalty of the military, but it was Suárez who performed the political manipulations that brought the military around. A military loyal only to the king would be insufficient in a democracy; it had to become loyal to the entire political system, of which the king was only a part. This conversion was Suárez's task.

The military had understood that the kind of transition to which they had reluctantly agreed would reform but not destroy the Francoist regime. On September 8, 1976, only two months following his appointment as prime minister, Suárez met with the highest-ranking officers of the three branches of the armed forces, including the three military ministers in his cabinet. (During the early transition, Suárez maintained a cabinet similar in makeup to those in the Franco regime. Each branch of the armed forces—army, navy, air—had its own minister in that cabinet.) In a masterful performance in which he gave the officers all the respect they were accustomed to receiving, he described the changes that he and the king wanted to make, including the legalization of political parties and the holding of elections. Suárez allegedly promised that the Communist party would not be legalized and that the military itself would not be reformed. With what they took as Suárez's word of honor, the military ministers in the cabinet accepted his Political Reform Law on September 10, 1976. Within days, however, it became known that the Communist-led Workers' Commissions would be included in the negotiations that were to lead to the Trade Union Reform Law. On September 22, Lieutenant General Fernando de Santiago, possibly the most influential officer in the army (and thus, in the entire armed forces), resigned from his post as first deputy prime minister for defense, enraged that the reformers would traffic with Communists. Suárez took the opportunity to replace the archconservative de Santiago with the reform-minded General Manuel Gutiérrez Mellado. Although a part of that military elite himself, he was cut from rather different cloth. A comment he made to a reporter provides an insight into Mellado's reformist orientation:

> I don't mind being called a liberal if that means that I admit to not being utterly right all the time, that I am ready to discuss things with whoever wishes to discuss things, that I prefer that there should be no more fratricidal wars, that I want Spain to belong to all Spaniards, that I regard it as suicidal to want to start all over again from scratch, throwing overboard all that had been gained up to now, and that I think one has to look to new and brighter horizons, not restricting oneself with transient ideas and institutions that have been outdated by the reality of a young, restless, vibrant Spain which aspires to a better and juster world.[7]

To many of his fellow officers, however, Gutiérrez Mellado was a turncoat, whose reforms of the armed forces were considered to be treachery. Gutiérrez Mellado made the chiefs of staff of the three military branches the commanders of their respective services and brought them together in the newly created Joint Chiefs of Staff (Junta de Jefes del Estado Mayor—JUJEM). JUJEM and its chairman became an advisory body to the minister of defense and the prime minister. Also newly created was the chief of the defense staff (Jefe del Estado Mayor de la Defensa—JEMAD), the highest-ranking figure in the military hierarchy. The JEMAD is in the direct line of military command and works with the minister of defense in the creation and implementation of defense policy. In wartime, the JEMAD would be commander-in-chief of the armed forces, directly responsible for conducting military operations.[8]

Gutiérrez Mellado was instrumental in abolishing the hated and feared Social Investigation Brigade, and set in motion the creation of new Military Ordinances (Reales Ordenanzas) and the reformation of the Military Code of Justice. The new Ordenanzas (which replaced those that had been in force since the reign of Carlos III, 1759–1788) came into operation in 1979. They released military personnel from swearing a personal oath to the monarch; allowed for the refusal of subordinates to carry out orders that violated the Spanish constitution or international law; and forbade discrimination in recruitment based on class, religion, gender, or political affiliation. The reformed Military Code of Justice came into being in 1981, during the administration of Calvo Sotelo. The new code limited military jurisdiction to strictly military offenses and brought military personnel accused of crimes under civilian jurisdiction. It also provided for the appeal of verdicts of the courts-martial in the civilian Supreme Court.

In addition, Gutiérrez Mellado set in motion reforms that affected promotion and retirement. The military could at last remove officers from active duty because of physical or psychological disorders and professional incompetence. The retirement age was lowered from 66 to 64, and the government, under certain circumstances, allowed officers early retirement, setting up, for the first time, an active reserve for those who were forced to retire sooner than they had expected. Top-ranking officers retained most of their perquisites, however, and retired on or near full salary. Promotions beginning at the rank of major would henceforth depend on qualifications and accomplishments and not solely on seniority, as they did throughout the Franco regime.

But Gutiérrez Mellado's most symbolic action—and that for which his military colleagues were probably the most unforgiving—was his role in creating the first civilian minister of defense since 1936, Agustín Rodríguez Sahagún. Gutiérrez Mellado remained deputy prime minister in charge of defense until Suárez's resignation in 1981.

The events in September 1976, the legalization of all political parties except the Communists in February 1977, the legalization of the rights to strike and to form trade unions in March 1977, the abolition of the National Movement, the legalization of the Communist party in April 1977, and the reforms initiated by Gutiérrez Mellado galvanized the *ultras* within the armed forces and led to their subversive activity that would eventually culminate in the attempted coup d'état on February 23, 1981 (which will be discussed later). The diehards accused Suárez of breaching his word and betraying Spain to "godless communism."

For the military *ultras*, the crusade against communism was matched in intensity only by their obsession with the unity of Spain. *España: Una, Grande, Libre* ("Spain: One, Great, Free") was one of Franco Spain's mythic slogans that proclaimed the historical unity of Spain. In tension with that unity, however, was Spanish regionalism, of equal historical validity and expressed in the ancient *fueros* that had, in the past, guaranteed degrees of autonomy for the various peoples of Spain. The Second Republic had been committed to the recognition of regional rights, and some form of autonomy either already existed (in Catalonia) or was in the making (in the Basque provinces and Galicia) when the Civil War broke out. The Nationalist victory was the death knell for regional rights, and Franco maintained a relentless, often ruthless, centralism for the entirety of his dictatorship. In his commitment to unity over regional rights, he was avidly supported by the military. As a result, one of the key elements of anti-Francoism was opposition to centralism.

After the death of Franco, the fervent supporters of a new democratic Spain included equally fervent supporters of regional autonomy. Both Juan Carlos and Suárez realized that their plans for the transition to democracy had to include a commitment to some form of regional self-determination. Not only would democracy in its Spanish form be incomplete without that guarantee, but the transition itself would be impossible without the support of regionalists. To secure their support, the king and Suárez acted even before the constitution was created and ratified. The king issued preautonomy decrees to Catalonia (September 1977), the Basque provinces (December 1977), and Galicia (March 1978) that made the recognition of regional rights an accomplished fact, which the drafters of the constitution could later refine but not effectively reject. Once the three "historical nationalities," as they are called, had been granted preautonomy decrees, however, it became apparent that similar claims, while not historical, could not be denied the remaining parts of Spain. Therefore, Valencia, the Balearic Islands, Extremadura, Old Castile (now called Castile-León), New Castile (now called Castile-La Mancha), and Murcía were granted decrees late in 1978. Within short order, Spain was divided into seventeen regions, each seeking autonomy to one degree or another.

In the Basque provinces, demands for autonomy reached a volume and intensity unmatched elsewhere in Spain. The leaders of the reborn, pre–Civil War, bourgeois party—the PNV—were willing to sit down and make a pact with the national government and the constitution-makers, but new left-wing political groups were seeking radical change. Several of these disparate, fractious leftist groups, some extremely dangerous, came together in the loose association called the Patriotic Socialist Front (Koordinadora Abertzale Sozialista—KAS, translated from the Basque language, Euskera or Euskara). The front's goal, Alternativa KAS, called for total amnesty for all political prisoners; the expulsion of the national army, the police force, and the Civil Guard from Basque territory; and the unification of the Spanish and French Basque provinces into a single, independent, Marxist nation-state. KAS's goal was virtually nonnegotiable for the national government and the constitution-makers in Spain. A description and analysis of the groups and parties that made up the Koordinadora are beyond the scope of this study, but the most notorious are ETA, which itself split into the moderate and tractable ETA-político-militar, and the violent ETA-militar, which is intimately linked with the political party Herri Batasuna.

The framers of the constitution made no attempt to accommodate the demands of Alternativa KAS. What was offered to *all* the Spanish peoples was the opportunity to create autonomous communities that would remain integral parts of the nation-state, thus maintaining Spanish unity while providing for a regionalism just short of federalism. Two routes to autonomy were set forth—a fast route designed to be used by the three "historical nationalities" and a slow route to be used by the remaining regions. With the acceptance of the constitution by all Spaniards, including the Basques, the shape of the new Spain was fixed.

For the unregenerate *abertzales* ("patriots"), the creation of the Autonomous Communities was an abomination because it accepted the fait accompli of the constitution and of the indivisibility of the Spanish nation-state. The *abertzales* reacted with an acceleration of violence that has not stopped to this day. For the unregenerate military *ultras*, the creation of the Autonomous Communities was an abomination because the very existence of the regions, even within the indivisible Spanish nation-state, threatened the mythic unity of Spain. Moreover, the most extreme of the regionalists, the Basque *abertzales*, were Marxists, uniting in a single enemy the two most passionate hatreds of the military *ultras*—communism and regionalism. The primary victims of *abertzale* violence were members of the military, the police, and the Civil Guard—the guardians of the unity of Spain. Therefore, each killing was not only a symbolic blow to that unity but also a goad to those who had protected that unity for forty years but were now estopped from doing so by what the military diehards believed to be the treachery of the new democratic leaders. The *abertzales* hoped to provoke the military to overthrow the fledgling democracy, thereby fulfilling the prophecy of the extremists who declared that the military would never allow Spain to be free.

The Beginning of the End

The ire of both the *abertzales* and the military *ultras* was focused in Adolfo Suárez. The *abertzales* condemned him for preventing the ultimate choice of self-determination—independence for the Basque provinces. The *ultras* condemned him for supporting any self-determination in whatever form and for preventing the forces of law and order from crushing, once and for all, the perpetrators of violence. Perhaps by this time (the end of the 1970s), no one could have maneuvered Spain through the treacherous political landscape; perhaps it would take the traumatic attempted coup d'état on February 23, 1981, to break the deadlock and allow the transition to move forward. In the meantime, however, Suárez's star was rapidly dimming. With the constitution in force and the first government elected under its rubrics in place, Suárez, who continued as prime minister, seemed increasingly overwhelmed by Spain's domestic problems: the souring economy, inflation, unemployment, escalating ETA terrorism, turmoil in the process of autonomy, and growing conspiracies plotted by the *ultras*.

Suárez became more and more isolated, absenting himself from parliament and refusing to hold press conferences. He sought refuge in the Moncloa Palace, surrounded by what came to be called his *fontaneros* ("plumbers")—hatchet men or yes-men who did little to dispel the growing public opinion that Suárez was becoming increasingly autocratic (often the posture of the insecure). Paul Preston offers an interesting insight into the possible causes of Suárez's withdrawal. Preston suggests that the prime minister, a man of modest social background, lacked confidence in his parliamentary skills—the kind needed for the free-for-all of democratic legislative debate. He compared unfavorably to a large number of his colleagues, many of whom were lawyers, former university professors, or high-ranking civil servants. Those in the latter two groups had succeeded early in their careers in *oposiciones* ("oppositions"). The route to university chairs and the upper reaches of the civil service, *oposiciones* were grueling public academic debates, much like gladiatorial combats, that weeded out all but the most agile and facile. Suárez lacked the necessary educational background, and the consociational skills that had served him so well in the early years of the transition were less useful in the more open, confrontational arenas of postconstitutional Spanish politics.[9] And on top of it all, the press was beginning to reveal the carefully guarded secret that Suárez was suffering from serious dental problems, which made it increasingly difficult for him to speak

Further complicating his already deteriorating political environment were early signs of the collapse that would eventually destroy the UCD from within even before it was destroyed from without by the elections of 1982. The families that made up the UCD felt less and less compelled to keep the artificial union together once the common task of creating the constitution had been accomplished. The natural differences among Christian Democrats, Social Democrats, and Liberals began to extrude at the very time that Suárez, hitherto the catalyst for unity, was himself wearing down, like an ailing patriarch no longer able to command loyalty and respect. The fact that these families had existed before Suárez came along strengthened their convictions that they could once again survive without him. The family leaders began to turn against Suárez and reestablish their own separate identities. His handling of the autonomy process in Andulucia revealed the erosion of his political skills, a weakening that gave his party peers a taste for blood. As mentioned earlier, the fast route to autonomy (article 151 of the constitution) had been designed for the Basque provinces, Catalonia, and Galicia—the "historical nationalities," as they are called; the slow route (article 143) had been planned for the remaining regions. Andalucia, though not a historical nationality, sought to pursue autonomy by the fast route. As the leader of the UCD and an early protagonist in the battle for autonomy, Suárez should logically have supported the Andalucian quest by whatever route the region chose to take. Moreover, Andulucia was a Socialist stronghold; Suárez's support for autonomy would have helped the UCD in this less-than-friendly territory. But Suárez had another agenda, caught as he was between separatist terrorism and military conspiracy. In an attempt to assuage the military *ultras*, he decided to slow the process of autonomy for areas beyond the three "historical nationalities." He set the stage for his scheme by removing from the cabinet his minister of culture, Manuel Clavero Arévalo, who had once been minister for the regions, and replacing him with a former chief censor in the Franco regime and the "official" biographer of the caudillo, historian Ricardo de la Cierva. With the proper sympathizers and sycophants in position, Suárez began his campaign to convince Andalucians to abstain from voting in the referendum scheduled for February 23, 1980. Under the terms of article 151—fast route—a majority in each province within a region seeking autonomy must vote yes if the referendum is to carry. But in Andalucia, the vote in Almería fell short of the majority, thereby shifting Andalucia to the slow route. (Andalucia finally achieved autonomy, the fourth region to do so, in December 1981, but by that date, Suárez was no longer prime minister, and the abortive coup d'état in February 1981 marked the crisis of Spain's transition to democracy.)

The Andalucian vote in February 1980 was a pyrrhic victory for Suárez. It delayed autonomy for Andalucia, but it did not assuage the *ultras*, and it gave credence to the terrorists' claim that the government was the enemy of the people. The vote also severely weakened the UCD in Andalucia and revealed Suárez's narrowing political vision and his willingness to sacrifice his party for his own policy. Moreover, it showed that Spain's democratic politics were too closely bound to the person of Suárez. Consequently, the personal political dilemma from which he seemed unable to extricate himself—caught as he was between terrorism and conspiracy, between the *abertzales* and the *ultras*—seemed to be the political dilemma of Spain itself, from which the nation might not be able to escape democratically.

Suárez's debacle in Andalucia was followed over the following months by costly UCD defeats in the Basque provinces and Catalonia. In the first elections for the newly created Basque parliament on March 9, 1980, the UCD was humiliated by coming in fourth. The plurality victor was the PNV, with 38 percent of the vote; second place went, ominously, to Herri Batasuna, the extremist nationalist party closely allied with the ETA-militar; third place went to the PSOE. On March 20, 1980, the first elections for the Catalan parliament gave the plurality victory to the Convergencia i Unió, the bourgeois Catalan nationalist party that was a spiritual cousin to the PNV; the Socialist Catalan party, Partido Socialista de Cataluña (PSC), came in second; the Communists third; and the UCD fourth.

By late 1980, Suárez realized that his effectiveness had come to an end, and he believed that his party was moving too far to the right for comfort. On January 29, 1981, at the party conference in Mallorca, he resigned as prime minister. In his address to the delegates, he urged that the UCD remain a centrist party and stressed that to do otherwise would betray the voters' confidence. He declared that a move to the right would fundamentally alter the character of the party. The conferees responded by choosing Leopoldo Calvo Sotelo, a conservative centrist, as its nominee for prime minister. The party presidency, formerly held by Suárez, went to Agustín Rodríguez Sahagún, Suárez's brother-in-law and a dedicated centrist.

THE CRISIS OF FEBRUARY 1981

Juan Carlos nominated Calvo Sotelo for the premiership. Voting for confirmation took place in the Congress on February 10, 1981, but Calvo failed to receive the necessary majority on the first balloting. The second round was scheduled for February 23, 1981, but as the voting was in progress, all hell broke loose. Antonio Tejero Molina, a lieutenant colonel in the Civil Guard, burst onto the floor of the Congress, armed and accompanied by other armed guardsmen. Together, they held the entire political leadership of Spain hostage—all the deputies and all the members of the cabinet. (Eventually, they freed the female deputies.) José María de Areílza recalls: "The worst thing was the lack of information. ... The soldiers took all our transistor radios and cut the telephone lines. We were completely isolated, prisoners. So far as we in the Cortes knew, Spain had become a military dictatorship again."[10]

A second conspirator—General Jaime Milans del Bosch, captain-general of the military region of Valencia—simultaneously mobilized the units under his command and placed Valencia under martial law. In fact, he had put tanks on the streets of the city of Valencia and had declared martial law throughout the region of Valencia half an hour before Tejero captured the parliament. In Madrid, a third conspirator—General Alfonso Armado Comyn, who had tutored the young Juan Carlos in the 1950s and 1960s and who had been a close friend of the prince—sought to implicate the king in the plot. Armado telephoned Juan Carlos and offered to appear at the palace to help the sovereign arrive at a decision about the coup. The plan devised by Tejero, Milans, and Armado was to convert Juan Carlos to their cause, overthrow the government with his approval, and set up an authoritarian monarchy under the protection of the armed forces. Almost immediately, the plot became apparent to the king; some say it was Queen Sofía rather than Juan Carlos who first figured that Armado was the mastermind, hoping to insinuate himself into the palace under the guise of helping the monarch make up his mind. By phone, the king sought the counsel of his father, Don Juan, at his home in Estoril, Portugal. Don Juan told the king: "Stay in the palace. Hold your ground, whatever the cost. Do not leave under any circumstances, whatever the promise, whatever they threaten. If you give up one inch, all will be lost."[11] The king then contacted the remaining ten regional commanders and informed them that the conspirators did not have his support. Two of the commanders spontaneously pledged their loyalty; the king had to persuade several of the remaining eight before they all came around. Juan Carlos had used a specially designed communications system, which he had had installed in the palace, that gave him direct access to the commanders of Spain's eleven military districts. It bypassed the regular communications system, which might have been vulnerable to sabotage or capture in time of crisis.[12] In fact, the conspirators had taken over the Madrid television station, and it was not until troops loyal to the government had retaken the station that the king was able to address the nation. At close to 1 A.M. on February 24, Juan Carlos, in an address taped earlier in the evening, reassured the Spanish people that the coup had been put down and that democracy remained intact.

The extraordinary day wound to an end in a particularly poignant and intimate way that demonstrated the king's deep commitment to Spanish democracy and to the Bourbon dynasty. At about 3 A.M. on February 24, Juan Carlos called for his son and heir to the throne, the thirteen-year-old Felipe. An observer recalled the scene for correspondent T. A. Allman eleven years later:

> Juan Carlos put his arm around his son's shoulder and said, "Felipe, I want you to remember this moment." Then the king took the boy, step by step, through everything that had happened. He explained about the elections, and how an elected parliament was the representation of the people's will. He explained how the military was the defender of the people—and therefore the greatest treason the military could commit was to turn against the elected representatives of the people.
>
> Then he explained about the monarchy. He told his son that, while the first duty of a king was to serve the people, a king's ultimate duty was to be the people's last defense.
>
> It was nearly four by the time the king finished. ... Things had started to calm down. Besides the king, the queen, and Prince Felipe ... there were only a few other people still there. You know ... we all felt terribly privileged to have been at the king's side that night.[13]

The events showed just how fragile democracy was in Spain, since it appears that the decisions of one man alone could have taken the country back to dictatorship. F-23, as the event is now referred to in Spain, proved that the transition was not yet over. It had, however, passed through its most severe crisis and was still alive.

The coup d'état had been building since events during the early days of the transition convinced the diehards in the military that the demolition of the Franco regime and the transition to democracy were in earnest. The legalization of the Communist party and the appointment of Gutiérrez Mellado to replace de Santiago were the catalysts that mobilized the *ultras*. From 1977 to 1981, conspiracy seemed to proliferate among the military diehards, but information about them remains murky. By their very nature, plots of this type defy analysis. They are mazes within mazes, and those who lie at the hearts of the mazes most often never come to light. In fact, the purpose of the maze is to make penetration difficult, if not impossible. Even writing about plots is problematic because describing them from genesis to completion suggests a purposeful, linear development, and in many cases, no such development occurred. Like Topsy, conspiracies typically "just grow." In this study, I will look at the three best known military conspiracies, alluding to others that are thought to have existed. Another caveat is needed here: "Best known" implies a depth of knowledge, but in reality, the best knowledge remains rather superficial. One fact does appear to be solid, however: several of the same plotters appear in all the conspiracies, the most notorious ones as well as others that remain obscure.

From September 13–16, 1977, a group of high-ranking *ultra* military men met at the home of de Santiago at Játiva, in the region of Valencia— three former ministers of the army, a former minister of the navy, and, among other officers, General Jaime Milans del Bosch. Ostensibly, they met to celebrate a wedding. What they talked about and what they alleg- edly proposed is not known. But it is conjectured that they planned to ask the king to set up an emergency military government or, failing that, to convince him to dismiss Suárez and indefinitely suspend parliament. Was it a conspiracy? Or were they simply a group of deeply disaffected men who talked but did not plot? The question remains unanswered to this day, but government intelligence learned of the meeting, which soon was labeled the "Játiva Conspiracy," and informed Suárez. His response could be called either cautious or timid, but in any case, the dilemma that would eventually entrap Suárez could be said to have begun there. Perhaps Suárez was cautious because the first legislative elections since 1936 had taken place only three months earlier and ground was being prepared for the creation of a new constitution. To discipline military leaders for a con- spiracy that may or may not have been in the making may have triggered a military uprising that could have stopped the transition cold. Perhaps Suárez was too timid and should have risked decisive action that would have established civilian primacy once and for all, relying on the king to keep the military allegiant. But fear won out, and little was done. The most conspicuous action taken against the men at Játiva was the reassign- ment of Milans del Bosch from the command of the armored division at Brunete, just outside Madrid, to the command of the military region of Va- lencia. The elite Brunete Division, a hotbed of antidemocratic sentiment, was the key link in the chain of armed garrisons throughout the country, created by Franco to maintain "domestic tranquillity"—that is, to put down insurrection. In the hands of a rebellious commander, the Brunete unit was strong enough to bring down a government.

In late 1978, the first direct plot against the government took shape: Operación Galaxia, named for the *cafetería* ("coffeehouse," "bar," or "café") where the conspirators met. The leaders of the plot were Captain Ricardo Sáenz de Ynestrillas of the Armed Police and Lieutenant Colonel Antonio Tejero Molina of the Civil Guard. The exact number of coconspir- ators is not known, but some of the men involved in the Játiva Conspiracy and in F-23 were active in Galaxia. The plan was to seize Suárez and the rest of the cabinet as they met at the Moncloa Palace, thereby creating a power vacuum that the military would then fill. The plot was to be carried out on November 17, 1978, while the king and queen were in Mexico on a state visit and while the minister of defense, Gutiérrez Mellado, and many high-ranking officers were out of Madrid. Further, the overthrow would coincide with the Madrid gathering of 150,000 right-wing militants to commemorate the third anniversary of Franco's death. Events in other parts of Spain appear to have been synchronized with those in Madrid. On the day the plot was to be put into action in Madrid, Gutiérrez Mellado addressed the senior officers of the southeast region (the Levant) of the Civil Guard in Cartagena. In the course of the speech, he was inter-rupted by the regional commander, General Juan Atarés Peña, who shouted, "La constitución es la major mentira! Arriba España! Viva Franco!" ("The constitution is the biggest lie of them all! Up with Spain! Long live Franco!"). Atarés was vigorously applauded. Gutiérrez Mellado ordered Atarés and everyone who believed as he did to leave the room. General Milans del Bosch, who was a part of the Játiva Conspiracy and who would play a central role in F-23, was in the audience. He rose and ac-companied Atarés out of the room, while Atarés hurled epithets at Gutiér-rez Mellado: "Freemason! Pig! Traitor!" Atarés, a close friend of Milans, had been Tejero's commanding officer when both men were stationed in the Basque region of the Civil Guard. The experience in the Basque prov-inces is said to have further radicalized these already reactionary men.

Suárez was informed of the plot on November 16 by the chief of the intelligence service of the Civil Guard, and Tejero and Sáenz were ar-rested. They were court-martialed eighteen months later, in May 1980, charged with "conspiracy for and proposing military rebellion." They were convicted, but the sentences were a mockery given the severity of the charge: Tejero received seven months of confinement; Sáenz six months and one day. Both were reassigned to duty immediately upon re-lease. Atarés was also court-martialed for indiscipline but was exonerated on all counts. The general in charge of the Atarés court-martial, Luis Caruana López (who was the military governor of Valencia) would, in the 1981 coup, refuse the order to arrest Milans del Bosch, one of the key con-spirators.

Once again, as with the Játiva Conspiracy, Suárez reacted with ap-parently little concern. Operación Galaxia was clearly a conspiracy, how-ever, and could not be explained away as the meeting at Játiva had been. It was rather offhandedly referred to as the work of "four crazy guys in a cafe." The *ultras*, in particular, dismissed it in this way because it left them with clean hands to conspire again. One could evidently conspire with im-punity; at least, this is what the diehards could assume.

From Operación Galaxia to F-23, there is evidence that several conspiracies were plotted by some of the same men, including Tejero and Milans del Bosch, but none came to fruition.[14] An explanation for the fail-ure of the preceding conspiracies to get as far as the attempted coup in

1981 did may perhaps be found in the writings of Stanley Payne, who believes that the Spanish military historically has intervened in politics only when civilian control is weak or has totally broken down and when popular support has collapsed.

> Historically, notable acts of military intervention have taken place only against relatively unpopular governments, those that denied reasonable access to major national political sectors, or those facing severe internal division or breakdown. Major instances of intervention against a national consensus or a clear majority of public opinion have been rare to nonexistent. Therefore, despite the generally Francoist sympathies of Spanish military officers, they would not be likely to block or to try to overthrow a democratization that (1) enjoyed firm and effective leadership, (2) was constitutional and carried out through legal channels without major disruption of public order, (3) was therefore able to establish its national legitimacy, and (4) received strong support from public opinion.[15]

The conspirators finally struck in 1981, at the only moment since the death of Franco when Spain had no leader. Suárez has resigned, and Calvo Sotelo had yet to be chosen prime minister. On the first ballot in the legislature, Calvo Sotelo failed to receive enough votes to win. In the midst of the second balloting on February 23, the conspirators took over the *Cortes.*

Perhaps we will never know how deeply the conspiracy extended into the armed forces and into the social, economic, and ecclesiastical elite, nor just how much information—if any—the government had on the plot. The Socialists were particularly severe in insinuating that the UCD ministers could not have been caught totally by surprise, for the PSOE leaders, without access to the state intelligence network, had already deduced that something was brewing. Unlike the previous conspiracies, which had been discovered by the intelligence services before they could be carried out, the attempted coup d'état was actually put into operation. Had the intelligence services been caught unaware? Had their investigative skills atrophied? Were the investigators themselves involved in the plot? Was Suárez oblivious to what was going on? An enigmatic statement made by Suárez in his televised farewell address to the nation deepened the mystery: "I am going because I do not want democracy to be a little parenthesis in the history of Spain." On the day following the most dangerous and traumatic event since the assassination of Carrero Blanco in December 1973, Suárez went on his planned holiday as if nothing had happened. Many questions remain unanswered, questions that go back to Játiva.

When the F-23 conspirators were finally sentenced in June 1982, after military trials during which the top-ranking accused sat on magnificent high-backed chairs upholstered in red velvet, the three central plotters—

Tejero, Armado, and Milans—were each sentenced to thirty years in prison and expelled from the service without pay. But the sentences given to the remaining twenty-nine military conspirators and one civilian were so light that they caused a national uproar and led Calvo Sotelo to appeal the sentences to the civilian Supreme Court.

The coup cannot be neatly appraised. Did it reveal the weakness or the strength of the military, the government, and democracy itself? The very fact that it took place reveals that the military contained dangerous antidemocratic elements. But the fact that the coup was not successful also reveals that most military elites remained committed to the democratic system, even though the king had to use all his powers of persuasion to convince some of them to do so. Perhaps above all, the coup revealed the utmost importance, almost the indispensability, of the king to Spanish democracy at that time. "At that time" is appended because today, it is hoped that the monarch's presence, though invaluable, is no longer indispensable for the survival of democracy. That one nonelected, politically nonresponsible individual should stand between the continued existence of democracy and the reversion to authoritarianism shows the precariousness of democracy in Spain in 1981. Yet those who created the constitution realized full well that the king would possess enormous authority and might some day have to use it to preserve the system.

In effect, many of the actors who took part in the abortive coup played predictable roles: the unregenerate diehards within the military who sought a return to Francoism; the ambiguous within the military, pulled between the memory of Francoism and the reality of democracy; and the converted within the military who had accepted the reality of democracy (for either pragmatic or ideological reasons). The king played the role it had been hoped he would play, and democracy survived. Perhaps survival itself, irrespective of how problematic it may have been, is all that matters. It is possible that too much emphasis has been placed on the absence of a total commitment to democracy on the part of the entire military elite—as if there should have been a kind of instantaneous mass conversion to democracy on the date the constitution came into force. It is unrealistic to think that the military, pampered and cossetted for four generations and encouraged to consider its members heroes of Spain, should suddenly embrace an ideology that would severely limit its prestige and threaten its existence. That most of its officers rallied to the new democracy is the single important reality. Robert Graham believes that Spain might even owe the conspirators a debt:

> In an odd way, Spaniards can be grateful to General Milans del Bosch and ex-Colonel Tejero for exposing the anachronism of military adventurism and the hollowness of the extreme right's nostalgic patriotism. The trial of

these rebel officers revealed just how out of touch they were with the reality of modern Spain and how incapable they would have been of governing the country. The high turn-out in the 1982 general elections and the resounding victory of the Socialist Party must be interpreted in the light of the abortive coup. It was a firm endorsement of the democratic process and showed the military that the spectre of an irresponsible "Red" government—standard propaganda of the Nationalists—was no longer taken seriously by the electorate. The divisive image of the Republic had been buried for good and Spain had largely come to terms with its past.[16]

The behavior of the government subsequent to the abortive coup is also open to conflicting judgments. The government of Calvo Sotelo attempted to downplay the importance of the coup, dismissing it as an isolated event spearheaded by individuals in an otherwise politically loyal military. By taking this stance, the government appeared both naive and conciliatory to military sensitivity, and conciliatory responses are usually made only to individuals or groups that can in some way hurt the appeasers. The government's behavior was thus a display of fear and weakness at a time when strength and audacity might have been more appropriate; perhaps the government should have gambled on the continuing forbearance of those who had rallied to the king and to the system and established, once and for all, the subordination of the military to political control.

Soon after the coup, the government seemed to go even further in placating the military, this time joined by the leading party of the opposition, the PSOE. Except for communism, nothing enraged the military more than what it considered to be the dismemberment of Spain into autonomous regions. The demands of the various nationalities of Spain— particularly the Basques and the Catalans but also the Galicians and the Andalucians—were illegitimate to the military diehards. At the time of the coup, both the Basque provinces and Catalonia had achieved autonomy, and in April 1981, two months after the coup, Galicia was granted autonomy. Then, in 1981, after reaching an agreement with the PSOE opposition in what was called the Pact of Autonomy (Pacto Autonómico),the UCD government presented to the Congress the Organic Law for the Harmonization of the Process of Autonomy (Ley Orgánica de Armonización del Proceso Autonómico—referred to by its acronym, LOAPA). The Pacto Autonómico did not include the parties of the Basque provinces or Catalonia: Their futures were to be renegotiated without their inputs. Although LOAPA was ostensibly a device to harmonize and regularize the extraordinarily complex and lengthy process of devolution, it was seen, especially by the Basques and the Catalans, as a law designed to curb or reverse autonomy that had already been granted.[17] And for many other

Spaniards, irrespective of region, it was seen as a sop to the centralist obsession of the military diehards who had masterminded or supported the attempted coup.

Basque and Catalan leaders tried to block passage of the law; when they failed to do so, massive popular demonstrations took place in Bilbao (Basque provinces) in October 1981, in Barcelona (Catalonia) in March 1982, and throughout both regions in September 1982. During the electoral campaign that would put the Socialists into power in October 1982, Basque and Catalan leaders organized the Anti-LOAPA Front, which sought to defeat any candidate who had voted for the hated law. As objects of the anti-LOAPA animus, the Socialists fared little better than did the members of the UCD. The problems of regionalism, accompanied by the problems of terrorism, would plague the Socialist administration for years.

LOAPA was immediately challenged in the Constitutional Court. In August 1982, the Court, to the shock of the UCD government, declared unconstitutional significant sections of the law, in particular those clauses stating that national law was superior to regional law in those areas where the Basque provinces, Catalonia, Galicia, and Andalucia (granted autonomy on December 12, 1981) had been given powers denied to the other regions of Spain. If, as it appears, LOAPA had been cynically designed to purchase the armed forces' continued support of Spanish democracy by sacrificing regional rights to the military's fixation on the absolute power of the central government, the Constitutional Court's declaration could have triggered a renewed military conspiracy against the system.

By contrast, one decision made by the UCD government in the waning months of its tenure in office (before the stunning victory of the PSOE in October 1982) could be interpreted, in part, as a strategy to counteract that possibility and to rein in the still fractious armed forces. In December 1981, the Spanish government was invited to join NATO—an invitation it accepted in June 1982. (The debate about the ramifications and repercussions of the government's acceptance of the invitation will be discussed in Chapter 12, where I analyze the referendum on NATO presented to the people by the Socialist government in 1986. The present discussion relates membership in NATO in June 1982 to the fallout from the abortive coup in February 1981.)

For many politicians, membership in NATO, like subsequent membership in the European Community, would signify Spain's acceptance as an equal in the family of democratic Western European nations. For many military men, membership in NATO would mean acceptance into the world's most prestigious military club. There was more enthusiasm for this in the navy and air force than in the army, but all the branches were self-conscious about their professionalism when compared to the armed forces of the existing NATO members. The army, by far the largest of the three Spanish services, was especially sensitive. It had spent the past forty-odd years primarily keeping domestic order, and when compared to battle-ready European and U.S. armies in NATO, it was soft, indulged, and woefully untrained. Neither the air force nor the navy was combat-ready by NATO standards, but the outlook of these two services was more professional than that of the army. Moreover, neither the navy nor the air force had been used as domestic police, and neither was as politicized as the army. These reservations aside, however, for many among the elite of the three services, despite their branches' inadequacies, the lure of professional comradeship with the elite armed forces of the leading Western powers was powerful.

But the armed forces of existing NATO members played by democratic rules and accepted the subordination of the military to political control. The Spanish military would have to play by the same rules and accept the same subordination if it was to be received as a professional equal by its peers in NATO. Thus, NATO membership presented something of a dilemma to the Spanish military: Either it had to forgo the political role it had played since the middle of the nineteenth century, which had no future in the new democracy except one based on conspiracy, or it had to accept a new nonpolitical role as the servant of the democratic system and receive as its reward not precarious and illegitimate political power but professional recognition and respect, both within Spain and abroad. As we shall see, the Spanish military seems to have chosen the second option.

DISINTEGRATION OF THE UCD

For a brief period after the attempted coup, the various groups within the UCD huddled for self-protection and rallied around Calvo Sotelo, who, after the interruption on February 23–24, had finally been elected prime minister. The moratorium on infighting quickly passed, however. The catalyst that triggered the final breakup of the UCD was the conflict swirling around the divorce bill sponsored by Francisco Fernández Ordóñez, the minister of justice and the leader of the social democratic left wing of the party.

It may be difficult for an outsider to appreciate the passion that surrounded the divorce issue in traditionally Catholic Spain. Not only did divorce profoundly affect the family, the most sacred social institution in Spain, it also undermined the supremacy of the male in one of the most patriarchal societies in Western Europe (in terms of male dominance and of the male mystique as captured in the word *machismo*). Divorce symbolized the newly liberated, permissive, open post-Franco society, and it was embraced by many, excoriated by others. Moreover, in a society in which illegality as defined by the state and sin as defined by the church had often been synonymous, divorce was not only sinful but also illegal during the Franco regime. The divorce bill was approved in the Congress and then went to the Senate, where it was amended to allow a judge to deny a divorce if either party claimed it would cause undue suffering because of age, health, or length of marriage. But the Senate's version would have emasculated the bill, and the amendment was voted down after the bill returned to the Congress for final disposition. The UCD broke ranks on the vote, ignoring a warning from Prime Minister Calvo Sotelo not to do so. With PSOE, PCE, and the rebel UCD votes, the bill became law on July 20, 1981, amid the dire predictions of the church and its mouthpieces in the *Cortes* (primarily the AP and the Christian democratic right wing of the UCD) that Spain and the family were on the road to perdition.

After the passage of the divorce bill, the UCD relentlessly tore itself apart in a struggle for control between the supporters of Calvo Sotelo, who favored a conservative policy that would pull the party further to the right, and the supporters of Suárez, who sought to hold firm at the center. On July 25, 1981, 39 UCD deputies from the Christian democratic wing signed a letter to their party president, Sahagún, decrying the party's drift to the left, citing the divorce bill as primary evidence. A "pacification" document presented by Sahagún the following September, which defined the UCD as a "reformist, progressive, center party," achieved none of its conciliatory goals. Fernández Ordóñez had already resigned as minister of justice in August, and in November, after Sahagún's "pacification" had failed, Fernández Ordóñez abandoned the UCD, accompanied by 8 other deputies. Their attempt to form a new social democratic parliamentary group in Congress failed, and they were forced to join the mixed group of unaffiliated deputies. In that same November, 3 more deputies left the party to join the AP, and Sahagún resigned as the UCD's president. The party presidency went to Prime Minister Calvo Sotelo. Adolfo Suárez then announced that he, too, might leave the party. The exodus continued until, by early January, UCD membership in the Congress had fallen to 150 deputies.

In late March 1982, Fernández Ordóñez created a new party, the social democratic Democratic Action Party (Partido Acción Democrático—PAD). In July 1982, Antonio Garrigues Walker abandoned the UCD and formed the Liberal Democratic Party (Partido Democrático Liberal—PDL); Oscar Alzaga left the UCD to form the conservative Christian democratic Popular Democratic Party (Partido Democrático Popular—PDP); and Calvo Sotelo resigned the UCD party presidency. The position went not to Suárez but to Landelino Lavilla, the majority leader in the Congress and a member of the Christian democratic wing of the party. Finally, on July 29, 1982, Adolfo Suárez, after failing to regain control of the

UCD, resigned from the party he had created and announced that he was forming a new one, the Democratic and Social Center (Centro Democrático y Social—CDS). By August 1982, UCD membership in Congress had fallen to 122 deputies. With the party's left and right wings now gone and the center contested by the CDS, the UCD had become a vaguely centrist party under the control of conservatives located at various points to the right of center. The once powerful party had become an amorphous remnant totally incapable of political leadership. Spain could not endure seven months of governmental inaction awaiting the expiration of the legislative mandate in March 1983. Therefore, on August 27, 1982, following the request of the prime minister, Juan Carlos dissolved the *Cortes* and called for new elections to take place the following October.

SWING TO THE LEFT

The preelectoral polls had predicted that the PSOE woud be victorious, but even so, the final tally after the election of October 28, 1982, was almost inconceivable for Spain. The turnout was 78.8 percent of the 26,517,393 registered voters, and the abstention rate was lower than in any previous electoral contest or referendum. The PSOE won 202 of the 350 seats in the Congress, giving it an absolute majority. The AP won the second highest number, with 106. The next closest party, the UCD, won only 13 (compared to 168 in 1979). Suárez's new party came in seventh with 2 seats. For the total breakdown of votes, see Table 6.1.

Several aspects of the electoral results merit comment. The extremist regional parties were weaker in 1982 than when they first appeared in 1979. The HB lost a seat, giving it only 2, and the EE managed only to hold on to the single seat it had. By contrast, moderate regionalist parties, the CiU and the PNV, gained strength, the former going from 8 to 12 seats, the latter from 7 to 8. The PCE—allied for the election with its Catalan counterpart, the Unified Socialist Party of Catalonia (Partido Socialista Unificado de Cataluña—PSUC)—was almost wiped out at the national level, falling from 23 seats in 1979 to 4 in 1982.

The political posture of the Spaniards demonstrated in the national elections in 1982 was maintained in the municipal and Autonomous Communities' elections held throughout Spain on May 8, 1983. Of the 57,908 contested municipal council seats, the PSOE won 21,545; the AP (in alliance with the PDP and the Liberals) won the second largest number, 16,521. The closest rival, the PCE, won only 2,462. In the 52 provincial capitals (including Ceuta and Melilla), the PSOE won control in 38, the AP in 10, and the PNV in 3; the PCE won in Córdoba. In the 13 Autonomous Communities in which elections were held, the PSOE won 389 of a total of 764 legislative seats; the AP won the second largest number, 272. The PCE

TABLE 6.1   Results of the 1979 and 1982 Elections

Political Party	Number of Votes in 1982	Seats in Congress	
		1982	1979
PSOE/PSC	10,127,392	202	121
AP/AP-PDP	5,543,107	106	9
UCD	1,425,093	12	168
CiU	772,726	12	8
PNV	395,656	8	7
PCE-PSUC	844,976	4	23
CDS	600,842	2	0
HB	210,601	2	3
ERC	138,116	1	1
EE	100,326	1	1
Independents, Others	648,346	0	9

Source: Reproduced from Keesing's Contemporary Archives (now published as Keesing's Record of World Events) (March 1983), p. 32012.

won 27; the CDS, 8; and the PDL, 2. All other parties and independents combined won 66 seats. In an unprecedented situation for Western Europe, a Socialist party was in the majority at every level of government: national, regional, provincial, and municipal.

The results of the 1982 national elections and their reaffirmation in the regional and municipal elections in 1983 offered an optimistic prognosis for Spanish democracy. In only their second national election under the new constitution and after less than seven years since the transition to democracy began, the Spaniards, despite being relatively unpracticed in politics, had sufficient faith in their political system and in the platforms of their major parties to reject the rightist incumbent and elect the strongest party on the Left—a transition that was accomplished without a breakdown of the democratic process. (It took the supposedly more politically sophisticated and experienced French thirty-six years, from 1945 to 1981, to do the same thing. And for the first time since the creation of their republic in 1946, the Italians had a Socialist government in the summer of 1983, not as the result of direct electoral mandate, as in Spain and France, however, but as the consequence of cabinet reshuffling.) In Spain, the Center disappeared, the PSOE controled the government, and the AP, which seemed on its way to extinction after the 1979 elections, became the opposition.

After public opinion polls indicated that the PSOE's dazzling sweep to power in Andalucia in May 1982 would probably be duplicated at the next national elections, magazines, newspapers, and scholarly journals were filled with articles written by men and women loyal to the political center who feared the possible polarization of Spanish politics that might occur as a result of the October elections. These authors did not consider themselves to be alarmists when they urged their fellow Spaniards to reembrace the center and avoid a move either to the right (to the AP) or to the left (to the PSOE or PCE). They were acutely aware of the history of the Second Republic, in which the hatred between those at the two poles erupted on the left in 1934 and then on the right in 1936. A repeat of these confrontations had to be prevented, and the writers believed that only a rigorous stance at the center—almost an act of will and self-discipline—would avert disaster. Moreover, they believed that the center deserved to be rewarded and perpetuated because of its extraordinary accomplishment: the transition to democracy culminating in the constitution of 1978 and the elections of 1979.

These warnings notwithstanding, the electorate rejected the center and moved toward the left and right. The Spaniards repudiated the ignominious UCD rump. The party's ideological identification in the election of 1982 was not cut from whole cloth but was pieced together out of what was left after the constituent parts had pulled away. The electorate rejected even more adamantly the new centrist party created by Adolfo Suárez, which appeared to be more the dull reflection of politics past than the bright image of politics to come. Suárez looked like the old man of politics: In the 1970s, he had been a paladin; in 1982; he seemed an opportunist. By contrast, the AP, particularly after the defection of its right wing, appeared to be a muscular yet allegiant conservative alternative, vigorously (if not abrasively) championed by Manuel Fraga Iribarne—seen by many as a stalwart and worthy opponent of Felipe González.

NOTES

1. *Informaciones,* February 9, 1979, p. 31.

2. Ibid., February 28, 1979, p. 3.

3. For an explanation of consociationalism, see Arendt Lijphart, "Typologies of Democratic Systems," in *Comparative Political Studies,* vol. 1, no. 1 (April 1968), pp. 3–44. See also Kenneth McRae, ed., *Consociational Democracy* (Toronto: McClelland and Stewart, 1974), pp. 70–89, and Arendt Lijphart, *Democracy in Plural Societies* (New Haven and London: Yale University Press, 1977), pp. 21–53.

4. McRae, ed., *Consociational Democracy,* p. 79.

5. Ibid., pp. 80–82.

6. Richard Gunther, "Democratization and Party Building: The Role of Party Elites in the Spanish Transition," in Robert P. Clark and Michael H. Haltzel, eds., *Spain in the 1980s: The Democratic Transition and a New International Role* (Cambridge, Mass.: Ballinger Publishing, 1987), p. 59.

7. John Hooper, *The Spaniards: Portrait of the New Spain* (Middlesex, England: Viking, 1980), pp. 72–73.

8. Eric Solsten and Sandra W. Meditz, eds., *Spain: A Country Study* (Washington, D.C.: Library of Congress, Federal Reserve Division, 1990), p. 295.

9. Paul Preston, *The Triumph of Democracy in Spain* (London and New York: Methuen, 1980), p. 173.

10. T. A. Allman, "The King Who Saved His Country," *Vanity Fair*, vol. 55, no. 8 (August 1992), p. 162.

11. Ibid., p. 163.

12. Hooper, *The Spaniards*, p. 45.

13. Allman, "The King Who Saved His Country," p. 163.

14. Thomas D. Lancaster and Gary Prevost, eds., *Politics and Change in Spain* (New York: Praeger, 1985), p. 111.

15. Stanley G. Payne, "The Role of the Armed Forces in the Spanish Transition," in Clark and Haltzel, eds., *Spain in the 1980s: The Democratic Transition and a New International Role* (Cambridge, Mass.: Ballinger Publishing, 1987), p. 85.

16. Robert Graham, *Spain: A Nation Comes of Age* (New York: St. Martin's Press, 1984), pp. 278–279.

17. See Goldie Shabad, "After Autonomy: The Dynamics of Regionalism in Spain," in Stanley G. Payne, ed., *The Politics of Democratic Spain* (Chicago: Chicago Council on Foreign Relations, 1986), pp. 111–180.

7

The Political System

Spain is a constitutional monarchy with a parliamentary government in the form of a bicameral legislature. The state is unitary and indivisible, but the constitution recognizes the creation of autonomous regions within the state. These regions are forbidden to federate with one another, and their power and authority emerge from the constitution and remain subject to it. In other words, no region, irrespective of its history or its preeminence, may claim that the right to autonomy predates the constitution. All political rights in Spain today were born with the constitution of 1978.[1]

THE MONARCHY

Juan Carlos I is the first monarch of the new Spanish polity, and his status arises exclusively from the constitution. Yet at the same time, he is the recognized descendant of the historical Bourbon house, whose continuity was broken by the Second Republic in 1931. After 1936, the house was restored in name only by Franco, who ruled absolutely and single-handedly for thirty-nine years with no monarch present on Spanish soil. Franco decreed that Spain had never ceased being a monarchy, on the valid basis that Alfonso XIII had never officially abdicated in 1931 but had, instead, simply gone into exile. Franco chose Juan Carlos, the grandson of Alfonso XIII, as his successor, though Alfonso's son, Don Juan de Borbón, was still alive. Eventually, Don Juan swore allegiance to his son and renounced his claim to the throne. Is Juan Carlos king of Spain because of heredity, because of Franco, or because of the constitution of 1978? In fact, he is king for all three reasons and thus occupies a unique position. The next king or queen of Spain will reign only because of the constitution, even though he or she will ascend to the throne as the heir of the first king of the new regime, Juan Carlos I. Juan Carlos can also be seen as the last king of the old regime, whether the old regime is interpreted to be that of Franco or that of the Bourbons.

The complex position of Juan Carlos I both maintains continuity and breaks it at the same time, changing Spain fundamentally in political ways while leaving the centerpiece, the king, untouched. To repudiate the new democratic regime, one must repudiate Juan Carlos and, hence, both the legacy of Franco, whose heir he is, and the Bourbon dynasty. To accept Juan Carlos, one accepts the new democratic constitution that established him. Those loyal to Franco, the Bourbons, or both—particularly the extreme Right and the military—could not extricate themselves from this dilemma—a situation that has contributed mightily to the stability of the political system.

The Spanish monarch is not sovereign in the way the British monarch is, playing out a meaningful but fictional role as the embodiment of sovereignty under a "constitution" that exists only as a collection of laws and judicial decisions. The Spanish sovereign exists *within* the constitution. Furthermore, the Spanish monarch does not possess a reserve of power above the state to be used in times of emergency, as the president of France does. The Spanish sovereign exists *within* the state. In Spain, sovereignty, as set forth in the constitution, lies in the people from whom the power of the state emanates (article 1). Part of sovereignty—the operative part (or the efficient part, to use Walter Bagehot's term)—is entrusted to the parliament for a specified period of time (articles 66, 67, 68); parliament, in turn, places its own governance in the hands of a prime minister, the head of government whom the parliament may remove (articles 99, 114). Another part of sovereignty—the symbolic part (or the dignified part, again using Bagehot's term)—is entrusted to the monarch, the head of state, for his or her lifetime. The people's entrustment gives the head of state an unmistakably populist nature, and there is something very Spanish about this democratization of authority. In prayers, Spaniards address God as "tu" ("you"), an informal form of address usually reserved for family and close friends, as if even the Supreme Being has to be brought down to earth a bit. In the kingdoms that existed before the formation of the Spanish nation, the form of address used by nobles in communicating with the monarch went something like this: "We, who are as good as you are, address you, who are no better than we." Similarly, in the 1978 constitution, the people honor the king with their generosity: He is their king because they allow him to be, and he, in turn, embodies their collective munificence. All of this reflects that rather marvelous mix of humility and hauteur that typifies the Spanish character.

Under the 1978 constitution, the monarch has a variety of duties (articles 62, 63): to sanction and promulgate the law; to summon and dissolve the Cortes and call for new elections; to call for a referendum in the cases provided for in the constitution; to propose a candidate for the presidency of the government (prime minister); to appoint and dismiss the members of the government; to issue decrees; to execute supreme command of the armed forces; to grant pardons; and to declare war and make peace. These duties may be carried out only with the countersignature of the prime minister or of an appropriate minister, who by signing, assumes responsibility. The person of the king is inviolate. The monarch's only opportunity to use power at his or her own discretion occurs when no party has a clear majority in the *Cortes,* and the monarch must choose from among contending party candidates in order to start the process of creating a government. All of these duties are almost identical to those of the head of state in any parliamentary democracy, whether a republic or a monarchy.

In the area of foreign policy, however, the current Spanish monarch, though unable to make policy, has come to play a conspicuous role, different from that of his fellow heads of state. But the role belongs exclusively to Juan Carlos; it cannot be played by his successors. The role does not exist constitutionally. Rather, it has been assumed extraconstitutionally by Juan Carlos, with the enthusiastic approval and encouragement of his prime ministers from 1976 until the present. Juan Carlos has become Spain's foremost actor on the world stage, and since February 23, 1981, when he single-handedly saved democracy in Spain at the time of the attempted coup d'état, he has been honored as one of the great modern democratic heroes, not only in Spain but also throughout the democratic world. He has virtually telescoped time and given democratic Spain a worldwide legitimacy that otherwise might have taken decades to achieve. Juan Carlos has helped to make the world forget Franco and the repressive, regressive Spain he ruled. He has come to personify the democratic stability so necessary for both domestic eminence and foreign investment, which has helped transform Spain into the world's eighth greatest economic power.

Juan Carlos plays another role that most likely cannot be transferred; in fact, this role may be even less transferable than his role as Spain's international spokesman. The monarch is commander-in-chief of the armed forces, but as with his other constitutional duties, this duty, too, must be sanctioned by the government, which thereby takes responsibility. But Juan Carlos has a very special relationship with the armed forces, particularly the older military elite, that transcends the constitution: He is the *personal* link to Franco, a kind of Saint Peter chosen by the caudillo to lead the nation. It was this special relationship that Juan Carlos called upon to save Spain's fledgling democracy on February 23, 1981. It will be impossible for his successor to maintain this almost spiritual relationship with the military.

Juan Carlos's successor is his son Felipe, the prince of Asturias. Under the Salic law, which historically has governed succession in the Bourbon royal house (in Spain, as well as in France), a woman may not ascend

His Royal Highness Prince Felipe de Borbón,
heir apparent

the throne. It was, in fact, Ferdinand VII's flagrant disregard of the Salic
law in 1835 that precipitated the civil wars that tore Spain apart for the
next forty years and that some say broke out again in the Civil War in
1936. Under the terms of the 1978 constitution, the Salic law no longer
governs succession, but its spirit lingers in the preference shown for male
heirs. If the reigning monarch has both sons and daughters, the eldest son
succeeds to the throne. If there are no sons, the eldest daughter ascends. If,
however, the eldest son has married and has children and dies before as-
cending the throne, his children will succeed, with sons taking precedence
over daughters. If all legal lines of succession cease to exist, the *Cortes
Generales* (the joint session of the Congress and Senate) chooses the successor to the throne.

What the king possesses incontestably is authority, and Juan Carlos
is building this quality strongly and wisely, setting precedents from which
his heirs (if they have any sense at all) will profit. It is generally conceded

that the transition to democracy from Francoism could not have taken place without Juan Carlos's deep commitment to democratic values and without his practical understanding of present-day politics. He has performed the royal role superbly, making himself almost indispensable as a source of wisdom and moderation to be consulted at every crucial step in the political process. As we have already seen, his behavior at the time of the attempted coup d'état in February 1981 is credited with saving the regime.

THE GOVERNMENT

The government or cabinet is composed of the prime minister ("president of the government" is the official title), the deputy prime minister (vice president), and ministers (article 98). The constitution left unspecified the number of ministries and their areas of competence. Even less detail was given to the role of the deputy prime minister, whose position and duties were left to the discretion of the prime minister. The 1983 Organizational Law of the Central Administration of the State (Ley de la Organización de la Administración Central del Estado) helped to fill the voids left in the constitution. The law named the ministries that make up the cabinet, and, though maintaining the prime minister's discretion over the tasks of the deputy prime minister, it formalized the existence of the position by providing that the deputy prime minister temporarily assume the duties of the prime minister if the latter should die, be sick or incapacitated, or be out of the country. It would appear that under the law, the prime minister cannot choose to leave the position unfilled. As we shall see, when this post was occupied by Alfonso Guerra, it took on enormous importance in Felipe González's government.

But the position of singular concern is that of the prime minister, who, once accepted by the Congress, has the exclusive power to form the government. The candidate for this position is presented by the king to the Congress for approval. If one party has an absolute majority in the Congress, the king's choice, in practice if not in theory, would be limited to that party's leader. If there were no clear majority, the king's discretion would increase in proportion to the complexity of the party composition in the lower house, with the monarch freely choosing, even from outside the Congress, that man or woman who seemed capable of putting together a working coalition. If, on the first balloting, the Congress accepts the king's nominee by an absolute majority, the sovereign then proclaims the nominee prime minister. If an absolute majority is not obtained, the second balloting on the same candidate takes place forty-eight hours later, and the nominee becomes president of the government if he or she wins a simple majority (receiving more yes than no votes). If this majority is not reached, a new nominee is presented by the king. Should no candidate be able to win approval after two months using the system just described, the king, with the approval of the president of the Congress (the equivalent of the U.S. Senate majority leader), dissolves both houses of the legislature and calls for new elections (article 99). Once approved, the prime minister is free to compose the cabinet as he or she sees fit with no further legislative approval, placing in it anyone that political reality permits. The constitution allows the prime minister to go outside the *Cortes* to select members of his cabinet, but in practice, the overwhelming majority of cabinet appointees have come from within the legislature. The prime minister may dismiss members of the cabinet with the same freedom, yet once formed, the cabinet becomes a collegial body. No single minister or group of ministers may be removed by legislative action. The legislature may remove the prime minister, but when this occurs, the entire cabinet goes, too.

The constitution makes the tenure of the government very secure. The life of the cabinet (or, more precisely, that of the prime minister) is designed to last through the four-year term of the Congress. The cabinet normally meets once a week on Friday, either in a decisionmaking capacity (*consejo decisorio,*) in which decisions are usually arrived at by vote, or in a discussional capacity (*consejo deliberante*), which is usually unstructured and freewheeling. But increasingly, authoritative decisions are made not by the full cabinet but by cabinet committees, much like those in Great Britain, whose number and membership have been spelled out by royal decree (1981) and whose functions have been spelled out in the Organizational Law of the Central Administration of the State (1983). Called delegated committees of the government (*comisiones delegadas del gobierno*), cabinet committees were originally conceived to coordinate information and expertise among related ministries; now, however, the cabinet committees make authoritative decisions that do not have to be approved by the full cabinet, even though, as in Great Britain, the full cabinet must take responsibility.

The prime minister, along with the deputy prime minister, is the connecting link among the committees, and he alone is privy to the activities of all the committees. In Spain, however, the cabinet committees are less mysterious than in Great Britain, where the number, membership, and activity of each cabinet committee is created by and known only to the prime minister and his or her staff. In other words, in Great Britain, members of one cabinet committee are, in theory, unaware of the existence or activities of the other cabinet committees—a situation that adds greatly to the power of the prime minister. Policy is made by a smaller and smaller number of elites in Great Britain, focusing on one person, the prime minister. In Spain, the number, membership, and activity of each committee are public information, but the prime minister, his deputy, and their staffs are privy to all the cabinet committees; this situation is similar to that in Great Britain, and it has increased the power of the prime minister. The five cabinet committees and their members are: (1) Autonomous Communities (minister of justice, minister of economy and finance, minister of public Administration, secretary of state for the Autonomous Communities); (2) Economic Affairs (minister of economy and finance, minister of public works, minister of labor and social benefits, minister of industry and energy, minister of agriculture, fisheries, and food, minister of transport, tourism, and communications, and the undersecretary of state for the economy); (3) Education, Culture, and Science (minister of education and science, minister of culture, secretary of state for universities and research); (4) Foreign Affairs (minister of foreign affairs, secretary of state for foreign affairs); and (5) State Security (minister of foreign affairs, minister of justice, minister of defense, minister of interior, director-general of State Security). Each of these committees may call upon other individuals for special expertise.

The prime minister may be removed before his four-year tenure is finished only by an act of censure, which is difficult to execute. The procedure, borrowed, in part, from the constitution of the French Fifth Republic and from the Basic Law of West Germany, must be initiated by a petition signed by no fewer than 10 percent of all the deputies. The motion must include the name of the candidate who would replace the incumbent prime minister if the action were to succeed. If the attempt to censure fails, those deputies who signed the petition are foreclosed from initiating another motion during that legislative session. Voting by the Congress may take place no sooner than five days from the presentation of the motion, and during that time, the candidate for the prime ministership (for whom a substitute may be named during the first two days) presents his or her program for debate. The censure is successful if it receives the approval of an absolute majority of deputies. Following that, the incumbent president of the government would resign, and the king would present the victorious candidate for approval. A prime minister may attempt to strengthen his or her own position by calling for a vote of confidence in periods of stress or following a major shift in policy or a cabinet reshuffle. The success of the vote is measured by attaining a simple majority from the deputies present (more yes than no votes). Failure to receive that majority means that the prime minister and the entire cabinet must resign. The process of finding a new prime minister follows the pattern already described.

A prime minister may attempt to extend his or her mandate (and that of his or her party) by dissolving just the Congress or both the Congress and the Senate and calling for new elections. This weapon may not be used by the prime minister while a censure motion is in progress, nor may it be employed earlier than a year following the preceding motion (except if a new president of the government cannot be found within two months after the president who dissolved the legislature is repudiated at the polls).

These devices strengthen the hand of the president of the government vis-à-vis the legislature, while protecting the latter's ultimate control of the political future of the state. The prime minister's dominance is also felt in the legislative process, which gives bills originating with the government (*proyectos de ley*) priority over bills originating with the legislature (*proposiciones de ley*) (article 89). The government has exclusive budgetary initiative, and any alteration in taxation or expenditures by the legislature must have prior governmental approval (article 134). This has been interpreted to mean that all budgetary proposals must come from the government but may be amended by the legislature; once the budget has been approved, however, it may not subsequently be altered by the legislature without the permission of the cabinet.

The government may also pass decree laws in times of "urgent and extraordinary necessity" (article 86). These laws, put into operation at the government's discretion, are subject to several restrictions. A decree may touch neither the basic institutions of the state nor the basic civil rights of the people; a decree must be immediately submitted to the Congress for debate, which must take place during the thirty days following the decree's promulgation; and Congress may accept or reject a decree or may treat it as if it were a governmental bill and handle it as a matter of urgency (article 90).

The power of the Spanish and British prime ministers is comparable when the former has an absolute majority in Parliament. If the Spanish prime minister presides over a coalition government, his tenure would, of course, be less secure than that of his British counterpart but more than that of his Italian counterpart, who can be ousted with the same ease as were the premiers of the French Third and Fourth Republics. The Spanish prime minister would, however, be as secure as the French prime minister in the Fifth Republic or as the German chancellor, given the constitutional provisions that make dismissal difficult. The Spanish prime minister is certainly more powerful than the French prime minister when the party of the latter is also the party of the French president. In those circumstances, the French prime minister is really second in command, subordinate to the president. A situation like that in France, where the president and the prime minister could be of different parties, could not exist in Spain. The Spanish prime minister, regardless of the extent of his or her power, is not the equivalent of the French president, who has powers beyond any prime minister anywhere. The bicephalous nature of the French executive makes it impossible to draw an exact comparison to systems like the British, German, Italian, or Spanish, where the head of state is essentially a powerless figurehead.

THE LEGISLATURE

There are two houses in the legislature—the lower, called the Congress, and the upper, called the Senate. Together, they constitute the *Cortes*. When the two houses act in joint session, they are called the *Cortes Generales*. The Spanish constitution, typical of most post–World War II constitutions, limits the powers of the Senate. The Congress dominates the legislature, and the government is responsible solely to the lower house.

The size of the Congress is established in article 68, which sets the minimum number of deputies at 300 and the maximum at 400. The Electoral Law of March 1977, updated by the Electoral Law of June 1985, set the number of delegates at 350. The deputies, who serve for four years, are chosen in the fifty provinces into which Spain is divided. All citizens eighteen years old and over enjoy free, equal, direct, and secret suffrage. Each province (plus Ceuta and Melilla) is guaranteed a minimum of one deputy (which rewards the sparsely populated provinces), and the remaining seats are distributed among the provinces according to population. The provincial seats are then distributed by party in proportion to the number of votes each party receives. The key words here are "by party" because the electoral system calls for closed and blocked ballots; citizens must vote a straight ticket and accept the order of the candidates as they appear on the ballot.

The size of the Senate is established in article 69, and there are two categories of senators, those representing the provinces and those representing the regions. The provinces, the historical divisions of Spain, are contained within the newly created Autonomous Communities, and no province may be split by regional borders. Each mainland province receives four senators (once again, sparsely settled provinces are rewarded); Ceuta and Melilla each receive two senators; and the two insular provinces (the Balearic Islands in the Mediterranean and the Canary Islands in the Atlantic) receive a total of sixteen. Like the deputies, the senators are elected for four years by citizens eighteen years old and over through free, equal, direct, and secret suffrage, but the constitution allows an organic law to determine how senators are to be chosen. At the present time, a majority system has been adopted, but this could be replaced in the future, for the electoral system is not constitutionally fixed. Each Autonomous Communuty is guaranteed at least one senator plus one additional senator for each one million inhabitants. As each community achieves autonomy, it, too, is guaranteed at least one senator plus one additional senator for every million inhabitants.

The Congress and the Senate operate in similar fashion. Each chamber has a party structure, a president (majority leader), a Mesa (executive committee), a Junta de Portavoces (a board of party representatives), and a system of committees and subcommittees.

Parties dominate the life of the *Cortes*, and through the party structure, the executive, in turn, dominates the legislature. This works despite the constitutional prohibition on party discipline—*mandato imperativo* (article 67)—which, in theory, makes each representative independent—an anachronism in a political system that stresses its social or group nature. Making deputies free agents follows in the tradition of liberal, individualistic, nineteenth-century European democracies. In practice, the desire to progress within one's party and to have its support at election time makes the deputy accept discipline, by whatever name, in the Spanish system.

Upon entering Congress, each deputy joins a parliamentary group (the equivalent of a parliamentary party in Great Britain). To reduce the number of groups, none may have fewer than five members (ten in the Senate). Parliamentarians join the group that most closely approximates their political beliefs, if the group is agreeable. And naturally, each of the major parties constitutes a group unto itself. The *Cortes* provides facilities like meeting rooms and secretarial help for the convenience of all groups, and all are subsidized by the *Cortes*. Part of the funding is given in equal shares to each group, and part is distributed in proportion to group size.

If a deputy is elected by a party that cannot put together the minimum number of members, that representative must join either an existing ideologically defined group (if that is acceptable to both) or the "mixed group," which amounts to a kind of catchall or grab bag unit. Any deputy who changes group affiliation during a session of parliament must join the mixed group; he or she may choose either to remain there or to join an existing group at the next session, provided that the group agrees. If there is massive defection from a group and the membership falls below the minimum, that parliamentary group ceases to exist and becomes absorbed in the mixed group. A great part of the legislative activity is carried out by parliamentary groups; the legislator rarely acts as an individual, which makes the prohibition against party discipline even more difficult to comprehend.

Each chamber is headed by a president elected by its members. To win on the first ballot, a candidate must receive an absolute majority of the votes cast; otherwise, a runoff takes place between the top two candidates, with the post going to whoever receives a simple majority. In theory, the victor becomes the president of the whole chamber; in practice, he or she becomes the voice of the majority. The president regulates debate, recognizes those who have been granted prior permission to speak, and exerts discipline to keep order. The president chairs the Mesa, which operates collegially, with four vice presidents and four secretaries in the Congress and two vice presidents and four secretaries in the Senate. In the Congress, the four vice presidents are chosen simultaneously, and each deputy is allowed to cast only one ballot. As a result of this voting procedure, it is almost certain that the major parliamentary groups will be represented. The same procedure is used in the Congress to choose the four secretaries, and an almost identical system is used in the Senate. A Mesa presides over each house of the legislature. It establishes the rules of parliamentary procedure, sets the agenda of the full house and all its committees, drafts the budget of the chamber and monitors its administration, and decides on the admissibility of parliamentary papers. The Mesa is assisted by nonpolitical legal advisers (*letrados*), experts in parliamentary procedure who help the president in the daily operation of each house, including the running of debates and voting; with the president's approval, they also determine the official record of the meetings of the full house, the Mesa, and the Junta de Portavoces.

Each parliamentary group is represented on the Junta de Portavoces in proportion to its size. The Junta, dominated by the majority party or majority coalition, is the policymaking organ of each house and gives the Mesa its political direction.

Each chamber works as a full house and in committees, but with few exceptions, tasks are performed in committees, particularly in permanent committees. These are the most important of the three congressional classifications: permanent, special, and investigatory. In the Senate, the names differ, but the functions are similar. There is a permanent committee for each of the departmental ministries in the cabinet, plus several other committees with more general competency. Each parliamentary group chooses its representatives on the permanent committees in numbers proportionate to the size of the group. Each committee then chooses its chairperson from among the members, so seniority (as it exists in the U.S. Congress, for example) does not apply. The committees (which break down into subcommittees that also maintain party proportion among their members) examine and discuss all *proyectos de ley* and all *proposiciones de ley*. However, governmental bills have priority under article 89, and all budget proposals and all bills relating to economic planning originate with the government (articles 134 and 131). Any bill may be amended in committee, but budgetary bills, once they have been passed into law, may not be altered without the cabinet's approval.

These are the only restrictions on the power of the legislature to exert ultimate control over the government. All bills are debated by the full house as they emerge from committee. The Spanish government lacks the constitutional power of its French counterpart to call for a single up or down vote on all or part of a bill under discussion, retaining only the amendments proposed or accepted by the government. There is no constitutional division, as there is in France, between "laws," which may be regulated by the legislature, and "rules," which may be regulated by the executive. Within the general restrictions of the constitution, the legislature is competent to deal with any kind of law.

The Spanish constitution borrowed from the Italian in giving the permanent committees powers they do not have in most democracies. Except in matters relating to constitutional amendments, treaties and other international understandings, organic and basic laws, and the budget, the chambers may delegate full legislative power to the permanent committees, obviating the necessity of having the bill debated or voted by the full house. Each house may recall that delegation at any time, however (article 75). For those who think this process might be less than democratic, it should be remembered that in composition, the permanent committees are small-scale models of the whole chamber.

When debate does take place on the floor of the Congress or Senate, freedom to speak is severely limited. No parliamentarian may take the floor without securing permission from both the president of the chamber and, in most cases, the chairperson of his or her parliamentary group. Under many of the rules of each house, it is not the individual deputy who is granted permission to be heard but the parliamentary group, which then chooses a spokesperson. Once on the floor, the parliamentary member may not be interrupted, but he or she may not wander from the topic being debated nor talk beyond the allotted time. After two warnings from the president of the chamber on either of these counts, permission to speak may be revoked, making a filibuster impossible.

A bill that has passed the Congress—either by vote in the full house or, when delegated, by vote in permanent committee—then moves to the Senate, where it goes through a similar procedure. Within the limit of two months, the Senate may either approve, amend, or totally reject the bill. If the bill is rejected in toto, the Congress may immediately overturn the veto by ratifying the original bill by an absolute majority or, two months after the receipt of the veto, by a simple majority—the same majority it takes to accept or reject senatorial amendments. If, after two months, the Senate does nothing, a bill becomes law by default. In the Spanish constitution, there is no equivalent to the U.S. conference committee, but then, logic would tell us that a conference between unequals (the Spanish Senate is much less powerful than the Congress) would be politically meaningless. Because the Senate is unable to kill legislation and because the government has near total control of the Congress, a deputy in opposition in either house who wants to obstruct the passage of a bill will seek an opinion from the Constitutional Court on the bill's constitutionality. There is no appeal from this court; an opinion that a bill is unconstitutional would require its promoters to begin the legislative process all over again. Unfortunately, the absence of a strong upper house that is able to check majoritarian decisionmaking in the lower house draws the Constitutional Court into the *political* process, an involvement unforeseen by the creators of the constitution.

What devices do the two chambers of the *Cortes* have to keep the government alert to their moods and opinions, considering that the party structure puts the president of the government in almost full control of the political process? The presidents of both houses are effectively agents of the majority, and although the Mesa and the Junta de Portavoces represent many parties, the majority is also dominant in those bodies due to proportional representation. The prime minister has control over the majority through his power to call for votes of confidence and to dissolve parliament. What, then, are parliament's weapons? The most powerful, of course, is censure, but this procedure is available only to the Congress and is difficult to accomplish. Far less draconian are the powers to: (1) investigate (article 76), (2) command the presence in the chamber of cabinet members, including the prime minister (article 110), (3) question or interpellate, (4) "initiate legislation," and (5) delegate to the government lawmaking funcitons normally given to the *Cortes*.

A question (*pregunta*) comes from an individual deputy and must be posed through the Mesa. The questioner specifies if he or she wants a written or an oral answer. If the request is for an oral answer, the appropriateness of the question will be determined by the Mesa before it is placed on the agenda of the full house. An interpellation (*interpelación*) is somewhat more urgent than a *pregunta*, and it may originate with an individual deputy or with a parliamentary group. Like the *pregunta*, it must be submitted to the Mesa for approval, but unlike the *pregunta*, the *interpelación* must be accompanied by the reasons for questioning the general policy of the government or a particular ministry. The *interpelación* is often presented as a motion to be debated in the full house; like the question, it is used to draw public attention to a deputy, a party, or an issue (article 111). The right to initiate legislation is guaranteed not only to the government but also to the Congress and the Senate (article 87). Note, however, that the initiative rests with the chamber and not with the deputies or senators. Private member bills become bills of the respective chamber. This does not eliminate the pork barrel, for there is nothing to prevent a chamber from accepting all private member bills out of formality, but this is unlikely to occur, and even if it did, governmental bills always have priority. Finally, the legislature may give the government lawmaking functions that normally belong to the *Cortes* (article 82), by decrees called *decretos legislativos.* (*Decretos leyes* are governmental in origin). Although the decrees represent an abdication of legislative duty in favor of the executive, the legislature itself takes the initiative to place the burden and responsibility on the government.

THE CONSTITUTIONAL COURT AND THE OMBUDSMAN

The drafters of the 1978 constitution borrowed from the post–World War II constitutions of France, Germany, and Italy to create the Constitutional Court, an innovation for all four political systems. Separate from the regular court system, the Constitutional Court exists solely to interpret the constitution. The makers of the Spanish constitution wanted to avoid the kind of multiplicity of functions that encumbers the U.S. federal judicial system, in which the Supreme Court is a court of original jurisdiction, the highest court of appeals, and a constitutional court. The Spanish court is made up of twelve members, each of whom must be a lawyer with at least fifteen years of experience. He or she may not be an elected politician, a civil servant, or an officeholder in a political party or a trade union. Once appointed, the court member must give up all private practice. Each member is appointed formally by the king for a nine-year term of office, with one-third of the total membership replaced every three years. The Congress and Senate each choose four members by three-fifths majorities, which lessens partisanship; two members are chosen by the government (which, of course, is partisan); and two are selected by the General Council of the Judiciary Power (Consejo General del Poder Judicial—GCJP). The council is made up of the president (chief justice of the Supreme Court, the highest court in the regular court system), twelve other judges, and eight lawyers chosen by the *Cortes*. It functions to appoint judges and to maintain ethical standards within the legal profession.

The court hands down decisions concerning the constitutionality of national and regional laws and of international treaties. It also hears appeals of protection (*amparo*) brought by an individual who alleges that his or her civil rights have been violated by either the national or regional governments and their officials. In addition, the court settles conflicts of jurisdiction that arise between the federal government and the governments of the Autonomous Communities, all of which have constitutionally specified powers (article 161).

The Constitutional Court has been drawn (in a manner possibly unforeseen by the founding fathers) into the political process by opposition parties in the *Cortes* that have used the court to delay the implementation of laws passed by the parliamentary majority. It takes only fifty deputies or senators to bring a charge of unconstitutionality before the court (article 162).[2] This constitutional challenge is a two-edged sword, however.

Since access to the Constitutional Court is not available to an individual seeking to challenge constitutionality, action by minority representatives serves to check possible majoritarian abuse. On the other hand, the same action can be used to delay the expression of legitimate majority will through the legislature. No device exists to distinguish between partisan political machinations and legitimate constitutional concerns.

The drafters of the 1978 constitution borrowed from the Scandinavian countries (as Great Britain did following World War II) to create the post of defender of the people, or ombudsman (*defensor del pueblo*) (article 54), activated by an organic law in April 1981. The holder of the office, a jurist of outstanding reputation, is chosen by both legislative houses acting jointly. He or she is to stand guard over the rights set forth in article 1 of the constitution. Anyone in public office may come under scrutiny, and everyone in public service must aid in the ombudsman's investigation.

AUTONOMOUS COMMUNITIES

Article 2 of the constitution declares Spain to be an indissoluble unity and then, in the same sentence, recognizes and guarantees the right of the nationalities and regions that make up the nation to proclaim their autonomy—without mentioning what this seemingly anomalous hybrid would be called. This omission was not an oversight; definition is dangerous where certain words—federalism or separatism, for example—may trigger an explosive reaction. The reticence to be clear has roots deep in Spain's past, for the forces of centralism and regionalism have fought bloody battles for centuries. The brief history of Spain sketched in the early chapters of this book was written, in part, to catalog this contest and to lay the background for an understanding of the struggle that still goes on today. Except for problems with the Basque extremists, fortunately, the struggle is now taking place within a peaceful and constitutionally established arena.

The unity that Rome brought to Spain and that, after the fall of Rome, the Visigoths reestablished under a single monarch ended with the Islamic invasion. The reestablishment of that harmonious unity has, in many ways, been the goal of all subsequent Spanish history. Since the Reconquest, there have been recurrent periods of unity, but these cycles have been achieved most often by the suppression of local rights. Recall that Muslim Spain was a single entity only during the brief reign of Abd ar-Rahman III. Before his reign, various Muslim kingdoms on the peninsula had defied Al-Andalus, and seventy years after his death, the caliphate had once again shattered into independent, warring *taifas*. Christian Spain was not unified until the reign of Ferdinand and Isabella, and even then, the two monarchs maintained their separate kingdoms after their marriage created Spain by bringing the kingdoms together. The Catholic Kings did not destroy the *fueros* that had been so doggedly obtained from their ancestors. Their Hapsburg descendants ruled a unified nation-state but recognized the rights of the *fueros*, bowing to political reality.

It was the Bourbons, emulating their French relatives, who brought modern unity to Spain by tearing down most of the regional *fueros* (those of Catalonia, Valencia, Aragon, and the Balearic Islands) and emasculating those that they left standing (in Navarre and the Basque provinces). The history of the Bourbons is rife with conflict between Madrid and the regions that would not stay suppressed. The First Republic was committed to federalism, but it lasted only a year (1873–1874), and its constitution never came into force. The restored Bourbons tightened the centralization of the country. The Second Republic (1931–1936) recognized the validity of regionalism and had begun decentralization when the Civil War broke out, partly over this very issue. The victorious Franco—even though he himself was a native of one of the regions demanding recognition, Galicia—crushed all resistance to his rule from Madrid, even forbidding people to speak their regional tongues in the privacy of their homes.

The constitution of 1978 recognizes the centrifugal forces of the nation (the regions attempting to pull away from Madrid), but it also acknowledges the centripetal forces of the state (Madrid attempting to pull the regions under the hegemony of a single sovereignty). Both forces have histories too long for their validity to be denied: The unity of Spain is as much a heritage as is racial and regional separateness. The constitution does not predetermine what the new Spain will be like when the regions seeking autonomy make their claims. Article 143 makes autonomy voluntary, although all the provinces of Spain have now been grouped into regions. Few restrictions limit autonomy. One requirement is that each province seeking to join with others to form a region must have a contiguous border with at least one of the other provinces. Article 145 prohibits the federation of regions. Article 143 stipulates that regions are to be formed by several provinces with historical, cultural, or economic backgrounds in common, but article 144 provides for a region made from a single province where the preconditions of article 143 cannot be met (Asturias, Cantabria, La Rioja, Madrid, Murcia, and Navarre).

Two ways were established to achieve autonomy: the fast way (article 151) and the slow way (article 143). The slow pace seems favored by the constitution, but the rapid path is made available for those impatient provinces whose identity has long been recognized and whose people are overwhelmingly committed to autonomy. Most of the areas of Spain do not have this kind of identity, and the slow pace was preferred in those provinces that would need time to create a viable region. For the slow track, the initiative to begin the process must be approved by the legisla-

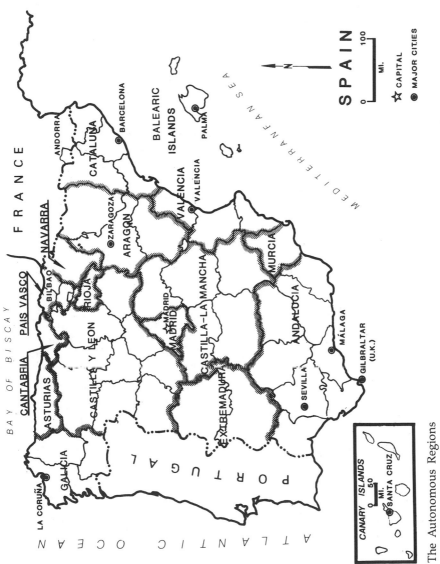

The Autonomous Regions

tures of the interested provinces and by two-thirds of the voters in those municipalities whose population represents a majority of the electoral census of the province (the capital cities).

The fast route to autonomy is more difficult; it requires a massive commitment by the provinces that seek to use it. As with the slow route, the initiative rests with the provincial legislatures, but the percentage of voters necessary to begin the process is raised to three-quarters in the municipalities whose population represents at least a majority of each province's electoral census. After these requirements have been met, the initiative is submitted to referendum in the provinces involved, and it must be accepted by an absolute majority of the electors of each province.

If the initiative (fast or slow) is successful, a statute is formulated by the legislatures of the provinces involved together with the deputies and senators representing the provinces in the national *Cortes*. The statute is then submitted to the *Cortes* for enactment into law, and with the king's signature, an Autonomous Community is born. The fast track, which would bring immediate full autonomy, was available only for the three "historical nationalities"—the Basque provinces, Catalonia, and Galicia. The slow track, which would delay full autonomy for five years following approval of the statutes of autonomy by the *Cortes*, was available for all the other provinces that chose to create Autonomous Communities. The Basque provinces and Catalonia held referenda in October 1979, and their statutes of autonomy were approved by the *Cortes* in December 1979—for Euzkadi, the Statute of Gernika; for Catalonia, the Statute of Pau. In Galicia, the referendum was held in December 1980, and its statute of autonomy was approved by the *Cortes* in April 1981—the Statute of Santiago. By mid-1983, all the remaining provinces had chosen to pursue autonomy, creating fourteen more Autonomous Communities and bringing the total to seventeen.[3]

Of the fourteen more recent Autonomous Communities, Andalucia was treated differently under the terms of the section of article 151 that provided for those provinces that did not qualify as "historical nationalities" but whose people supported immediate full autonomy. Under these terms, the councils of each province seeking to form an Autonomous Community had to approve the creation of the region. Three-fourths of the municipal councils within each of these provinces also had to approve; a popular referendum would then follow, which had to be approved by the affirmative vote of a majority of the electorate in each province. With this approval, a regional constituent assembly would create a statute of autonomy, which had to be submitted to the electorate for approval. Andalucia did not make it through this gauntlet for reasons I have already discussed, but by October 1981, a compromise was reached that granted Andalucia its statute of autonomy two months later.

Special reference should be made to Navarre. It had been a separate kingdom until it was conquered by Ferdinand in 1512 and made a part of Spain, the last piece necessary to complete the modern Spanish nation-state. Like the three Basque provinces—Alava, Guipúzcoa, and Viscaya—to which it is linguistically and culturally related, Navarre enjoyed special treatment throughout most of Spanish history, guaranteed by its *fueros*. Unlike the Basque provinces, however, it continued to enjoy special privileges even under Franco. The Basque provinces remained loyal to the Republic, but Navarre went over to the Rebels and was rewarded by Franco for its fidelity, even to the extent of being allowed to raise its own taxes. During the time of constitution-making in 1977–1978, the Navarrese were torn between maintaining their separateness or joining the three Basque provinces to form a single political entity (the latter option was strongly urged by the Basques). Navarre chose to maintain its own identity, and it followed the slow route to autonomy but still maintained the right to raise its own taxes.

The section of the constitution entitled "Concerning the Autonomous Communities" clearly demonstrates the tension that pervaded the constituent assembly. The call for a strong central government was imperative, but the demand for regional self-determination was equally exigent. A balance had to be found without alienating either the centralists or the regionalists; terminology had to be carefully chosen or specificity sacrificed if the document was to be ratified. *Federalism,* for example, was a taboo word, and the details of how the national government would exert its supremacy over the Autonomous Communities were never spelled out. Under a true federal system, in which the component units enjoy full power from the moment the political system comes into existence, each federated unit has the same power within itself and the same relationship between itself and the national government. When full autonomy finally comes to all the regions of Spain, it would appear that the nation will have what amounts to a federal system, irrespective of terminology or of the nature of each regions's birth. In the meantime, Spain is a quasi-federal system whose component parts are in various stages of autonomy.

Despite regional disparity, however, all seventeen Autonomous Communities have certain characteristics in common. All are subject to the national constitution and to their respective statutes of autonomy, which amount to regional constitutions. Each statute of autonomy may include elements unique to a particular region, and all are approved by the *Cortes* in the same manner. If the statutes are amended, all must follow the same procedure, which requires approval by an absolute majority in the *Cortes.*

Article 152 stipulates that each Autonomous Community will have a unicameral legislative assembly with deputies elected for four-year terms by universal suffrage, using a system of proportional representation. Even though political parties are not mentioned, they have come to dominate all elections, both for and within the regional legislature. The assembly nominates one of its members as president (or prime minister), who is, in turn, appointed by the king. The Council of Government (or cabinet) is also chosen from among the members of the assembly. The constitution is silent on the method to be used to appoint ministers, but practice within the region leaves the prime minister free to choose his or her own cabinet. Together, the president and the council constitute the executive, which is politically responsible to the assembly and can be removed by it. As in the national legislature, the regional prime minister can be ousted by a successful constructive motion of censure; the motion must include the name of the replacement and be approved by an absolute majority of the chamber. Like the *Cortes,* the regional legislature may operate either as a whole house or in committee. The principal function of the regional assembly is to make regional laws, but it also has three important functions in regard to the national government. It elects the senators who represent the Autonomous Community in the national Senate (article 69); it may initiate legislation (*proposiciones de ley*) before the national Congress (article 87); and it may present appeals (*recursos de anticonstitucionalidad*) before the Constitutional Court if it believes that an Autonomous Community's rights have been infringed by actions of either other Autonomous Communities or the national government (article 161). In addition, article 152 allows each Autonomous Community to create a high court of justice to resolve judicial conflict within the borders of the region, without in any way prejudicing the nationwide authority of the Supreme Court in Madrid. Article 152 applies only to those regions that take the fast route to autonomy (article 151), but logic tells us that the provisions will be extended to those that take the slow route (article 143).

Article 149 lists the areas that are the exclusive responsibility of the central government: nationality and immigration; international relations; defense and the armed forces; customs and tariffs; the monetary system; general, overall national planning; and the calling of national referenda. Article 148 lists the powers and responsibilities that belong to the Autonomous Communities, which include: the regulation of municipal boundaries; city planning and housing; highways, railways, and public works within their borders; private airports and marinas (recreational facilities only); irrigation, canals, and flood control within their regions; forestry and reforestation; public health and sanitation; social welfare; environmental protection; libraries, museums, and cultural activities; the fostering and teaching of the regional language (where applicable); and tourism.

Tensions among the regions of Spain and between the individual regions and the national government occur over (1) the implementation of the sections of article 149 that deal with delegated powers, and (2) the section of article 150 that transfers lawmaking powers from the national *Cortes* to the regions and permits the regularization or harmonization of these transferred powers among the regions. Article 149 lists the powers that belong exclusively to the central government but that may be delegated, without surrendering national sovereignty, to the Autonomous Communities. These deal primarily with regional transportation and traffic control—air, sea, rail, and road; telegraph and radio communications; the post office; meteorological service; cultural activities, such as the restoration and preservation of national monuments; and the regulation of academic and professional titles.

Perhaps the provisions most likely to produce conflict between the central government and the Autonomous Communities reside in article 150, which allows the *Cortes* to permit one or all of the regional assemblies to make laws in areas normally reserved for the national legislature. The *Cortes* may also transfer, to one or all of the regional cabinets and bureaucracies, functions that normally belong to the national executive. In addition and most potentially troublesome of all, article 150 permits the national government to pass laws that regularize the authoritative decisions of the Autonomous Communities, even in those areas reserved for the latter's competence, if the national common good demands it. Obviously, the potential for conflict between the national and regional governments is enormous; the *common good* can be a highly contentious term. The Organic Law for the Harmonization of the Process of Autonomy was a powder keg of constitutional and political contention.

To protect the regions from the possible encroachment of the central government, article 150 requires that the national government obtain an absolute majority vote in each chamber of the *Cortes* before it may act to regularize the behavior of the Autonomous Communities. To protect the central government from the improper behavior of an Autonomous Community, the article stipulates that the laws passed at the regional level under the delegated power of the national government will be subject to scrutiny by the *Cortes*. (Of course, the constitutionality of any law passed at any level is subject to the challenge in the Constitutional Court.) An administrative or executive function transferred to a regional government under article 150 will be monitored by the national prime minister and the cabinet, with the higher executive level overseeing the lower. Administrative oversight, in general, will fall to the government's delegate, provided for in article 154 of the constitution. The delegate, appointed by the government, is the liaison between the central government and the Autonomous Community and directs the bureaucratic functions of the national government in the that region; where necessary, the delegate coordinates the administrative functions of the two entities.

Finally, under article 155, the national government has a reserve of control to be used in extraordinary circumstances. If an Autonomous Community does not conform to the obligations of the constitution or acts in a way that gravely threatens the national interest, the national government may take "the necessary steps" to compel the region to fulfill its obligations or to alter its behavior. Before it acts, however, the national government must first warn the president of the Autonomous Community. If the warning is ignored, the government may then take action once it has received the approval of the absolute majority of the Senate, the chamber that represents the Autonomous Communities in the *Cortes*.

The financial viability of the Autonomous Communities is guaranteed in articles 156, 157, and 158 of the constitution. The communities may levy taxes; they may be reimbursed with part or all of certain national taxes; they may be awarded funds from the national government so that essential public services are properly carried out throughout the entire country; and they may receive monies out of the Interterritorial Compensation Fund (Fondo de Compensación Interterritorial—FCI), a kind of equalization grant designed to compensate the poorer regions.

As state functions are transferred from the national to the regional level, funds from the national treasury will also be transferred to carry out these functions. The Basque regions and Navarre have special rights under their *fueros*. Though historical in origin and reinstated by the 1978 constitution, the *fueros* have no existence apart from, behind, or beyond the constitution. There is nothing in the constitution that would prevent the national government extending these rights to the remaining fifteen Autonomous Communities. Under the *fueros*, the Basque region and Navarre collect not only their own regional taxes (just as do the other regions) but (unlike the remaining fifteen regions) they also collect all the taxes that would otherwise be collected by the national government, such as personal income tax, corporate tax, and national sales tax. The two regions then transfer to the national government a set amount, renegotiated every five years, for the cost of those national services that have not been transferred to the two regions.

To help rationalize the economic function of the national and regional governments in their various relationships of exclusivity, sharing, and delegation, the 1980 Organic Law on the Financing of the Autonomous Communities (Ley Orgánica de Financiación de las Comunidades Autónomas—LOFCA) set up the Council for the Fiscal and Financial Policies of the Autonomous Communities (Consejo de Política Fiscal y Financiera de las Comunidades Autónomas), made up of the national minister of finance, the national minister of public administration, and the finance ministers of the seventeen Autonomous Communities. The council is advisory only and seeks to consolidate national and regional policy regarding public investment and public debt, the cost of public services, and the allocation of public funds to the various regions.

THE PROCESS OF AUTONOMY: AN APPRAISAL

Tension between the center and the periphery has dogged Spain since the creation of the "state of autonomous communities" (*el estado de las autonomías*) was concluded in the winter of 1983.[4]. This tension is certainly not unique to Spain; it is endemic to all nonunitary states where power is divided and shared. The combative relationship between Washington and the states, which began early in the U.S. republic and continues unabated today, is but one example among the federal systems of the world. (It is a pity that the word *federal* cannot be used to describe the regime in Spain because all comparative examples are based on the federal-unitary dichotomy. The special reasons why the term had to be eschewed by the constitution-makers have already been discussed, but be that as it may, what exists in Spain today is effectively a federal system.)

In Spain, however, the relationship between center and periphery has been made more complex still, not only because of the country's distant history but also because its recent history made the demand for regional rights (states' rights, as one would say in the United States) a part of the battle cries of freedom against Franco's oppression. The center in Spain, Madrid, thus represented both the political dictatorship and the cultural, linguistic, and ethnic hegemony of Castile over the rest of the country. The sense of oppression was most acute in the three "historical communities"—the Basque provinces (now Euzkadi), Catalonia, and Galicia, and especially in Catalonia and Euzkadi. As a result, when it was decided early in the transition that autonomy would be a part of the democratization of Spain, Catalonia, Euzkadi, and Galicia were given special treatment, which they believed was deserved because of their historical uniqueness: Autonomy was their birthright. When the possibility for autonomy was then constitutionally offered to the rest of Spain, irrespective of the lack of historical identity among any particular people or area, the three "historical communities" believed that their own autonomy had been somehow debased—in a kind of psychic, relative deprivation that made them less special. As Goldie Shabad observes, "In the view of Catalan and Basque nationalists the distinctive culture of the two regions and their historical experience with self-government justified their position as 'privileged' autonomous communities which ought not to be diluted by equalizing the degree of autonomy across all regions."[5]

This denial of uniqueness has poisoned the relationship between Madrid and Euzkadi and Catalonia, particularly the former. It has also contributed to extremist assertions by some regional nationalists that the rights of autonomy set forth in the constitution logically allow for extending autonomy to independence, despite the constitutional provision that Spain is indivisible (article 2). (The relationship between Madrid and Galicia has been far less conflictual.) The extremist stance assumed by regional parties like Popular Unity in Euzkadi and Republican Left (Esquerra Republicana—ER) in Catalonia has forced the larger, more moderate bourgeois regional nationalist parties like the Basque Nationalist Party and Convergence and Unity in Catalonia to move toward extremism to avoid being outmaneuvered on their flanks. The latter two regional parties are large enough to win seats in national elections; their presence in the *Cortes* in Madrid has often been more confrontational than their socioeconomic attitudes would suggest.

Although the call for independence may be discounted as going beyond the limits of political debate, the call for the transfer of full decision-making authority from Madrid to the Autonomous Communities falls very much within those limits. Since no regions actually existed prior to the constitution (even though preautonomy agreements had been made with the three "historical communities"), all power under the constitution belongs to the state, that is, to the national government. For autonomy to be meaningful, it was therefore necessary for part of that power to be transferred from the state to the regions. The amount of power and the pace of its transfer was undefined, however. The three "historical communities" and the others that took the fast route to autonomy initially received the fullest complement of transferred power, but they continued to demand more. The remaining Autonomous Communities have demanded equal treatment. The problem has arisen because each region that chose the slow route received autonomy on an ad hoc, region-by-region basis; the number of functions and the amount of power transferred, therefore, varied by region. A 1982 attempt by the *Cortes* to regularize the transfer of power and make uniform all regional authority was, in large part, declared unconstitutional by the Constitutional Court (in The Organic Law for the Harmonization of the Process of Autonomy).

It was the "historical communities," especially Euzkadi and Catalonia, that were most opposed to LOAPA. Their leaders reasoned that the law, as they interpreted it, would necessarily have removed power that had already been transferred to those regions in order to make equal the power transferred to all regions. Euzkadi and Catalonia felt that LOAPA was a threat to their very autonomy.

After the declaration of unconstitutionality, the issue of transferability lay unresolved. Not until 1992 were the problems inherent in Title XIII of the constitution—Concerning the Territorial Organization of the State (articles 137 through 158)—seemingly settled once and for all. The pact between the PSOE government and the PP, the leading party of opposition, harmonized and increased the power transferred to the regions that had chosen the slow route to autonomy—Madrid, Castile-La Mancha, Extremadura, Castile-León, Murcia, Rioja, the Balearic Islands, Cantabria, Asturias, and Aragon. The transference of the control of education, with its billion-peseta price tag and involving the positions of some 250,000 public servants, was the last and most formidable hurdle to be surmounted by the government and the PP. Control of education would pass to the regions just mentioned, with the achievements in educational reform made by the various national governments since 1978 accepted and respected by those regions. (Control had already passed to the remaining regions.) Health care, on the other hand, would remain as it was, "given the complexity and the slight interest shown by the Autonomous Communities because of its financial consequences."[6]

Money has been a major bugbear throughout the process of establishing regional autonomy. Although the choice to create Autonomous Communities was discretionary under the constitution, it was inevitable that all of Spain would elect to divide into regions. It was not logical to think that some people would choose to remain directly ruled from Madrid and that others would choose self-rule. But self-government and the transference of power from Madrid to the regions would cost a fortune, not only to set up the infrastructure of autonomy at the outset but also to pay, from that time forward, the expenses of self-government: construction and maintenance of public buildings, salaries for all elected and appointed officials in the three branches of government, and funds to carry out the functions transferred from Madrid. For the richer regions—of which Euzkadi and Catalonia are the richest—the costs would be manageable. But for the poorer regions—by far the majority—the costs could prove to be beyond their capacity. To help equalize the burdens and to establish some degree of parity among the seventeen Autonomous Communities, a fund was established for interterritorial compensation and a supplementary fund was set up for interim compensation (Compensación Transitoria—CT). As might be expected, Euzkadi and Catalonia were not happy with the arrangement because they would pay into the fund more than they would receive. Galicia, on the other hand, being one of the poorest regions in Spain, benefited significantly from the fund.

The funds would not be dispersed according to some fixed plan, however. They would be forthcoming as a result of periodic negotiations between the national and regional governments. The last such negotiations took place in February 1990 and would remain in force until a definitive reform of the funding system was initiated.[7]

NOTES

1. For the complete document, see *Constitución Española* (Madrid: Boletín Oficial del Estado, 1989).

2. Article 162, section 1 reads: "The following are empowered to bring charge of unconstitutionality, the Prime Minister, the Public Defender, 50 deputies, 50 senators, the collegial executive organs of the Autonomous Communities, and in the appropriate case, the Legislatures of the same."

3. See Goldie Shabad, "After Automony: The Dynamics of Regionalism in Spain," in Stanley G. Payne, ed., *The Politics of Democratic Spain* (Chicago: Chicago Council on Foreign Relations, 1986).

4. Ibid., p. 112.

5. Ibid., p. 119.

6. *El Pais*, International Edition, February 3, 1992, p. 11.

7. Ibid., February 26, 1990, p. 23.

Part Three
Political Forces

8

Political Parties

The UCD disintegrated in 1983 following the general elections of October 1982, which empowered the PSOE to form the government with an absolute majority and made the AP the leading party of opposition. The PSOE and the AP, now called the PP, continued to occupy the same positions in parliament after the general elections of 1986 and 1989. As we shall see in Chapter 12, the PSOE lost its absolute parliamentary majority in the general elections in 1993, but it remains the dominant party in the legislature, and the PP is still the leading party of opposition. In this chapter, I will discuss the disappearance of the UCD and the accession to power and opposition of the PSOE and the AP (now PP), respectively— two parties that, in the early years of the transition, would have been considered the least likely to have achieved such eminence. At that time, the people perceived both parties to be extremist, the PSOE because of its yet unreconstructed Marxism-Leninism and the AP because of its ostensible links to Francoism. The electorate translated its fears into votes for the more centrist UCD. (It also relegated the Communist party to the periphery of Spanish politics.) As we shall see later in this chapter, first the PSOE and then the AP went through vigorous self-examination, prodded by a concern that the public's perception of them would result in continued electoral rejection unless the two parties transformed themselves.

The PSOE began its move toward the center in 1979. By the general elections of 1982, the PSOE had drawn sufficiently close to the center to pull former UCD voters into its ranks and thus assure a Socialist victory. It took trouncings in the 1982, 1986, and 1989 elections to finally goad the AP into self-appraisal. (Table 8.1) That appraisal, though not as dramatic as that of the PSOE, detached the party from its right-wing moorings and initiated its move toward the center. (Even the Communist party has gone through self-analysis, but the outcome has so far been less clear cut than that of the PSOE and PP.)

The distance that now separates the PSOE from the AP (PP) has become too narrow to accommodate a new centrist party—as proven by the failure of Adolfo Suárez's party, the CDS.

TABLE 8.1   Distribution of Seats in Congress Following National Elections
in 1982, 1986, and 1989

	1982	1986	1989
PSOE	202	184	175
PP (AP, CP)	106	105	106
CDS	2	19	14
CiU	12	18	18
IU	4	7	18
PNV	8	6	5
HB	2	5	4
EE	1	2	2
PAR	0	1	1
AIC	0	1	1
CG	0	1	1
UV	0	1	2
PA	0	0	2
Others	0	0	0

Source: The figures for 1982 and 1986 are from *Keesing's Contemporary Archives* 32 (December 1989), p. 34822. The figures for 1989 are from *Keesing's Record of World Events* 35, no. 10 (December 1989), p. 36984.

The centripetal process of moderation in the two major national parties is the key element to understanding Spanish political parties since 1979. I will elaborate on this process in this chapter and then describe the proliferation of parties in the Spanish multiparty system, at both at the national and the regional levels.

DISCONTINUITY IN THE SPANISH PARTY SYSTEM

The major characteristic of the system is its youth; for all practical purposes, Spanish political parties came into being after January 1977. Even the PSOE, created in 1879, and the PCE, created in 1921, are "new," transformed in a manner that their militants in the 1920s and 1930s would scarcely recognize. Except for these two national parties and two regional parties—PNV and the Republican Left of Catalonia (Esquerra Republicana de Catalunya—ERC)—none of the other parties active at the outbreak of the Civil War still exists. The twentieth-century development of Spanish parties (most of them corrupted by the political system in which they operated during the last decades of the nineteenth and the early decades of the twentieth centuries) was interrupted by the dictatorship of Primo de Rivera from 1923 to 1929. Continuity was shakily reestablished during the brief and chaotic Second Republic (1931–1936) and then finally broken completely after 1939, when the Civil War ended. In reality, parties had already been destroyed in those parts of Spain that had fallen under Franco's control as the fighting progressed. On September 13, 1936, two months after the outbreak of hostilities, the Junta de Defensa Nacional, then the governing body of Nationalist Spain, outlawed all political parties. The ban stayed in force, except for the official FET y de las JONS (later renamed the National Movement), until February 1977. Note the absence of the detested word *party*. For Franco, political parties were the scourge of Spain and the cause (not the result) of Spanish divisiveness. His attack on parties during the war and his relentless pursuit of their remnants after the war was over effectively ended party activity for 36 or 39 years, depending on whether one dates from 1939 or 1936.

When parties were legalized in 1977, almost no one could link the present to the past. In contrast to Franco, who ruled for almost forty years, Hitler ruled for just twelve years (1933 to 1945) and Mussolini twenty-one (1922 to 1943). Therefore, when parties were resuscitated in Germany and Italy after World War II, there were many politicians ready to begin again who had been active before the dictatorships: Konrad Adenauer and Alcide di Gasperi, to name only two. In Spain, there were very, very few. One was Santiago Carrillo, the Communist leader. His forty years of exile had put him out of touch with the reality within Spain, however, and after his triumphant return home in December 1976, his work as party leader (in contrast to his personal contribution in easing the transition to democracy) can only be called a failure. Dolores Ibárruri, the legendary La Pasionaria of the Civil War, also returned, but she was in her eighties, and her years of exile in the Soviet Union made her value to the emerging Spanish democracy little more than symbolic. The authors of the Foessa report make the following comments on the discontinuity of Spanish parties: "The relative discontinuity has positive aspects. The present-day parties are less affected by the myths of the past, that is, by the problems and failures that preceded the Civil War. But there are also some negative aspects: the absence of the historic memory of past errors and above all the lack of democratic, parliamentary experience of the new political class."[1]

Finally, a few words should be said about the attitude of the average Spaniard toward political parties at the beginning of the transition to democracy in 1975. When asked by pollsters about their liberties, the Spaniards placed the need for parties fifth on a list of essential political ingredients. First was freedom of the press, followed by freedom of religion, freedom to create labor unions, and freedom to create private universities. Much of this attitude has been attributed to the four decades of propaganda poured out by Franco on the evils of parties. This prejudice, the result of a socialization that was deeply planted and difficult to root out, continues even today, and many in Spain who think seriously about politics feel that this mentality obstructs the development of faith in democracy. Many Spaniards misunderstand just what politics and political parties can and cannot accomplish in a free society.

PARTIES OF THE TRANSITION

Unión del Centro Democrático (UCD)

The UCD was the preeminent party of the transition. Ahead of its time, it was a fortuitous creation that enabled Spain to survive Franco. But ultimately, it would die because it was alien to the Spanish political environment at the time (and perhaps it would be alien even in the 1990s). It was a kind of catchall party in an emergent democracy whose societal elements had not yet found a common denominator (or denominators) for the long haul of democracy. At its inception, the UCD was an incarnation of the hope that temporarily transcended a heterogeneity too vast to be accommodated by a single political party. Once that hope—the creation of a democratic Spain—became a reality, the day-to-day political will necessary to make the creation thrive proved too taxing for the elements that made up the UCD. Moreover, the political ambitions of the men who had subordinated themselves to Suárez in order to bring about the transition to democracy reasserted themselves after the transition was in place, engaging in what became internecine destruction.

The UCD began as a federation called the Unión del Centro (Center Union), composed of fifteen parties that reflected mostly Christian democratic, social democratic, or liberal (in the European usage of the term) philosophies. The ties that held them together were their rejection of Francoism and their commitment to political change, but the nature of the change and the shape that the new political system would take were obscured by ideological differences. It is unlikely that this motley association would have had the great political force it came to possess if Adolfo Suárez had not announced, in early May 1977, that he would run for congress in the June 1977 elections and join the Center Union as an independent, unaffiliated with any of the constituent parties. Until his announcement, Suárez had had no political identification; he was prime minister in a personal, not a party, capacity, appointed by and loyal only to the king. With Suárez now a member, the Center Union changed its name to UCD and changed its position from an anti-Franco to a prosystem one. The system was represented by the king, Suárez, and the governmental associates the prime minister brought with him into the party. The new UCD became the party of those *in* power—the party of the incumbents, who have the advantage in any political system. José Maravall writes: "The UCD was a combination of three different sectors: a traditional Right attached to the machinery of the state and unwilling to let it go; a democratic Right with a conservative Christian ideology; and a reformist sector which although small was well aware of its importance for the Centrist electorate."[2]

Adolfo Suárez

The marriage of convenience between Suárez and the affiliates of the
Center Union was mutually beneficial. The members of the Center Union
got immediate access to executive power through Suárez and a preemp-
tive competitive advantage in the upcoming parliamentary election.
Suárez got access to electoral constituencies. This was especially important because his and the king's grand design for the restructuring of Spain
needed support in the new constituent assembly if the plan was to be successful, yet Suárez had no links to the electorate. Even though the Center
Union and its successor, the UCD, lacked a grassroots organization that
could turn out the voters, the affiliated parties were intimately identified
with political notables whose personal electoral attraction was potent.
Suárez hoped for success by association and was rewarded in the legislative elections in 1977. He turned the resources of the state to the advantage of his and his party's electoral campaign. Moreover, in a country

where deference to those in power had been instilled in the people for decades, this fusion of political power and democratic commitment gave the
UCD enormous political strength. The UCD blatantly used the state bureaucracy for its own electoral benefit, and during the campaign, radio
and television (which were then owned and operated by the state and
should have remained nonpartisan) brazenly favored the UCD. The opposition parties cried foul but to little avail.

The UCD became even more dominant when it won the largest
number of votes in the 1977 elections and the largest number of seats in
the Congress. It won only a plurality, not an absolute majority, however,
and Suárez formed a minority government, which called on all his negotiating skills. To secure a solid base from which to bargain with the other
parties in parliament, he moved to consolidate the UCD behind him and
on June 23, a week after the elections, announced that the coalition of
parties that made up the UCD would merge to form a single entity.
(Suárez did not want to spend valuable time having to negotiate *within* the
UCD.) The formal creation of the new UCD took place on August 5, 1977,
and the party held its first congress the following October. By his action,
Suárez effectively cut the ties between the leaders of the formerly separate
parties and their now disbanded organizations. These leaders, whom the
media came to call the "barons," continued to speak for their respective
political viewpoints but were now deprived of an institutionalized base
outside the UCD. They became totally dependent upon Suárez, who alone
controlled the access to power.

The new consolidated party was essentially a pragmatic, centrist organization whose primary goal was to win and keep power. Because of
the diverse backgrounds of its members, however, its philosophy was
somewhat amorphous and free-form, designed to attract as many voters
as possible. Luis García San Miguel describes the party in two different
ways. First, he notes that "the UCD presented itself as the resultant of a
kind of triple synthesis: between forces emerging out of Francoism and
forces emerging out of the opposition; between ideals and aspirations
from the right and others from the left; finally among Christian Democratic, Social Democratic, and Liberal ideologies."[3] Then García San Miguel remarks, "As Gasperi said of the Christian Democracy (in Italy), the
UCD was a party of the center, playing the politics of the left with votes of
the right."[4]

The party believed in a state that was strong and positive but meanwhile protected civil and human rights; it believed in the unity of Spain
but supported regionalist claims. The UCD stood for the separation of
church and state but recognized the special place of Catholicism in Spanish society. Its foreign policy sought to integrate Spain into a democratic
Europe while maintaining close ties with the United States. As García San

Miguel says, if we equate the Right with capitalism and the Left with socialism, then "we would have to say that the program of the UCD is clearly rightist, much like the program of other Liberal and Christian Democratic parties in the West."[5] If the Right is proreligion and the Left is antireligion, then, again, the UCD would have to be considered rightist. Still, Suárez took a tolerant stand on the legalization of divorce and the decriminalization of adultery, positions similar to those of the Left, and it was he who legalized the Communist party, called for the first free elections in forty-one years, and supported amnesty for terrorists.

Obviously, the party suffered from internal tension from the very beginning, and that stress eventually pulled the party apart. Once the initial transition to democracy seemed to be under way, the efferent forces within the party to begin the struggle to restructure it in their own images. For the Social Democrats, the party was too rightist: too slow to reform society; too willing to allow the Francoist infrastructure (the bureaucracy, the police, the armed forces, the university system, and the world of banking and finance) to stay in place; too committed to unalloyed capitalism. For the Christian Democrats, the party was too leftist: too willing to secularize; too tolerant of permissive behavior like divorce, adultery, and abortion; too ready to join with the Left, the policy of consensus. Exacerbating the ideological fractionalization and perhaps providing the added impetus needed to pull the pieces apart were the personal ambitions of the "barons," who often disguised their ambition by calling it doctrinal fidelity. Richard Gunther cites interviews with Spanish political actors at the time. One former secretary-general of the UCD, quoted by Gunther, said,

> There were no ideological problems, except on some point like regulation of schools or the divorce law. There were no ideological problems, but there was a pure and crude struggle for power. ... The "barons" were jockeying to become prime minister. For me, this was a pure struggle for power. I believe that they thought the UCD was a full consolidated party with which one could play as they play with the DC in Italy. Those same conditions did not exist within the UCD to permit them to play political games to that extent. The only thing they succeeded in doing was breaking up the party.[6]

In short, the UCD was insufficiently institutionalized to withstand the enormous stress that the "barons" placed upon it. The party was too young, too weak, and too shallowly planted to survive the turmoil within it.

Partido Socialista de Obrero Español (PSOE)

The Spanish Socialist Worker's Party is the oldest party in Spain, but the discontinuity mentioned earlier robbed it of most of its ties to the past.

The PSOE was effectively reborn in October 1974, at the 26th Party Congress, held in Surenes near Paris. Control of the party went to a group of young men and women of the post–Civil War generation whose ideology was Marxist and revolutionary. The "young turks," of whom the most prominent was the thirty-two-year-old labor lawyer Felipe González, had never lived in exile but had identified with the party in exile as the living embodiment of classic Spanish socialism. The young activists, still operating beneath the surface in Spain, had come out of the fertile, anti-Franco environment of the universities and the liberal professions and were prepared to transform the country radically once Franco was gone. They made up the majority at the congress in Surenes. Called *renovados* ("those wanting to renovate the party"), they outmaneuvered and outvoted *históricos* ("old guard"), and took over the party from them. For the most part, the *históricos* were moderate socialists, some with social democratic leanings, and many of them had lived outside Spain for years. Both *renovados* and *históricos* wanted to seize the magical initials PSOE, freighted with emotionally charged historical memory. When the party was legalized in Spain in February 1977, the *históricos* were the first to register their application with the government, and for a short time, they carried the official Socialist label. The anomaly was soon corrected, however, and the government recognized the majority *renovados* as the legitimate heirs to the party's name and mystique.

This was not the only party speaking for socialism, however. During the Franco regime, men of great stature within Spain, particularly in the universities and in journalism, had begun to oppose his rule. Their careful opposition was usually played out within the limits of what the regime would tolerate, but these activists were living in Spain, not out of harm's way in exile. They were equally vulnerable to suppression by the regime and to attack from the party in exile, which accused them of opportunism. They were, in fact, closet socialists. An open avowal of socialist beliefs could have led to even more draconian punishment than was meted out to the eminent professor Enrique Tierno Galván, whose attacks on the regime became so intense that, in 1965, Franco had him removed for life from his university chair. When political parties were legalized in 1977, Tierno and his followers felt they had earned their places in the political system that Suárez and the king were creating, and they rejected the claim of the PSOE that it alone was the voice of socialism in Spain. Tierno organized a socialist alternative to PSOE called the Popular Socialist Party (Partido Socialista Popular—PSP), which presented its own lists of candidates in the elections of June 1977.

The PSOE, not the PSP, galvanized the non-Communist Left, and the PSOE declared its principles at the 27th Party Congress, the first held on Spanish soil in over forty-one years. Prime Minister Suárez had allowed the congress to convene in Madrid in December 1976, two months before the party became legal. Attending as guests were most of the great names in European socialism: Pietro Nenni (Italy), François Mitterrand (France), Willy Brandt (West Germany), Olof Palme (Sweden), and Michael Foote (Great Britain).

The PSOE claimed that it was "a class party, and as a consequence a Marxist and democratic party of the masses."

> We are a class party because we defend and fight for the historic project of the working class: the disappearance of the exploitation of man by man and the construction of a classless society. ... We are Marxist in that we believe in the scientific method ... and that class conflict ... is the motor of society. We define ourselves as democratic because we are in agreement that the internal organization of the party should be scrupulously democratic. ... The PSOE defines itself as socialist because its program and behavior lead to the takeover of the means of capitalist production through the assumption of political and economic power by the working class and the socializing of the means of production, distribution, and monetary exchange. We understand socialism to be both a goal and a process that leads to that goal, and our beliefs compel us to reject any accommodation with or simple reform of capitalism.[7]

For the first time in its history, the PSOE had openly defined itself as Marxist, and its leader, Felipe González, pledged that the party would irreversibly change Spain: It would put an end to the exploitation of man by man, create a classless society, and replace the apparatus of the state by workers' self-management. "Let it be clear to each and everyone that the party will never renounce its goal."[8] Yet by 1979, the party that had apparently been ready to do battle for a total break with the Francoist past, in accordance with rigorous Marxist ideology, became in behavior and philosophy (if not in name) a social democratic party, accepting parliamentary democracy, limited monarchy, and capitalism. Why had the PSOE so vehemently embraced Marxism in 1976 and then so dramatically reversed itself fewer than three years later? Reasons and interpretations abound, but I belive that the most trenchant explanations of what occurred and why it did are found in the writings of Santos Juliá.[9]

Until PSOE's stunning showing in the elections of June 15, 1977, the Socialists had been overshadowed by the Communists both as the keeper of the leftist flame and as the nemesis of Francoism. Communism, the Communist party, and Communists had become the mythic opponents of Francoism. This idea was kept before the public by Franco's ceaseless propaganda campaign depicting the Civil War as a crusade against communism and communism as the greatest of all the potential threats to his regime. Francoist dogma was given additional credence when the United

Felipe González

States obtained bases in Spain in 1953 in order to contain communism—
which by then was not only the scourge of Spain (Franco's hoary contention) but also the scourge of the world. Communism's place in the
Francoist demonology was ironic since it had been the weakest of all the
forces on the Left during the Second Republic and had become prominent
in Spain only after the Civil War broke out and aid from the USSR to the
Republic was made conditional on Republican acquiescence to Soviet
domination. Once the war was over, however, communism disappeared
in Spain as an active political force (driven out or underground by the victors), and sympathy for communism as such was initially weak among
Spaniards who opposed the Franco regime. But with Franco's persistent
contention that it was his primary enemy, communism (whether in exile
or underground in Spain) grew in stature among anti-Franco Spaniards
not because of its ideology but because of its position as the preeminent
enemy of the regime—as Franco himself declared. Among the most force-

ful ways to be anti-Franco was, therefore, to be pro-Communist. Moreover, Communists underground in Spain eventually did become subverters of the Franco regime when they infiltrated the labor sectors of the syndicates through the Workers' Commissions, which became full-fledged unions after the collapse of Franco. Spanish Communists in exile throughout the world kept the party embers stoked abroad. Self-declared martyrs of Spanish democracy, they proudly accepted Franco's epithet, "enemies of Spain." With the passage of time, some of them—like Santiago Carrillo and, above all, Dolores Ibárruri—grew to legendary proportion.

The Spanish Socialists appeared lilliputian when compared with the larger-than-life Communists. It would seem that neither in exile nor underground in Spain had they paid their dues to anti-Francoism. And even though it was, in many ways, Franco himself who had paid the Communists' dues by endowing them with prowess they did not really possess, the Communists seemed to be the great force on the Left that would lead Spain out of Francoism and into the future. The *renovados* who captured the Socialist party in Surenes in 1974 believed that if the PSOE was to compete against the Communists for the support of the Left in post-Franco Spain, it would have to prove its good faith in Marxist theory—thus the fervent commitment to Marxism at the 1976 congress in Madrid. For a brief moment, it appeared that the PSOE would be the only major party on the Left. When all other parties were made legal in February 1977, the Communist party remained illegal. If the illegality had continued, the PSOE would most probably have received the major part of the leftist vote. But when the Communist party was legalized in May 1977, the competition on the Left was on, with the Communists the odds-on favorites over the Socialists in the elections to the constituent assembly in June 1977.

The elections of June 15, 1977, were a stunning endorsement of the Socialists and an equally stunning repudiation of the Communists. No party won an absolute majority. The plurality was won by the UCD (34 percent of the vote and 165 seats in the 350-member Congress). The Socialists came in second (24.9 percent of the vote and 118 seats); the Communists came in a distant third (9.3 percent of the vote and 20 seats). A working-class nation had given the plurality of its support to a Center-Right coalition whose vocabulary and platform was comfortingly temperate. At the time of the election, polling information was already revealing the moderation of the Spanish voters, who tended to locate themselves at the middle of the ideological spectrum. It was believed, however, that those who would choose to vote further to the left would reward the Communist party for the reasons I have presented. But the Spanish people who voted on the left chose, instead, to reward the Socialists, primarily because the PSOE alarmed the electorate less that the PCE did, irrespective of the hard line taken by the Socialists at the 27th Party Congress.

Voting patterns in the election revealed to the PSOE that if the party was to increase its percentage of the vote (and thus its number of seats in the legislature) in the future, it would have to pull votes from its right flank, not from its left. Committed Communists were not likely to switch allegiance and vote for the PSOE, no matter how far to the left it might move. But just to the right of the PSOE, the allegiance of most supporters of the UCD was far more fluid, given the amorphous nature of the party. As we have already seen, the UCD was, in fact, far more a loose electoral federation than a clearly defined, institutionalized party. Its constituencies could be attracted to other parties whose beliefs and platforms were sufficiently accommodating. Therefore, the most logical and potentially beneficial direction in which the PSOE could move to increase its vote was to the right. Moreover, the 1977 election put the PSOE securely *within* the political system, no longer marginalized by the prosystem parties or suffering from an inferiority complex vis-à-vis the Communists. The people had placed the PSOE tantalizingly near enough to power to suggest that it should rethink its radical Marxist commitment if it wanted electoral victory in the future.

Party leaders faced a dilemma: either maintain fidelity to the resolutions of the 27th Party Congress and risk defeat at the polls or recast the 1976 resolutions, vigorously pursue victory at the polls, and risk the accusation of electoralism (which places electoral victory ahead of doctrinal purity). For the political purists, electoralism is the unforgivable sin. Felipe González and his cohorts—particularly his alter ego (some say his Mr. Hyde), Alfonso Guerra—opted for electoral success and began to move the party away from socialism and toward social democracy.

Shortly after the elections, González began to demonstrate his accommodative skills. In October 1977, he negotiated with Prime Minister Suárez and the other major political leaders in parliament to create the Moncloa Pacts, whose articles accepted a reformed, capitalist, free market economy at odds with socialist doctrine. In late May 1978, when the Socialists and the Centrists arrived at an impasse in their negotiations on the draft of the constitution, Suárez and González instructed their seconds-in-command to work out a compromise—the crucial Suárez-González agreement—thereby ensuring the successful passage of the draft through the *Cortes*. Earlier in the year, González had begun to mend the rift between the PSP, which had performed poorly in the 1977 elections, and the PSOE. Then, In April 1978, the PSOE absorbed the PSP, making Tierno Galván honorary president of the PSOE. A few days later, González broached the topic that clearly revealed his commitment to moderation and to moving his party away from ideological militancy. He proposed that at the next congress of the PSOE, to be held in May 1979, the adjective *Marxist* be dropped from the party's definition. In the meantime, the party once again went to the polls on March 1, 1979, in the general elections called by Suárez following the nation's acceptance of the constitution in the December 1978 referendum. The ideology presented by the PSOE to the electorate during the campaign was the same as that presented in 1977: Until a new party congress decided otherwise, the declarations of the 27th Party Congress remained in force. Perhaps González believed that his pragmatic behavior since the last election would convince the voter that the party itself had changed, in actions if not in words. The people remained unconvinced, however, and their response in 1979 was almost identical to that in 1977. The UCD won 35.5 percent of the votes and 167 seats in the Congress (34.8 percent and 165 seats in 1977); the PSOE won 30.8 percent of the vote and 121 seats in the Congress (29.4 percent and 118 seats in 1977). The lingering fear of Marxist extremism in an unregenerate PSOE was expertly manipulated by Adolfo Suárez, to the great advantage of his party. On the last day of the campaign, he went on television to reassure the people that the UCD offered "Christian humanism," in contrast to the PSOE's "Marxist, socialist materialism."

The PSOE held its 28th Party Congress in May 1979 to battle internally for control of the party. On one side were the Marxists—the *críticos* ("critical sector")—who believed that the failure of the party to defeat the UCD earlier in the year was due to González's conciliatory behavior; they felt he had compromised the party's ideology in order to accommodate what they considered to be a capitalist, bourgeois political system. They argued that the remedy was to reiterate and pursue with conviction the party resolutions set forth in the 27th Party Congress in 1976. Confronting the *críticos* were González and the *felipistas*, who wanted, once and for all, to rid the party of outworn theories, which they were convinced were keeping the PSOE from the ultimate political victory: control of the *Cortes*.

The *críticos* were in the majority at the congress, and they succeeded in maintaining the party's Marxist orientation. They realized, however, that without González, the party could not survive electorally. In the public's mind, the PSOE and Felipe—who at this time in his career, was referred to by his first name only, as if the surname was superfluous—were one and the same. The *críticos* wanted González to remain as secretary-general while the party remained Marxist. The paradox was compounded by the fact that the *críticos* condemned personalism (*personalismo*), which transforms a party into one person's fiefdom. González relished the *críticos'* dilemma, and in a masterfully executed coup de main, he resigned as secretary-general, leaving the party leaderless. (He, of course, still remained leader of the PSOE within parliament.) Fully aware of the power of his celebrity, González gambled that the party would demand his return, on his own terms. His calculation carried good odds. When his resignation was announced to the delegates in the convention hall, they erupted into a prolonged chant: "Fe-li-pe, qué-da-te!" ("Felipe, stay!" which rhymes in Spanish). Remarkably, this demonstration came from delegates who had just voted to retain Marxism!

In the meantime, while the battle over leadership and party doctrine captured the attention of the congress and of the country through the media, an organizational committee of the congress adopted a motion made by the *felipistas* that would severely curtail dissent within the PSOE. The motion confirmed the party's rejection of "tendencies" (organized factions) within the party and extended the prohibition to include even unorganized "currents of opinion." Under the rules and regulations adopted by the 1976 congress and now readopted, party members could be expelled for several reasons: making public pronouncements that might damage the party's image, committing acts of indiscipline, slandering another member, or provoking a major conflict within the party.[10] The *críticos* were too divided among themselves to stop the passage of the motion, which was approved by 92 to 72 vote with 10 abstentions. The *felipistas* at the congress also managed to change the procedure by which delegates would be chosen to future congresses. No longer would they be directly elected at the local level, where Marxists were most vocal; henceforth, they would be chosen in a three-tiered selection process—local, provincial, regional—designed to weed out radicals and produce moderate delegates who were supportive of González.

After González resigned, the stalemated congress was not officially declared closed, which would have made all resolutions (including the reinstatement of Marxism) binding. Rather, González and Alfonso Guerra maneuvered to halt closure and set up an interim governing body—the *comisión gestora*—that would tend to party affairs until the convening of an extraordinary congress the following September. That congress was expected to resolve the problems of leadership and ideological orientation. Richard Gunther writes:

> In the four months between the 28th Congress and the Extraordinary Congress, González and Guerra traveled extensively throughout the country holding meetings with provincial executive committees (which were much more *felipista* than the majority of delegates at the 28th Congress) and coordinating their efforts to control more effectively the selection of delegates to the Extraordinary Congress. They were greatly assisted in their endeavors by the implicit blackmail of the party inherent in González' resignation. ... As a result of their efforts, González and Guerra were in a position to dominate the Extraordinary Congress and secure approval of changes in the party's ideology.[11]

At the extraordinary congress, González was reelected secretary-general, and the term *Marxism* was skillfully finessed. "The PSOE considers Marxism to be a critical, theoretical, nondogmatic instrument for the analysis and transformation of society using the various Marxist and non-Marxist contributions that have come together to make socialism the great liberalizing alternative of our time, fully respecting personal beliefs."[12] The PSOE had effectively been transformed from a Socialist to a Social Democratic party, and this orientation became the new orthodoxy. With rules that prohibited not only "tendencies" but also "currents of opinion" and with the selection of delegates to future party congresses structured to return moderate *felipistas*, Gonzáles was now in absolute control of the party. Electoralism and personalism, the scourges of the "old" PSOE, had become reality in the "new" PSOE. From González's perspective, the party was now ready to prepare for its run for the gold in the next general election.

The 29th Party Congress of the PSOE held in October 1981, exactly one year before the next general election, consolidated González's control of the party. There was some resistance to him, primarily from regional party leaders, but support was so overwhelming that González chastised the delegates for their failure to be more freethinking. (Like the rich man who disdains money, perhaps González encouraged criticism because he was essentially unassailable.) In the voting, the executive report was accepted by 96.6 percent of the delegates, and González was reinstated as secretary-general by 100 percent. Richard Gillespie comments: "Together with the reality of decision-making being in the hands of a few heads of delegation, and few delegates even bothering to attend congress sessions, the picture that emerged was of a Stalinist party, replete with personality cult, strong party apparatus, rigid internal discipline, a ban on tendencies, and the persecution and expulsion of dissenters."[13] An analysis of the PSOE from its electoral victory in 1982 to the present will be given in Chapter 12.

Partido Comunista Español (PCE)

The Spanish Communist Party has perhaps received more credit than it should for its role in the transition. The PCE's poor showing in the elections of 1977 and 1979 indicates that the party was not a potent force among the electorate, and the 1982 elections almost eliminated it completely from national politics, at least for the time being. But the mystique of the party and the bravura of its leader, Santiago Carrillo, made its voice one of the most carefully heeded in the early period of the transition—before the 1977 elections showed that the PCE's approval or disapproval of political change had not been that important. Students of Spanish history

Santiago Carrillo

and politics should not find this surprising, for the party has never played a significant role in Spanish politics. Its part in the Second Republic was minor. It elected no deputies to the 484-member **Cortes** in 1931, only 1 in 1934, and just 17 in 1936. Only after the Soviet Union intervened in the Civil War at the request of the desperate Republic (which sought but received no aid from the United States, France, or Great Britain) did Communist influence increase enormously in Spain—the price the Republic paid for Soviet help. Because Franco proclaimed that he was fighting to save Spain and the world from communism and because the Communists willingly accepted the mantle of the thwarted savior of the Spanish democracy—defeated by the intervention of the Axis powers and by the neglect of the Western democracies—communism's aura grew in Spain and throughout much of the world, nourished by the exiles who fled Spain after Franco's victory in 1939. To their credit, the Communists organized the most effective underground opposition to Franco in the early years of his regime. And in later years, it was the Communists who organized the covert Workers' Commissions that infiltrated the official trade unions (the syndicates), that structured and controlled labor. These efforts did not legitimize the Communists electorally in post-Franco Spain, however. The Spanish Communists (and most political observers as well) had expected that their courageous, clandestine activity in Spain during the Franco years and their posture as heirs to the Republic would accomplish for them what underground activity had accomplished for the French and Italian Communists—generous rewards at the polls after World War II for their commitment to these nations and for their heroism.

Even if the party itself was less then successful, its leader, Santiago Carrillo, was undeniably a powerful presence in post-Franco Spain, and his moderation contributed significantly to Spain's relatively smooth transition to democracy. This is especially true in terms of his acceptance of the monarchy, his approval of the highly symbolic new Spanish flag, and his role in the creation of the constitution. Coming home after almost four decades of exile, Carrillo made a dramatic first public appearance in Madrid in December 1976. His arrest on December 22 and unexpected release on December 30 symbolized the joyful yet painful return of all the men and women who had ever been hounded by Franco. Carrillo was free, and he was a hero. As already described, the cry from those who supported freedom for his party became the cry for freedom for *all* political persuasions, no matter how heretical.

Even before his return to Spain, however, Carrillo had already begun to temper his ideology, whether out of a true commitment to liberalization or out of opportunism in his quest for political power. In July 1976, he spoke in what later would be labeled Eurocommunist terminology, separating himself from Moscow's domination:

> Yes ... we had our pope, our Vatican and we thought we were predestined to triumph. But as we mature and become less of a church, we must become more national, closer to reality. We must see that each individual has his private life, his individual sense of things. I told the last party executive meeting that a person's preference of friends, of music and literature, whether to be religious or atheist, has nothing to do with the party. The party can only be concerned with problems of politics and social struggle. ... And why not make a comparison with Luther. ... Nowadays, he wouldn't be burned by the Inquisition. Heretics usually turn out to be all right. They are ahead of their time, but after all they are right. We want communists to be heretics. When we are conservatives we are no longer right. ... We want a type of socialism with universal suffrage, alternation of government, not control of power for the communists but an alliance of forces that in no way would allow a communist monopoly. ... We mean the Communist party could be in a

one coalition government and if it lost out in the next elections it would be outside.[14]

Carrillo spoke these words before his return to Spain in December 1976. But after the legalization of the PCE in April 1977, the Spanish party made no modification in its statutes to reflect his new philosophy. In fact, the PCE went into the 1977 elections with its Marxist-Leninist ideology intact and won only 9.3 percent of the vote and 20 seats in the Congress. In a move similar to that later made by Felipe González, Carrillo acted to demonstrate to the electorate that he and his party were worthy of trust. He took part in the negotiations that led to the Moncloa Pacts in October 1977, many of whose articles were contrary to communist economic theory. Then, in April 1978 while the draft of the constitution was being hammered out, Carrillo officiated at the historic Ninth Congress of the PCE, which eliminated the word **Leninist** from the party's self-definition. "Today," the party announced, "it is no longer fitting to consider Leninism to be the Marxism of our time."[15] The delegates also excised the concept of the dictatorship of the proletariat and embraced Carrillo's Eurocommunist philosophy. The party was then redefined as Marxist, revolutionary, and democratic.

The PCE presented itself to the electorate in the elections of March 1, 1979, under its new Eurocommunist banner, but the response from the people was little different from that in 1977. The PCE won 10.9 percent of the vote and 23 seats in Congress, compared to 9.3 percent and 20 seats in 1977. The new face of the party had not convinced the Spanish people that its heart and mind had changed as well. A great part of the popular skepticism could be attributed to the internecine war that had begun to rage within the party itself. Ideological differences were compounded by other, more personal cleavages: a generational split between older comrades-in-arms, veterans or victims of the Civil War who eagerly accepted rigid Marxist-Leninist discipline and expected everyone else to do likewise, and younger members who were less blindly obedient; and a social or class split between laborers and intellectuals. Regional splits, though not unique to Spain, were more commonplace there than in other countries. The Catalan Communist party founded in 1936, the Unified Socialist Party of Catalonia, had considered itself separate from the national party centered in Madrid from the beginning, but with regionalization in Spain becoming a reality, the Communist parties in the various autonomous communities were seeking increasing latitude from Madrid. Three factions contended for the leadership, which did not shift, however, until after the party's debacle in the national elections of October 1982. The PCE, electorally linked with the PSUC, received only 4.1 percent of the vote, which gave them only 4 seats in the Congress, down from 23 after the 1979 elections. One faction was pro-Soviet and attributed the party's plight to the adulteration of its classic doctrines. Why should the people vote for a Eurocommunist program when there was already an almost identical one offered by the PSOE? A return to basics would swing the national leftist vote back to the Communists. A second faction was pro-Eurocommunist but against Carrillo, who, it claimed, ran the party like an autocrat, allowing no dissent and purging those who dared challenge him. Like the pro-Soviets, this group wanted to oust Carrillo, but whereas the former felt he had corrupted the party, the latter felt he had deceived it, showing one face to the public and another to the party's militants. This group wanted the democracy exhibited externally to be practiced internally, and it attributed the party's electoral weakness to its internal contradictions. The third faction was made up of those loyal to Carrillo.

After the 1982 elections, Carrillo resigned as secretary-general of the PCE and picked Gerardo Iglesias as his successor. Carrillo, who remained on the Central Committee, calculated that the relatively unknown and in-experienced Iglesias would soon demonstrate his inadequacy and that the party would demand Carrillo's return. But Iglesias proved more talented and tenacious than Carrillo had expected, and he resisted Carrillo's mach-inations to undermine his authority. In March 1985, when Carrillo and his followers refused to cease their opposition to Iglesias and adhere to the discipline of democratic centralism, Iglesias and his supporters had suffi-cient votes to dismiss Carrillo from the Central Committee. The PCE, still with its Eurocommunist orientation, remained the national, mainstream Communist party in Spain.

In October 1985, Carrillo left the PCE and founded his own party, the Revolutionary Marxist Communist Party of Spain (Partido Comunista de España Revolucionario Marxista—PCERM). Before the general elections in 1986, this organization gave way to Carrillo's newer party, the Round Table for Communist Unity (Mesa para la Unidad Comunista—MUC), which went to the polls under the name Communist Unity (Unidad Comunista—UC).

Carrillo was not the first schismatic, however. In January 1984, Ignacio Gallego had left the PCE and created the Communist Party (Partido Comunista—PC). Later renamed the Communist Party of the Peoples of Spain (Partido Comunista de los Pueblos de España—PCPE), it was an orthodox, Marxist-Leninist, pro-Soviet party, recognized by the Kremlin as the official Communist party in Spain and widely believed to receive generous funding from Moscow. Thus, Spain had three national Communist parties, in addition to regional Communist parties like the PSUC in Catalonia and the Communist parties in Andalucia and Galicia. The latter two were theoretically autonomous, with their own names and symbols, but remained electorally affiliated with the PCE, as did the "independent" PSUC.

Recognizing the electoral impotence of the individual pieces of the fractured nonsocialist Left, two of the national parties, the PCE and the PCPE, came together in April 1986 to create the United Left (Izquierda Unida—IU). This was a sociopolitical movement whose adherents would maintain their separate identities but contest the 1986 general election as a single entity. The IU presented itself as a broad-based, progressive association linking most of the major forces left of the PSOE. Carefully maintaining it was not a party, the IU also included the Socialist Action Party (Partido de Acción Socialista—PASOC); the Progressive Federation (Federación Progresista—FP); the Carlist Party (Partido Carlista—PC); and several small ecologist and anti-NATO groups. The Progressive Federation and the Carlists had curious backgrounds. The FP was the creation of Ramón Tamames, the eminent (some say the preeminent) Spanish economist who had risen to professional prominence during the later years of the Franco regime and who, after the caudillo's death, declared himself to be a Communist. The Carlists, reactionaries during the Second Republic, had been absorbed by Franco's FET y de las JONS. With the coming of democracy, the Carlists reemerged, transmogrified into a party of the Left. The third national Communist party, Santiago Carrillo's MUC, remained aloof from the IU and went to the polls alone, identified on the ballot as Communist Unity.

If the preceding exposition does not suffice to demonstrate the exotic complexity of the Spanish nonsocialist Left, a nostalgic footnote should add further spice. Shortly before the 1986 elections, still another Communist party, the pro-Soviet Spanish Worker's Party (Partido Comunista Obrero Español—PCOE) rejoined the PCE; its chief, Enrique Lister, mythic Loyalist hero of the Civil War, had abandoned the PCE when the latter, under Carrillo's leadership, distanced itself from Moscow.

In the 1986 elections, the IU won 4.6 percent of the vote and 7 seats in Congress, 3 seats more than the PCE alone won in 1982. Carrillo's party won only 1 percent of the vote and no seats in Congress.

In 1989, the still fragmented nonsocialist Left once again faced a general election. The PCE (since 1988 headed by Julio Anguita, who had succeeded Gerardo Iglesias), the PCPE, and the PASOC remained associated in the IU. Still fighting alone, Santiago Carrillo created yet another party after the MUC's 1986 debacle, the Workingmen's Party of Spain (Partido de los Trabajadores de España—PTE). In the 1989 elections, Carrillo's party proved no more attractive to the electorate than had the MUC, but the IU increased its percentage of the vote to 9.05 percent (from 4.6 percent in 1986) and won 18 seats in the Congress (up from 7 in 1986); its support came primarily from the PSOE. An analysis of the election will be given in Chapter 12.

In October 1991, Carrillo, now seventy-five years old and worn down, declared his party dissolved, absorbed into the PSOE. This was a rather stunning integration given the fact that the most severe critics of the PSOE claim it has become not merely social democratic but liberal in the classic European meaning of that word, at least in its economic policy. In a defiant self-exculpatory valedictory, Carrillo declared that with the fall of communism in Eastern Europe and the Soviet Union, Communist parties elsewhere would soon "follow the same path."

A crisis of identity had already struck the PCE, not only as it looked into itself but also as it looked at itself within the IU. The crisis was both a philosophical and an electoral dilemma. What purposes did Communist parties serve in stable, capitalist democracies following the repudiation of the ideology in its own birthplace? If they have lost their revolutionary purpose and remain simply parties of radical change offering themselves to the people as governmental alternatives, could or should the PCE continue as a separate entity when electoral success eluded it except when it was allied with other nonsocialist, leftist parties? In 1986, the IU had outperformed the PCE alone in 1982, and in 1989, the IU had dramatically bettered its own showing in 1986.

Yet it was undeniable that within the IU, the PCE was the largest and most potent contingent, and its defection from the alliance would most likely bring down the IU in its present form. Thus, the PCE was too powerful an entity to be ignored. Furthermore, the dilemma was compounded by the presence of Julio Anguita, who was not only secretary-general of the PCE but also coordinator-general of the IU. Within the PCE, a minority of the Central Committee wanted to dissolve the party and see it absorbed into the IU, which would then be converted from a sociopolitical movement into a new, single party that could be a viable choice for those on the Left who were growing weary of the ten-year incumbency of the PSOE. As in all countries, the useful vote (**voto útil**)—the vote that has a chance of winning—is an important determinant of electoral choice in Spain. The majority in the Central Committee supported Anguita, who insisted that the PCE retain its separate identity, perhaps converting the IU from a somewhat vague sociopolitical movement into a confederation of parties. But Anguita sent out seemingly conflicting signals about both the PCE and the IU. In October 1991, he declared, "All power to the IU." But then he went on to say, "First of all, the PCE should develop itself within the United Left and the United Left itself should also develop itself in every way. Apart from that, I don't really know. Nothing is eternal."[16] Anguita was, of course, also fighting to maintain his power both within the PCE and within the IU, buttressed by a tough nostalgia for the PCE that, as he said, possessed a patrimony made up of the "personal investments and sacrifices" of its militants, past and present.

A minority of members in the IU, as in the PCE, wanted the alliance to be converted into a party. They therefore formed a group within the IU that they labeled the New Left (Nueva Izquierda—NI), headed by Nicolás Sartorius. In early December 1991, Anguita, in a carefully (some say cynically) designed ploy, resigned as coordinator-general of the IU and also as the head of the parliamentary group of the IU inside the Congress. The parliamentary position was taken by Sartorius, the chief spokesman for the New Left. Thus, the potential existed for conflict within the IU both outside and inside parliament. Anguita said that he resigned in order to be "at liberty" to pursue his vision of the future of the IU, which would become a federation of autonomous parties. At the 13th Congress of the PCE in December 1991, he was reelected secretary-general, and 80 percent of the 700 delegates at the congress voted to maintain the PCE's separate identity. Five months later, at the Third Assembly of the IU in May 1992, Anguita accepted his reelection as coordinator-general, making clear that his vision about the future of the PCE and the IU had been confirmed by a majority of the delegates at the PCE congress the previous December. But though past selections of the coordinator-general had been made by acclamation, Aguita won with only the support of his militants. Approximately 60 percent of the IU supported his vision of the future for the IU, and approximately 40 percent supported Sartorius and the New Left. Thus, the fissure within the IU deepened.

In the months following the Third Assembly, Anguita consolidated his hold on the IU, removing New Left supporters from the movement's governing body and even "deauthorizing" Sartorius as the spokesman for the group. The differences between the two men moved into a bigger arena when they took opposing stands on the manner by which Spain would chose to accept or reject the Maastricht Treaty, which would further extend European unity. Anguita adamantly demanded a popular referendum, but Sartorius supported a decision by parliamentary vote. Anguita's intransigence threatened to break the IU apart. Caught by his own dependance on the existence of the IU as the host for the PCE, he backed off, temporizing.

The Spanish parliament accepted the Maastritch Treaty (Anguita and the IU outside parliament seem to have been the only major force in Spain seeking a referendum). Although the conflict between Anguita and Sartorius has since quieted, the struggle for power and the future of the IU continues.

Manuel Fraga

Alianza Popular (AP)—Coalición Popular (CP)— Partido Popular (PP)

The Popular Alliance is synonymous with Manuel Fraga Iribarne, perhaps the most complex personality in contemporary Spanish politics. Fraga was considered a liberal when he served Franco as minister of information and tourism from 1962 to 1969, and his name became a household word when he engineered the first opening up of the regime with the Press Law of 1966. He was purged from the ministry in 1969 by Franco, who insinuated that his policies to liberalize the media, including entertainment, and to attract tourists had begun to corrupt public taste and morals. In reality, Fraga was only a liberal when compared to the conservatives who made up much of the Franco establishment. After the caudillo's death, Fraga's natural conservatism came forth amid the liberalizing elite that was moving into predominance after the resignation of prime minister Arias Navarro. Many agree with British historian Raymond Carr and coauthor Juan Pablo Fusi that Fraga's hardening political stance became more pronounced after his experience as minister of the interior (in charge of the police and internal security) in the Arias governments; in that post, he was forced to deal with the violence that continued to sweep Spain.[17] Perhaps it was then that Fraga's strategy for the transition took shape, a strategy rejected when Juan Carlos chose Suárez to head the government that replaced Arias.

Fraga's plan for political change would have maintained the positive things that had come out of Francoism. After all, the unprecedented national prosperity of the 1970s had come about as a result of decisions made by the generalisimo in the early 1950s. But the Civil War and Franco were realities that had to be accepted without any wish to recapture the past, as the extreme Right proclaimed it wanted to do. Fraga intended to modify the Francoist system slowly, keeping intact its basic structure, probably including even the syndicates. This strategy differed from that of Suárez, who was using the existing Francoist laws and institutions to restructure the system totally, abiding by the letter of those laws but not by their spirit. Finally, Fraga would have closed the system permanently to certain parties and groups: the Communists, above all, but also those who sought to weaken the unity of the state, such as the regional extremists.

Fraga's program became the basis for his own political group, Democractic Reform (Reforma Democrática), which in October 1976 federated with six other rightist groups to form Alianza Popular. AP celebrated its first congress in March 1977, two months before the June elections. Its platform was right-wing, formulated by leaders who, with one exception, had all served at one time or another as ministers in Franco's cabinets. They took pride in their identification with the former regime, while maintaining that they sought no nostalgic revival and intended to play by the democratic rules of the game. This was interpreted to mean that if the AP won the elections, it would not use its power to reconstruct Francoism. However, the party's reassurance failed to convince the electorate, which gave the AP only 8.4 percent of the vote and 16 of the seats seats in the Congress in the 1977 elections.

The two sources that the party had counted on for support turned out to be far weaker than expected: the residual appeal of Franco, which party members felt was still very strong among the people, and the vote of the many functionaries to whom Franco had given employment—a veritable army of doorkeepers, building superintendents, janitors, porters, cleaning women, and lottery ticket salespeople (reserved for the handicapped) who were barely employable even in the early years of Francoism. If democracy put an end to featherbedding, many in this group would face unemployment.

The Popular Alliance held together while the constitution was being created, and Fraga's was the dominant voice from the Right on the Committee on Constitutional Affairs. At times, he raised his voice viciously against those articles in the drafts that he considered to be "red." Yet after the constitution was approved by the *Cortes*, Fraga urged AP supporters to follow his example and vote their approval in the December referendum. The reasons for this about-face (called duplicity by the party's right wing) are not fully known, but Fraga probably realized that his future in the political system that the constitution was about to usher in would be spent permanently in the backwater of the extreme Right if he did not approve the document and move toward the center.

Fraga's action provoked the departure of two of the AP's most conservative members: Gonzalo Fernández de la Mora, whose ideology was very close to that of the extreme Right (and thus close to opposing the democratic system), and Federico Silva Muñoz. This withdrawal automatically made the AP more moderate, a posture already endorsed by some younger members who spoke for a tempered and civilized Right at the party's second congress, held in January 1978. Fraga's sympathy with this more moderate, centrist position can be seen in the following remarks: "Obviously the center is one thing, and the UCD of Suárez is something else. The center includes many people, and the UCD is only a small bureaucratic machine that Suárez has set up and manipulates for his own convenience. ... With respect to the right, we are not going to speak about the right but about the center-right which is what we are and have always said we have been."[18]

In the elections of 1979, the centrist electorate stayed loyal to the UCD. The AP fared even more poorly then it had in 1977, dropping to 5.8 percent of the vote (8.4 in 1977) and 9 seats in the Congress (16 in 1977). The AP seemed to be in an irreversible decline, yet in the elections of 1982, the UCD was obliterated. The PSOE won the plurality of votes and the absolute majority of seats in the Cortes, and the AP that had appeared moribund just three years earlier emerged as the second largest party in Spain.

As a result of the 1982 elections, the AP achieved prominence by default, but it lacked the clear vision of itself that could parley that prominence into a viable alternative to the PSOE. The electorate simply did not see the party as the Center-Right, where Fraga said that it was in 1982 and always had been since its creation in 1977. Moreover, the presence of Fraga himself posed a dilemma for the future of the party—a dilemma that could not be solved as long as he was party president. Without doubt, he was the most popular politician on the Right in Spain. Because of him, the AP could count on approximately 4 to 5 million hard-core rightist voters. But also because of him, the AP could not attract voters who were closer to the center. Regardless of his positive role in the transition to democracy and in the making of the constitution, Fraga was, in the minds of uncommitted voters, too identified with the Franco regime to be an acceptable leader of the Center-Right. Furthermore, his autocratic personality did little to persuade undecided centralists that he was sufficiently flexible for the rough-and-tumble of democratic politics, despite his vaunted intelligence, acknowledged even by his political opponents.

In 1986, Fraga's behavior during the national debate on Spain's continued membership in NATO revealed a cavalier attitude toward the electorate, which he apparently thought had no memory or no mind. A passionately anticommunist cold warrior, Fraga had supported the UCD government when it negotiated Spain's membership in NATO in 1982. In March 1986, the PSOE government, fulfilling an electoral pledge, called the public to a referendum to decide whether Spain should remain in NATO. (Details of this referendum will be discussed in Chapter 12.) In an attempt to discredit the government, which was supporting continued membership in NATO, Fraga urged his supporters to abstain from voting in the referendum: The government's defeat in the referendum could likely lead to its defeat in the upcoming general elections. Was Fraga risking national security for his own party's political advantage? Did he expect the public to forget that until the national debate on the referendum, he had wholeheartedly supported Spain's membership in NATO?

This serious miscalculation of the public's gullibility contributed to the AP's poor showing in the general elections in June 1986, three months after the referendum, which kept Spain in NATO. Seeking to broaden its appeal, the AP went to the polls in an electoral coalition with other right-of-center parties. The Popular Coalition (Coalición Popular—CP) embraced the AP, the Christian democratic, Popular Democratic Party (Partido Democrático Popular—PDP), and the Liberal Party (Partido Liberal—PL). But once again, as in 1982, the PSOE swept to victory, winning 44.3 percent of the vote and an absolute majority of seats in parliament. The CP received 26.2 percent of the vote, giving the coalition 1 seat less than the AP (in alliance with the PDP) had won in 1982. The coalition had not even reached what political experts were saying was the electoral ceiling for the right wing in Spain, approximately 30 percent of the vote.

Soon after the elections, the PDP pulled out of the CP, and in the new legislature meeting for the first time on July 15, 1986, the PDP deputies joined the Grupo Mixto. To what became known as the "critical sector" (sector crítico) in the AP, Fraga was the prime cause of the party's stagnation and the coalition's erosion. Moreover, the economic elites organized in the powerful Spanish Confederation of Business Organizations (Confederación Española de Organizaciones Empresariales—CEOE) were deeply concerned that with Fraga at the head of the largest conservative political force in Spain, the AP had little chance of becoming a viable alternative to the PSOE. Although the CEOE and the AP were separate and independent organizations, the AP was the principal electoral outlet for a majority of the CEOE's member.

During the summer of 1986, the critical sector came up with a plan whereby Fraga would be finessed out of control of the AP: He would be encouraged to run for the mayoralty of Madrid. If he were successful in his electoral bid, his energies would be consumed in the task of running the capital city; if he were unsuccessful, he would be discredited as the leader of the AP and could be replaced. The strategy was a gamble for the critical sector, and it backfired. When Fraga learned of the movement against him, he retaliated in early September 1986 by summarily dismissing the most notable of the critics, Jorge Verstrynge—secretary-general of the AP, deputy in parliament, and Fraga's putative heir apparent. (Verstrynge left the party and joined the Grupo Mixto in parliament.) Fraga's subsequent behavior aptly demonstrates why the problems and fear caused by his autocratic leadership of the AP evolved. He chose as Verstynge's successor a relatively inexperienced, young, right-wing hothead. His defiantly capricious choice was a poorly calculated move to persuade potential centrist voters that the AP should become their electoral home. Fraga almost seemed to be saying, "This is my party, and I can do with it as I damn well choose." The new secretary-general, twenty-seven-year-old Alberto Ruiz Gallardón, was described in *El Pais* as a "bespeckled, every-hair-in-place, brightest-boy-in-the-class grind" (what Americans would today call a "nerd").[19] Ruiz's description of the magazine *Madriz*, an official publication of Madrid's city government, gives a nice example of his mentality: "Repugnant, pornographic filth, blasphemous in the juridical sense of the word, contrary to morals and the family."[20]

In the following month, October 1986, the Liberal Party broke away from the CP and joined the Grupo Mixto in parliament. The CP had effectively ceased to exist, leaving the AP as the sole major voice of the Right in Spain, which now more than ever needed to expand its electoral base. Yet in this period of party and coalition disarray, Fraga suddenly resigned as AP president, in December 1986. Miguel Herrero y Rodríguez de Miñón, spokesman for the AP group in parliament, was made acting president. An extraordinary congress of the party would be held in February 1987 for the express purpose of electing a new permanent president. A seasoned, nationally known politician, Herrero was expected to be chosen for the post, but the delegates to the congress bypassed him and elected, instead, thirty-five-year-old Antonio Hernández Mancha, AP president in Andalucia but virtually unknown outside the region. Neither the AP president nor the secretary-general had seats in parliament. At this juncture, not one of the historical figures of the AP was in a decisionmaking position in either the party or the parliament.

The incredible, almost naive lack of focus, compounded by inept leadership, persisted for almost two years, portending of disaster for the party in the next general election. In October 1988, Fraga began a campaign to regain the presidency of the AP, stating that in his new bid for power, he would be different: "No tengo el propósito de ser el mismo que fuí" ("I do not intend to be the same as I was").[21] His charisma, intelligence, and influence intact, Fraga "persuaded" Hernández Mancha, against his will, not to run for reelection at the next party congress in January 1989, with assurances that there would be no reprisals on Hernández's supporters should Fraga be reelected. And reelected he was, by an overwhelming 86 percent of the vote of the delegates to the congress. They also chose to rename the AP as the Popular Party (Partido Popular—PP), with the clear goal of moving the party toward the center and form a viable Center-Right alternative to the PSOE.

Fraga informed the congress that he would soon begin an orderly succession to his leadership, implying a rather short tenure as president of the PP. In July 1989, he announced that the search for a successor had begun, instituting a kind of audition whereby each of the seven vice presidents of the party would play "president for a week" under Fraga's rigorous scrutiny. In early September 1989, Fraga anointed José María Aznar, PP president of Castile-León, whose name would be placed at the head of the PP parliamentary ticket for Madrid in the upcoming general elections, thereby making Aznar the PP candidate for prime minister should the party be victorious at the polls. Fraga announced that he would continue as president of the PP until the next party congress but also let it be known that his energies in the next several months would be spent in Galicia; there, he would head the PP ticket in the regional elections for the Xunta, the governing body of Galicia. Thus, Fraga was removing himself from the national scene and giving way to Aznar, who would be the center of attention in the PP's national campaign.

In the general elections held on October 29, 1989, the PP performed in much the same way as its predecessors had in 1986 and 1982. The party received 25.83 percent of the vote (compared to 26.2 percent for the CP in 1986 and 26.6 percent for the AP/PDP in 1982) to win 106 seats in the Congress (compared to 105 in 1986 and 106 in 1982). Seven years after the election that made the AP the second party in Spain, its successor, the PP, was back where the AP had started, with an expanded electorate still elusive. In December 1989, the PP won an absolute majority in Galicia, making Fraga the new president (prime minister) of the Xunta. For the sixty-seven-year-old Fraga, it was the first elected position he had ever occupied, after twenty-five years in public life.

José María Aznar

Aznar was elected president of the PP at the party's national congress, held in Seville from March 31 to April 1, 1990. He had, however, already begun to act like the maximum leader, demonstrating a flexibility of policy that could attract the centrists so desperately needed for victory at the next general election in 1993. Earlier in March 1990, Aznar laid the groundwork for what he said would be a "normal and regular" dialogue with the Catholic hierarchy in Spain, but he also made it clear that the party was not confessional, that is, that it would not become the political voice of the Spanish church. "My mission as a politician is not to turn the party into a parish. I want the Popular Party to represent the interests of as many citizens as possible, not those of a particular group, whether the CEOE [the employers' federation] or the Church. And, another thing, if relations with this or that group should get better, I'd be delighted."[22] Aznar would not paint himself into a corner on the explosive issue of abortion, the bête noire of the Catholic episcopacy he was courting. He allowed himself room to maneuver for whatever future alliances he might forge. Although he said he was not in favor of expanding the circumstances under which abortion could legally take place, he accepted the fact that abortion was legal and would not spin his wheels seeking to have the law repealed. "I do not like abortion, but I support *that which is possible.* What we cannot do is support that which is impossible."[23]

Aznar's overtures to the church were made not only to find supporters within the religious community but also and more importantly to attract those voters who identified themselves as Christian Democrats but who no longer had a viable party for which to vote. Christian democracy had become a persuasion without a home. In December 1990, at the meeting of the Christian Democratic International held in Dublin, which he attended as an observer only and not as a delegate, Aznar went as far as he was likely to go in declaring the PP sympathetic to Christian democracy. To the congress, he said that the PP "would promote not only the ideas but also the principles and values of Christian democracy both within the political system and within Spanish society."[24]

Aznar also held out the party's hand to the liberals, both those primarily opposed to governmental interference with economic rights and those who were primarily opposed to governmental interference with civil rights. Although both wings of Spanish liberalism (and European liberalism, in general) resisted what they considered governmental encroachment, the emphasis of each wing was quite different. Aznar, in a highly adroit two-step from the statism with which Fraga and his party had been identified, sought to court those of both liberal persuasions, all of whom were without a viable party by then.

It took Aznar time to overcome the reticence of the powerful economic liberals organized in the CEOE. Their fear of Fraga's statism and his deadly electoral hand made them leery of his handpicked successor. But by late spring 1992, a delicate consensus had been reached between the PP and the CEOE regarding their opposition to the economic policy of the PSOE government. Aznar, after meeting with the directorate of CEOE in June 1992, declared that a "period of normality"[25] between the two organizations had begun, all the while stressing the independence of each group. The relationship was still tentative, however. Only three days before the meeting, the president of the CEOE, José María Cuevas, had said that his organization would not be a party to the "pursuit and destruction" of the government;[26] Aznar countered, accusing Cuevas of "a certain uncommendable political frivolity."[27] The PP office let it be known that the three million voters needed to defeat the PSOE would not be won by "blindly following big business."[28] Still, each organization needed the other if the PSOE was to be defeated in 1993, and the PP was proving to be far more attractive to the CEOE than Fraga and the AP had been.

In response to the public outcry against the spreading scourge of drugs in Spain, the PSOE government introduced a bill in 1991 that would, among other things, allow the police to enter the dwelling of a suspected drug trafficker without warrants and to apprehend and hold suspects without identifying themselves. Officially titled the Law of Citizen's Security (Ley de Seguridad Ciudadana), it is popularly called the Corcuera Law, named for the minister of the interior, José Luís Corcuera, who introduced the legislation. Aznar's response to the bill might have stunned his tough law-and-order predecessor. In the statist conservatism of the AP and Fraga (as well as in the social conservatism of the Roman Catholic Church), community rights take precedence over individual rights if the well-being of the whole is undermined by a defense of the rights of the few. Yet in an attempt to attract those liberals who resisted government interference with civil rights (like the sanctuary of one's domicile), Aznar and the PP, in a dramatic about-face from the social philosophy of AP, became the champion of those opposed to the Corcuera Law and to the party that had sponsored it. Aznar's courtship of the defenders of civil rights clarifies in retrospect his stance on abortion: Individuals who would not want the government breaking down the front door of the house would also not want the government breaking down the door of the bedroom or the door of the abortion clinic. Aznar's pragmatism was doubtlessly encouraged by the results of a poll taken by *El País* in early January 1992, which revealed that 40 percent of those polled were against the police entering a home without authorization, regardless of the rationale. Out of that 40 percent could come the numbers needed to propel the PP to victory in 1993. Aznar was already beginning to anticipate this outcome when he announced, in July 1992, that his pollsters were telling him that the PP would be within 4 percentage points of the PSOE (35 percent—PSOE, 31 percent—PP) if the elections were held at that time.[29]

In a fishing expedition designed to cast his electoral net even further and to narrow the percentage between the PP and the PSOE, Aznar bruited that, should the PP and its allies be victorious in 1993, he might be willing to cede his position as the next prime minister of Spain to Jordi Pujol, the eminent president (prime minister) of Catalonia and founder of the largest regional party in Catalonia (and in Spain), Convergence and Unity. Aznar was, in effect, telling potential regional party allies that their leaders had access to national power through cooperation with the PP. Repercussions in the PP caused Aznar to pull the net back in somewhat, but his offer revealed his relentless commitment to move the PP from its rightist orientation and make it electable in 1993.

In November 1992, Aznar announced that the next party congress would be held in February 1993, earlier than had been expected. He wanted the public to witness the PP's renewed commitment to his leadership, thereby further strengthening his hand for the upcoming general elections. His hand was already strong, however. Immediately upon assuming power in April 1990, he began to apply an iron grip on both party political leaders and party bureaucrats throughout Spain. Under his leadership, there would be new professional and operational criteria by which the provincial party bureaucracy would be judged and held accountable. Each provincial manager had to report daily by telefax to the central office in Madrid, which, in turn, controlled and coordinated the activities of all the managers. Moreover, provincial party executives were gradually brought under Aznar's authority. They were told that, in the future, their value to the party would be measured not by their capacity to win points at congresses but by their capacity to win votes in elections. Aznar's autocratic behavior soon came under attack from the national party's executive committee, which included not only the president and the general secretary but also members elected by the national congress. The committee demanded a more consensual decisionmaking process, but Aznar offered only to discuss policy on a one-to-one basis. He did not even entertain the notion of collegiality.

The treatment of Juan Hormaechea, PP president (prime minister) of Cantabria, demonstrated Aznar's determination to control the party nationwide. Hormaechea had severely criticized both Aznar and Fraga and was censured by the party for indiscipline. Supported by certain members of the Cantabrian PP, he fought back, refusing to resign or to stop his attacks. But Aznar was willing to sacrifice his party's prime ministership in Cantabria rather than tolerate what he considered Hormaechea's subversion. With the support of other members of the Cantabrian PP, Aznar cut a deal with other parties in the legislature and brought down Hormaechea with a vote of no confidence. Hormaechea was replaced by Jaime Blanco, a PSOE deputy whose party had been the essential player in the bargain with Aznar. From Aznar's point of view, it was better to have an avowed opponent in the PSOE as prime minister of Cantabria than a dissident colleague in the PP. Only party unity would produce the electoral results he envisioned for the PP. In July 1992, he boasted, "No one today can dispute the homogeneity of the PP compared to the heterogeneity of the PSOE."[30]

Today, it is apparent that Aznar has been attempting to reconstruct the center that had been occupied by the UCD before its demise in 1982–1983 and has remained vacant ever since. He is seeking to attract to the PP elements that had been a part of the UCD—Christian Democrats and Liberals—that are now persuasions without political homes. But the nature of the PP today and the nature of the UCD in its day are very different. The UCD was a unified party in name only. Even though its component parts had theoretically been dissolved when Suárez created the UCD, it was, in effect, a confederation of programmatic parties that never lost their identities. Once the task of making the constitution and of acting as midwife to the transition to democracy was finished, the leaders of the various components of the UCD reasserted their individual sovereignties; not for nothing were they called "barons." When their "king," Adolfo Suárez, resigned in 1981, his replacement, Calvo Sotelo, was more like the regent of a contested succession that a ruler in his own right, and one by one, the fractious "barons" withdrew their allegiance.

By contrast, Aznar is attempting to create a catchall party with electoral rather than programmatic goals. Its adherents are loosely held together by commitments to a less active role for government, the privatization of some (but certainly not all) state-held properties, a defense of individual civil rights (particularly attractive to potential liberal voters), and a concept of lo español ("that which is Spanish")—a notion of the integrity of Spain that also recognizes the legitimacy of the "nationalities" that make it up. The PP is the political home for most practicing Catholics (although, as we have seen, it eschews any hint of confessionalism and has sought to avoid reopening the issue of legalized abortion). By contrast, the PSOE's tolerant indifference toward religion makes practicing Catholics feel uneasy with socialist permissiveness. The PP can also be counted on to champion the state's continued subvention of private education (of which the largest part happens to be Catholic)—an issue to which potential Christian Democratic voters are particularly sensitive. The party has mended fences with the business elites who, though pleased with the PSOE's embrace of neoliberalism, are more comfortable with a party that emerges from the Right; even though it has moved toward the center, the PP is the "natural" home for the entrepreneurial class.

For Aznar, winning has become everything.

REGIONALIST PARTIES

In addition to the nationally organized parties that have been discussed, regional (also called nationalist) parties are prominent throughout Spain. In fact, in Euzkadi and Catalonia, nationalist parties dominate regional government. The PNV, the largest nationalist party in Euzkadi, won the plurality in regional elections in 1980, 1984, and 1990; in the regional election in 1986, it won second place, following the PSOE. The CiU, the largest nationalist party in Catalonia, won the plurality in the regional election in 1980 and the absolute majority in regional elections in 1984, 1988, and 1992. For all their importance regionally, however, an in-depth analysis of nationalist parties is beyond the scope of this study. Nevertheless, they must be mentioned here because many of them have seats in the Cortes, both in the Congress and in the Senate.

The following regionally organized parties have had representation in the Cortes at some time since the first postconstitutional election in 1979. The most prominent (or, in the case of HB, the most notorious) are described briefly.

1. The Basque Nationalist Party (Partido Nacionalista Vasco—PNV) was founded in 1895 by Sabino Arana. The party is conservative and Catholic, drawing support from the middle to lower middle classes, farmers, and the clergy. During its history, it has taken various positions on regional autonomy, from independence to conciliation with the central government in Madrid. In the early transition, its position was relatively accommodative with Madrid, but radical parties to its left compelled it to take a harder line so as not to be outdone by its electoral competitors. PNV won seats in Congress in 1979 (7), 1982 (8), 1986 (6), and 1989 (5).

2. The Basque Left (Euzakadiko Ezkerra—EE) was founded in 1977 by Francisco Letamendía out of several nationalist groups. It is a noncommunist party of the Left that has evolved from a radical separatist to a leftist nationalist party, committed to the profound transformation of Spanish society and state through the existing political system. It has been deeply opposed to ETA violence but equally opposed to excesses of the law enforcement agencies of the central government. EE won seats in Congress in 1979 (1), 1982 (1), 1986 (2), and 1989 (2).

3. Popular Unity (Herri Batasuna—HB) was founded in 1978. It is a coalition of Marxist and nationalist groups committed to a five-point program called Alternativa KAS. In reality, this is a challenge to the existing Spanish political system calling for self-determination for Euzkadi; the inclusion of Navarre in Euzkadi; the withdrawal of all Spanish military and police forces from Euzkadi; amnesty for all political prisoners (meaning all jailed members of ETA); and the profound socioeconomic transformation of Euzkadi. Because HB does not recognize the legitimacy of the Spanish state, its deputies from 1979 to 1989 refused to take their seats in the *Cortes;* in 1986, four of the party's candidates ran for national office while in prison and were victorious. HB won seats in Congress in 1979 (3), 1982 (2), 1986 (5), and 1989 (4).

4. Basque Solidarity (Euzko Alkartasuna—EA) was founded by Carlos Garaikoetxea after the general election in 1986, in which the PNV lost 25 percent of its seats in Congress. The new party maintained that it offered a nationalist, progressive alternative to the PNV (from which it had defected), the EE, and HB. Garaikoetxea, former prime minister (*lendakari*) of Euzkadi, had been the spokesman for the critical sector of the PNV, opposed both to the leadership of the former *lendakari*, Xabier Arzallus, and to the stance of the PNV in regard to Basque autonomy. EA described il-

Jordi Pujol

self as profoundly nationalist; *sabiniana* (that is, faithful to the politics of the founder of the PNV, Sabino Arana); progressive (more to the left of PNV but not as far left as EE); and democratic, calling (as does HB) for self-determination by the Basque people. EA won seats in Congress in 1989 (2).

5. Convergence and Union (Convergencia i Unió—CiU), founded in 1974 by Jordi Pujol, is the largest nationalist party in Catalonia (and in Spain). It is considered to be the spiritual successor of the first regionalist party in Catalonia—the Catalan Regionalist League (Lliga Regionalista Catalana), founded in 1901 by a group of Catalan industrialists, businessmen, financiers, and lawyers. CiU is modern, progressive, and supportive of free enterprise. In power—as it has been at the regional level, either in coalition from 1980 to 1984 or alone with an absolute majority since 1984—it has produced efficient government. Because there is no radical nationalist party to its left and because there have been no rebellions from within,

it has been able, with both grace and toughness, to champion and expand Catalan autonomy, all the while maintaining good working relations with the government in Madrid. It appeals to a broad electorate spread across the center, including many non-Catalans who have gone to work in Catalonia from other regions in Spain. CiU won seats in Congress in 1979 (8), 1982 (12), 1986 (18), and 1989 (18).

6. The remaining nationalist parties in the Cortes, past and present, are:

- The Aragonese Regional Party (Partido Aragonés Regionalista— PAR), which won seats in Congress in 1979 (1), 1986 (1), and 1989 (1).
- The Galician Coalition (Coalición Gallega—CG), which won seats in Congress in 1986 (1) and 1989 (1).
- The Valencian Union (Unión Valenciana—UV), which won seats in Congress in 1986 (1) and 1989 (2).
- The Canary Independence Association (Agrupación Independiente Canaria—AIC), which won seats in Congress in 1986 (1) and 1989 (1).
- The Union of the Canary People (Unión del Pueblo Canario— UPC), which won 1 seat in Congress in 1979.
- The Andalucian Party (Partido Andaluz—PA), which won 2 seats in Congress in 1982.
- The Republican Left of Catalonia (Esquerra Republicana de Catalunya—ERC), which won seats in Congress in 1979 (1) and 1982 (1).

Nationally organized parties dominate the politics of all the Autonomous Communities except Euzkadi and Catalonia, two of the three "historical communities" and the richest regions in Spain. But in Euzkadi, regionalist sentiments are so divided among contending the regionalist parties that the PSOE, the strongest national party in Euzkadi, wins sufficient votes to make coalition with the Socialists a necessity in the regional parliament. Under normal circumstances, the PNV, the largest Basque party, and the PSOE would make strange bedfellows: The former draws its support from the bourgeoisie and from practicing Catholics, whereas the latter is supported by the working classes. Together, the several regionalist parties would have sufficient seats in the Basque legislature to exclude the PSOE from government. But local parties are too mutually antagonistic to work with each other, separated primarily over their attitudes toward autonomy and their willingness to cooperate with Madrid. Although several Basque parties are strong enough to elect deputies to the *Cortes* in Madrid, their divisiveness fragments Euzkadi's voice at the national level. In fact, Basque regionalist groups and parties cannot put aside differences long enough even to celebrate the sacred regional holiday, *Alberri Eguna* (in Spanish, *Dia de la Patria Vasca,* or Basque Homeland Day). In 1988, to use but one example, the following discordant groups were heard at the official ceremony held beneath the historic Gernika oak: Partido Nacionalista Vasco, Herri Batasuna, Euzkadiko Ezkerra, Euzko Alkatasuna, Euzkal Batasuna, and Ezker Mugimendu Albertzalea.

By contrast, Catalan regionalist sentiment is expressed overwhelmingly in the CiU, which has had an absolute majority in the Catalan parliament since 1986. The party is a major contender in national politics as well, and the absence of any prominent conflicting Catalan voice gives the region a powerful presence in the *Cortes* in Madrid.

Surprisingly, meaningful regionalist sentiment failed to materialize in Galicia. The major political voice in this poor and religious third "historical community" is the PP, at both the regional and national levels.

By contrast, the absence of a significant regional voice in Andalucia is not surprising. The region is not one of the "historical communities," and its self-identity, though strong, never manifested itself in separatist or even autonomous sentiments. The people's desire to be treated as equals in the process of autonomy after 1978 prompted them to make Andalucia a separate region, but if Euzkadi, Catalonia, and Galicia had not demanded special treatment, it is unlikely that Andalucia would have sought autonomy on its own. In both regional and national politics, the overwhelming voice of Andalucia is the PSOE. In fact, poor but developing Andalucia is the very heartland of Socialist strength.

NOTES

1. Fundación Foessa, *Informe sociológico sobre el cambio político en España, 1975–1981* (Madrid: Editorial Euramérica, S.A., 1981), p. 343.

2. José Maravall, *The Transition to Democracy in Spain* (London: Croom Helm, 1982), p. 64.

3. Luis García San Miguel, "Las ideologiás políticas en la España actual," *Sistema* 40 (January 1981), p. 64.

4. Luis García San Miguel, *Teoría de la transición* (Madrid: Editora Nacional, 1981), p. 141.

5. Ibid., p. 118

6. Richard Gunther, "The Parties in Oppositon," in Stanley Payne, ed., *The Politics of Democratic Spain* (Chicago: Chicago Council on Foreign Relations, 1986), pp. 60–61.

7. *Resoluciones del Congreso del PSOE de 1976,* Madrid, 1977 (folleto del Partido).

8. Ibid.

9. Santos Juliá, "The Ideological Conversion of the Leaders of the PSOE," in Frances Lannon and Paul Preston, eds., *Elites and Power in Twentieth-Century Spain* (Oxford: Clarendon Press, 1990), chapter 14.

10. Richard Gillespie, *The Spanish Socialist Party: A History of Fractionalism* (Oxford: Clarendon Press, 1989), p. 346.

11. Gunther, "The Parties in Opposition," p. 20.

12. Antonio Bar, "El sistema de partidos en España: Ensayo de caracterización," *Sistema* 47 (March 1982), p. 24.

13. Gillespie, *The Spanish Socialist Party*, pp. 363–364.

14. *New York Times*, July 7, 1976.

15. *Cambio 16*, April 2, 1978.

16. *El Pais*, International Edition, October 7, 1991.

17. Raymond Carr and Juan Pablo Fusi, *Spain: Dictatorship to Democracy*, 2d ed. (London: George Allen and Unwin, 1981), pp. 212–213.

18. *Cambio 16*, February 26, 1978.

19. *El Pais*, International Edition, September 8, 1986.

20. Ibid.

21. Ibid., International Edition, October 31, 1988.

22. Ibid., International Edition, March 12, 1990.

23. Ibid.

24. Ibid., International Edition, November 17, 1990.

25. Ibid., International Edition, June 15, 1992.

26. Ibid.

27. Ibid.

28. Ibid.

29. Ibid., International Edition, July 13, 1992.

30. Ibid.

9

Violence and Terrorism

Violence continues to haunt Spanish democracy. Indeed, according to a poll taken in 1992, it was the people's most compelling public concern. Left-wing violence erupted in the latter days of the Franco regime, designed to help destroy the dictatorship. But violence did not wither away after the regime's demise. The terrorists' goal then became the destruction of democracy, which they believe is the facade of the illegitimate Spanish state. ETA, the most notorious of the leftist terrorist groups, calls the existing government "the military government" (*"el gobierno militar"*), as if it were an alien, occupying force within the Spanish territory. For these terrorists, true democracy would free the many Spanish nations, each of which would then create its own state.

Also on the Left is the smaller, less known, but equally vicious First of October Anti-Fascist Resistance Group (known by its acronym, GRAPO). In December 1982, the last of its original members not in captivity was gunned down by the police in Barcelona. The organization was then thought to be dead, but it had died before and, like the phoenix, risen again. In 1988, it resurfaced, announcing its arrival by a killing in Galicia in May and more killings the same month in Galicia and Asturias. In 1989, attacks in Valencia and Madrid were attributed to GRAPO, and in September 1990 in Madrid, it planted bombs in the stock exchange, the ministry of economy, and the Constitutional Court building. Two months later, the group struck again, exploding bombs in the ministry of the treasury. Its profile has been lower as of late, but the organization might well still exist.

For the terrorists on the Right, democracy was also an abomination because it stood in the way of the return to the authentic Spain, as personified in Franco. With myopic vision, the right-wing terrorists saw a deep nostalgia among the people for a Spain that they considered to have been perverted by democracy. For these terrorists, the last words of Franco, made public at his death, still ring with full resonance: "Do not forget that the enemies of Spain and of Christian civilization are watching, and you should lay aside all personal gain in favor of the goals and interests of our homeland and of the Spanish people. Continue striving to obtain social justice and education of all Spaniards and make use of the rich multiplicity of its regions as a fountain of strength for a continued united Spain."[1]

Right-wing terrorism reached its apogee with the abortive military coup d'état on February 23, 1981. Some dozen or more nonmilitary groups, most quite small, existed in the late 1970s and early 1980s, but they have apparently now disappeared. The most violent was the Youth Front (Frente de la Juventud), made up of about 150 activists. The founders had split away from the New Force (Fuerza Nueva), the right-wing party of Blas Piñar, which won no seats in the 1982 elections and has since disbanded. The most chilling fact about the Youth Front (if one can compare degrees of cold-bloodedness) was the age of many of its soldiers: "Of the forty-two youngsters who joined the Nazi organization in the first three months of 1982, two were under fourteen years of age, fourteen had not yet turned fifteen, and ten were about to celebrate their sixteenth birthday."[2] Without doubt, the most exotically named group on the Right was the Guerrilla Fighters of Christ the King, the Guerrilleros de Cristo Rey (whose motto could easily have been "Kill a Commie for Christ").

The guerrillas saw themselves as God's militant laymen and laywomen, and a number of clergy were among the ranks of the terrorists. It is estimated that approximately 3 percent of Basque priests were sympathizers or supporters of ETA.[3] Most did not carry arms or directly take part in the violence, but many were certainly accomplices to mayhem, murder, and kidnapping. The pro-ETA clergy aided the terrorists by maintaining hideouts and places of refuge, furnishing locations for arsenals, and lending monasteries, convents, sacristies, and churches for clandestine meetings. They propagandized at public religious ceremonies, such as weddings and funerals. Some, however, gave up the cassock to wear the wardrobe of militant ETA soldiers, and of these, a few were arrested—one for killing a retired civil guardsman. The most notorious of all the outlaw priests was Eustaquio Mendizábal, who was shot and killed by the police in 1973.

The Basques are the most religious people in Spain, and their region produces a larger number of priests per capita than any other in the country. In 1979, non-Basque Spain produced 3.2 priests per 1,000 inhabitants; in Euzkadi, the percentage was 5.2, and in Navarre 7.1. Among these devout men, however, were some who (like the Guerrillas for Christ the King on the Right) also killed for God. They rationalized their conversion to bloodshed by declaring that there is a state of war between Euzkadi and the rest of Spain. They believed that they were not helping ETA but were, instead, aiding an occupied people, just as the members of the underground in Europe during World War II helped their fellow citizens against the Nazis. In their own minds, the Basque priests who placed their faith in ETA were not monsters but heroes.

The past tense is used in the preceding sentences because the profile of the Basque clergy involved with terrorism is lower today than it was in the 1970s and the early 1980s. But as late as 1987, Juan Carlos, in his traditional televised Christmas Eve message, lamented the deaths of those brought down by terrorists and condemned those who take part in violence in whatever capacity: "We must show neither weakness nor fear nor doubt in rejecting with conviction those who spill the blood of Spaniards in their criminal attacks and those who aid, excuse, or justify them irrespective of their political, social, or religious position."[4]

Less than two weeks earlier, the Basque bishops had issued a pastoral letter entitled "Dialogue and Negotiation for Peace" ("Diálogo y negociácion por la paz"); this was only two days after an ETA attack in Zaragoza that left eleven people dead. The bishops condemned the violence but supported political demands espoused by ETA and Herri Batasuna, calling for the right of each people to self-determination. This right translates for the Basques as the right to secede from Spain by ballot; this would be equivalent to the people of Texas or Louisiana or Maine having a right to withdraw from the United States if they so voted. Such a vote is unconstitutional in Spain, and to support it is to trifle with the very existence of the Spanish nation-state. The bishops also asked both the Spanish government and ETA terrorists to make concessions in order to bring about peace. An editorial in *El País* sums up the moral ambiguity of the Basque bishops: "We are asked to accept as something natural that the legitimate democratic institutions make concessions to the requirements of those who demand 'a political price'—in the words of the bishops—before the killing stops."[5]

ETA began as a single organization, but it split into ETA-militar, (military), which is totally committed to revolution, violence, and bloodshed, and ETA-políticomilitar (political-military), which is more moderate and more willing to negotiate and take part in the political process but still prepared to kill for its cause. ETA has said that it originally resorted to violence because it was the only way to be heard by Franco, who had turned deaf ears to the supplications and demands of the Basque people. Many observers believed that once Franco was dead, the unfortunate plight of the Basques (and of other repressed Spanish peoples, such as the Catalans and the Galicians) would at last be alleviated. Hope for a peaceful solution increased when the men who guided the transition to democracy, in particular Juan Carlos and Adolfo Suárez, acknowledged the legitimacy of regionalist claims. Autonomy began to be actualized first through preautonomy decrees issued by the monarch, then through provisions for autonomy written into the constitution, and finally through the creation of regional legislatures and governments by elections that took place beginning in the spring of 1980. The violence of ETA did not subside, however. On the contrary, terrorism increased, particularly on the eve of elections, referenda, and the formation of new governments.[6] Through bloodshed, ETA revealed its opposition to any political process that took place under the auspices of the national government and that would legitimize the Spanish state. It became apparent that ETA, in particular ETA-militar, would settle for nothing short of independence for Euzkadi, followed by a Marxist revolution within the new state.

In the beginning, ETA had aimed its violence primarily at the hated symbols of Spanish national sovereignty: the police, the army, and, above all, the Civil Guard that patrols the provinces. But as its campaign grew more fanatical, more ambitious, and more costly, ETA unleashed violence against fellow Basques. Sophisticated modern weaponry purchased in the international black market of arms and munitions is enormously expensive, and money had to be found. Thus, kidnappings for ransom, especially of Basque industrialists and entrepreneurs, reached epidemic proportions. Extortion became even more widespread, amounting to nothing less than protection money wrenched from ordinary citizens. Initially, the major sources of the "revolutionary tax" (*impuesto revolucionario*), as the money is called by the terrorists, were doctors and other professionals who earned large incomes.[7] But as time went on and expenses increased, the "tax collectors" began to hit humble folk as well, particularly small shopkeepers and bar and café owners—people dependent upon the public for their livelihoods.[8] Those who refused to donate to the cause of revolution ran the risk of having their businesses boycotted, having their premises destroyed or damaged, or even losing their lives. Eventually, ETA terrorists expanded their extortion targets from individuals to large commercial enterprises, especially banks.[9] In April 1982, for example, directors of the banks of Vizcaya, Santander, Hispano-Americano, and Guipuzcoana received letters from ETA-militar demanding a total of 1,000 million pesetas. Banks that refused to come up with the money risked being bombed.

Panic was spread among the rest of the Basque population when anyone who had contact with the police was labeled a *chivato* ("stool pigeon"), thus frightening away even those citizens who had legitimate complaints unassociated with terrorism. Law enforcement and the judicial process were thereby undermined, and the entire social, economic, and political infrastructure of the system was gradually eroded in the Basque provinces. Professionals such as doctors and lawyers left the region. Owners abandoned their houses, particularly those located in the remote countryside. Businesses closed their doors, and foreign investment began to dry up. Tourism had already died in parts of Euzkadi, and it is now seriously hurt throughout Spain. ETA has bombed department stores, hotels, restaurants, supermarkets, clinics—anyplace where people gather. Resorts that cater to tourists have been favorite targets. The terrorists hope that violence will destroy the tourist industry, Spain's most important source of revenue and foreign exchange. In 1992, ETA announced that it would make the World's Fair in Seville and the Olympic Games in Barcelona principal targets (although the events passed with no incidents).

The vast majority of the Basque people abhor the violence. Moreover, the Marxist revolution sought by ETA extremists would destroy the capitalist economy of the Basque region; along with Catalonia, it is the richest region in Spain, and most of the citizens are comfortably bourgeois. Yet the Basque people were caught in a terrible dilemma. Fear prevented most of them from acting against ETA, and a crisis of conscience prevented the rest from condemning ETA outright. At the beginning, the members of ETA were willing to risk their lives to defend the Basque language, culture, and ancient *fueros.* ETA militants were heroes who then turned into criminals. Some people called ETA the Basque mafia, but the Basque people cannot forget what the group once stood for or what it was once willing to die for. Perhaps the words of Marenchu Echeverría best expressed the inner conflict. Echeverría was the deputy mayor of Tolosa in the province of Guipúzcoa and the daughter of a Loyalist who fled to exile during the Civil War and finally returned to Spain in 1977. She herself had been active in creating the *ikastolas,* the underground schools designed to keep the Basque language and Basque nationalism alive during the Franco regime. The schools now operate openly and are demanding their share of public funding from the national government. "We will have to go after them [ETA] with our own police force, and I'll be in favor of jailing and bringing them to trial. ... But I could never bring myself to inform on them, not now, not ever, not for any amount of money. It just isn't something I could do after all these years."[10]

The moral dilemma gradually began to abate as the Basques finally became sickened with the wanton violence ostensibly done in their behalf. In the first ten years of democracy (1977–1987), ETA killed 475 people, and the numbers have continued to mount to this day.[11] Relentless but unpredictable attacks have kept the nation on tenterhooks: a soldier here, a civil guardsman there, a policeman somewhere else. From time to time, the assassins struck the uppermost military hierarchy—an eighty-one-year-old general and a vice admiral, Cristóbal Colón (the Spanish translation of Christopher Columbus). The admiral—a direct descendant of the great explorer, one of the mythic heroes of Spain—was the highest-ranking naval officer assassinated since Carrero Blanco. His killing carried enormous symbolic weight. ETA terrorists even reached into the entourage of the king and queen: In 1987, a bomb was planted in the hotel housing the royal couple's bodyguards at a ski resort in the Pyrenees. The assassins seemed to be saying, "No matter who you are or where you are, we are there." Sometimes, a single person was killed; often, it was two or more. And frequently, an innocent bystander would be added to the body count. In an attack in 1986, ten civil guardsman were killed in Madrid, and in another attack in Zaragoza in 1987, five girls, two women, and four more guardsmen were blown to pieces. In 1991, the two-year-old son of a civil guardsman was killed by a car bomb. Since 1978, ETA has killed twenty-one children and adolescents, not as direct targets but as incidental victims of attacks on others. But the terrorists have remained remorseless: "The life of one terrorist is worth five times the life of the child of some *txakurra* (a disparaging term for policeman in the Basque language)."[12]

Attempts on the part of the government to reach some agreement with ETA proved futile. The government long denied that it had any contact with the organization other than the publicly made offer to allow ETA members to come in from the cold to return home and be accepted into Spanish society—reinsertion (*reinserción*), as the policy is called. ETA, however, equated an acceptance of reinsertion by any of its members or ex-members as treason. The most notorious act of retribution was the execution of María Dolores González Cataráin, a former ETA leader who wanted to leave the netherworld of violence. Known by her nom de guerre, "Yoyes" (all ETA militants have underground names), she was called a "traitor to the Basque people" and an "accomplice" of the Spanish authorities.

> ETA—Revolutionary Socialist Basque Organization of National Liberation—assumes responsibility for the execution of María Dolores González Cataráin (Yoyes), collaborator with the repressive plans of the oppressive Spanish state and traitor to the process of national liberation that the Basque Working People are bringing about. The treason must be measured by the Basque people as a function of her collaboration, both in politics and in law enforcement, with the genocidal plans which the forces of occupation of the oppressive Spanish state have worked out for the Basque people.[13]

In 1987, the government finally admitted that there had been sporadic contacts in Algeria between its representatives and those of ETA, but González denied that any negotiation had taken place. Nothing came from these and subsequent meetings, but given the reasoning of the terrorists, nothing could logically be expected. Violence, which had begun as a means to an end, had become an end in itself. Peace, *as defined by ETA*, could only come out of violence; any nonviolent negotiation could not, therefore, produce peace. Negotiations could produce compromise, but compromise was incompatible with peace. ETA would accept only unconditional surrender by the Spanish government to the demands of the organization.

The organization that would not bend had to be broken, for no sovereign democratic state can allow a minority to dictate terms to the majority. But breaking ETA would be enormously difficult. The sentiments of the Basque people first had to harden against what had initially been considered a heroic organization. Once this transformation had begun, ETA then had to be pursued, but the terrorists had eluded Spanish law enforcement agencies by fleeing to France. In the early years of ETA's existence, France had considered the militants to be political refugees and refused to hunt down ETA members on French territory. Indeed, France has historically offered itself as a haven to foreign political activists pursued by repressive regimes. But even after Spain became a democracy and ETA continued its violence, France persisted in declaring that ETA was an organization worthy of protection, rejecting Spain's contention that its members were common criminals who deserved extradition.

Only after the Socialists came to power in France (1981) and in Spain (1982) did France reappraise its policy and offer to cooperate with Spain in the capture and extradition of ETA members. When the conservatives gained control of the French legislature in 1986, the new prime minister, Jacques Chirac, reaffirmed France's commitment to Spain. With ever-increasing intensity, France searched out and captured ETA terrorists, moving closer and closer to the *Artapalo*, the generic name for the leadership. Domingo Iturbe ("Txomin") was taken in 1986; in 1987, Santiago Arrospide ("Santi Potros"); and in 1989, José Antonio Urrutikoetxea Berrgoetxea ("Josu Ternera"), the most important of *Artapalo* yet taken. After Ternera's capture, leadership moved to Francisco Múgica Garmendia ("Pakito") and José Javier Zabaleta Elósegui ("Waldo"). In September 1990, Waldo was detained by the French police. Pakito was then joined in the *Artapalo* by José Mariá Arregui Erostabe ("Fittipaldi") and José Luis Alvarez Santacristina ("Txelis"). All three were captured on March 19, 1992, in Bidart, a town not far from Bayonne, causing the most serious blow to ETA since its birth. In June 1992, the French police detained Iñaki Bilbao, considered to be Pakito's successor. If the backbone of ETA has not been broken, it has suffered such crippling injury that it might not survive. It is ironic that these almost faceless men and women with exotic nicknames have kept an entire country in trauma for half a generation and have had an impact on public life virtually equal to that of the legitimate authorities.

When and if ETA no longer exists, perhaps another mysterious terrorist organization will also disappear—the Anti-Terrorist Liberation Group (Grupo Anti-terrorista de Liberación—GAL). Since its targets are left-wing terrorists, it would probably have to be called a right-wing group, but it does not seek to restore the dictatorship. It acts more as an avenger for the military and police personnel killed by GRAPO and ETA. Many contend that the organization is made up of rogue law enforcement officials who have adopted the techniques of their opponents. In 1986, French television reported that GAL had, in fact, been created by high-ranking officials in the Spanish Interior Ministry, and allegations were later made that the ministry failed to investigate GAL even after it knew of police involvement with the group. In July 1988, after weeks of investigation, charges, and countercharges, a judicial inquiry found that funds from the Interior Ministry had been secretly diverted to GAL. The minister of the interior, José Barrionuevo, vehemently denied the accusation, and González supported his denial. In the same year, two police officials were imprisoned for having helped organize GAL.

NOTES

1. *New York Times,* November 21, 1975.
2. *Cambio 16,* August 30, 1982, p. 15.
3. Ibid., June 20, 1983, pp. 20–26.
4. *El Pais,* International Edition, December 28, 1987.
5. Ibid., December 21, 1987.
6. Spanish newspapers chronicle this escalation of terrorism with increasing desperation and frustration. They articulate what the public is less able to express: When will the killings stop? Scarcely a month passes without another anguished headline, another anguished article describing the wanton violence.
7. *Cambio 16,* January 17, 1983, p. 15.
8. Ibid., August 2, 1982, pp. 16–20.
9. Ibid., February 14, 1983, pp. 16–21.
10. *International Herald Tribune,* August 6, 1979, p. 2.
11. *El Pais,* International Edition, January 19, 1987.
12. Ibid., March 2, 1992.
13. Ibid., September 15, 1989.

Part Four
The Socioeconomic Context

10

The Economy

Until the 1960s, Spain was a poor country with 48 percent of its population living from agriculture, often at the subsistence level. The transformation of the country's economy in the past quarter century from penury to prosperity and from agriculture to industry was nothing short of phenomenal, and the Spanish "miracle" joined the Italian and German "miracles" as some of the major Western European economic events of the post–World War II era. Then suddenly, the Spanish "miracle" went awry. The threat to the Spanish economy was catalyzed by the action of the oil-producing cartel in the mid-1970s, but it was exacerbated in Spain by conditions of the country's own making.

THE TRADITION OF AUTARKY

A brief digression is necessary to put the situation into historical perspective. The Industrial Revolution did not reach Spain until the 1960s. There had been large-scale manufacturing in Spain since the last century, and certain areas of the country were even then classified as industrial: Catalonia with textiles and the Basque provinces with heavy industry (in part fueled by coal from Asturias). But the rest of the country was agricultural, the land worked primarily by a depressed peasantry. The largest commercial farmers were the aristocratic absentee wheat growers of Castile, who, together with the Basque and Catalan industrial elite, successfully pressured the state to protect their interests with tariffs that were the highest in Europe by the early twentieth century. Import duties kept out not only the goods and services that might have competed against those of the protected Spanish oligarchy but also the technology and mentality that might have transformed the essentially conservative, provincial Malthusian Spanish society into a modern, progressive one.[1] Spain became a tight little island effectively cut off from the rest of the developing Western world. There was some foreign investment in Spain (primarily in railroads, public utilities, and mining), but the Spanish laws that allowed foreign investors to bring money into Spain also allowed them to take out

233

profits earned within the country. They were not compelled to reinvest in the Spanish economy; instead, they were compelled to purchase domestic products, thereby entrenching protectionism and enriching the Spanish elite. By contrast, the Spanish masses profited very little from foreign investors. These investors seemed like state-sponsored carpetbaggers allowed into the country to reap their profits from essential services that the Spanish elite could not or would not supply; then they were ushered out of the country as if their presence would contaminate Spanish life. Isolation and self-sufficiency—a kind of spiritual and material autarky— seemed to be the ideal of those who ruled Spain, even if the price of national aloofness was a retrograde society.

Isolation by Choice

During the regime of Primo de Rivera, the Spanish state began to play a larger role in the pursuit of autarky. The government took over sectors formerly developed by foreign entrepreneurs, particularly investing in essential infrastructural development. This should not, however, be interpreted as an indication of a sudden concern for the welfare of the Spanish masses. The state was the public face of Spain's ruling elite, and the decision to move into large-scale public enterprise reflected the oligarchy's desire to use public moneys to finance activity too risky for private capital. Primo initiated an ambitious program of public works: road building, river navigation projects, irrigation, and land reclamation. He set up semiofficial banks to encourage investment in projects considered to be in the national interest. He created the Regulatory Company of Petroleum Monopoly (Compañía Arrendataria del Monopolio de Petróleos—CAMPSA) as a state concession to regulate the petroleum industry and to put into the national coffers the profits that had been going to foreign investors. Under Primo, the state also became the majority stockholder of what later would be named Iberia, an international airline originally created by amalgamating several smaller firms.

Given a ruling elite that included both the industrial oligarchy of Catalonia and the Basque provinces and the landed aristocracy of Andalucia and Castile, it is not surprising that in his urge to transform Spain, Primo left the anachronistic system of land tenure untouched. The *minifundio* was the small landholding typical of northern Spain (with the exception of certain regions of Aragon, Catalonia, and the province of Salamanca); at its most extreme, in Galicia, holdings of less 20 hectares (49.4 acres) were common. This acreage was often fragmented into a dozen noncontiguous pieces, requiring the farmers to move from plot to plot scattered about the countryside and making the use of modern machinery and technology almost impossible. Even rich soil did not yield at maximum productivity.

The *latifundio* was the large, often giant-sized holding characteristic of southern Spain—particularly Andalucia, Extremadura, and La Mancha, where holdings of 500 hectares (1,235 acres) per family was not uncommon, and where the duke of Medinaceli, for example, owned 30,906 hectares (76,338 acres). Most *latifundios* included large portions of grazing land unsuitable for farming. But even where the soil was rich and could be used for crops, it was often farmed at less than maximum capacity. Although the land lent itself to the techniques of large-scale production, the owners were only interested in producing enough to secure a lifestyle of elegance and leisure. And ironically, profits were spent in Seville or Madrid or Paris or London, not on the land. Land redistribution that might have allowed more families to own and till the land or a national agricultural policy that might have required the land to be used more productively were totally unacceptable alternatives to the landed gentry. And that gentry was one of the pillars of Primo's support at the beginning of the dictatorship.

During the short-lived Second Republic, little was done to change the basic structure of the Spanish economy. Whether the Republic might have accomplished more if its political forces had not spent their time tearing at one another is a moot question. During the Red Biennium (the period of leftist government from December 9, 1931, to December 31, 1933), laws designed to redistribute land were passed, but the program had barely gotten off the ground when the government of the Black Biennium (the period of rightist government from December 31, 1933, to February 16, 1936) reversed the process. The Civil War broke out too soon after the Popular Front came into power for its land reform policies to be carried out.

The Civil War devastated Spain, and the economy was still in tatters twenty years later when the Stabilization Plan was inaugurated in 1959. Gabriel Jackson estimates that 580,000 people died as a direct result of the war;[2] Hugh Thomas puts the figure at 600,000.[3] Ramón Tamames, the Spanish economist, goes further than either Jackson or Thomas in his appraisal of the total human and material cost of the war.[4] He estimates that during the last months of hostilities and immediately afterward, approximately 300,000 men and women fled into exile, most of them in their prime and many of them skilled and educated. Comparing prewar to postwar demographic statistics, Tamames deduces that during the conflict, the population fell another 500,000, more or less, because of the decline in the birthrate. He further calculates that 875,000 productive worker-years were lost in prison. To this incredible human loss he adds the material devastation: (1) the equivalent of $575 million worth of gold spent by the republicans to finance the war; (2) the complete destruction of 250,000 dwellings and the partial destruction of 250,000 more, out of a national total of approximately 6 million; (3) over 192 towns and cities more than 60 percent destroyed; (4) approximately 50 percent of all railway rolling stock and 30 percent of all merchant ships destroyed; (5) 34.2 percent of cattle, 32.7 percent of sheep and goats, and 50.4 percent of pigs dead; and (6) industrial production down approximately 31 percent, gross national income down approximately 25.7 percent, and per capita income down approximately 28.3 percent.

Isolation by Necessity

After World War II was over and Spain and the rest of Western Europe were ready to rebuild, the Franco regime was ostracized by the victorious Allies; refused admittance to the international political, social, and economic organizations that were being created; and ignored by the United States, whose largesse in the form of Marshall Plan aid put many European economies on their feet again. Franco embraced autarky because he had no other alternative, but in doing so, he followed a Spanish tradition that was already half a century old.

At the beginning, Franco doubtless believed that his economic policy would be successful. Spain had survived in the past and would survive again. When, for example, the world depression came after 1929, Spain suffered less than most countries because of its isolation from the main currents of international trade and finance. Franco's economic policies were similar to those pursued by the leadership in prerepublican Spain, so he was on relatively familiar ground. He also felt confident in his own economic decisionmaking. He regulated domestic production, exports, and imports and subjected the latter to rigid licensing; he applied currency restrictions and adopted fluctuating exchange rates dependent upon the nature of the buyer and seller; he rationed consumer goods and fixed prices. He resorted to protectionism for certain economic activities and put the state into the business of postwar reconstruction, for which private capital was either insufficient or unavailable.

Under Franco, the National Institute of Land Development (Instituto Nacional de Colonización—INC) replaced the Institute of Agrarian Reform (Instituto de Reforma Agraria—IRA) that had been created during the Red Biennium to oversee land redistribution. The INC was empowered to increase the area of cultivatable land—though not by expropriation—in order to feed a hungry nation. Eventually, the INC became the single largest landowner in Spain. Its role was to turn over to private ownership land acquired by the state. The breakup of the large estates, known as *latifundios,* made even less sense in postwar Spain than it had during the Republic, when political demands for land reform often ran counter to rational economic policy. If maximum agricultural output was the objective in postwar Spain, then large-scale farming was essential. The realities of economics and politics merged neatly here; the sanctity of private property was one of the pillars of Franco's belief system, and large landowners made up one of the pillars of the Franco regime. The Land Parcel Consolidation Service (Servicio de Concentración Parcelaria—SCP) was formed to help consolidate the tiny, separate holdings of the *minifundios* and thereby increase production by the use of machinery. The National Wheat Service (Servicio Nacional de Trigo—SNT) came into being to regularize the distribution of wheat and, incidentally, to protect the pro-Franco wheat growers from the vicissitudes of the market; the SNT was given exclusive power to buy wheat from the primary producers and could thus artificially determine what the going price of grain would be.

The state moved into industry through two public sector entities: the National Institute of Industry (Instituto Nacional de Industria—INI) and the General Directorate of State Assets (Dirección General del Patrimonio del Estado—DGPE). Both were originally conceived to supplement private investment in areas of particular national interest (armaments, for example) or in which an essential economic function might be insufficiently attractive to private capital. The INI was and is a state holding company owning shares in a number of incorporated Spanish entities, that is, corporations called Anonymous Societies (Sociedades Anónimas—SA). Through the DGPE the state directly holds shares in Spanish companies (unlike the indirect holdings in the INI.

By the mid-1980s, the state had shares in some 60-odd companies, which, in turn, controlled some 150-odd subsidiaries. Among the best known are the National Steel Enterprise (Empresa Nacional Siderúrgica, SA–ENSIDESA), of which the state holds 97.5 percent of the shares; the National Northern Coal Mining Enterprise (Empresa Nacional Hulleras del Norte, SA–HUNOSA), with 100 percent of the shares; the National Electrical Enterprise (Empresa Nacional de Eletricidad, SA–ENDESA), with 97.3 percent; Spanish Shipyards (Astilleros Españoles, SA–AESA), with 100 percent; Spanish Society of Touring Cars, (i.e., family cars) (Automóviles de Turismo, SA–SEAT), with 94.8 percent; and Spanish Airlines (Líneas Aéreas de España, SA–Iberia), with 99.5 percent. In addition, there are companies involved in food processing, ball bearings, fertilizers, sea and air transport, electronic and data processing, aluminum, and armaments and munitions, as well as various regional development corporations.[5]

By the mid-1980s, the state directly held shares in some 20-odd Spanish companies, of which the best known are the Spanish Export Bank (Banco Exterior de España), with the state owning 51.4 percent of the shares; Tobacco Enterprises (Tabacalera, SA), with 53.5 percent; and the National Telephone Company of Spain (Telefónica, SA) with 31.5 percent. In addition, the state directly owns shares in Spanish companies dealing in banking, agriculture, textiles, footwear, shipping, news gathering, film making, tunnel building, salt, and mercury.[6]

Under the sponsorship of the DGPE were the Iberian Petroleum Refining Company (Compañía Ibérica Refinadora de Petróleos, SA–Petroliber), which controls the refining of crude oil; the Leasing Company for the Petroleum Monopoly (Compañía Arrendataria del Monopolio de Petróleos, SA–CAMSA), a private corporation given the exclusive right by the state to distribute and market petroleum products; and the National Petroleum Enterprise (Empresa Nacional de Petróleos, SA–ENP), which controls the transport of crude oil. All three companies, in addition to seven other gas and oil companies, came under the control of the newly created National Institute for Hydrocarbons (Instituto Nacional de Hidrocarburos—INH), patterned on the INI and holding shares in a similar manner. The state holds 99.9 percent of the shares of the ENP, 82.7 percent of Petroliber, and 97.5 percent of CAMSA.[7] (The INI, the DGPE, and the INH give the lie to the commonplace U.S. notion that only in Communist countries does the state own the means—or at least part of the means—of production.)

The INI became a power unto itself, wasteful and difficult to discipline. It perpetuated inefficient business enterprises whose low productivity was disproportionate to capital investment. Moreover, the resources of the INI came directly from the state, which resorted to the printing press when it got low on cash. These activities contributed mightily to the inflation that began to push Spanish prices beyond competitive levels internationally and beyond society's capacity to purchase domestically.

Autarky failed to keep Spain apace with Western Europe. Foodstuffs and raw materials were still in short supply in the 1950s. The state-sponsored programs were not achieving the goals for which they had been created; their activities were out of synchronization and often counterproductive. Spain was stagnating. It had to break out of its isolation or else join the ranks of what later came to be called the Third World. As Sima Lieberman writes: "The economics of the EEC [European Economic Community] were expanding; if Spain was to benefit from this expansion it had to shift rapidly away from policies of autarky and expand its trade with Western Europe. The pace of economic advance in most of Western Europe was progressively turning Spain into a more economically backward country."[8] When Franco adopted the familiar policy of autarky, he could not have foreseen the qualitative socioeconomic change that would soon be taking place in Western Europe. In the past, Spain could be isolated, autarkic, and aloof but still compare adequately to other members of the Western family of nations. But that family was beginning to change so radically by the mid-1950s that Spain, looking backward and inward, was quickly falling behind. It was rapidly joining another family: the underdeveloped, preindustrial nations of the Third World.

SPAIN REJOINS THE WORLD

Spain's isolation ended in 1953 when Franco negotiated aid agreements with the United States and the concordat with the Vatican. The economic plight of the country began to be relieved somewhat by U.S. funds, which came to over $1 billion by the end of decade. But the funds flowed into a socioeconomic system totally incapable of multiplying the windfall and making the expenditure of one peseta produce many more. On the contrary, the money was sucked into what Robert Graham, correspondent for the London *Financial Times,* called "paleocapitalism—primitive market skills operating in a jungle of bureaucratic regulations, protectionism, and pedaled influence."[9] The haphazardly spent funds temporarily eased the imperiled Spanish economy (and inadvertently propped up Francoism for another twenty years) and to an extent primed the Spanish pump. But it also led to spiraling inflation and depleted reserves. By the end of the same decade, foreign reserves had fallen to a paltry $6 million, having dropped by almost $50 million in a single year, 1958–1959.

If further priming was to take place, Spain needed a significant economic source to be made ready for renewed and sustained growth. A new economic policy had to be implemented, but Franco was out of his depth with anything more sophisticated than autarky. In February 1957, he made the momentous cabinet change that first brought into the government the young technocrats who were also members of the Opus Dei. These men, soon joined by other members of the Opus Dei society, authored the Stabilization Plan of 1959, designed to prepare Spain for entry into the outside world of trade and finance. It is said that Franco gave the aggressive innovators free rein, saying, "Hagan lo que les de la gana" (properly translated as "Do whatever you wish"). A more idiomatic translation would reveal Franco's impatience and frustration—forced as he was into a policy that he did not like and that he knew he could not freely control once engaged but that he could not avoid unless he were willing to settle for the pauperization of Spain: "Do whatever you damn well feel like doing."

The Stabilization Plan shut down the easy supply of money to entrepreneurs and increased the costs of goods and services essential to the
people, slashing their purchasing power. It restricted the expansion of private bank credit by giving the minister of the interior the power to regulate credit and the discount practices of private banks. The plan raised the
rates charged by the state-owned national railway, Red Nacional de
Ferrocarriles Españoles (RENFE); increased the cost of telephone service;
and upped the prices of lubricants, petroleum products, and tobacco. The
peseta was devalued, and the plan set in motion the machinery that allowed foreign investment to enter the country. Foreign capital could com-
prise up to 50 percent of the total capital of a Spanish firm; with the
approval of the cabinet, it could exceed the 50 percent limitation. Furthermore, dividends and capital and asset appreciation generated by foreign
investment could be repatriated.

Implementation of the Stabilization Plan caused an economic recession. Healthy firms were compelled to retrench when easy credit for new
investment was not forthcoming, and many weak firms went out of business. Production fell, and consumer demand decreased. When new legislation made it easier to fire employees, unemployment increased.[10] But
just as the planners had envisaged, imports fell and exports rose as the
cost of Spanish goods declined. The balance of payments improved significantly, providing Spain with foreign exchange. Lieberman writes:

> The Stabilization Plan of 1959 also stimulated economic growth through two
> major effects. By bringing the economy closer to a market system and by ex-
> posing Spanish firms to foreign competition, the Plan confronted domestic
> inefficient firms with the choice between increasing their productive effi-
> ciency or having to face probable business failure. It thus induced many
> firms to modernize their methods of production and to develop new prod-
> ucts. By liberalizing foreign trade and by opening up the economy to foreign
> investment the Plan allowed Spain to benefit from its geographical proxim-
> ity to the rapidly developing economy of western Europe.[11]

The plan readied Spain for the economic takeoff that occurred in the
1960s, but that takeoff would not occur in the free market economy recommended in the report from the International Bank of Reconstruction and
Development. The report had been requested by the Spanish government,
and the bank had sent its team of investigators to Spain in March 1961.
Perhaps, given Spain's history of state intervention in the economic process, the move to a free market economy would have been too severe a jolt
for the country to endure. Moreover, the economic elite that supported
Franco would not have tolerated the total exposure to competition that
such an economy would have demanded. Finally, the men of the Opus Dei

who were now in charge of Spain's economic regeneration would have lost a great deal of control if the free forces of the market, not governmental planning, determined Spain's economic direction.

In the place of a free market economy, the Opus Dei technocrats borrowed a scheme that had worked successfully in France and adapted it to Spain: indicative planning, a cooperative effort between the state and private enterprise. The government set out the general scheme, which private enterprise was free to either follow or ignore. Following the plan brought great benefits, however, including tax advantages, accelerated depreciation, special lines of credit, and subsidies. To encourage private investment in areas that the planners considered in need of development, the government designated certain national regions as Economic Poles and granted special benefits to private firms willing to operate within them. Development Poles were established in regions where a certain amount of industrialization already existed. Industrial Promotion Poles were created in regions with no or very little industrialization. And Poles of Industrial Decongestion (Polígonos de Decongesción Industrial) were established to relieve the pressure built up in cities like Barcelona and Madrid. At the beginning of the 1970s, the concept of poles was expanded to integrate urban planning with industrial development in Metropolitan Zones exceeding 750,000 inhabitants and in Urban Zones of more than 250,000. Finally, the activities of the INI were curtailed and coordinated with the overall development plans. The INI was to concentrate on risky, long-range activities: providing aid for private firms in temporary financial difficulty until the firms were again stable and protecting infant industries until they were strong enough to compete on their own.

Beginning in the 1960s, Spain's economic growth was spectacular. Table 10.1 gives Spanish growth rates compared to those of other Western countries. In 1953, the Spanish gross domestic product (GDP) was 14 percent of the French GDP and 23 percent of that of Italy; by 1965, the Spanish GDP was 22 percent of France's and 39 percent of Italy's. In 1974, the figures were 23 and 40 percent, respectively.

Between 1963 and 1971 (1963 = 100), Spain's net production per person nearly doubled (194), outpacing that of West Germany (150), Italy (153), the Netherlands (163), and Great Britain (134). And from 1964 to 1972, Spanish wages rose an average of 287.9 percent per year. Table 10.2 shows the growth of the gross industrial product from 1959 to 1971, and Table 10.3 compares the Spanish economy in 1960 and in 1970.

THE ECONOMIC MIRACLE FALTERS

Economic problems in Spain in the 1980s reflected the economic problems of the industrialized world as a whole. The following phenom-

TABLE 10.1   Average Annual Percentage of Growth of Gross National Domestic Product for Selected Western European Countries

	1965–1969[a]		1970–1973[b]	
	Total	Per Capita	Total	Per Capita
Spain	6.2	5.1	7.3	6.2
Belgium	6.4	3.7	5.2	4.8
France	5.7	4.9	5.2	4.3
West Germany	4.7	4.0	3.2	2.6
Italy	6.0	5.2	3.8	3.0
United Kingdom	2.4	1.9	3.2	2.9

[a]For France and West Germany, 1965–1970.
[b]For Belgium, Frnace, West Germany, and Italy, 1970–1974.

Source: U.S. Bureau of Census, *Statistical Abstract of the United States,* 93d ed. (Washington, D.C., 1972), p. 814, and 97th ed. (Washington, D.C., 1976), p. 876.

TABLE 10.2   Annual Growth Rate for the Gross Industrial Product, 1959–1971 (in constant pesetas)

Year	Percentage Increase
1959	0.2
1960	2.7
1961	13.6
1962	11.3
1963	12.2
1964	13.3
1965	9.4
1966	9.3
1967	4.5
1968	6.0
1969	11.4
1970	7.1
1971	3.9

Source: M. L. Ardura Calleja, "El sector industrial," in Juan Velarde Fuertes et al., eds., *La España en los años 70* (Madrid: Editorial Moneda y Credito, 1973), p. 329.

TABLE 10.3   The Spanish Economy in 1960 and in 1970 (in millions 1970 pesetas)

	1960		1970		Average yearly growth (%)
	Value	% GNP	Value	% GNP	
GNP	1,115.3		2,252.4		8.5
Available resources	1,193.8		2,636.0		8.2
Private consumption	766.3	68.7	1,522.2	67.6	7.1
Public consumption	141.8	12.7	249.5	11.1	5.8
Gross capital formation	177.0	15.9	521.3	23.1	11.4
Imports	78.5	7.0	383.6	17.0	17.2
Exports	108.7	9.7	343.0	15.2	12.2

Source: M. J. González, *La economía política del Franquismo, 1940–1970* (Madrid: Editorial Tecnos, 1979), p. 30.

TABLE 10.4   Causes of the Economic Crisis: Spain and OECD Countries

Economic Indicators	Spain (%)	OECD Countries (%)
Public spending as a percentage of gross domestic product; variation between 1971–1973 and 1961–1963	+42.8	+12.0
Average yearly increase of hourly wages between 1964 and 1973	14.7	8.2
Real growth rate of domestic demand in 1973	8.9	5.4
Real annual growth rate of gross industrial product for 1965–1973	6.5	4.8
Relative share of crude oil in energy consumption in 1973	66.9	55.0
Imports of petroleum products as a percentage of total petroleum products consumed in 1973	99.0	70.0

Source: *La economía española en la década de los 80* (Madrid: Alianza Editorial, 1982), p. 31.

ena, some of which originated in the mid-1960s, were responsible: the U.S. balance-of-payments deficit, which caused an enormous dollar glut on the international market; an increase in public sector expenditures, often financed by permissive monetary policy; an increase in both private and public demand that drove prices continually upward; and the demands of labor for higher and higher wages. In Spain, these problems were compounded, ironically, by the very success of the miracle that grew on cheap fuel, easy credit, and extensive foreign investment. Perhaps the miracle took place too quickly and was too dependent on events that were beyond Spanish control. Table 10.4 compares the effects of these factors on Spain and on the member countries of the Organization for Economic Cooperation and Development (OECD).

Spain was faced with high unemployment, rampant inflation, excessive dependence on foreign energy sources, and a lack of domestic savings and investment. Spanish economists were convinced that the country could not begin to pull out of the recession until private investment increased significantly. The percentage of gross national savings to gross national income fell from a high of 22.6 percent in 1973 to 19.4 percent in 1980, and the percentage of net national savings to net national income fell from a high of 15.8 in 1973 to 11.0 in 1980.[12] The explanation lies partly in the high cost of fuel, passed on to the consumer through higher prices that absorbed more disposable income. The answer also lies in the continued growth of consumption, irrespective of increasingly higher prices. Spain had become a consumer society, one of the consequences of the industrial revolution that began in the 1960s. It cannot be forgotten that for the first time in national history, the people as a whole had money to spend and enjoy; they were now more concerned about spending today than saving for tomorrow. Their savings dropped, and as a consequence, investment plummeted, too, from 27 percent in 1974 to 21.5 percent in 1980 (the percentage represents the ratio of gross capital formation to gross domestic product).[13] Juan Velarde Fuertes believes that Spaniards did not appreciate just how serious the problem had become.[14] The Great Depression in the 1930s did not hit Spain as hard as it did other countries; thus, the experience did not teach Spaniards the same sobering lessons that it taught other peoples.

In 1980, unemployment in Spain reached 12.6 percent, representing over 1.6 million unemployed out of an active workforce of nearly 12.9 million. The figure in 1974 was 3.2 percent, representing 434,000 unemployed out of an active workforce of almost 13.4 million. These figures compare dramatically with the years 1966 to 1969, when unemployment varied between 0.9 and 1.1 percent.[15] Most authors attribute the fall in the active workforce not only to longer periods of schooling and to the lowered age of retirement but also to disillusionment and disappointment among the young—many of whom gave up the search for work and fell back upon the family for their upkeep. In the first three months of 1981, unemployment among people between the ages of 16 and 19 reached 40.7 percent, representing 484,000 people; for those between the ages of 20 and 24, the percentage was 26.9, representing 467,700 people.[16] The unemployment problem became increasingly serious because more and more women were entering the workforce—29.2 percent of the population in 1980 compared to 12.1 percent in 1940 and 20.1 percent at the beginning of the economic miracle in 1959. Spanish laborers who went to work in other Western European countries and whose remunerations helped the balance of payments enormously from the mid-1960s to the mid-1970s began to return home. Their absence helped contribute to the low figures of unemployment, but economic problems in the host countries made life there increasingly difficult. Temporary emigration to Europe peaked in 1972. Between 1963 and 1979, close to 1.7 million people emigrated temporarily. Permanent emigration to Europe reached its highest level in 1971. Between 1963 and 1979, over 1 million people emigrated permanently. Overseas emigration was at its highest in 1963. Between 1963 and 1979, a total of 216,500 people emigrated overseas.[17]

Velarde Fuertes believes that unemployment was Spain's most serious problem not only for economic reasons but also for social and political ones.[18] Unemployment erodes national cohesiveness: It isolates the individual and encourages the selfish pursuit of one's own well-being at whatever cost. Unemployment statistics do not always show that in some regions of the country, the percentage is far higher than in others. People in depressed areas are particularly vulnerable to specious political argument, and unemployment in Spain undermined faith in the political system just when democracy was beginning to put down roots. There are those who contend that under Franco this situation would never have arisen and that if he were alive today, the situation would be corrected.

Moreover, the rural exodus contributed heavily to unemployment. Today, only about 15 percent of the workforce is engaged in agriculture, and agricultural employment fell steadily by about 4 percent per year between 1975 and 1985. In pursuit of a better and more exciting life, men and women from farms flocked to the cities, seriously (in some places, almost totally) depopulating the countryside and overpopulating the urban areas. Hundreds of thousands went to the cities unprepared to join the modern urban workforce; instead, they joined the growing lines of the unemployed.

Spain had an unfavorable balance of payments in eleven of the twenty years between 1961 and 1980. Because of the OPEC price hikes that began in 1973, a favorable balance of $557 million in 1973 turned to an unfavorable balance of $3.245 billion in 1974. In 1978 and 1979, the balance was again favorable, but in 1980, the unfavorable balance was $4.989 billion, and the estimated deficit for 1981 was $5 billion.[19] Not all of the blame can be placed on the increased price of oil, but it was certainly the major factor. In 1980, 65 percent of all the energy consumed in Spain came from petroleum, compared to 54.2 percent (1979 figure) in the nations of the European Economic Community, now called the European Community. The percentage had declined about 7 percent from 1976 to 1980 but was still among the highest of the developed countries. Spain's domestic production of oil is almost zero; its dependence upon imported oil is almost total. The economic miracle in Spain was purchased, in large part, with cheap fuel, and the nation's consumption of energy is based upon petroleum products. This usage could be converted to other sources only at enormous cost and over a long period of time.

Payments to oil producers are not the sole cause of Spain's almost chronic unfavorable balance of payments. Payments for royalties and for technical assistance are inordinately high, owing to insufficient domestic scientific research and development. This situation, too, will remain relatively unchanged until the educational system and the industrial community adapt to the reality of a modern technological society. In addition, the repatriation of profits on foreign investment in Spain and interest payments on Spain's foreign debt contribute heavily to the unfavorable balance, and though the tourist industry helps mightily to correct the imbalance, tourism has begun to fall off slightly, even though in 1981, a record 40 million visitors spent approximately $7.2 billion in Spain.[20] Finally, the return of migrant Spanish workers put an end to the checks from abroad that also had served to counter the outflow of money.

In the early 1980s, inflation continued to dog the Spanish economy. In 1975, the year Franco died, inflation stood at 17.0 percent. It rose to 24.5 percent in 1977, the year the Spaniards went to the polls to elect the constituent assembly—an unhappy juxtapostion of events. It declined to 15.5 percent in 1979, the year the people elected the first government under the constitution, and dropped to 14.0 percent in 1982, when the Socialists came to power. But inflation was still far too high, and it made a volatile campaign issue.[21]

THE ECONOMY AND THE SOCIALISTS: THE 1980s

Where, one might ask, had the genius and energy gone that had brought about the economic miracle almost twenty years earlier? It would seem that with the heavy hand of the dictator now removed, the economy should have soared once again. It must not be forgotten, however, that although Franco allowed the miracle to take place, he was not happy about his loss of economic control, and he never allowed a true market economy to take hold because it could have posed a serious threat to his political control. Moreover, the basic economic infrastructure of Spain remained relatively untouched by the economic reformers of the 1960s—particularly those in the private banking and financial worlds and the public sector world represented by the INI, the DGPE, and the latter's oil and gas subsidiaries (which later became part of the INH, created in 1981). In the worlds of business and labor, the syndicalist structure was still fully in place at Franco's death, in spite of its almost total dysfunction, and the negative effects it spawned would persist long after its demolition in the early years of the transition. In short, a thorough overhaul of the economy was called for before a new economic miracle could even be thought about. But after 1975, Spanish genius and energy were devoted not to an economic overhaul but to a political overhaul—in fact, to a political revolution that transformed Spain from dictatorship to democracy—all the while fending off the threats of counterrevolution that constantly menaced and finally became overt on February 23, 1981.

Even if the genius and energy could have been mustered and spent on economic reform to parallel political reform, consensus on the direction of that reform would not have been possible, given the highly fractionalized party that charted and negotiated the political transition. The UCD was of one voice only in its commitment to political democracy. It was deeply at odds internally about the social and economic transformation that would inevitably follow, and it fell apart when it attempted to address these aspects. With the absolute victory of the PSOE in 1982, attention could finally be turned to economic and social issues, particularly since democracy seemed, at last, to be safe after its successful baptism by fire, precipitated by the abortive coup in February 1981. If democracy was not absolutely safe, it was at least safe enough to allow attention to be focused elsewhere.

Running on the slogan "Socialism Means Freedom" and promising industrial renewal, economic modernization, and 800,000 new jobs, the PSOE, with Felipe González at its helm, swept into power with an absolute majority in Congress. It was confronted by: an annual GDP growth rate that had just moved into positive figures (1.2 percent in 1982 from -0.2 percent in 1981); inflation running at 16 percent per annum; public expenditure running even wilder (not just for social programs but also for subsides to parasitic public sector industries and services); a serious imbalance of international payments; the continued dependence on imported petroleum, the major fuel of the Spanish economy and society; and unemployment that was officially put at 20 percent. Moreover, when the PSOE came into power, it faced a restive workforce that expected the rewards promised in return for its support at the polls. For the first time in Spanish history, their "own kind of people" had taken charge of Spain; at least, that is how workers felt about Felipe (as he was then informally and affectionately called) and his fellow young turks. The workers considered themselves to have been grossly abused by the outgoing administration, and they expected the PSOE to right their wrongs. These sentiments were shared by all workers, despite their party or union affiliations. But of course, the feelings were strongest among the members of the General Workers' Union (Unión General de Trabajadores—UGT), independent but closely affiliated with the PSOE. The Communist union, the Workers' Commissions (Comisiones Obreras —CCOO), preferred that a party on the Left be in power rather than a party on the Right. But it never trusted the PSOE, as the UGT did initially. Nor did the CCOO trust the UGT. Relations between the organizations reached a bitter low after the UGT, in January 1980, signed the Interconfederal Outline Agreement (Acuerdo Marco Interconfederal—AMI) with the Spanish employers' association, the Spanish Confederation of Business Organizations (Confederación Española de Organizaciones Empresariales—CEOE). The CCOO called the UGT a "yellow" (i.e., company) union for having reached agreement with the CEOE, but the CCOO soon pulled back from its extreme leftist stance when it realized that the demands of the union elites were running ahead of its rank and file. Still, both the UGT and the CCOO were disgruntled with the UCD government and the existing economic system, and both looked to better days with the PSOE government.

The working classes considered themselves to have been Franco's greatest victims. During his regime, they had been deprived not only of their political rights but also of their economic rights—the rights to unionize, to bargain collectively, and to strike. The only major concession made to the workers was job security: It became virtually impossible to fire workers in Franco's Spain. In the later years of the dictatorship, worker unrest grew, and strikes became increasingly frequent. Comparing 1968 to 1974, the number of strikes went from 236, involving 114,355 workers, to 1,193, involving 625,971 workers, and the number of hours lost on strikes went from 2,224,100 to 18,188,895.[22] But the working classes remained dangerously vulnerable. They had few rights and little protection under Francoist law, and strikes could always be crushed. Moreover, strikes had to be motivated purely by economic demands; any hint of political demands could bring immediate reprisal.

Workers received full political and economic rights under the 1978 constitution, but the implementation of those rights was not immediately forthcoming. It was, in fact, not until March 1980 that the Workers' Statute came into force. In the meantime, laborers believed that they had carried the burden of the transition to democracy, just as they had carried the burden of Francoism and particularly of the economic miracle in the 1960s. The miracle had vastly enriched those elements of the bourgeoisie close to Franco, but it had kept the workers where they had always been, among the poorest in Europe. True enough, workers had benefited indirectly from the general rise in Spain's standard of living, but in relative terms, the middle class fared far better. Moreover, the workers were never partners in the transformation.

In a speech to workers in Barcelona in July 1970, Franco himself admitted that many of the poorer people in Spain had not shared equally in the benefits of the country's economic "miracle." Stanley Payne comments and then directly quotes Franco: "Franco declared that the average level of income had reached a satisfactory level but that the same could not be said of proportionate distribution, 'since some of the population gain a great deal, while other poorer sections remain behind.'"[23] The virtual explosion in the number of strikes in 1976, during the period of flux following Franco's death, gives us conclusive evidence that the workers were no happier than they were when Franco spoke in 1970. There were 1,568 strikes in 1976, involving 3,638,952 workers and the loss of 110,016,240 hours[24]

Workers were, to an extent, partners in the socioeconomic agreements made among the unions, business, and government in the early years of the transition, but they felt themselves to be unequal partners. Their demands were always compromised and whittled away by employers and the government, who evoked the specter of a military that might use such demands as an excuse to overthrow the government and crush the fledgling democracy. The wide-ranging Moncloa Pacts, signed in October 1977, partially addressed the workers' demands, but the agreement was *of* the workers and *for* the workers, not *by* the workers. The pacts were made between the political parties and the government; neither management nor labor was a direct participant, but management was kept far more apprised than was labor during the negotiations. The Acuerdo Marco Interconfederal was signed in January 1980 by the CEOE and the UGT but not by the CCOO. The agreement regulated collective bargaining and tied wage increases to productivity. The increases could fluctuate between 13 and 16 percent per annum but could be regulated downward from 11 to 15 percent in 1981, if the economy worsened or inflation dropped.

On June 7, 1981, on the heels of the abortive coup in late February, the National Agreement on Employment (Acuerdo Nacional Sobre Empleo—ANE) was signed by the UGT, the CCOO, the CEOE, and the government, their solidarity galvanized by the recently attempted putsch and the continued fear of possible future conspiracies. Wage increases for 1982 were set to fluctuate between 9 and 11 percent (a range lower than that set in the AMI two years earlier). Even the maximum wage increase would be two points *below* the projected inflation rate of 13 percent. This disadvantage was to be offset by the government's promise to create 350,000 new jobs, but this promise was like all promises—far easier to make than to keep. Moreover, the so-called wage increase would merely maintain the current wage level since the increase would be consumed by inflation. And there were no limits put on profits to be made by business. As a consequence, workers were convinced that, once again, they were made to sacrifice in order to help the government control inflation.

Each of the pacts just discussed had been designed to last only a limited time: Moncloa lasted for one year, and AMI and ANE each lasted two. The ANE was still in operation when the PSOE came into power in 1982, but from the party's accession until the end of the decade, only a single pact was agreed to by the government, the UGT, and the CEOE. It is important to distinguish how pacts were used by the UCD governments and by those of the PSOE. For the UCD governments, pacts were designed to hold off socioeconomic reforms until the constitution could be created and the fledgling democracy put on its feet. Political goals were uppermost. No one denied the exigency of socioeconomic reforms, but, as I have explained earlier, such reforms simply could not be faced until political reform had taken place. Moreover, the UCD never had an absolute majority in parliament and thus did not have the numbers to push through radical socioeconomic reforms, even if it had wanted to do so. By contrast, the PSOE had an absolute majority from the start and did not have to finesse the powers of any group outside parliament, whether business or labor. The PSOE was not vulnerable and did not have to make pacts. "The majoritarian government of Gonzáles ... was more concerned instead about the application of the mandate theory; it believed that it had the right and the duty to carry out policies conceived in terms of the 'general interest,' although agreements could be reached if they did not distort the main thrust of reforms."[25]

In 1980 and 1981, the legislature finally passed laws to implement the guarantees to labor set forth in the 1978 constitution. Because these laws implemented constitutional mandates, they were political in nature in spite of their socioeconomic content. Thus, they could be enacted without jeopardizing the political primacy of the UCD governments. The Workers' Statute came into force in March 1981. It ended the state's direct role in labor negotiations, henceforth to be conducted by representatives of labor and management. It also guaranteed a minimum wage and the right to have access to social security. In an attempt to help reduce unemployment, it shortened the workweek from 44 hours to 42 hours and limited the amount of overtime a person could put in from 20 to 15 hours per month. The statute made it somewhat easier for employers to dismiss redundant or inefficient employees, but the issue of part-time employment remained unsettled. Employers were asking to be able to hire part-time employees, who could be taken in when business increased but let off when business slackened without the obligations and penalties that regulated full-time employment (such as social security payments and workers' compensation). Employers finally obtained this right after the Socialists came to power. The Basic Employment Act (Ley Básica de Empleo—LBE) came into force in October 1981. The law defined what was meant by employment and protected the unemployed. It established a schedule of unemployment benefits related to the length of time employed and created additional benefits representing 75 percent of the officially guaranteed minimum wage (Salario Mínimo Interprofesional Garantizado—SMIG) for workers whose basic benefits had run out. In addition, Spanish workers who had been abroad and who were unable to find jobs within 180 days of their return to Spain were made eligible for unemployment benefits. Employers and employees finance 60 percent of unemployment insurance, and the state finances the remaining 40 percent.

Several factors contributed to the Socialist electoral victory in October 1982. The UCD had virtually fallen apart; only a remnant was left of the ruling party of the transition. Several national parties had emerged from the breakup of the UCD, but they were small, weak, and poorly organized. The Spanish voter had to look to other national parties, of which the Communist party (PCE), Socialist party (PSOE), and the right-wing Popular Alliance (AP) were the most important and best organized. Spaniards either feared or were highly suspicious of the PCE and the AP, the former because it smacked of rigid orthodoxy and association with totalitarianism (notwithstanding the party's profession otherwise) and the latter because it smacked of Francoism. The most viable alterative, therefore,

was the PSOE. This analysis is not meant to diminish the intrinsic attraction of the Socialist party and its electoral program. But the PSOE could
not have won the election by responding only to the classic leftist voter. Its
appeal was far beyond a narrowly Socialist sector. Moreover, its socialism
had become highly attenuated since the heady days of Surenes, and, as
shown in the chapter on political parties, by the elections in 1982, it had
become, in effect, a Social Democratic party. Only its unchanged name recalled its militant origin. The party could not, therefore, claim an electoral
mandate for profound, systemic, socioeconomic change.

Furthermore, two recent events gave the PSOE pause as it took control of Spain in 1982. At home, the attempted coup, which had occurred
only twenty months earlier, had left a gnawing fear among the people that
the military might try again if political, social, or economic change went
too far. Abroad, in France, the ill-fated Mitterrand experiment in muscular
socialism was already running into trouble by the time the Socialists came
to power in Spain, and the eminent French Socialist had begun to pull his
party toward social democracy, where it has remained ever since.

As a consequence, the PSOE government adopted a monetarist policy to reduce the budget deficit, lower inflation, and maintain a wage scale
below the rate of inflation. The 800,000 new jobs promised during the election campaign would emerge, in the long run, from a strengthened and
growing economy. In the short run, however, unemployment would have
to rise, part of its impact to be alleviated by unemployment compensation
provided in the Basic Employment Act of October 1981. Increased unemployment resulted from several factors. The Socialists' orthodox industrial policy would trim fat from heavily featherbedded public sector industries (and would lower budget deficits by reducing subsidies to those
public sector industries that had survived only through governmental largesse). Old, labor-intensive industries—such as ship building, steel production, coal mining, and textiles—would be shut down, merged, or consolidated, and new industries that demanded a smaller but more
sophisticated workforce—such as electronics, food production, and transport vehicles—would be encouraged. Unemployment increased, too, as a
result of the influx of laborers from the countryside who were looking for
the good life in the cities but were ill equipped for urban unemployment
(except in the underground economy). Further, Spanish workers returning from abroad, where they were no longer needed, added to the already glutted labor market.

Although official employment figures were dangerously high, it
should be pointed out that unofficial figures were perhaps closer to the
truth, and they made the problem of unemployment, if still daunting,
somewhat more tractable. Estimates vary, but some analysts believe that
almost one-third of the nearly 20 percent of the workforce that was unem-

ployed actually worked in the underground economy, sometimes call the "black economy." In it, neither the worker nor the employer pays social security, nor does the worker pay income tax. The black economy was found primarily in labor-intensive businesses: agriculture, construction, and domestic service (maids, nannies, gardeners, cooks, chauffeurs, and so on).

Early in its first term in office, the Socialist government confronted the economic infrastructure that had remained essentially untouched since the days of Franco, in particular, public sector industries and banking. In 1982, the behemoth—the INI—employed some 217,000 workers, 7 percent of Spain's industrial labor force, in 60-odd companies and their 100-odd subsidiaries. The INI conglomerate generated sales of over $10 billion a year, of which 34 percent came from exports. Many of the companies were profitable, but losses were running over $1 billion a year, primarily in coal mining, steel production, ship building, capital equipment, aeronautical construction, and Iberia, the Spanish international airline.[26] Young socialist economists, such as Miguel Boyer (minister of the economy and treasury in González's first government) and his successor Carlos Solchaga, made it clear that the state would no longer keep dying industries artificially alive with subsidies. By contrast, firms that were sick but capable of new life were either to be restructured and kept in Spanish hands or sold to multinational corporations, which had vast resources for research and development. Privatization of the whole lot (i.e., selling public sector companies to Spaniards on the open market, in the spirit of Margaret Thatcher) was not a ready alternative. The Spanish stock market was (and remains) relatively small for a country of Spain's size, and it was unable to accommodate large volumes of trading. Moreover, Spaniards, new to prosperity and to the willingness to risk that results from prosperity, were timid investors; they put their money in the tried and true, like electrical utilities and the telephone company. As a consequence, investment would be the largest part of the answer, but infrastructural change within Spain would also be important.

To begin with, the government announced that by 1993, the most unproductive coal mines of HUNOSA would be shut down, costing some 6,000 jobs, and another 6,000 jobs would be cut in the steel mills of ENSIDESA. Even these reductions would not make these vast, heavily subsidized, state-owned industries self-supportive, much less profit making, but economic reality had to be weighed against political reality. The working class voted overwhelmingly for the PSOE and could exact retribution at the polls, even though the loss of employment was sweetened by retirement at full pay up to the year 2002.

Banks are the primary source of capital in Spain, but they already owned too much of Spanish industry and were reluctant to invest more, particularly in industries that were economically shaky. When industry reeled from the blow delivered by OPEC in the mid-1970s, banks—as major investors in industry—reeled, too. During the darkest days of the banking crisis, 1978–1983, some fifty banks had to be rescued by the Deposit Guaranty Fund (Fondo de Garantía de Depósitos—FGD), set up in 1977 to protect depositors. Since 1980, the fund has also functioned as a state-run banking "hospital," the Banking Corporation (Corporación Bancaria).[27] In this capacity, the corporation sought out healthy banks that could take over and revitalize ailing ones. Finding insufficient purchasers in Spain, the FGD looked abroad, where foreign banks were only too eager to move into Spain—if not through the front door, than through the side. Under Spanish law, a Spanish bank may have only three branches, but a foreign bank buying a Spanish one acquires all the latter's branches as well. Thus, foreign banks multiplied throughout the country. After 1982, the PSOE government made it even easier for foreign banks to enter Spain. In 1985, for example, National Westminster bought 49 percent of Banco de Gerona, and Chase Manhattan bought 91 percent of Banco de Finanzas.[28]

SPAIN JOINS EUROPE

Joining Europe had been a national obsession since the beginning of the transition to democracy. Membership in the EEC, now the EC, was more than economically important. Politically and, more deeply, psychologically, membership meant Spain's acceptance by fellow Europeans as a full-fledged democracy. Spain at last became a part of Europe on January 1, 1986, when it joined the EC. After so many years, it would no longer be "different"—the adjective used by Franco to mean superior, by tourists to mean exotic, and by progressive Spaniards to mean retrograde. No longer would Europe end at the Pyrenees, an observation that had dismissed Spain as a remote and backward place that was more a part of Africa than of Europe. Today, Europe begins at Gibraltar!

But joining Europe was painful, and in the accession treaty signed in 1985, the EC drove a hard bargain. Spain was not prepared for what it was getting into. All political parties had been strongly supportive of membership, but the political elites had not educated the public about the impact that membership would have on Spanish life, particularly economic life. The gradual integration of Spain into the EC would be carried out over a seven-year period, beginning January 1, 1986, when Spain opened its doors to competition from the EC traders and to investment from the EC companies. Customs duties on EC products were to be phased out by March 1, 1988, and tariffs on industrial goods from third countries (i.e., non-EC members) were to be reduced to the EC average (approximately 5 percent) by January 1, 1993. With some exceptions, import quotas were to disappear immediately. National assistance to industry (like the subsidies paid to companies in the INI, the DGPE, and the INH) would be subject to strict EC regulations, and the EC antitrust rules came into force immediately. Further, Spain was obliged to comply with consumer, product, and environmental protection standards set by the EC. As of January 1, 1993, Spain's workers would be able to seek employment anywhere in the EC, but reciprocally, workers from the other EC member nations could seek work in Spain. Immediately upon admittance on January 1, 1986, Spain was required to levy the value-added tax (VAT), which is the EC's major source of revenue. The tax was particularly hard on the Spanish laboring classes, for whom food was the major expense. The prices of milk and bread jumped 3 to 4 percent overnight; the costs of other basic commodities rose from 6 to 7 percent. (The VAT is a tax applied to the additional value created at a given stage of production and calculated as a percentage of the difference between the product value at that stage and the cost of all materials and services purchased as input.[29])

The burden of membership could have been lightened considerably had Spain been able to make money within the EC in those areas where it was most competitive: fresh fruits and vegetables, olive oil, and wine. But it was precisely in this area that the terms of admission were most stringent, made that way primarily by France and Italy (Spain's major agricultural competitors). These potentially lucrative farm products would not be accommodated under the EC's Common Agricultural Policy until 1996, three years beyond the seven-year period of adjustment for all other economic activity. Only in regard to fishing were the Spaniards able to make a better deal. Spain has one of Europe's largest fishing industries (both fish and shellfish), and along with the Scandinavian countries, it is Europe's largest consumer of things from the sea. Spain has been enormously defensive about any attempts to restrict fishing. Moreover, much of the industry is located in Galicia and the Basque provinces (Euzkadi), two of the highly sensitive Autonomous Communities that look upon attempts to limit their fishing industry as attempts to limit their autonomy. Furthermore, the PSOE is strongly challenged politically in these regions by the PP (formerly the AP) in Galicia and by various regionalist parties is Euzkadi. The PSOE could not afford to alienate these regions by agreeing to an EC fishing policy that would burden Spain unduly. Under the terms of admission, Spain got a 40 percent increase in the number of trawlers allowed to fish in EC waters and gained a 128 percent increase in the quota of hake (*merluza*, in Spanish), the country's favorite and most frequently consumed fish. The EC also agreed to help Spain modernize its fishing industry.[30]

Catching up with Europe was the preeminent economic concern of Felipe González and his ministers throughout his second and third administrations, and they would catch up using whatever economic strategy proved effective. The PSOE won the absolute majority again in the elections of 1986, and in the 1989 elections, the party won exactly half the seats in Congress. In 1984, just two years beyond the party's first victory, González had said that macroeconomics had no ideology, that it spoke neither to nor for the Left or the Right. In June 1987, one year after his party's second victory, González reiterated his economic pragmatism. Gone were even allusions to the old socialist shibboleths. Words such as "the Left," "the Right," and "class struggle" had been excised from his vocabulary. Yet he said that the PSOE still needed the workers, adding that the workers also needed the PSOE. He warned workers and unions that their indiscriminate attacks on the government would strengthen the opposition and could lead to its possible future victory at the polls. He said the Britain of Harold Wilson and James Callahan had given way to the Britain of Margaret Thatcher, and the Germany of Willy Brandt and Helmut Schmidt had given way to the Germany of Helmut Kohl. In France, Mitterrand had been forced to cohabit with Chirac following the conservative victory in the 1986 legislative elections.

Even though there was no one of the stature of Chirac, Thatcher, or Kohl within the Spanish opposition, González said that politics, like nature, abhors a vacuum. Incessant criticism from the workers and their unions would weaken the government and produce a power void. He said that Thatcher and the Conservatives had won in 1979 not because of their merit but because the unions had virtually hounded the Labor government out of office, making ever more exorbitant demands that the citizenry finally came to reject by evicting the Labor government from power.[31] González, with ill-concealed conceit, told the workers and their unions that irrespective of what the government might have to do to prepare Spain for January 1, 1993, the working class was far better off with the PSOE in power than with anybody else. In effect, he told them to back off. Out of his casual clothes and into his suits and ties, González no longer seemed "one of our own kind" from the worker's point of view. He was no longer Felipe, the ordinary guy in the corduroys and sweaters.

The estrangement would characterize the relationship between González and the unions for the remainder of the decade and into the 1990s. Unions and workers felt that they were being taken for granted but realized that there was no viable alternative to the PSOE government. Such a realization did not, however, lessen frustration and resentment. In fact, it exacerbated them, much like an unhappy marriage for which divorce is not an option. Once again, labor felt it was carrying the burden for Spain's admission to Europe, just as it had borne the burden of the miracle in the 1960s and of the transition to democracy in the late 1970s and early 1980s.

Strikes and protests became a regular part of Spanish public life during the late 1980s and the early 1990s. Construction workers, students, miners, and transport workers struck in March 1987, and a general strike was averted only by a single vote in the CCOO. But sentiment for a general strike continued to brew. The causes of labor's bitterness included not only what it considered inadequate wages but also the vast disparity in the standards of living from one region of Spain to another—an imbalance that was difficult for laborers to accept given the egalitarian goals once espoused by the PSOE and still espoused by the UGT and the CCOO. In November 1988, the government declared that, in spite of growing opposition from the unions, it would not alter its economic policy, and Carlos Solchaga, the minister of economy and treasury, accused the unions of pursuing political rather than economic ends, thereby attempting to usurp the function of the democratically elected government put into power to serve all of Spain, not just the workers. Nicolás Redondo, leader of the UGT, spoke of an incipient divorce between the PSOE and the UGT, and in a mocking reminiscence, he commented that Felipe González would scarcely recognize the man who once called himself "Isidoro,"—González's nom de guerre in the anti-Franco underground.[32]

On December 14, 1988, the long-threatened general strike paralyzed Spain. It was the first such strike since 1934. Approximately 90 percent of the working population, some 8 million people, responded to the call of the UGT and the CCOO, which effectively brought Spanish life to a halt. From the workers' point of view, the strike was the only alternative left, given what they perceived as the unwillingness of the political system to respond to their needs. As members of the European working class and as citizens of a country now a part of the EC, Spanish laborers looked to their European counterparts and saw individuals far more advanced economically and socially than they themselves were. Even though Spain's fellow EC members were, by economic necessity, pulling back from the full extension of the welfare society that had been grafted to European capitalism after World War II, workers elsewhere in Europe were still far ahead of their Spanish counterparts. It was the Spanish workers' conviction that the PSOE government was retreating even before it had advanced in the achievement of the socioeconomic democracy that they saw as the essential corollary of political democracy.

In October 1991, a general strike took place throughout Asturias in reaction to the government's decision to shut down coal mines that were no longer economically viable. A projected 40,000 jobs would be lost. The high cost of extraction from deep, almost exhausted mines meant that coal could be imported even from great distances far more cheaply than it could be produced domestically. For workers, however, the decision meant increased unemployment in an already deeply troubled region.

Six months later, in April 1992, a general strike totally paralyzed Galicia, one of the poorest regions in Spain. It was called in yet another attempt to force the government to reconsider its economic policy. Redondo lashed out at the government: "In that sanctuary of raging monetarism that is known as the ministry of economy, they are trying to make devils out of the unemployed, calling them parasites and bums." He added, "They ought to hunt down fraud and corruption rather than go after those people out of work."[33]

On May 28, 1992, a nationwide general strike closed down industry for half a day, but unlike the general strike in 1988, it had little effect on daily life. Moreover, the police seemed unusually conspicuous at the time of the strike, prompting Redondo to accuse González of using excess force against the workers. He went on to warn: "Authoritarianism can be dangerous, to which our very recent history can give testimony."[34] He then increased his dosage of venom and called the government "the accomplice of the corrupted elites." He added: "Everyone should be measured by the same instrument. ... One should not be hard on the weak and reverential toward the powerful."[35]

The rationale for almost every socioeconomic decision made by the government since the Socialists took Spain into the European Community on January 1, 1986, was the need for the nation to reach European par. The issue of convergence with Europe swept aside almost all other considerations. But according to the government's long-range plan, by January 1, 1993, all Spaniards would be able to redeem the sacrifices they had been called upon to make, to their great benefit. But late in 1991, Spain entered into yet another agreement with Europe that called for renewed sacrifices and, from the vantage point of the working class, a postponement of that national well-being that had been promised by 1993. The European Union came into existence on December 11, 1991, at Maastricht, the Netherlands, with the goal of achieving political and monetary union by 1999. Spain's reasons for joining the European Union were complex (as were its reasons for joining the EC in 1986). Once again, Spain had the opportunity to define itself as a European democracy, this time, however, with far more self-assurance than it had possessed in 1986. Spain joined the union not as a supplicant (its posture in 1986) but as an equal. Moreover, it had fulfilled the monumental task assigned it in 1986 and had proved its mettle. Furthermore and, in many ways, most important of all, Spain was now redeemed, and to the governing elite, if not to the masses, the sacrifices already made and those yet to be made were more than justified. The ghost of Franco was finally exorcised at Maastricht and with it, all questions of

Spanish moral worth and national expiation. It is ironic that it was the So-cialists who finally got Spain out of purgatory.

The obstacles to be surmounted this time are solely economic; noth-ing else must be proved. For Spain to be accepted in the projected mone-tary union, it has to meet four very concrete criteria: (1) Inflation cannot be higher than 1.5 points above the average of the three member nations with the lowest rates of inflation; (2) interest rates cannot be higher than those in the three member nations with the lowest rates of interest; (3) the deficit cannot be higher than 3 percent of the GDP; and (4) the public debt cannot be higher than 60 percent of the same GDP. The fourth criterion should be the easiest for Spain to pass; at the time of the signing at Maastricht, the Spanish public debt was only 44.7 percent of the GDP.[36]

The other criteria remain formidable, and meeting them once again renews the debates within the Socialist party itself and between the Social-ist party and the unions and workers. These debates focus on how much socialist orthodoxy is called for versus how much pragmatism; phrased another way, they pit the workers' demand for higher wages, extension of social democracy, and the solution to chronic unemployment against the government's relentless and pragmatic pursuit of neoliberalism.

In June 1992, inflation was the highest it had been in four years, hov-ering around 6.5 percent.[37] More ominously still, employment figures showed that 1,200 people were losing jobs every day.[38] In August, the Bank of Spain pronounced the country to be in terrible economic health, and polls revealed that 55 percent of Spaniards were opposed to the gov-ernment's economic policy.[39] Three months later, in November 1992, the peseta was devalued again, this time by 6 percent, for a total devaluation of 11 percent in three months.[40] The following month, Solchaga sat for an interview with *El Pais*. The newspaper described him as a man who had gradually modified his image from that of the detached professional econ-omist and technocrat to that of a first-rate politician concerned not only with progressive fiscal policy but also with the lack of opportunity for many Spaniards and with the problems of poverty and marginality.[41] Per-haps the PSOE government was beginning to make adjustments in its own image in preparation for the general election that, by law, had to take place no later than October 1993.

THE PSOE'S ECONOMIC PERFORMANCE: AN EVALUATION

The PSOE came to power in 1982 prepared to make good its electoral pledge to bring about the socioeconomic democracy that would comple-ment the political democracy ushered in by its predecessor. The new gov-ernment was unprepared, however, for the dimensions of the economic problems it would face: massive budget and trade deficits, a serious imbalance of payments that had resulted in the near depletion of foreign currency reserves, mounting unemployment, rising inflation, and falling foreign investment. Under classic socialist theory, socioeconomic reform should be achieved at the expense of economic efficiency if a choice between the two goals had to be made, but the PSOE had renounced classic socialism in 1979. Moreover, the 1978 constitution had established Spain's commitment to a market economy (article 38). Further, the pragmatic new prime minister believed that with the party's overwhelming electoral mandate, there was a national, general interest to which his government had a duty to respond. González's government would, therefore, pursue economic efficiency in order to reverse Spain's economic decline and to position the country favorably for taking off in the future. Meanwhile, however, the Socialists began to make good their own promises of social and economic change: university reform (Ley de Reforma Universitaria) in 1983; social security reform (Ley de Pensiones) in 1985; public educational reform, which included regulation of the relationship between public and private schools (Ley del Derecho a la Educación) in 1985; trade union reform (Ley de Libertad Sindical) in 1985 (González continued the democratic labor legislation that had begun under Suárez—Estatuto de los Trabajadores and Ley Básica del Empleo); health care reform (Ley General de Sanidad) in 1986; and later, after the 1986 election, extension of the school-leaving age to sixteen and expansion of vocational education (Lay de Ordenación General del Sistema Educativo) in 1990. These socioeconomic guarantees would, in part, be paid for through a more equitable tax system; the reduction of the massive, featherbedded bureaucracy inherited from the Franco regime; the lowering of inflation through tight money (i.e., raising interest rates); the reforming of capital markets; and the restructuring and reconversion of the highly subsidized, state-owned industrial sector (Ley Sobre Reconversión y Reindustrialización, 1983).

Unemployment proved more intractable. The PSOE had promised 800,000 new jobs in the 1982 electoral campaign, but these did not materialize. In fact, unemployment grew in the early years of the Socialist administration. But unemployment itself was perhaps not quire so societally destructive as it might have appeared. It affected young people and women primarily, but in 1984, for example, 73 percent of the unemployed lived in families with employed male workers. José Maravall observes: "Wages did not suffer, in aggregate terms, from economic reforms. The average income per worker grew 13 points in real terms in the period 1977–82 and, although in much more moderate terms, it still went up by 5.5 points between 1982 and 1989. That is, for the beginning of the economic reforms, the buying power of wages went up .09 percent per year."[42] Moreover, the loss of income for those who lost jobs and for those who could not obtain them was partially counterbalanced by the increase in "social income" (brought about by the new socioeconomic legislation) that was available to everyone: state-funded health care, education, social security, unemployment compensation, and in those cases that qualified, housing subsidies. Irrespective of these attenuating circumstances, however, unemployment remainded massive, and those looking for work remained unmollified.

Maravall aptly sums up the Socialists' economic achievements and problems:

> The "final" effects of economic reforms in Spain began to emerge from the second quarter of 1985, a few months before the country became a full member of the European Community. The fall in the price of oil and the depreciation of the dollar helped economic recovery, while the reforms had put the Spanish economy on much better grounds in terms of inflation, the public deficit and industrial competitiveness. In the following five years, the rate of growth was, on average, twice that of the European Community as a whole—around 5% per year. The inflation differential vis-à-vis the European Community was cut from five to 1.5 points, and the public budget deficit came down to 1.9 percent of the GDP. Unemployment fell by six point, as the very large numbers of new jobs overcame the continuing expansion of the active population. By the end of the decade, however, the Spanish economy was experiencing, as other Western European countries, new problems with inflation (it went up to 6.9 percent in 1989) and with the current account deficit. The Gulf Crisis aggravated the situation: Spain had not reduced its energy consumption over the decade and was largely dependent on imported oil. Reforms had taken the economy out of a difficult situation: it was now more open and competitive and the state was solvent; the problems were increasingly similar to those other Western European economies, although the Spanish economy still lagged behind most of them.[43]

NOTES

1. *Malthusian* refers to the concept that the good things of life are in short supply and that one must husband the little one has out of fear that even that might be consumed too quickly. The mentality leads to a narrow, unimaginative life in which risk of any sort is minimal.

2. Gabriel Jackson, *The Spanish Republic and the Civil War, 1931–1939* (Princeton: Princeton University Press, 1965), pp. 526–540.

3. Hugh Thomas, *The Spanish Civil War* (New York: Harper & Row, 1963), pp. 631–633.

4. Ramón Tamames, *La república, la era de Franco* (Madrid: Alianza Editorial, 1973), pp. 349–358.

5. Pete J. Donaghy and Michael T. Newton, *Spain: A Guide to Political and Economic Institutions* (Cambridge University Press, 1987), p. 141.

6. Ibid., p. 143.

7. Ibid., p. 146.

8. Sima Lieberman, *The Contemporary Spanish Economy: A Historical Perspective* (London: George Allen and Unwin, 1982), p. 201.

9. Eric Solsten and Sandra W. Meditz, eds., *Spain: A Country Survey* (Washington, D.C.: Library of Congress, Federal Research Division, 1990), p. 141.

10. After the Labor Charter came into being in 1938, it was very difficult for an employer to dismiss an employee; in part, this protection had been guaranteed to workers to compensate them for the loss of all the rights they had possessed prior to the charter.

11. Lieberman, *The Contemporary Spanish Economy*, p. 215.

12. Servicio de Estudios, *La economía española en la década de los 80* (Madrid: Alianza Editorial, 1982), p. 43.

13. Ibid., p. 56.

14. Juan Velarde Fuertes, "Economía," in *Cinco años después: Cual es la balance?* (Barcelona: Ediciones Acervo, 1980), pp. 60–90.

15. Servicio de Estudios, *La economía española*, p. 68.

16. Ibid., p. 69.

17. Ibid., p. 77.

18. Velarde Fuertes, "Economía," p. 65.

19. Servicio de Estudios, *La economía española*, p. 96.

20. *The Europa Yearbook 1983–1984: A World Survey* (London: Europa Publications, 1983–1984), p. 1071.

21. Keith G. Salmon, *The Modern Spanish Economy: Transformation and Integration into Europe* (London and New York: Pinter Publishers, 1991), p. 6.

22. Stanley Payne, *The Franco Regime, 1936–1975* (Madison: University of Wisconsin Press, 1987), p. 555.

23. Ibid., p. 55; Franco quote is from *Pensamiento político*, vol. 2, pp. 515–516.

24. Payne, *The Franco Regime, 1936–1975*, p. 555.

25. José M. Maravall, "Economic Reforms in New Democracies: The Southern European Experience," Estudio/Working Paper 1991/92, June 1991, Center for Advanced Study in the Social Sciences, March 1991, Instituto Juan March de Estudios e Investigaciones.

26. "Spain Survey," *The Economist*, March 1, 1986, p. 14.

27. Donaghy and Newton, *Spain: A Guide*, p. 210.

28. *The Economist*, 1986, p. 19.

29. Solsten and Meditz, eds., *Spain: A Country Survey*, p. 386.

30. *The Economist*, 1986, p. 26.

31. *El Pais*, International Edition, April 20, 1987.

32. Ibid., November 21, 1988.

33. Ibid., April 13, 1992.

34. Ibid., June 1, 1992.

35. Ibid.

36. Ibid., December 16, 1991.

37. Ibid., June 13, 1992.
38. Ibid., June 29, 1992.
39. Ibid., September 24, 1992.
40. Ibid., November 23, 1992.
41. Ibid., December 28, 1992.
42. Maravall, "Economic Reforms in New Democracies," p. 36.
43. Ibid., pp. 36–37.

11

Culture and Society

The surface of Spanish life has changed spectacularly since Franco was buried in November 1975. Spaniards may now legally divorce; have abortions; smoke, snort, or otherwise ingest dope; swim naked at the beach; and openly indulge their most elaborate sexual fantasies, with pornography available at kiosks, bookshops, movie houses, and live theaters. But by and large, Spain's leading newspapers no longer carry personal advertisements for the purchase and sale of sexual gratification in whatever combination the reader could want. Things have now become far more sophisticated. John Hooper, correspondent for the *Guardian,* tells of an enterprising married couple in Barcelona—one party an accountant, the other a child psychiatrist, no less—who opened a house of pleasure for other couples bored with their partners and itching to switch. Temporary new liaisons could go from flirtation to consummation without leaving the premises. In rooms arranged in a progressive order of intimacy, couples could move from barroom to ballroom to petting room, furnished only with sofas, then to the last room, carpeted with wall-to-wall mattresses.[1] The order could not be reversed, and one could not skip a grade. It is not surprising that the Catalans are known for their business acumen!

Perhaps this account plays too heavily upon things sexual, but sex and politics were the two greatest taboos in Franco's Spain. Now that politics is constitutionally accessible to almost everyone, the present sensual indulgence suggests that a new Spain is in the making—one that is quickly joining the mainstream of Western culture and life, with all of its benefits and drawbacks.

SPANISH CULTURE UNDER FRANCO

The contrast to what was the officially trumpeted culture and life of the Franco regime could scarcely be more dramatic. Spain's culture was a Catholic antique, complete with symbols and ceremony inspired by Ferdinand and Isabella, Charles V, and Philip II. Catholic morals and ethics (and philosophy, too, to the extent that more profound elements crept into official Francoist thinking) undergirded all public life and all private life that came under the influence of the state—particularly education, whose content was almost totally shaped by the Spanish Catholic Church. Foreign influences obsessed Franco, and he sought to eradicate anything that he judged had corrupted Spanish society since its heyday during the Siglo de Oro, the golden sixteenth century. Cosmopolitanism had wreaked havoc upon Spanish values. According to Franco, "The spirit of criticism and reservation is a liberal thing that has no roots in the soil of our movement, and I repeat to you once again that its tone is military and monastic and to the discipline and patriotism of the soldier must be added the faith and fervor of the man of religion."[2] Speaking of the nineteenth century—which to Franco and his disciples, was the zenith of the "anti-Spain" that had started to take shape during the Enlightenment of the eighteenth century—Franco asked, "Doesn't a century of defeat and decadence demand a revolution? It does indeed—and a revolution in the Spanish sense that will destroy an ignominious century of foreign inspired doctrines that have caused our death. ... In the name of liberty, fraternity, and equality and all such liberal trivia our churches have been burned and our history destroyed."[3] In his speech announcing the creation of the FET y de las JONS, Franco recalled the Carlists in the nineteenth century as defenders of an ideal Spain fighting "the bastardized, Frenchified, Europeanized Spain of the liberals."[4]

These atavistic sentiments found their way into all official positions on culture and society and found expression in proregime magazines and revues like *Jerarquía*, *Vértice*, *Escorial*, and especially *Arbor*, the publication of the powerful and influential High Council for Scientific Investigation (Consejo Superior de Investigaciones Científicas—CSIC), with its orthodox Catholic bias.

Franco turned his back on the mainstream of Spanish culture that had been renewed in the "Generation of '98" (1898), named for the year that Spain was humbled by the United States in the Spanish-American War. The talented members of that generation sought to rediscover the indigenous roots of a once magnificent civilization, now fallen to disgrace, that might be refertilized to produce a new, authentically Spanish culture for the twentieth century. These men and women did not seek to resuscitate some epoch in Spain's past and pump it back to artificial life, as Franco did forty years later. They sought, instead, to rediscover in the treasure trove of Spanish history those elements that had once made Spain culturally great and that might again inspire the nation to cultural eminence.

Angel Ganivet began the national self-examination with his essay on the nature of Spanishness, "Idearium español," published in 1896. Other notables of the Generation of '98 were Miguel de Unamuno, essayist and professor of Greek; writers Azorín (José Martínez Ruiz), Pio Baroja, and Ramón del Valle Inclán; poet Antonio Machado; painter Ignacio Zuloaga; and essayist Ramiro de Maetzu, who later became a right-wing apologist. In some ways, these men followed in the spirit of their older contemporaries: Santiago Ramón y Cajal, the histologist who won the Nobel Prize for medicine in 1906; historian Marcelino Menéndez y Pelayo; Joaquín Costa, the social and legal historian; and Pablo Iglesias, the father of Spanish socialism.

The generation that followed that of '98 took a different approach to the quest to build a Spanish culture for the twentieth century, a route that took its adventurers into Europe. The foremost name among the Europeanists, a group that also included Gregorio Marañon and Ramón Pérez de Ayala, was José Ortega y Gasset, whose essay "The Revolt of the Masses" made him internationally famous. Ortega became the lodestar for the generations of liberal intellectuals who followed him—if by *liberal* one suggests an inquisitive, restless, passionate, nondogmatic dedication to truth. Only later did members of the Spanish intelligentsia begin to respond to the beat of a different drum, primarily from the Left. Perhaps best known of these new intellectuals was Juan Goytisolo. During the Franco years, however, Ortega the Europeanist and Unamuno the Hispanicist represented, for those suffocating in the orthodox, incensed air of Francoism, everything that had been and that one day might again be sublime in Spanish culture—in Ortega's words, "the iridescent gem of the Spain that could be."

It would not be fair to say that Spain under the Franco regime was a total cultural wasteland, but few of the artists, writers, and intellectuals who chose to remain in Spain achieved international recognition, whether they created within the Catholic sanctuary or outside it. Worldwide honor went, instead, to those identified with the great Spanish cultural heritage who had gone abroad after the Civil War began or who were already living abroad when the war broke out and refused to return to Spain while Franco was in power. Pablo Picasso was the most resplendent of these personalities; others included motion picture director Luis Buñuel; cellist Pablo Casals; guitarist Andrés Segovia, and Juan Ramón Jiménez, who received the Nobel Prize for literature in 1958 while living as an expatriate in Puerto Rico. Among those less celebrated internationally but eminent in their fields who spent many of their creative years away from Spain are historian Américo Castro, who taught at Harvard; educator Fernando de los Rios; Claudio Sánchez Albornoz; and poets Luis Cernuda and Jorge Guillén.

Special mention should be made of three world-renowned artists who do not fit into the preceding categories. Poet and dramatist Federico García Lorca, who finally holds the place in the pantheon of Spanish

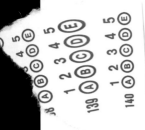

that was denied him by Franco, was executed by the rebels early in
[Ci]vil War. For those who opposed Franco, both inside and outside
[ ]Lorca symbolized the creative Spanish spirit that had been snuffed
[ ]the rebellion. The painter Joan Miró, the greatest Spanish artist of
[twe]ntieth century after Picasso, returned to Spain following the Civil
[ ]e had attacked the rebels through his art early in the war and remained unrepentant. Perhaps Miró's fame protected him from reprisal,
but his work was totally ignored by the regime, and his country honored
him—as the world had done long before—only after Franco died. At
Miró's death in December 1983, he was eulogized by both king and com-
moner. Three years later, in July 1986, Salvador Dalí, another Spanish artist spurned by Franco, was honored with the opening of a plaza in Madrid
that had been designed by the artist himself.

Freethinking intellectuals fought an uphill battle during most of the
Franco years. There was some intellectual activity, however, and as the regime aged, that activity became more challenging. Of course, no frontal
attacks against the system were ever tolerated—the censors saw to that—
and those who dared to make incursions along the flanks always ran the
risk of punishment. Antonio Tovar, the rector of the University of Salamanca, and Pedro Laín Entralgo, the rector of the University of Madrid,
were both summarily removed from their posts when their voices of protest grew too bold. Had they been seen as enemies of the regime, neither
would have been appointed to such exalted academic-political positions,
but even these men were subject to discipline when they "forgot their
place."

Some of the earliest dialogue that quietly and obliquely questioned
the regime took place among progressive, Catholic elite academics. In the
early 1950s, Laín Entralgo and José Luis Aranguren, a distinguished professor of ethics and sociology, took part in roundtables devoted to the
works of Jacques Maritain and Teilhard de Chardin, the most celebrated
living exponents of liberal Catholicism. Liberal Catholicism goes back to
the middle of the nineteenth century, and since that time, its criticism of
orthodox Catholicism has furnished a rich source of debate within the
church and among its intellectual faithful. Joaquín Ruiz Giménez, the minister of education in Franco's fourth cabinet, also moved toward liberal
Catholicism (it was he who had appointed Tovar and Laín to their rector-
ships). He fell from Franco's grace in 1956 and became a part of what Juan
Linz calls the "alegal opposition," described in Chapter 4.

Novelists began to write critically about Spanish society, not openly
against the regime as such but against the quality of life in Franco's Spain.
Its ugliness and violence were described in Camilo José Cela's *La familia de
Pascual Duarte* (1943); its materialism and furtive sexuality in Cela's *La
colmena* (1951); its hypocrisy and moral putrefaction in Carmen Laforet's

Nada (1944); its inanity and vacuity in Rafael Sánchez Ferlosio's *Jarama* (1956). In films, Luis García Berlanga and Juan Bardem tried to bring to the screen something both Spanish and intellectually challenging, but they rowed against a powerful current of kitsch. Movies were (and remain) enormously popular in Spain, but during the Franco era, those relatively few films that were produced domestically were either mindless musical comedies or innocuous folkloric dramas that relived, in melodramatic unreality, the "glorious days of Spanish history." Foreign films, particularly U.S. films, dominated the screen, but the censors scrutinized them for a glimpse of stocking, a bit of décolletage, or an exposed thigh (a word, by the way, that was expunged by the censors from the dialogue of a stage play by José María Pemán). One famous incident has been told and retold. In *Mogombo*, Ava Gardner was changed from Clark Gable's mistress to his sister in the dubbed dialogue of the film, to avoid the suggestion of adultery. The possibility of incest was obviously less shocking.

Spain has also had its share of those who created in the self-quarantined world of inner migration, what Ralf Dahrendorf calls the "romantic attitude" in describing German intellectuals.

> Here we encounter a political attitude of retreat from politics. In its hierarchy of values not only civil society but the state as well is superseded by the "true" virtues of inner perfection, of profundity, of the world of the mind. ... Although it sentimentally deprecates reality there is no serious evaluation of the world involved in their approach; the inner emigrant is not a fighting man but likes to leave reality to its own resources in order to withdraw himself to the refuge of "truth."[5]

Those who emigrate inwardly are difficult to judge, for they obviously are able to create in any atmosphere, rendering the politics of the country in which they live unimportant to them. A person who can create while the world around him sickens is either larger or smaller than human dimension. Perhaps Miró was larger, as was Vicente Aleixandre, the poet who won the Nobel Prize for literature in 1977. Raymond Carr and Juan Pablo Fusi believe so: "For Miró the years of Francoism were a scratch on the skin. His image of Spanish culture ... is of a carob tree deeprooted and evergreen. The award of the Nobel Prize to Vicente Aleixandre was not merely a reward for an unsullied and outstanding talent. It was a recognition that Spanish culture had survived. Or to put it another way, it had proved impossible to cut Spain off from the modern world."[6]

POST-FRANCO CULTURE AND SOCIETY

In October 1985, Belgium honored Spain at Europalia, a festival created in 1969 to reflect the cultures of the members of the European Community. At the time of the celebration, Spain had already been voted into the EC and would join officially on January 1, 1986. The festival, with events held in all the major Belgian cities, featured Spanish painting, sculpture, photography, design, architecture, theater, music, and dance. The exposition was inaugurated by the heir to the Spanish throne, Felipe, prince of Asturias, and the king and queen of the Belgians, Boudouin and Fabiola (herself a Spaniard). It was enormously successful. But the chief cultural critic for Le Soir, the leading newspaper in Brussels, said: "Europalia gives us a conventional image of Spain," and a contributor to the weekly magazine Le Vif noted, "Spain has made a great effort to present the classics, but there are aspects of young life that are missing."[7]

Both critics were accurate, but both missed the most significant aspect of Europalia: Spain was coming back to Europe after forty years of ostracism during the Franco regime and almost countless decades of moldering on the periphery of the continent prior to Franco's rule. Moreover, Belgium, as the host country, played a deeply symbolic role. Like all their fellow Europeans, including Spaniards, Belgians have vivid and immediate historical memories, and their memories of Spain are, for the most part, bleak. The Low Countries, of which Belgium is a part, were ruled by Spain during the Siglo de Oro, when Spain was the preeminent country in the world. And Spain's repression can be recalled in Belgium as if it were yesterday. In essence, at Europalia, Belgium pardoned Spain for its excesses, including the excesses of Franco, who had been aided in his victory by the modern-day oppressor of Belgium, Nazi Germany. It is all terribly convoluted, but then, the European mind is convoluted. And at Europalia, Belgium said, "Welcome!"

The critics were correct in their appraisals of Spanish culture in 1985, but Spain had showed itself in the only way in which it felt secure: as classic Spain. New Spain was in the making, but it was not yet ready for inspection, although many creations of the new Spain were present at Europalia. In the 1980s (and even today, but with less frenzy), Spain culturally was like an adolescent discovering the forbidden modern world, and discovery was an end in itself. Everything was in flux, and the experience was exhilarating. The phenomenon was called la movida—"the movement"—but this did not imply some organizational context; the term would be more precisely translated "the moving"—around, up, down, backward, forward, wherever movement can take the individual.

Spanish artists, in particular its creative artists, were at the heart of this "moving" and have been in the vanguard of what has followed now that la movida has settled down somewhat. Spain has certainly had its share of great performing or interpretative artists in the past forty years; many have become near icons: Pablo Casals, Andrés Segovia, Monserrat Caballé, Victoria de los Angeles, Plácido Domingo, Pilar Lorengar, Alfredo Kraus, Teresa Berganza, José Carreras, and Alicia de Larrocha, among others. But interpretative artists are different from creative ones, and, apart from their *personal* convictions (like those of Casals and Segovia who went into exile), they are not so constrained artistically by the political system within which they perform or chose to live. By contrast, creative artists, who deal directly with ideas, are profoundly affected by the political environment in which they work or aspire to work, and the Francoist environment was suffocating. The new environment of freedom that came after his death was enormously exhilarating, but it took a great deal of getting used to, like sunlight after confinement. Moreover, the environment was precarious until the failed coup d'état in 1981 seemingly put to rest the possibility of a regression to dictatorship.

The plastic arts—painting, sculpture, drawing—have seen the most exuberant creativity in the post-Franco era. In fact, the arrival in Spain of one of the masterpieces of twentieth-century painting defined the early period of artistic discovery. In accordance with Picasso's wishes, *Guernica* came home at last from the Museum of Modern Art in New York City, where the artist said it should hang until democracy returned to Spain. By now considered the greatest artistic expression of the horrors of the Spanish Civil War, its arrival was a poignant and symbolic event proudly shared by countless thousands of Spaniards who came to see it for the first time. Until 1992, it hung alone in an enormous room in a building adjacent to the Prado, protected like an icon behind bulletproof glass. It was an unfortunate setting because the painting was diminished by its strange, almost surreal isolation, but such protection was deemed necessary for fear that some pro-Franco zealot would attempt to deface it. But the painting also challenged the official taste of conservative, classic Spain because it was a piece of modern, abstract art, the kind that was derided and ignored by orthodox Spanish critics during the Franco dictatorship.

In 1964, a museum honoring the person and works of Picasso discreetly opened in a restored townhouse in Barcelona. The collection of works, primarily graphics and a few paintings, came from Jaume Sabartes, Picasso's intimate friend and former secretary. The opening was gingerly handled because Picasso was an avowed enemy of the Franco regime, and no mention of his name could be made. In fact, the civil governor of Barcelona had even said that while he was in charge, no museum dedicated to Picasso would ever exist. The opening was billed as the "Restoration of the Berenguer de Aguilar Palace, Exposition of the Sabartes Collection," and the "museum that wasn't a museum" became known only by word of mouth because officially, the "Picasso Museum" did not exist and therefore could not be publicized. Even its whereabouts were difficult to determine for a visitor unfamiliar with Barcelona. Moreover, the building was identified only by the street number. Discovery became part of art appreciation.

Modern art could be seen in Spain during the Franco years only by making a trip over difficult roads to Cuenca, a small, isolated city some ninety miles east-southeast of Madrid. There, the painter Fernando Zóbel created the Museum of Abstract Spanish Art out of a series of connected "hanging houses" (casas colgantes) for which Cuenca is famous—ancient houses cantilevered on mountainsides that hang over gorges below. Not a great artist himself, Zóbel nonetheless maintained the only sanctuary in Spain for the creation and display of modern art. Out of this sanctuary came names that have achieved world eminence: painters Antoni Tàpies and Antonio Saura and sculptor Eduardo Chillida. Between these and the younger post-Franco generation not associated with Cuenca are Luis Gordillo, Guillermo Pérez Villata, and Chema Cobo, whose reputations are now solid. Those causing excitement in the younger post-Franco generation—in Madrid and Barcelona and, more important in terms of international acceptance, New York City—are painters Miguel Barceló and José María Sicilia and sculptor Cristina Iglesias.

Madrid now has it own museum where some of these artists already hang in the permanent collection and where younger ones might aspire to hang. In 1990, the Queen Sofía Center of Art (Centro de Arte Reina Sofía—CARS) opened after years of restoring and renovating a vast, eighteenth-century hospital down the street from the Prado. It will house a permanent collection, space for traveling shows, library and documentation center, and workshops, plus the now de rigueur gift shop and restaurant. The Socialist government, in addition to paying for the nearly $60-million renovation, also has spent some $52 million on acquiring works for the permanent collection. Given the astronomical prices that works of modern art command today, Spain is probably too late to amass a collection of modern masters, but it stands ready to begin collecting the masters of tomorrow. The centerpiece of the museum is Guernica, which was moved to the Reina Sofía over the protests of Picasso's heirs, who said that the master wanted his work to hang beside those of the other Spanish immortals in the Prado (whose directors also resisted the move).

More old masters and some new ones arrived in Spain in 1992. In December 1988, after months of negotiations with the Spanish government, Baron Hans-Heinrich Thyssen-Bornemisza, a resident of Switzerland, announced that the major part of his art collection would go to Spain for ten years, with a strong probability that it would remain there permanently. The highly complex and controversial negotiations resulted in what looks very much like a lease-purchase agreement. The baron came out handsomely rewarded for his "generosity," but Spain received a large part of what is considered the greatest private art collection in the world after that belonging to Queen Elizabeth II of England. A final total of 803 paintings would go to Madrid, the major recipient, and to Barcelona after appropriate buildings were restored and remodeled to house them: the Villahermosa Palace in Madrid and the Monastery of Pedrables in Barcelona. The Villahermosa Palace, close by the Prado, was finally ready in May 1992, and it opened to the public on October 10, 1992. The baron's decision to take the collection to Spain was strongly encouraged and perhaps initiated by the Baroness Thyssen, Carmen Cervera, the baron's Spanish wife; her urgings gave Spain an advantage, edging out competing countries for the most extraordinary artistic coup in memory. And though Spain paid an extraordinarily high price for the collection, there were many other countries and many other museums (like the Getty, which is rumored to have offered a preposterous sum of money) that would have been only too happy to have had the opportunity to negotiate for it.

Even as foreign art was entering Spain either on visits or for semipermanent residence, Spanish art, primarily from the Prado, was beginning to travel the globe, propelled by an exuberant sense of Spanish pride. During the Franco regime, no major museum in the world would have negotiated with the Spanish government even for paintings from the Prado, arguably the world's preeminent picture gallery, nor would Franco have allowed the works to move. But in 1978, paintings of Francisco Zurbarán went to the Metropolitan Museum in New York, as did works by Diego Velásquez, the supreme Spanish master (some say the greatest painter ever) in 1989. In 1992, paintings by José de Ribera went to the Metropolitan. And in 1987, Queen Sofía opened an exhibition of Spanish art in Paris.

In Spain, corporate funding is beginning to support the arts, which for centuries had been helped solely by the state. The Fundación Juan March, established by the Spanish financier Juan March Ordinas, began to underwrite exhibits, as did corporations and banks, such as La Caixa, Banco Exterior, and Banco de Bilbao. Significant in terms of popular support for the arts and artists, strictly private, noncorporate groups like the Friends of Culture (Amigos de la Cultura) have been created. In 1991, the Prado received a totally unexpected bonanza: Manuel Villa Escusa, a real estate developer, was killed in a car crash and left his entire fortune— some $40 million in Madrid real estate—to be used solely for the acquisition of paintings. One can understand why Madrid was chosen the European cultural capital for 1992.

With the World's Fair in Seville and the Olympic Games in Barcelona, the arts of Spain came under world scrutiny. The fair and the games were pure theater, and as such, they can be considered a part of the Spanish cultural renaissance. The two events proved that Spain, hitherto known primarily for intense individualism, could produce a joint effort that was a succès fou, as the French would say—a delirious success. And though artistic quality cannot be measured by extravaganzas like the fair and the games, reality tells us that a country unable to bring such events off successfully simply cannot aspire to international cultural standing.

Beyond the plastic arts, Spain has had other very impressive successes. Surely the most talked about and perhaps the best young film director in Europe today is Pedro Almodóvar, the enfant terrible of Spanish cinema. The Spanish movie industry may not have high international rank (even though it has an enormous market in the 320 million people of the Spanish-speaking world), but Almodóvar has achieved international fame. Even before him, however, post-Franco Spanish filmmakers were being honored internationally. The Spanish film *Volver a Empezar* (To Begin Again) won an Academy Award in the United States in 1983, and two Young Director Awards at the Cannes Film Festival. And even during the Franco regime, Carlos Saura was able to produce films of high artistic quality that were seen in the non-Spanish-speaking world. Of course, no one has yet reached the heights of Luis Buñuel, but he is one of the giants of the universal film industry: Not many of his sort appear anywhere at any time.

Camilo José Cela won the Nobel Prize for literature in 1989, partly in recognition of his talent and partly to reward his creative courage under Franco. His was the fifth such prize to a Spaniard and the first since that won by poet Vicente Aleixandre in 1977. But for the most part, Spanish writers have not yet achieved the international acclaim of their Latin American counterparts, such as Gabriel García Márquez, Mario Vargas Llosa, Jorge Luis Borges, Octavio Paz, or Manuel Puig. And the great novel about the Spanish Civil War has yet to be written and probably can only be written by a Spaniard (*pace* Ernest Hemingway).

With major commissions around the globe, two Spanish architects have moved into the international arena: superstar Ricardo Bofill and the increasingly celebrated Santiago Calatrava, about whom the *New York Times* wrote: "His designs for bridges and railroad stations in Switzerland, Germany, and his native Spain have set the standard by which contemporary public works projects will be judged."[8] And yet another Spanish architect is gaining international recognition, José Rafael Moneo, who designed the Thyssen Collection.

Spanish theater has not produced a great playwright since Lorca. This perhaps is understandable in the most public and the most exposed of the arts. During the Franco regime, authors like Antonio Buero Vallejo created works that often defied the censors, but their daring was relative to the strictures of the time. Dramas and comedies considered provocative under Franco would no longer play convincingly either in Spain or abroad, and today's young dramatists have yet to produce works with international viability. Fine acting and imaginative production and direction can often salvage weak writing, however, and I remember exciting nights in the theater in Madrid thanks to the extremely gifted actress-director Nuria Espert. In recent years, her talents have begun to receive recognition beyond Spain. In 1986, she directed Glenda Jackson to great acclaim in a London production of Lorca's *The House of Bernarda Alba*, and in 1988, she directed *Rigoletto* and *Madame Butterfly* at Covent Garden.

Few professions suffered greater ignominy than journalism during the Franco dictatorship. Compelled to pander to the regime, its practitioners saw whatever critical faculties they may have possessed atrophy under a censorship that lasted longer than any other in Western Europe in this century. The free press that exists today is remarkable, given the wasteland out of which it emerged, and among Spain's many fine newspapers and journals, one newspaper has become exceptional by world standards. In 1991, the *Gannett Center Journal* of Columbia University published an article by John Merrill, professor of journalism at Louisiana State University, listing the twenty best newspapers in the world: It included *El Pais*, the Madrid daily. At the time of the accolade, the paper had been in existence only fifteen years but had already begun to receive international recognition. In 1986, the Roosevelt Foundation for the Four Freedoms honored *El Pais*, which was represented at the ceremony in Holland, the home of the foundation, by then editor Juan Luis Cebrián. In presenting the award, William J. van den Heuvel, president of the foundation, called *El Pais* "one of the most outstanding daily newspapers of the free world. ... Its leadership and intellectual honesty have given it influence far beyond the borders of Spain."[9] Two years later, Cebrián himself received a gold medal from the Spanish Institute in New York City. Eric Javits, president of the institute, made the award, noting that *El Pais* had become "an open forum for dialogue in a Spain evolving toward democracy. In this sense Cebrián helped to alter the direction of Spanish journalism and reinforce the transition to democracy and at the same time the relation between Spain and the United States."[10] The influence and power of the newspaper has continued to grow. *El Pais* and the Italian newspaper *La Repubblica* purchased 30 percent of the British newspaper *The Independent* in 1990, and these three newspapers together with the German newspaper *Süddeutsche Zeitung* formed a consortium to cover events in the "new" Europe that came into existence on January 1, 1992.

Even Spanish sports figures have become known across the world. Golfer Severiano Ballesteros won the British Open for the third time in 1988, and in the same year, cyclist Pedro Delgado won the Tour de France. Another Spaniard, Miguel Induráin, won the tour in 1991 and 1992.

Divorce and Abortion

The divorce bill became law on July 20, 1981, prevailing over the relentless lobbying of the Catholic hierarchy and the fierce opposition of the conservative lay elite. The college of bishops issued this verdict following the bill's passage: "Rather than being a remedy for evil, divorce is converted into an open door for the generation of evil."[11] General Fernández Posse, speaking at a religious ceremony, lamented the old society that he felt was being destroyed by the new, permissive legislation:

> We are at war, a special subversive dirty war. They are trying to destroy our spiritual and moral values, penetrating all our social establishments, showing the lowest tastes. ... A stubborn enemy has infiltrated the media, the church schools and universities. ... It seeks to propagate pernicious ideas which bring parents and children into conflict in order to destroy the family, the basic cell of all civilized society and the foundation of Christianity.[12]

Those who supported the legalization of divorce called their lay and clerical opponents hypocrites, pointing out that members of the elite had long been able to end their marriages through annulments engineered by a compliant church hierarchy. The prodivorce advocates also noted that the same conservative elite and the same church hierarchy had resisted earlier liberalization that struck down jail sentences for adultery and decriminalized the sale of contraceptives. When the Socialists came to power in 1982, many articles in the civil code dealing with the relationship between the sexes had remained unchanged from the Franco era. For example, under existing law, the mother of a child born out of wedlock was not allowed to establish the father's identity. A female lawyer in Madrid explained it this way: "There are many men who have illegitimate children who do not want to recognize them. And since the Church believes in the indissolubility of marriage it would have to accept the legality of two families."[13]

It had been estimated that 300,000 to 500,000 couples would rush to the courts to initiate proceedings once divorce became legal. (The law allows divorce by mutual consent after two years of separation.) But one year after the law came into effect, only an estimated 28,000 couples had started legal action; most were middle-aged, had had an average of fifteen to twenty years of married life, and came primarily from the middle classes. An ironic exception was Franco's granddaughter, María del Carmen, the young duchess of Cádiz, who separated from her husband, a cousin of Juan Carlos, and later divorced him.

The fact that Spaniards did not invade the courts once divorce became legal did not dissuade the opponents of abortion from asserting that abortion was a mortal sin and that once it was legalized, demand for the operation would become epidemic. Led by the hierarchy of the Spanish church, the crusaders cried out once again that the Socialists were perverting Spanish morals. The archbishop of Cuenca announced: "Assassination committed by a terrorist is less a crime than the killing of a defenseless child [fetus]."[14] In February 1983, the Spanish bishops denounced the abortion bill as "gravely unjust and totally unacceptable" and declared that abortion "could not escape the moral qualification of homicide."[15] The church put into a textbook used in parochial schools a statement that classified abortion as "a violent act comparable to terrorism and war." Another text that was not published ranked abortion with "systematic torture, concentration camps, and nuclear war."[16] The Socialist government countered that its sponsorship of permissive legislation was not changing the moral climate of Spain but was reflecting in law the changes that had already taken place. Estimates show that before 1983, approximately 300,000 abortions a year took place in Spain and that more than 100 women died each year at the hands of bungling, backstreet abortionists. According to sources in England, 75,000 Spanish women had aborted in the British Isles between 1977 and 1983.[17] The Socialists reminded their conservative opponents that upper-class women had always had a remedy for ridding themselves of offspring produced from socially unacceptable liaisons: Article 410 of the penal code mitigated the crime of murder committed by the mother of a newly born child if the killing were perpetrated "to hide her dishonor" (ocultar su deshonra). Her punishment would be minimal. A lower-class woman, on the other hand, could not easily avail herself of this defense because, by custom, it was assumed that a lower-class woman had no honor to protect. The Socialists removed article 410 from the code and replaced it with a new law that removes the classist insinuation but still treats infanticide committed by a distraught mother more leniently than other killings between close kin.[18]

In April 1985, the Constitutional Court declared unconstitutional the Regulation of the Voluntary Interruption of Pregnancy (Regulación de la Interrupción Voluntaria del Embarazo), popularly called the Abortion Law, passed by the PSOE government in October 1983. The law allowed abortion under three conditions: ethical abortion (aborto ético) if pregnancy had occurred as the result of rape; eugenic abortion (aborto eugenéstico) if the fetus was deformed; therapeutic abortion (aborto terapéutico) if there was a threat to the mother's life. The court did not seem opposed to ethical abortion, but because the law contained only a single article encompassing all three conditions, the entire law was declared unconstitutional. The declaration of unconstitutionality did not challenge the government's right to make law in regard to abortion, but it rejected what the court considered to be the law's failure to protect the rights of the unborn adequately, as guaranteed under article 15 of the constitution. The decision was curious. It was based on the fetus's right to life. Yet if the three conditions had been covered in separate articles, the court apparently would have accepted the constitutionality of abortion if life had begun as the result of rape, declaring abortion unconstitutional only under the other two conditions. If a fetus has a constitutional right to life, why would fetal life resulting from rape be unprotected but deformed fetal life be protected and the life of the mother be unprotected?

A new law that sought to overcome the court's earlier objections went into effect in early August 1985. Abortion would be legal in the first twelve weeks if pregnancy resulted from rape and in the first twenty-two weeks if the fetus was deformed. The law also allowed for abortion if the mother's life was in danger, but it went on to include threat to her mental or physical health as well. The law stipulated that abortion could be carried out only by doctors in state-regulated clinics and only after permission was granted by a panel of examining physicians at the clinic.

The law guaranteed a woman the right to abort under the three conditions but did not, however, guarantee her the ability to find doctors and medical personnel willing to perform the operation. Doctors, nurses, and other medical technicians at the public clinics sought the right to refuse to comply with the law when their consciences commanded; they also sought the right to perform the operation when their consciences relented. This effectively gave them a veto not only over the law but also over favorable decisions made by the panel of examining physicians at approved clinics. As a consequence, most women went to private clinics, where abortions were performed clandestinely. Women seeking abortions in private clinics and doctor, nurses, and other medical technicians performing the operations in these clinics came under relentless bombardment by local authorities. Medical records were seized, undermining doctor-patient confidentiality; telephones in private clinics were tapped; and patients, doctors, nurses, and other medical personnel were detained in local jails. Local authorities and antiabortion groups like Family Action (Acción Familiar) and the Association for the Respect of Life (Asociación pro Respeto a la Vida), taking advantage of legal actions, hauled the owners of private clinics, their practitioners, and their patients into court.

In late 1986, the government sought to ease restrictions on legal abortion. By decree (*decreto real*), the government did away with the examining committees in regulated clinics to minimize chances for a delay that could put the woman beyond the protected weeks during which abortion could take place. The decree also removed the requirement that all surgical interventions take place in operating rooms: Women less than three months pregnant for whom the procedure posed little risk could have surgery performed in clinics without such facilities. However, the courts immediately suspended enactment of the decree, once again citing article 15 as the pretext. In issuing the decree, the government had declared that no woman would ever again be jailed for having an abortion, implying that those who had already been imprisoned would be pardoned. The government could not prevent the court from issuing such sentences, but the court could not force the government to carry them out.

After the court's suspension of the royal decree, the government accredited a limited number of private clinics, allowing them to come under the protection of the law passed in August 1985. Since doctors, nurses, and other medical personnel in private clinics had no crises of conscience, the abortions in these clinics could go ahead with no further legal obstruction.

By 1988, the court had become more supportive of the administration (or perhaps had come to accept the reality of life in present-day Spain), and it reversed the suspension of the decree made in 1986. Following directives from the World Health Organization, the court declared that the health of pregnant women demanded the immediate enforcement of the decree. Further, a new law was in preparation stipulating that the list of factors considered to threaten a woman's mental or physical health would now include a precarious economic situation that would be exacerbated by the addition of another child. In September 1992, the government announced that in the new penal code being prepared, a fourth condition for obtaining a legal abortion would be added: if pregnancy would lead to anguish (*angustia*—the Spanish translation of the French word *detresse*, which appears in the French abortion law). Since 1985, most women seeking abortions have cited a threat to their mental and physical health as the reason, but the new concept of *angustia* or *detresse* is far more ambiguous and simpler to document. Under the new penal code, abortion for reasons of anguish could only take place in the first twelve weeks of pregnancy and had to be certified by a physician other than the one performing the procedure. But the certification process was simpler than that required to document a threat to a woman's mental or physical health. The latter required certification by a specialist, but the certification for anguish could be given by any doctor other than the one performing the abortion.

The restricted right to abort did not, of course, satisfy Spanish feminists, who continued to call for abortion on demand. But the gradual liberalization of access to abortion probably would eliminate any need for a repeat of the highly theatrical but deadly earnest act of defiance by feminists in 1985. At that time, two illegal abortions were performed at a feminist convention in Barcelona to demonstrate opposition to the limited nature of Spanish abortion rights. The entire membership—four thousand women—declared themselves willing *jointly* to take responsibility.

Probably more clearly than anything else, the battle over abortion and related sexual issues demonstrates the severely declining moral authority of the Catholic Church in present-day Spanish society. The political power of the church had already been lost with the creation of the democratic constitution. Today, Spaniards are simply not listening to the church, whose voice had carried with it the force of law until the death of Franco. When abortion became legal, the church declared that anyone involved in any way in the procedure would be excommunicated, but in a population where church attendance has fallen dramatically, the threat was a weak deterrent. In 1990, the pope urged Catholic pharmacists not to sell contraceptives, but the Spanish Federation of Pharmacists (Federación de Empresarios Farmacéuticos de España) announced that its members would ignore the plea, stating that a pharmacy served *all* the public.

The Spanish episcopacy excoriated the government for its "moral indifference" and "moral turpitude" because of its attitude toward the use of condoms and its secular educational process that, according to the church, sought to remove all moral and ethical values. (The government had recently endorsed an advertising program urging people to carry condoms and use them.) The document in which the church's broadside appeared was the first pronouncement from the Spanish hierarchy after Cardinal Angel Suquía was chosen by his fellow bishops to be president of the Spanish episcopacy. The document was a part of forty folios cataloging the church's attack on the government, coming out of the Episcopal Conference held in November 1990.[19] Some say that the episcopal outburst resulted, in part, from pique felt by the cardinal: González had kept him waiting for over six months before receiving him at the Moncloa Palace. According to the document, Spain had become a "huge casino" filled with political irresponsibility, influence peddling, corrupt practices, improper use of public funds, and ideological discrimination. The document lamented that "true ethical criteria are being replaced in the public conscience ... by a majoritarian dialectic and the force of votes, by social consensus which is changing the mentality of the public as a result of legal provisions."

José María (Txiki) Benegas, organizational secretary for the PSOE, called the document aberrant and antidemocratic, and Luz Sánchez-Mellado, the government's spokesperson, stated, "The document is so harsh and so unjust that as spokesperson of the government and having given the publication a first reading I prefer to calm down somewhat (*tener el ánimo más sosegado*) before I can give the evaluation the documents deserves."[20] In essence, what the episcopal hierarchy was criticizing was not so much the Socialist government but modern society and politics in general. However valid the document may or may not have been, the church revealed itself to be an institution that simply could not adjust to the fact that its influence had plummeted in post-Franco Spain. Writer and philosopher José Luis López Aranguren put it very well: "It is an error to hold the socialist government responsible for present-day secularism. The government merely reflects the attitudes of society. ... It is true that we live in a tremendously materialistic time, but the church itself, through people like Archbishop Marcinkus, financial advisor of the Vatican, has projected a lamentable image."[21]

Drugs

While the debate over abortion polarized both the decisionmakers and the citizenry, the Socialist government was also attempting to deal with yet another reality that has become part of Spanish society: drugs. In April 1983, the parliament passed legislation that made Spanish drug laws among the most lenient in Europe, altering prior legislation that had been among the most severe. Trafficking in drugs remains a serious offense, but the possession of drugs in small quantities for personal consumption has been decriminalized. Once again, the Socialist political leaders were charged with destroying the moral fiber of the nation. And once again, the Socialists contended that they were only attempting to handle an existing social phenomenon and were not creating the problems through legislation.

In March 1984, El Pais reported that until 1976, drug arrests relating to heroin distribution involved grams of the drug; after 1977, the amounts were measured in kilograms. In 1982, the total amount of drugs confiscated weighed 109 kilos and 395 grams, and the number of traffickers reached 11,000—figures similar to those for the preceding three years.[22] By the late 1980s, heroin was still the drug causing the greatest number of social problems, but cocaine was making enormous headway among Spain's drug users. In 1990, authorities seized more cocaine than heroin from traffickers: They confiscated 5,382 kilos of cocaine (up 189 percent since 1989), 886 kilos of heroin (up 24 percent from 1989), and 70,075 kilos of marijuana (up 9 percent from 1989), the latter most often used socially by adolescents.[23] In 1983, there were officially 83 deaths from drug overdosage, primarily in Madrid, Bilbao, and Barcelona. In 1990, 431 persons died of drug overdoses in the five largest cities alone: Madrid, Barcelona, Valencia, Seville, and Bilbao. The amount of drugs consumed in Spain is not precisely known, but the amount confiscated in 1983 already placed Spain at the top of the list in Europe.[24] In March 1984, three articles in El Pais gave some indication of the scope of drug addiction and trafficking in Spain. One article concerned a twelve-year-old boy in Barcelona who was undergoing treatment; a second told of three boys—aged nine, thirteen, and sixteen—who were arrested in Granada for holding up a bookstore to get money for drugs. The third article told of a young heroin addict in San Sebastián who committed suicide after holding ten people hostage for two hours in a bank.

As drug addiction and its twin scourge, crime, increased dramatically, the PSOE government reacted by raising the penalties for drug trafficking; especially severe punishment was prescribed for those who dealt drugs at health centers and schools or who were involved with minors in any way. In the penal code being prepared in late 1992, new drug-related crimes were added: the making, possession, transportation, or distribution of anything going into drug production. In addition, more severe laws were drawn up to deal with the laundering of drug money. But as in all other democratic societies (where draconian antidrug measures are precluded), longer jail sentences have been no deterrent whatsoever. On the contrary, drug addiction and trafficking seem to be increasing almost exponentially.

In 1988, experts in drug prevention and treatment—advisers to the National Drug Plan (Plan Nacional Sobre Drogas)—testified that, in their opinions, existing drug policy based on criminalization had been a complete failure, and they suggested that controlled decriminalization might bring better results. The attempt to control drug trafficking by legal means "is ineffective and arbitrary because like all other crimes that occur as response to unsatisfied social demand, like abortion, the effective rate of control is extraordinarily low."[25] Another expert on drug prevention said, "While the focus remains on criminalizing the trafficking in drugs, drug prevention becomes impossible. Whether we recognize it or not drugs are attractive to those groups at highest risk because they have about them a halo both magic and transgressive and put into motion mechanisms of social exclusion that make rehabilitation difficult."[26]

But even as experts were questioning the effectiveness of criminalizing of drug trafficking, Spaniards were calling for *more* criminalization. According to a poll taken by the Center of Sociological Investigations (Centro de Investigaciones Sociológicas—CIS) in October 1991, 79 percent of those interviewed were in favor of criminalizing the consumption of drugs—a policy that the PSOE leadership rejected, claiming it would further marginalize the addict and make prevention and treatment even more difficult.[27] A poll taken by *Demoscopia* for *El Pais* in January 1992 revealed that Spaniards considered terrorism, drug addiction, unemployment, and criminal activity the four most serious problems facing the nation—problems that appeared to defy solution.[28] By then, citizens had already started to take the law into their own hands, faced with what they felt was inadequate governmental action. In big cities around the country, neighborhood vigilante groups patrolled the streets on the hunt (*a la caza*) for drug users (who, of course, were not breaking the law), bodily throwing them out of the neighborhoods when found. In Valencia, there were bloody confrontations between vigilantes and police, whose task is to control not only criminals but also those who take the law into their own hands, irrespective of motive. At the same time, however, José Luis Corcuera, minister of the interior and commander-in-chief of all police forces, condemned judges who were, in his opinion, overly scrupulous with those detained because of possession (possession for personal use is not illegal). He also labeled journalists who decried police excesses in relation to drug enforcement as "pseudointellectuals" and excoriated the "yuppies" who go to parties where "lines of cocaine are drawn on silver platters."[29]

The response to the epidemic of drugs was pitting elected officials, citizens, and law enforcement agents against one another while the scourge continued to spin out of hand, seemingly immune to any deterrent force. And to compound the already frightening problem, Spain had to live with the reality that, along with Portugal, it had become the major European gateway for cocaine. Between the two countries, there are twenty-two ports through which cocaine can move onto the continent, handled by Latin American criminals who, speaking the same languages, disappear easily into the populace.

SPANISH CULTURE REINVENTED

For those familiar with Spain's history, particularly with the details of the country's last democratic experience during the Second Republic, the soberness with which the Spaniards have undergone change is remarkable. Even the most intense conflicts—over divorce, abortion, and educational reform—had been fought according to the rules of the democratic game. The inveterate Spanish recourse to rage has seemingly become aberrant. The attempted coup d'état in February 1981 was not successful, and the violence committed in the Basque lands or perpetrated by Basque terrorists in other parts of Spain is now unacceptable even to the majority of the Basques, let alone the rest of the citizenry.

Where is the Spaniard who, according to Salvador de Madariaga, acted first and thought later?[30] What has become of the Spanish man about whom Elena de la Souchère has commented: "While he pays his respects to another through the formulas of refined courtesy custom demands of him, at that very moment the Spaniard is miles away from even conceiving of the other person's point of view."[31] Where is the Spanish stranger the trenchant Hispanophile V. S. Pritchett once listened to on a train? "His whole performance illustrated the blindness of Spanish egotism. The speaker stares at you with a prolonged dramatic stare that goes through you. He stares because he is trying to get into his head the impossible proposition that you exist. He does not listen to you. He never discusses. He asserts. Only *he* exists."[32]

Where are the passionate Spaniards for whom the constraints of democracy were intolerable, and where are the political doctrines into which they once poured their wrath? Where are the anarchists and the Communists? According to William Plaff, the anarchists now vote Socialist, and the Communist party has lost its appeal. What Fascists still exist count for little today. The Socialists in power since 1982 are behaving more like the Social Democrats in Northern Europe than like Socialists in the other Latin nations.

> Today Spain has dramatically changed. It has become a land of relentless moderation as well as capitalism, a conspiracy of modernism, enlightenment and moderation incorporating king and leaders of every party, all of them scrupulously democratic in everything they say, polite in the criticisms of others, invariably positive and constructive. It is the last thing a veteran of the Civil War might expect to find. ... Possibly the Spanish have learned from history, a lucky exception among nations. Perhaps the Civil War was just too awful. Perhaps 1936 was simply another Spain, another epoch. Perhaps Franco should be credited that he put wounded Spain into a coma where everyone forgot. ... Perhaps it is simply necessity. The past had to be obliterated. Spain today is a country resolutely without a memory. It has reinvented itself. For all that one might tell from the Spain of today time began on the day in 1975 when Juan Carlos became king.[33]

NOTES

1. John Hooper, *The Spaniards: A Portrait of the New Spain* (Middlesex, England: Viking, 1986), p. 283.

2. *Palabras del Caudillo* (Madrid: Ediciones de la Vicesecretaría de Educación Popular, 1953), p. 317. The translations of Franco's words are mine.

3. Ibid., p. 54.

4. Ibid., p. 11.

5. Ralf Dahrendorf, *Society and Democracy in Germany* (New York: Doubleday, 1969), pp. 288–289.

6. Raymond Carr and Juan Pablo Fusi, *Spain: Dictatorship to Democracy* (London: George Allen and Unwin, 1979), p. 133.

7. *El Pais*, International Edition, October 7, 1985.

8. *New York Times*, April 9, 1993.

9. *El Pais*, International Edition, September 22, 1986.

10. Ibid., November 21, 1988.

11. *Macleans*, October 26, 1983.

12. Ibid.

13. *New York Times*, April 11, 1980.

14. *Macleans,* October 26, 1983.

15. *Diario 16,* February 5, 1983.

16. *New York Times,* October 8, 1983.

17. *Macleans,* October 26, 1983.

18. *El Pais,* October 19, 1983.

19. Ibid., International Edition, November 24, 1990.

20. Ibid.

21. Ibid., International Edition, December 2, 1990.

22. Ibid., March 22, 1984.

23. Ibid., International Edition, October 21, 1991.

24. Ibid., March 27, 1984.

25. Ibid., International Edition, October 31, 1988.

26. Ibid.

27. Ibid., International Edition, October 28 and December 2, 1991.

28. Ibid., January 6, 1992.

29. Ibid., October 14, 1991.

30. Salvador de Madariaga, *Englishmen, Frenchmen, Spaniards,* 2d ed. (New York: Hill and Wang, 1969).

31. Elena de la Souchère, *An Explanation of Spain,* Eleanor Ross Levieu, trans. (New York: Vintage Books, 1964), pp. 20–30.

32. V. S. Pritchett, "Spain," *Holiday* 37 (April 1965), p. 63.

33. *Los Angeles Times,* March 20, 1983.

Part Five

Spain in the New Europe

12

The PSOE in Power

In their tough, unsentimental political biography of Felipe González, *La ambición del César*, José Luis Gutiérrez and Amando de Miguel make the following indictment:

> Protected by the famous ten million votes that boosted the PSOE to the pinnacle of power, the party "invaded" society with sweeping arguments that disfigured the contours of what was thought to be a western democracy. For González, an absolute majority in the two houses of parliament, in almost all of the Autonomous Communities, and in thousands of city halls throughout the country was not sufficient. The PSOE wanted to dominate every aspect of public life, from the media to cultural and civic and recreational associations. This "totalitarianizing" passion was intended to expand merely formal democracy and to capture for the party an historic opportunity to remain in power for at least a generation—for all practical purposes, making impossible alternation in power or even access to it by the parties of the opposition. Incidentally, the process followed by the Socialist party was linked in certain essential aspects to clearly antidemocratic behavior like that of Mexico's multimansioned PRI [Mexico's single-party dominant Institutionalized Revolutionary Party—Partido Revolucionario Institucional].[1]

The sheer hubris that energized the party and its leaders leaves one somewhat awestruck. But if their ambition was to remain in power for a generation and if a generation is defined as thirty years, they were nineteen years short. The PSOE lost its majority in the election held on June 6, 1993.[2] Pollsters had already been indicating that after the next general election, the PSOE could well have to share its power, possibly even giving it up entirely.

ACCOMPLISHMENTS

Polls taken in late December 1992 put the PP only 6.8 percent behind the front-running PSOE. One year earlier, the distance had been 18 points.[3] Even though the PSOE maintained its majority over the years, there had been a gradual erosion in popular support for it, which made the shrinkage seem less precipitous.

The exhilarating 1982 election first put the party into power with 48.7 percent of the valid votes, producing 202 seats in the 350-seat Congress. In the 1986 elections, the PSOE, while still holding an absolute majority of the seats in Congress, saw its percentage of the valid votes drop to 44.3 percent, producing 184 seats. And in the 1989 election, the PSOE ultimately won only 39.55 percent of the valid votes, producing 175 seats, exactly half the total number. One says, "ultimately" because voting irregularities in Barcelona, Murcia, Melilla, and Pontevedra and challenges before the Constitutional Court kept the final political conformation of the Congress unresolved until March 1990. In the interim, new elections had to be held in the disputed constituencies, and the government was not securely ensconced until the vote of confidence on April 5, 1990. With its minimal half of all seats, the PSOE was still able to govern with relative ease because the four Basque deputies from Herri Batasuna had not taken their seats. They were continuing their boycott, maintained since 1982, of what they considered to be the government of an illegitimate political system. This time, however, the Constitutional Court ruled on March 29, 1990, that the HB deputies would never be allowed to sit unless they swore the conventional allegiance to the constitution. No longer would the HB deputies themselves be able to decide arbitrarily when and if they would take their seats.

International Achievements

Its erosion notwithstanding, the PSOE could claim some spectacular successes since 1982, and nowhere is this more evident than in the international arena, where Spain has finally come into its own. Credit must be given to the preceding, foundation-building UCD governments, but the triumphs took place while the Socialists were in power, and to them goes the glory—and they have exulted in it. (Though it is difficult to describe in a study of this sort and certainly impossible to document, I have been gently amused observing the tyros of the new governing elite taking their places as equals at the conference tables of their long-established European counterparts. Observing them is like watching hesitant young peacocks as they gradually, then triumphantly spread and raise their resplendent tail feathers.) Under PSOE leadership, Spain joined the European Community (treaty signed on June 12, 1985, and activated on January 1, 1986); the recently revived Western European Union (November 1988); and the European Monetary System (June 1989). In November 1991, it also signed the Maastricht Treaty, along with its fellow EC members. Spain had joined NATO in March 1982, in the waning days of Calvo Sotelo's tenure as prime minister, but it was Felipe González who secured that membership in the referendum held on March 12, 1986, six weeks after Spain's admission to the EC.

The strategy used by González reveals a great deal about the transformation of the PSOE from a Socialist to a Social Democratic party, already discussed, and about the transformation of Spain into a major international player. The success of the referendum was a coup de théâtre, with a bravura performance by González. When membership in NATO was rushed through Congress by Calvo Sotelo and the ruling UCD party, González and the PSOE were stridently opposed. Although the deradicalization of the PSOE had long since been under way, certain holdovers from its ideological past still existed and could be manipulated for electoral advantage, among them, anti-Americanism. In the minds of many, many Spaniards, NATO was synonymous with the United States, and the U.S. military presence in Spain was a constant reminder of the Franco dictatorship. Many on the left blamed the United States for the last twenty years of Franco's rule, for aid to Spain in 1953 had come at a time when the regime appeared to have been most vulnerable and perhaps ripe for overthrow. Whether this appraisal by Franco's enemies was realistic is conjectural, but many believed it to be true, and they harbored a deep resentment of the United States for its infusion of what, for then destitute Spain, were staggering sums of money that shored up a seemingly tottering political system.

In 1982, the PSOE went to the hustings pledging, among many other things, that if it came into power it would give the Spanish people the opportunity to decide for themselves, via referendum, whether Spain should remain in NATO. The party expected that the people would say no to continued membership, thereby validating PSOE's anti-NATO stand. But governing was quite different from campaigning, and as we have already seen in discussing the economy, the electoral base of the PSOE victory was broader than its Socialist core, which was both anti-NATO and anti-American. For short-run electoral gains, the PSOE was able to tap the reluctance of many Spaniards to become involved in the Cold War and in East-West rivalry. But once in power, the PSOE found its long-range goals could be seriously undermined if it continued to champion Spain's abandonment of NATO. González and his government were passionately determined to take Spain into the European Community and accomplish what neither Franco nor the UCD governments had been able to bring about. But all the EC member nations were, at the same time, either full-fledged members of NATO or, like France, affiliated with it. Thus, applying for membership in the EC while planning to ask the Spanish people to repudiate continued membership in NATO were incompatible goals. Although, strictly speaking, Spain could be a member of one organization and not of the other, political reality said otherwise. Yet the PSOE government was committed by electoral pledge to put the issue of continued NATO membership before the people in a national referendum: It could not renege on its pledge without leaving itself open to accusations of unvarnished opportunism. However, the pledge included no specific timetable, nor did it prevent the PSOE government from changing its mind about Spain remaining in NATO. As we have already seen, pragmatism was the force that moved the PSOE from a Socialist to a Social Democratic party, and in the decision to finesse Spain's continued membership in NATO, pragmatism was in full operation.

The referendum was finally held on March 12, 1986, almost four years after the Socialists had come into power. But the date was hardly fortuitous. While González and his colleagues were abroad, negotiating Spain's membership in the EC, government representatives at home began to build support for Spain's continued membership in NATO, seeking to siphon popular enthusiasm for the former to fuel the latter. Then, with the almost universal approval of the Spanish people, Spain became a member of the EC on January 1, 1986. A little over two months later, González held the referendum on NATO, making a yes vote not only a vote of approval for NATO but also a kind of vote of confidence for the performance of the PSOE government. Moreover, the wording of the referendum was shrewdly crafted to make a yes vote on continuing Spain's membership in NATO encompass, as well, provisions that would keep Spain free of nuclear arms and would mandate the reduction of the U.S. military presence on Spanish soil. Consequently, U.S. political leaders who were eagerly supporting Spain's continued membership in NATO could not urge a negative vote, yet a positive vote would greatly strengthen the PSOE government's bargaining position vis-à-vis the United States, increasing Spain's stature in the international arena. The referendum reads as follows:

> The Government considers it in the national interest that Spain remain in the Atlantic Alliance and resolves that established on the following terms:
>
> 1. The participation of Spain in the Atlantic Alliance will not include its incorporation in the integrated military structure.
> 2. The prohibition on the installation, storing or introducing nuclear arms on Spanish territory will be continued.
> 3. The progressive reduction of the military presence of the United States in Spain will be proceeded with.
>
> "Do you consider it advisable for Spain to remain in the Atlantic Alliance according to the terms set forth by the Government of the nation?"[4]

Of those taking part in the referendum, 52.3 percent voted yes, 39.84 percent voted no, and 1.09 percent cast blank ballots. It is interesting to note that since the referendum was viewed as a kind of national vote of confidence for the PSOE in a year that, by law, would also see a general election, Manuel Fraga, leader of the major party in opposition (the AP) asked the Spanish people to abstain. The AP was caught in an intriguing dilemma. As a party on the right, it had enthusiastically supported NATO membership in 1982, but at the time of the referendum, it was the Socialists who were urging a positive vote. Yet a yes for NATO would be interpreted as a yes for the Socialists. In an attempt to wriggle out of the predicament without having to support withdrawal from NATO, the AP urged the Spanish people to abstain from taking part in the referendum, hoping thereby to weaken the credibility of the PSOE government—a cynical strategy that seemed particularly reprehensible for a party that prided itself on its moral integrity. The strategy was not successful. The PSOE rode to victory in the general election, which González called less than three months after the successful NATO referendum. The party won, in large part, because of the international accomplishments of its leaders.

In January 1988, after two years of often bitter negotiations, Spain and the United States agreed to move U.S. F-16s out of Spain from Torrejón, the U.S. air base on the outskirts of Madrid. The installation was seen by Spaniards as emblematic of their country's international inferiority; they often asked how Americans would like to see a Spanish air base on the outskirts of Washington, D.C. González received high praise for holding firm against the U.S. colossus, and the PSOE's success in the elections of 1989 can be partly attributed, once again, to the government's international accomplishments, which helped offset its domestic shortcomings. Between June 25, 1991, and March 24, 1992, seventy-two F-16s were flown out, ending almost forty years of the U.S. presence near the Spanish capital. The departures symbolized Spain's new position on the international scene: It was now a worthy player, no longer to be taken for granted.

Midway between the first and last departures of the F-16s, Spain enjoyed the first perquisites of its new status. It was asked to be the host of the extraordinarily important Mideast peace talks among Israel, Egypt, Jordan, and the Palestinians, overseen by the United States and Russia. The meeting took place in Madrid in late October and early November 1991.

Less than one month after the last F-16 left Spain, the International Exposition opened in Seville, on April 20, 1992, and on July 8, the Olympic Games began in Barcelona. The decisions to hold both events in Spain were made by international committees charged with judging Spain's suitability. Actually, those decisions had been made several years earlier, when Spain's international status was far less impressive, but the opening dates could not have been more opportune. Spain presented itself to the world in a manner unparalleled in this century, and both celebrations were spectacularly successful. Barcelona's sophisticated beauty and ambiance—an amalgam of the antique and the contemporary—came alive on television screens across the globe. And Seville, from whose port Columbus had set sail in 1492, shook off centuries of picturesque dust to lay claim to world-class status. To ice the cake, Madrid was declared the cultural capital of Europe for 1992. Felipe González, his government, and his party could and did take deserved credit for these achievements.

Success has, however, eluded the Socialist government in its efforts to resolve two enduring problems of foreign policy. (In the government's defense, it has to be pointed out that success also eluded its immediate predecessors and *their* predecessors for at least 250 years.) Spain has wanted Gibraltar back since it was transferred to British sovereignty in 1713 under the terms of the Treaty of Utrecht, which ended the War of the Spanish Succession. But Spain also wants to keep two city-states on the coast of what is now Morocco—Melilla and Ceuta—which came into Spanish possession in 1497 and 1581, respectively. Morocco now wants them, but Spain is as reluctant to relinquish them as Great Britain is to give back Gibraltar. One cannot say that Morocco wants to "take back" the two cities, for they became Spanish centuries before Morocco was created. Indeed, they were not part of any existing nation-state. In other words, to the Spanish, Morocco cannot take back what it has never possessed. Gibraltar, on the other hand, was an integral part of a long-existing nation-state, which now wants it back. Such niceties do not, however, convince either the Moroccans or the British. Moreover, Spain's argument to acquire Gibraltar could be used by Morocco in efforts to take Ceuta and Melilla.

To the Socialists' credit, Spain's relations with Morocco are better now than they have been in a very long time, due, in great part, to the largest loan Spain has ever made a foreign country—125,000 million pesetas—negotiated by González and the king of Morocco in 1988. But the problem of Ceuta and Melilla has merely quieted down; it has not gone away.

Spain's relations with Great Britain have been complicated by both nations' membership in NATO and the EC. How are conflicts over sovereignty resolved between members, if neither is willing to give up claims to disputed territory? There is no facile answer. For both countries, Gibraltar is a quaint but troublesome legacy from colonial times—a symbol of national pride and grandeur and a reminder of a glorious past now gone.

National Achievements

Military Reform. After 1982, González continued the reforms that had begun under Suárez and Calvo Sotelo. Under the Socialist administration, the Spanish armed forces at last became the counterpart of the military in the other democratic countries of Europe and the world: It was now the loyal servant of a civilian government.

The PSOE government reduced the size of the military and restructured its deployment throughout Spain. By 1991, the army had been reduced from 280,000 (when the PSOE took office) to 195,000, and by the same date, the army officer corps had been reduced from 41,983 (in 1985) to 35,213. Distinctions were wiped away between those forces designated for external defense and those designated for internal security, and the authority of the eleven military districts into which the nation is divided was reduced. Today, all Spanish males must complete military service (*mili*), but the PSOE reduced the number of obligatory months from between fifteen and eighteen to between twelve and fifteen, and conscientious objectors could be excused. In October 1986, for the first time in Spanish history, the PSOE appointed a civilian to command the Civil Guard, and in the following month, it reinstated those members of the Democratic Military Union who had been court-martialed and removed from the armed forces. Finally, in February 1988, the PSOE government issued a decree-law that permitted women to enter the armed forces and the military academies.

Economic Growth. Despite the socioeconomic problems facing the PSOE government in late 1992 and the prospects of electoral reprisal by the people in 1993, the party could point to statistics that showed Spain to be among the most successful advanced industrial nation-states. Once again, credit must be given, in part, to the preceding UCD governments and even to Franco. But the economy flowered under the PSOE governments, and the Socialists, like all incumbents, have taken the credit themselves. Table 12.1 illustrates the strong showing Spain had made in commercial and industrial development by the mid-1980s in comparison to other Western nations, using indicators of commercial and industrial development. Spain's ranking in the top quarter of the countries graded in number of persons per telephone (2.7 in 1985, compared to 1.3 for the United States)[5] and in the number of viewers per television set (3.8 in 1986, compared to 1.7 in the United States)[6] reflects the improvement in the nation's standard of living.

In 1986, the per capita GNP annual growth rate was 3.2 percent, well above that of Spain's European neighbors; out of 157 countries, Spain ranked 46 (the United States ranked 68).[7] It ranked first among 62 coun-

TABLE 12.1   Ranking of Spain Among Western Nations in Industrial Development

	Spain	Other
Motor vehicle production (1985)[a]	8	United States-2
Cement production (1988)[a]	9	United States-4
Steel production (1986)[a]	11	United States-3
Mineral production (1986)[a]	13	United States-33
Iron ore production (1985)[a]	15	United States-5
Coal production (1986)[a]	15	United States-2
Fish caught (1985)[b]	17	United States-5
Fruit production (1986)[c]	8	Italy-4; France-7
Vegetable production (1986)[c]	9	Italy-7; France-12
Home ownership (1988)[d]	100	United States-75
Nuclear energy (1987)[e]	9	United States-1
Railroad trackage (1987)[a]	18	West Germany-3; UK-7; France-9; Italy-16
Length of paved roads (1987)[f]	12	United States-1; France-9; West Germany-10; UK-11
Size of merchant marine (1986)[a]	20	United States-5
Air passenger miles (1986)[g]	12	United States-1; UK-5; France-6; W. Germany-8

[a]Source: UN Statistical Yearbook.
[b]Source: FAO Yearbook of Fishery Statistics.
[c]Source: FAO Production Yearbook.
[d]Source: UN Construction Statistics.
[e]Source: UN Energy Statistics Yearbook.
[f]Source: Road and Motor Vehicle Statistics.
[g]Source: Civil Aviation Statistics of the World.

tries in net direct foreign private investment, with $57 million dollars.[8] By the 1980s, the distribution of Spain's workforce among the three basic economic activities was very much like that in other developed nations: 17.6 percent in agriculture, 31.8 percent in industry, and 50.6 percent in services.[9]

If the statistics were good by the mid-1980s, they were spectacular from 1986—the year Spain joined the European Community—until 1991. In that five-year period, Spain relived the economic miracle of the 1960s. Unlike the earlier phenomenon, however, which took the country from near penury to modest prosperity, the new miracle took Spain to the threshold of the opulence already enjoyed by its neighbors to the north, particularly Germany and France. From 1986 to 1991, Spain grew faster economically than any other country in Europe, averaging more than 4 percent a year and reaching a vertiginous 7 percent in 1987.[10] In 1987 and 1988, capital investment grew by 15 percent,[11] and foreign investment reached $10 billion in 1989 alone.[12] From 1986 to 1990, Spain shared (along with Ireland, Portugal, and Greece) almost $8 billion a year in grants from the EC to raise living standards and provide infrastructure growth in backward regions.[13] And Spanish gross domestic product per capita leaped from $5,991 in 1986 to $15,149 in 1992.[14] *The Economist* puts Spain in perspective:

> Assume Spain's GDP per head is already within, say, ten points of the EC average, what difference does it make? One difference is that, on this reckoning, Spain's economy is already bigger than Canada's. According to official figures, on a purchasing power-parity basis, Canada's GDP is only 7 percent larger than Spain's. That gap would disappear once the black economy was included. Canada, remember, is a member of the G7 club of rich industrial countries. Spain would have an excellent case for a place at what is, in effect, the world's economic High Table. The G7 might become the G8.[15]

THE PSOE IN TROUBLE

The new economic miracle began to lose its luster in 1991. Already in 1990, the economic growth rate had fallen to 3.5 percent rather than the 4 percent that had been projected, and in 1991, the growth rate slipped even lower, to 2.5 percent rather than the projected 3.6 percent.[16] In November 1992, the Bank of Spain announced that the growth rate had slowed to less than 1 percent in the third quarter of the year.[17] The dramatic increases in the per capita GDP peaked in 1991 and remained virtually unchanged in 1992. To compound the dire statistics, the fiscal deficit in 1992 was 4.4 percent, rather than the projected 4.0 percent.[18] (It should be remembered that to qualify for acceptance in the European Monetary Union projected at Maastricht for 1999, the fiscal deficit by that date could be no higher than 3 percent of the gross domestic product.) Although inflation dropped from 6.9 percent in 1989 to 5.5 percent in 1991 and 5.4 percent in December 1992, economists concurred that the decline simply confirmed the economy's downturn.[19] By contrast, the rate of unemployment continued to climb, reaching 15.5 percent by 1991 and 18.4 percent in the third quarter of 1992.

The catalyst of the economic downturn was the Gulf War, which caused petroleum prices to soar. For Spain, whose primary source of energy is petroleum (virtually all of which must be imported), the price increases further unbalanced an economy that was already showing signs of instability. But the roots of Spain's economic problems went deeper than the oil crisis. Spain and the PSOE government had believed that membership in the European Community would be the economic panacea, and, as we have already seen, membership did bring immediate and dazzling results. But Spain soon discovered that membership also had its hidden costs. Spain had to compete with the EC powerhouses, Germany and France, which could produce and deliver with more quality and more efficiency than could Spain. "We were seduced into believing we were in the major league," said Jaime Mariátegui, a business consultant. "But when you are racing a Spanish SEAT against a Mercedes, eventually you get to face reality."[20]

To compete, the PSOE government knew that Spain had to reduce the encumbrances that increased the cost of the nation's goods and services—among them, continued subsidies to long-subventioned, state-owned enterprises and newly assumed entitlements that Spaniards, like all other Western Europeans, had come to expect (payments for health, education, housing, social security, family benefits, unemployment compensation, and more). All EC members are encumbered to one degree or another, but the richer members with strong economies could shoulder the expenses more easily than could the poorer ones with troubled economies. (Even the richer members, however, had already begun to reappraise their costs, particularly their entitlement payments.)

The PSOE government was caught between the desire to pursue economic efficiency and increase Spanish competitiveness and the desire to fulfill electoral pledges to further socioeconomic democracy—pledges that could not be ignored, even given the PSOE's transformation from a Socialist to a Social Democratic party. Cutting subsidies to troubled publicly held industries would lead to further unemployment within the very class that is (or at least had been until then) the bedrock of PSOE support. I will cite but one example. The state-owned HUNOSA coal mines had amassed losses of over $1.2 billion, even though they had received subventions of over $2 billion since 1988. Yet closing down the deep, almost exhausted mines, which had not shown a profit in years, would put thousands out of work.[21] Cutting entitlements would affect all citizens but particularly the working class, which was already vociferously complaining that cuts were being considered even before Spaniards had achieved the level of coverage already reached by their fellow EC members. A German or French citizen, even with reduced entitlements, would be better off than a Spaniard of similar status before cuts were made.

Perhaps there was a way for the government to come down from the horns of the dilemma without making painful and potentially dangerous cuts. In 1990, the government sought to increase state revenue by increasing property valuations for tax purposes. The program (to cost some $1 billion) called for aerially photographing all property in Spain. It was estimated that the first phase of the plan would have raised taxable value from 15 to 42 trillion pesetas ($446 million); the second phase would boost it to $122 trillion. But the daring plan was shelved, however, after the government was threatened with thousands of lawsuits from property owners, encouraged by the mayors of several large cities. The postponement was considered the most significant policy reversal for the PSOE government since it had come into power in 1982.[22]

Pursuing yet another approach to increase revenue, the PSOE government in 1991 raised the VAT, a regressive sales tax that hits the working class especially hard, from 12 to 14 percent, all the while lowering income tax rates, which benefits the more affluent.[23] (It would appear that in its relationship with its bedrock constituency—the workers—the PSOE both giveth and taketh away—or at least it *attempted* to give. The year before, in an effort to help the working class, José María Benegas—third in command in the PSOE after Felipe González and Alfonso Guerra—had proposed that the government compel banks to make mortgage loans at significantly reduced interest rates for the construction of 400,000 new houses for the working class over a four-year period.[24] The response to the proposal set in relief the philosophical differences within the PSOE between hard-liners and more traditional socialists [to be discussed below] that had come to the surface late in 1988. The monetarist hard-liner, Finance Minister Carlos Solchaga, immediately attacked the proposal as unworkable. González, though not publicly taking sides, is thought to have supported Solchaga's opposition, which carried the day.)

In September 1992, the PSOE government announced the most austere budget in its ten-year regime for 1993. The government was determined to reduce the fiscal deficit to 3.6 percent of the GDP from the 4.4 percent of 1992. The budget called for further privatization of state-held firms, cuts in defense spending, and curbs on public sector wages and salaries.[25] Although privatization in Spain had not been extensive, as it has been in Great Britain, for example, the PSOE had already begun to dispose of some state-owned industries. In 1989, 30 percent of Repsol Explorations, SA (an oil company) was put up for sale. Earlier, the government had sold the majority holding in SEAT to Volkswagen, AG.[26] Weak or depleated publicly owned enterprises such as HUNOSA are seldom attractive to private investors, however. Privatization is thus not always the way either to rid the state of obsolete industries or to put money into the state's coffers.

During the heyday of the second miracle, the government had kept interest rates high in order to attract foreign capital, but as a result, the peseta became strengthened to the point where Spanish goods were being priced out of the market. In addition, the nation's single largest source of foreign exchange, tourism, had begun to suffer, for Spain had ceased to be an inexpensive place to vacation. In 1990, for example, tourism brought in about $16 billion, but the number of visitors fell by 750,000 in the first six months of the year compared to that same period in 1989.[27]

The various attempts to reinvigorate the Spanish economy having failed, the government devalued the peseta by 5 percent in September 1992, and two months later, it was devalued by another 6 percent.[28] The decision amounted to a sobering, tacit admission by the government that

Spain could not yet keep up with its fellow EC members except by lowering the value of its currency—and along with it, the nation's pride and dignity.

Lowering Spain's sights on Europe was never considered as an alternative. The PSOE government had taken Spain into Europe and remained staunchly committed to the relationship, not only for the sake of Spain but also for the sake of the party's prestige and place in history. Moreover, the Spanish people were also committed to Europe, and the PSOE counted on their continued support regardless of how difficult the government's policies might prove to be. It was, however, an inauspicious time for the party to face the electorate. If James Carville had been running the 1993 campaign for Felipe González, as he did for Bill Clinton, he would have had to keep his famous sign tacked up in campaign headquarters (translated into Spanish, of course): "Es la economía, estúpido!"

Errors and Omissions

In this section, I will attempt to explain the disenchantment that seemed to suffuse the citizenry as national elections approached. Perhaps the length of time in office is part of the explanation; so, too, is the failure to reform where reform was necessary (and called for when the PSOE was in opposition before 1982). And surely the lack of meaningful parliamentary opposition contributed, as did the inner conflict within the PSOE.

Tenure in Office. Is there a cycle of power that a governing elite simply outlives? What happened to Thatcher and to Bush suggests that perhaps there is. The question troubles González, who believes that there is such a cycle but that the PSOE has not yet outlived it. This following quotation is extracted from an extended reminiscence that González shared with Juan Luis Cebrián, former editor of *El País,* over a leisurely lunch at the Moncloa Palace, in October 1992.

> I know that there are many who perceive that this period is coming to an end, with my party's eventual loss of the absolute majority. This perception floats in the atmosphere, and I cannot deny the atmosphere any more than I can deny that it's raining or that we have a drought. In addition, in many prestigious universities sociopolitical analyses are made according to which there is a ten-year turning point in every governing tenure, a point that produces a certain end of an era sensation or a crisis in confidence, or whatever. I don't know if they are right or not. But I tend to believe that it is truer for countries that have had a longer run than ours. In the case of Germany or post-war France the historic cycle came to twenty years. And in our case, for example, I can say that … the cycle is not yet closed. What we have accomplished that is positive is very fragile. I do not even speak about what is negative, for they are already throwing our failures into our face and every day demanding an accounting.[29]

Lack of Opposition. In January 1992, the leaders of the PSOE recognized that their biggest problem was the public's perception that their party was corrupt. Just the month before, *El Pais* reported that over 200 politicians had been indicted for some sort of misconduct since the Socialists came to power in 1982. All the alleged wrongdoers were certainly not PSOE members, but the majority were, given the overwhelmingly majoritarian presence of the PSOE for the past ten years at the national, regional, and local levels. The second most "corrupt" party was the PP (formerly AP), the closest thing Spain has to an opposition. The article went on to say that many of the accused retained their elected or appointed positions and that those who had left government had done so only as the result of pressure from their parties.

Why had the party that had so long dominated Spanish politics become corruptible, if not corrupted? Of course, the most facile (but not necessarily incorrect) answer might come from Lord Acton, who said that power corrupts and absolute power corrupts absolutely. And the PSOE has come as close as one can imagine to absolute power in Spain since it first entered office in October 1982. Cebrián has given a more rigorous explanation, perhaps the most cogent I have seen, and the following analysis expands on his seminal ideas.[30]

Essentially, the Spanish political system as it actually works is out of synchronization with the system as it was *designed* to work in the constitution. The Spanish founding fathers created a parliamentary monarchy to be operated by a multiparty system that would produce coalition governments; these coalitions would then offer most of the major parties and even some of the minor ones a voice in political decisionmaking. Indeed, it would have been virtually impossible for the founders to have envisaged anything else. It must not be forgotten that dozens of parties had sprung up in the aftermath of the legalization of political parties early in 1977, and the continued existence of a large number of them seemed inevitable. A system of proportional representation was therefore adopted as the most equitable way to achieve electorally the widest possible spectrum of political expression.

The results of the election in 1979 gave the UCD a plurality of the seats in the *Cortes,* and while the victory was lopsided, it did not throw the political system into dysfunction. The government's existence was, in fact, always somewhat precarious. In 1982, however, the PSOE won an *absolute* majority in the *Cortes* and repeated the success in 1986 even with a reduced percentage of the popular vote and a reduced number of seats in the Congress. In 1989, it won exactly half the seats. It is rare for a single party to win an absolute majority in a proportional system, much less to duplicate and then almost triplicate the feat. But the victory produced a governing party with virtually no checks and balances. In a properly functioning, multiparty, parliamentary system, each party checks the other; those that manage to reach agreement to create a governing coalition are essentially uneasy partners. The compromises made in order to reach consensus are constant reminders of the lack of fidelity to the integrity of the ideology or platforms of the compromising parties. (It would be more accurate to say the "compromised" parties, in the sense of having made dishonorable concessions.) Some piece of the programmatic whole cloth of each party must be cut away in order to create what amounts to a patchwork of concessions. There is constant tension within the coalition, which might not be good for policy output but which does prevent one party from overstepping its bounds. Coalitions constantly teeter on the verge of potential collapse, keeping power barely within reach. Moreover, the parties not in the coalition have a vested interest in its collapse, for they might be included in the coalition's replacement.

In a two-party-dominant parliamentary system, like Britain's for example, one party usually wins the absolute majority of seats in parliament, giving it total control over the legislature and producing a politically unified cabinet. The potential for abuse would seem palpable, but in the British system, a complex of checks has been created to keep power harnessed. The fact that these checks owe their origins and continued viability to British custom and tradition, not to constitutional or legislative enactment, does not weaken their force: For all practical purposes, usage has given the checks constitutional weight. The position of Her Majesty's Loyal Opposition is, in fact, a paid position, with a salary only slightly less than that of the prime minister. The duty of the leader of the opposition is simply that: to oppose at full throttle, within the limits of loyalty to the system embodied by the monarch. The leader of the opposition is aided by a shadow cabinet, which, though disembodied, acts as a looming presence over the actual cabinet. In the House of Commons, question time is one of the great traditional devices designed to keep the leadership vulnerable and exposed, and though questions may come from both the party in power and the party in opposition, they are essentially a weapon of the opposition. Even the prime minister must take questions personally once a week. In addition, the very workings of the two-party-dominant system that gives total power to a single party makes the governing party wary in the use of that power. The knowledge that the opposition could come into power at the next election constrains the party in power to act with prudence. Margaret Thatcher's administration may be the exception since she pushed her majority about as far it could be pushed. But even though her party has yet to suffer the consequences of such hubris, she herself already has. The Conservatives, fearing possible reprisals from a winning Labor party in the next election, sacked the individual most identified with what many came to see as an abuse of power.

Neither of the two preceding scenarios apply to Spain from 1982 until the present: The PSOE government has essentially been free from formalized opposition. Even the informal post of leader of the opposition, established in 1982, was downgraded in August 1983 by a prime ministerial decree entitled Rules in the General Priority of State Rankings (Reglamientos de Ordenación General de Precedencias en el Estado). In all official acts organized by the crown, the government, or the administration, the leader of the opposition ranks fifteenth. Moreover, since the PSOE controlled the *Cortes* absolutely until 1989, the legislature abdicated its duty as watchdog over the executive. The very first congressional investigatory committee in Spain's democratic history came into existence only in early 1992, to inquire into the behavior of Julián García Valverde, the minister of health. While head of RENFE (the national railroad company), he had engaged in what later was considered questionable behavior. It is significant that the congressional right to investigate was implemented only after the Socialist party lost its absolute control of the *Cortes* after the elections in 1989.

The PSOE certainly cannot be blamed for having won its overwhelming majorities in 1982 and 1986. It played by the rules but won more than the rules had been designed to accommodate. Perhaps hubris is an inevitable characteristic under such fortuitous circumstances, but democratic politics often extracts a terrible revenge for such overweening arrogance. The general elections in 1993 began to show how painful the extraction will be.

Failures to Reform

When a party gets the power to do what it has said all along that it wanted to do, the public expects that party to do it. Yet the PSOE has been accused of failing to reform adequately three systems that, while in opposition, it had claimed were long overdue for change: the bureaucratic, educational, and judicial systems.

The Bureaucratic System. Early in its first administration, the PSOE government put approximately half a million civil servants on a continuous workday—from 8:00 A.M. to 3:00 P.M., Monday through Friday, plus every other Saturday. This schedule now makes it impossible for those hired by the state to hold two jobs simultaneously during the normal workday. But for generations, it had been an accepted way of life for workers to leave a first job early in order to arrive late at a second job (thereby, often performing both jobs badly). This long-overdue change had a monumental impact on the Spanish workforce, but as I wrote in an earlier study, the changes were "only the tip of the reform that the bureaucracy must undergo,[31] and that iceberg resisting reform is still in place.

Particularly pressing was the need to restructure the recruitment and training of the prestigious and powerful upper echelons of the civil service called the *cuerpos*, closely akin to their French counterparts, the *grands corps*. The members of this body, overwhelmingly upper-middle-class males from the big cities (primarily Madrid), were left virtually untouched even by Franco. Yet a large percentage of the men at the top at the time of his death in 1975 were still there in 1982 and are still there today. In other words, the new democracy is, to a large degree, still run by men who operated the old dictatorship. And even though an authentic civil servant is supposed to be able to accommodate any master, that adaptability seems above suspicion only when all the masters share a similar commitment to democratic values. To serve a dictator and a freely elected executive with equal aplomb could make the bureaucrat an uncivil, self-serving servant. Many Spaniards believe this description fits the high bureaucracy perfectly.

In April 1987, Alfonso Guerra, then deputy prime minister and Felipe González's alter ego, declared that the basic promises made by the Socialists in 1982 had been fulfilled. "Democratic stability, economic rationality, and the end of Spain's international isolation have been achieved in the past five years."[32] He did not, however, include the reform of public administration. In fact, he berated those who criticized that failure to reform:

> When one does not have the responsibility to govern it is easy to move in the world of grand principles. Administrative reform is one of those principles. Everyone criticizes and says "This administration is no good, it must be reformed." But no one tells us how precisely to do it because few people know how to do it. The Spanish bureaucracy has in part a life of its own which eludes the political will of those who govern, at least in the short run.[33]

This was a rather extraordinary admission of weakness for the deputy leader of the party whose absolute majority had been renewed only a year earlier—a party that had brooked no interference in restructuring the country's economic system. Five years later, Felipe González, in his long monologue with Cebrián, talked about criticism and the presence of a still unreformed bureaucracy: "When the opposition criticizes us I very seldom have the feeling that it hits the mark. They do not see the things about which I criticize myself. ... But you already know that, in any case, I am not at all satisfied with the performance of the bureaucracy; I wasn't on the very first day, and I am not now."[34]

The Educational System. If the issues of divorce, abortion, and drugs caused a national furor, the Socialists' program for educational reform triggered an equally truculent reaction, drawing a bombardment of condemnation from the forces on the right, captained by the Spanish Catholic hierarchy and seconded by its lay lieutenants. Bishops, priests, devout laity, and Catholic newspapers, magazines, journals, radio stations, press services, and publishing houses entered the fray. The church and its faithful were fighting a rearguard action against a secular state empowered through the ballot to bring about reforms that would change Spanish society even more profoundly than the liberalization of divorce and abortion. Responsibility for the education and socialization of the Spaniard would pass from the church and its institutions to the state and its institutions. This would both follow the pattern established in all Western democracies and break a tradition that had endured longer in Spain than in any other Western European nation. With only a few short-lived breaks, the education and socialization of the Spaniard had been almost exclusively the preserve of the church since the days of the Catholic Kings.

The educational reform would operate at two levels: Primary and secondary education was covered by the Organic Law on the Right to an Education (Ley Orgánica del Derecho a la Educación—LODE), and higher education was covered by the Law of University Reform (Ley de Reforma Universitaria—LRU). The level at which change would have the greatest impact, especially upon future generations, was primary and secondary education. Here, the conflict swirled about the mutually contradictory guarantees in article 27 of the constitution. On the one hand, it said that "everyone has the right to an education" and that "basic education is obligatory and free." Such rights would be guaranteed through a general program of instruction, with the state "inspect[ing] and sanction[ing] the educational system in order to see that the law is fulfilled." The objective of teaching, according to the article, is to bring about "the full development of the human personality all the while respecting the democratic principles of social interaction and fundamental rights and liberties." On the other hand, article 27 also guarantees "freedom of instruction" to those who teach, and it affirms the right of parents "to have their children receive the religious and moral formation that is in keeping with the family's convictions." Moreover, "with the reservation that the principles of the constitution be respected, individuals and corporations have the right to create centers of learning," and "the public authorities are obliged to assist those centers of learning that meet all the requirements established by law."

Which of these rights take precedence? The Socialists were close to unanimity in holding that the fundamental right was that of the child-student to receive the best education possible in an academic atmosphere committed to democratic principles. These goals would be monitored by the state and would be achieved, first and foremost, in the public schools. The Right was almost equally unanimous in its belief that the fundamental right was the parents' right to have their children receive the religious and moral training appropriate to the family's convictions. For the overwhelming majority of those on the Right, this could only occur within Catholic schools, and the right of these schools to educate as their directors and faculty saw fit and to be subventioned by the state were set forth unequivocally in the constitution. Moreover, the Right resisted even the suggestion that the state had the right to oversee the expenditure of public moneys granted to the private schools. (During the Franco years, church schools had been given carte blanche to do whatever they chose, with no requirement to give an accounting to the state.) The Left did not deny that private education had a constitutional right to exist and be financially aided by the state, but the Socialists and their allies were adamant about maintaining rigorous control over all public moneys that went to support private education and about giving priority to public education. In the controversy over whose rights were paramount—the child-student's or the parents'—the Socialists cited the 1982 opinion of the European Court of Human Rights, which gave precedence to the child. The Right fought fiercely to stop the passage of LODE by the Senate, introducing 4,160 amendments in an attempt to block the final vote. But the filibuster action failed, and the bill became law in March 1984.

The Law on University Reform, LRU, increased the autonomy of each state university vis-à-vis the ministry of education and science, but within the guidelines of the ministry. (There are thirty state and four private universities in Spain; three of the latter four are operated by the Society of Jesus [Jesuits], and the remaining one is operated by the Opus Dei.) The LRU also weakened the control (some say the stranglehold) of the *catedrático*, the sole full professor in each department; this individual also possessed the chair that granted him (or her, but rarely) full command of the faculty. There was not even the suggestion of collegiality in decision-making. Above the *catedráticos* sat the rector, essentially a political appointee. (During the Franco regime, rectors and *catedráticos* could lose their positions if they ventured over the invisible line marking the limits of the regime's tolerance.) The LRU established that the governance of the universities would henceforth be placed in a university council (claustro constituyente) made up of professors of all ranks, including the *catedráticos*, the administrative staff, and, where appropriate, students.

The reform did not, however, alter university fees, entry examinations, curricula, or quality of education. As a consequence, by the middle to late 1980s, university education was in crisis. From January 20 to 23, 1987, 2.5 million university and secondary school students went on strike, railing against high fees and university entrance examinations. The constitution set forth the right of every Spaniard to receive an education (article 27), and students saw fees as an impediment to that right. They also deemed entry examinations to be prejudiced against those from the less privileged strata of society (presenting arguments of class bias similar to those made by minority students in the United States against the SAT and similar examinations). In February 1987, after the students' union had called off its strike, José Mariá Maravall, minister of education and science, presented the government's offer: Fees for the final four years in state high schools would be done away with; students coming from families with at least two children and earnings below 140,000 pesetas (then approximately $1,100) a month would be exempt from university fees; the number of state scholarship would be raised by 25 percent; an extra 67,480 school (not university) places would be provided; and the government would increase spending on education by 25 percent in 1987 and 40 percent in 1988. Maravall estimated that the reforms would cost about 40,000 million pesetas (then about $310 million).[35] His offer was immediately accepted by the student union. (In spring 1988, university professors went on strike, joining primary, middle, and secondary school teachers, all of whom sought pay increases that would put them on a par with nonteaching civil servants with the same classification.)

Beyond the immediate complaints of the students in 1987, there was a deeper disgruntlement about the suitability and quality of advanced education for the modern industrial and even postindustrial world into which Spain was moving. There were too few places to accommodate the demand in many academic disciplines, forcing students to major in specializations in which they had no interest or for which they had no talent. Universities were enormously crowded—over 100,000 undergraduates at the Complutense in Madrid and over 80,000 at the Central in Barcelona. In addition, the universities were often in bad repair and had poor facilities, laboratories, and equipment. Because very few of the universities had residences or dormitories, students were (and still are) compelled to live either at home or in rented facilities off campus. And the word *campus* is not really appropriate for Spanish universities, which, like many of their European counterparts, are really a collection of urban buildings rather than a place in which a full life can be lived, with housing, recreational, cultural, athletic, and medical facilities provided and extensive extracurricular activities available. In sum, the universities continued to offer education more suited to the old Spain than the new—focusing on the arts, medicine, and law, rather than the sciences (including computer science), business, and communications. And students were unhappy.

In April 1989, the government announced its program (White Paper—Libro Blanco) for restructuring elementary, middle, and secondary education. It would mandate that all Spaniards be schooled from ages six to sixteen (an increase of two years), and a newly remodeled high school curriculum leading to the *bachillerato* (a certificate of completion of high school following examination) would require two more years. University entry would still depend upon successfully passing entry examinations; possession of the *bachillerato* would not automatically provide access to advanced education. The government announced that the reforms would cost almost one billion pesetas. In 1990, the provisions of the White Paper were turned into the Law for the General Restructuring of the Educational System (Ley de Ordenación General del Sistema Educativo).

The Judicial System. In mid-1988, the government announced that it had fulfilled the pledges it made in 1982 to modernize the judicial system, most of which had been unchanged since the Franco regime and even before. The reforms included the provision for habeas corpus, asylum, legal defense of the accused, conscientious objection, and freedom of assembly and public demonstration. Changes had been made in laws dealing with the sentencing in criminal cases, and abortion under certain conditions had been legalized. But critics of the Socialist government provided a catalog of reforms that were still needed: Guarantees set forth in the constitution had yet to be implemented fully. Either nothing had been done where legal impediments did not exist, or legal impediments continued to operate that, in effect, negated constitutional provisions. The court system had neither been modernized nor sufficiently funded, and above all, the penal code created during the Franco dictatorship still remained in force. It was not until February 1992 that the PSOE government announced that a new code was in the making.

DISSENSION WITHIN THE PSOE

Early in 1990, the first insinuations of what would develop into the "Juan Guerra affair" became public. In a nutshell, Alfonso Guerra's brother Juan had gotten rich by using his fraternal relationship to great advantage. Juan allegedly used official office space in Seville, out of which he was accused of wheeling and dealing with the knowledge and tacit approval of Alfonso—who was deputy prime minister, deputy leader of the PSOE, intimate friend and collaborator of Felipe González, and the most powerful politician in Andulucia, the largest region in Spain. The scandal unfolded throughout 1990 and 1991. In February 1992, the Supreme Court of Andulucia exonerated Alfonso Guerra of any wrongdoing, but in December 1992, Juan Guerra was sentenced to one year imprisonment and a fine of 15 million pesetas for fiscal crimes. The scandal seemed to go to the very core of the dilemma of the Socialist party, caught as it was between adherence to doctrinal fidelity and the expedient pursuit of power. Juan

Guerra, the Socialist opportunist, corrupted (or appeared to corrupt) his righteous brother, Alfonso.

But by the time he was exonerated, Alfonso Guerra had long since resigned from the cabinet, giving up his position as deputy prime minister. (He retained his position as deputy secretary-general of the PSOE, however.) He announced his resignation on January 12, 1991, but Guerra's spiritual, psychological withdrawal from Felipe González and his entourage of political pragmatists had begun several years earlier. Some say the general strike in December 1988 marked the first visible break in the relationship of Felipe and Alfonso, the latter identified by the striking workers and their leaders as the keeper of the flame of the muscular brand of socialism that both González and Guerra had embraced early in their careers. And in fact, the resignation did make manifest the schizophrenia of the PSOE, which had been growing since the party's accession to power in 1982. Though both González and Guerra had re-created the PSOE in the years preceding and following Franco's death and though both men engineered the spectacular victories in 1982 and 1986 and the simple victory in 1989, the facile adaptability of González often ran counter to the stringent rigor of Guerra. Alfonso always played a kind of Thomas à Becket to Felipe's Henry II.

After the break on January 12, 1991, Guerra demonstrated the split personality of the PSOE. He announced that the party had been colonized by the powerful economic forces in Spain (like a virus colonizes a host) and that González had been kidnapped by those forces and had to be rescued. Guerra believed that the PSOE had been governing, for all practical purposes, in coalition not with other parties but with the socioeconomic "powers that be" (los poderes fácticos, as they are called in Spain). In the cabinet, Guerra's bête noire had been Carlos Solchaga, minister of economy and finance, who seemed to be the advance man of these forces. In March 1991, González, in the most extensive cabinet shuffle since he came to power in 1982, appointed three men who were closely identified with Solchaga to the ministries of agriculture, industry, and public works and transport.

Recriminations and accusations flew back and forth between felipistas and guerristas throughout 1991 and 1992, with party insiders saying that only an extraordinary congress of the PSOE could put an end to the family feud. Yet González and Guerra maintained that their friendship was intact even though Guerra claimed he had not resigned from the cabinet but had been thrown out by González. Internal discord of such dimension is threatening for a party at any time; in the beginning stages of an electoral campaign, it can be a mortal blow. In his long discussion with Cebrián in October 1992, González sought to reaffirm his attachment to Guerra:

Let's not go on talking about *guerrismo* or *felipismo* and mixing in personal relations that have nothing to do with the debate of renovators, party liners, etc., etc. I am convinced that in the event I run again Alfonso would be the first to support me, independent of any other consideration. And I am no longer speaking of him but of what I understand to be a more widespread feeling. ... The complexity that the PSOE has taken on as a result of its institutional responsibilities and of its broad view of society has made the PSOE, from my point of view, more a party of consensus than simply one that counts majorities.[36]

But in December 1992, a *mano-a-mano* between two men representing two visions of the Socialist party was fought with the entire nation watching, like spectators at the bullring. Alfonso Guerra, the deputy secretary-general of the party, faced off with Narcís Serra, who was deputy prime minister (Guerra's former position). In their respective tours around Spain, region by region, each man offered a political message—one pragmatic, the other leftist—and a political style—one colloquial, the other populist—all with the encouragement of Felipe González. "The PSOE needs a debate with other leaders and other points of view," González said.[37]

But González seemed as unresolved as his party. Toward the end of his rambling monologue with Juan Luis Cebrián, González began to muse; his mood was autumnal, like the day, somewhat out of keeping for the fifty-year-old man. He agreed with some observers that he was an old young man, and he spoke as if there were more than one personality within that man, a duality that perhaps matched the split personality of his party: "If one is up there on the rostrum one can lose the perspective of one's size. One must come down and see oneself from a distance, better to understand other people and not to write memoirs. Memoirs are always written by one of the two personages we carry around inside ourselves seeking to justify the other."[38]

THE 1993 ELECTIONS

The battle continued to rage as the party went to the polls in June 1993. But which party went before the electorate? Was it the pragmatic, colloquial one, or the leftist, populist one? The question remains unanswered. The election left the PSOE without a majority in parliament, but it was still the largest party in Spain. As leader of the plurality, González was once again asked by the king to form a government. He chose not to go into coalition but rather to preside over a minority government, a decision that showed a special kind of arrogance, like performing on the high wire without a safety net. A coalition indicates unequivocally that one's power depends upon the decisions of others; a minority government indicates much the same thing, but while the power lasts, it is solely one's own.

This uncertain leadership must be galling to Felipe González, who for eleven years had absolute power. To his 18-member cabinet, created in July 1993, he appointed 8 new ministers and 6 independents, mostly technocrats—not one *guerrista* among them. What a far cry they were from the jubilant young Socialists ready to "save" Spain who made up González's first cabinet in 1982! Moreover, it would appear that, irrespective of their undeniable accomplishments, the Socialists did not "save" Spain: The job still remains to be done. Economic conditions in 1993, for example, eerily recalled those in 1982. In the first quarter of 1993, the number of jobless reached 3.3 million, 21.7 percent of the workforce, with some 500,000 more people expected to lose their jobs before the end of the year. Unemployment would then be at 23 percent. In addition, inflation was rising at an annual rate of 4.9 percent. After several years of unprecedented prosperity under the Socialists, Spain was suffering the most serious economic strife in thirty years.[39]

Yet Spain would not be where it is today politically had the Socialists not taken their turn at power, demonstrating that the new democratic regime could be governed as responsibly from the Left as from the Right (or, more accurately, from the Center-Left and Center-Right). Mutual rejection of the Left and the Right, a potentially virulent legacy from the Second Republic, has been replaced by mutual accommodation of the Left and the Right, made real by the elections in 1982 that effectively brought to a close the transition to democracy that began with Franco's death in 1975.

DEMOCRACY REGAINED

Where, then, is democracy today in Spain, and where is Spain today in Europe and the world? These interrelated questions and their responses bring full circle the study of Spain set forth in the introduction to this volume.

It would be neither hyperbolic nor disingenuous to say that democracy in Spain is secure. There is little nostalgia for the past or yearning for some hypothetical alternative to replace the political system that came into existence on December 29, 1978. Moreover, Spaniards have awarded the system with a legitimacy that transcends governmental efficacy, and they seem to have wed themselves to democracy for better or for worse, for richer or for poorer, in sickness or in health.

During the last years of the UCD governments, a disenchantment had come over the Spanish people. Their initial euphoria during the early, heady days of the transition that preceded the creation of the constitution seemed to have given way to a disillusionment with the new democracy's ability to solve everyday problems, particularly those put on hold in the Moncloa Pacts. Many observers feared that the people's commitment to democracy would falter or even collapse in the face of the UCD governments' ineffectiveness and that they might be drawn to nondemocratic solutions.

> Allegedly, this *desencanto* was manifested in a variety of symptoms: most commonly, it was linked to demobilization and apathy, negative perceptions of democracy and democratic institutions, perceived inefficacy and insufficiency of government, frustrated political and economic expectations, a decline in voter turnout and the growth of antidemocratic attitudes. ... Although indications of these phenomena were not verified empirically, it was then common to state that *desencanto* was directly and negatively affecting the reserves of legitimacy of the new democratic regime—a development that was regarded as undermining the new regime's ability to survive potential challenges in the future.[40]

But the fears proved groundless, and the commitment to democracy remained steady. "In 1981 shortly after the attempted coup, the proportion of those who recognized the legitimacy of Spain's democracy rose to 81 percent and in 1982 after the victory of the *Partido Socialista de Obrero Español* (PSOE) it stood at a comparatively high 74 percent."[41] By 1990, 80 percent of Spaniards preferred democracy to any other form of government, up from 49 percent in 1980.[42] And the majority of both those who responded positively to the Franco regime (in 1989, 13 percent) and those who responded ambivalently (saying that the Franco regime had been partly good and partly bad—in 1989, 45 percent), acknowledged the legitimacy of the new regime.[43]

Moreover, Spaniards are able to distinguish between regime legitimacy and governmental efficacy, as illustrated in Table 12.2. Unlike their compatriots during Spain's first attempt at democracy—the Second Republic—Spaniards today no longer hold the political system hostage for governmental policies gone wrong or governmental policies that run counter to a particular political persuasion. Now, when political dissatisfaction demands remedy, alternation in government has replaced threats to the regime. Spain today plays the political game in much the same way as the other democracies of the world.

SPAIN IN THE WORLD TODAY

With democracy, Spain became free to fulfill a destiny that had been almost eclipsed for generations, perhaps even centuries. To borrow a phrase from psychology, democracy released Spain for self-realization, not only within itself but also within the world at large. Internationally,

TABLE 12.2   Legitimacy and Efficacy in Spain, 1978–1989: A Typology (in percentages)

	1978	1980	1985	1989
Democrats[a]	74	46	75	76
Critics	11	32	12	11
Satisfied	3	4	7	6
Antidemocrats	12	18	6	7
N	5,190	4,784	1,926	2,472

[a]"Democrats" are those who express a preference for the democratic regime and believe that it is efficacious; "critics" acknowledge the legitimacy but not the efficacy of Spanish democracy; "satisfied" respondents, on the contrary, acknowledge its efficacy but not its legitimacy; and "antidemocrats" reject both the efficacy and the legitimacy of the system.

Source: Montero and Torcal, "La cultura política," p. 60, as it appears in José Ramón Montero, "Revisiting Democratic Success: Legitimacy and the Meanings of Democracy in Spain," in Richard Gunther, ed., *Politics, Society, and Democracy: The Case of Spain* (Boulder: Westview Press, 1993), p. 154. Reprinted by permission of José Ramón Montero.

the liberated personalities of Spain are, like the national personas, multiple; of them, the European one has become dominant. "Spain was the spearhead of the European idea when she attempted to build a unified Europe in the sixteenth century. It became American when she discovered the New World five hundred years ago. It has been Mediterranean since the ancient times of Rome and Carthage."[44]

Mediterranean Spain

Spain is the major power in that part of the Mediterranean where its principal interests lie, the Maghreb (Algeria, Libya, Morocco, and Tunisia). As we have seen earlier, however, Spain is vulnerable there because of its policy regarding Ceuta and Melilla, cities on Morocco's Mediterranean coast that Spain considers to be as Spanish as any part of the Iberian Peninsula. It supports maintaining the status quo and has the military strength to do so should an attempt be made to take the cities by force. On the other hand, Moroccan nationalists call for the liberation of the two cities at any cost, and the conservative opposition party, the Istiqlal, has even asked the pope to intercede on Morocco's behalf. Further, the Spanish attitude regarding Ceuta and Melilla makes problematic the claim on Gibraltar, and it keeps Spain and Great Britain in contention.

Adding to the complexity, Spain's relations with its other North African neighbors have, of late, become strained as a result of the surge in immigration from these neighbors into Spain. It is ironic that a land known for expulsion and often obsessed with purity of blood should now be facing a crisis over aliens who consider Spain a land of opportunity. Although the number of illegal immigrants is estimated to be no more than 130,000 to 170,000, these newcomers take jobs away from Spaniards and are blamed (along with Latin Americans, many of whom pass undetected in Spain) for the increase in crime. "This is not yet France. If you go through Madrid it isn't the same urban landscape as Paris. But if we don't adopt a coherent policy with the economic crisis in North Africa and the movement of people in Europe we could become like France."[45]

At the other end of the Mediterranean, Spain has had a historical relationship with the Islamic countries of the Middle East, one that has assumed major importance today given Spain's almost total dependence on imported oil. That special relationship was recognized internationally when Spain was asked to host the Mideast peace talks in November 1991. Spain's belated recognition of Israel in 1986 met with the great displeasure of the Arab League, but the idiosyncratic position in regard to Israel seemed indefensible once Spain joined the European Community, all of whose members recognized Israel. Moreover, Spain's anti-Israeli policy was a holdover from the Franco regime, and it was tainted by that genesis.

American Spain

Spain maintains a deep emotional attachment to Latin America, based on a shared language and culture that, although diluted by time and by massive non-Spanish immigration into all of Latin America, is stronger than the cultural ties that link Great Britain to the United States, for example. After the return to democracy, Spain began to reestablish its presence in Latin America, and the pace of contact accelerated after the Socialists came to power in 1982. King Juan Carlos and Queen Sofía have visited most of the major Latin American nations, and visits between the Spanish prime minister and the various Latin American presidents have taken place on a regular basis, either in the Latin American countries or in Spain. In 1991, the first Summit Meeting of the Iberoamerican Community of Nations (including Portugal and Brazil) was held in Guadalajara, Mexico; the second was held in Madrid in July 1992. Juan Carlos and González have proposed that these meetings take place annually for the rest of the decade. The political objective of the summits is to create a single Iberoamerican voice in the international arena ("una sola voz en el concierto internacional").[46]

When there is friction between Latin American nations, Spain is always ready to offer its good offices. In October 1987, there were conversations in Madrid between the Guatemalan government and Guatemalan guerrillas under the auspices of the Esquipulas II understanding, the latter a peace plan for Central America put forth by Oscar Arias, president of Costa Rica.[47] In 1988, Daniel Ortega, president of Nicaragua, asked Spain to take part in the verification group to oversee the fulfillment of the pacification of Central America, also under the Esquipulas understanding.[48] In

April 1989, former Spanish Prime Minister Adolfo Suárez was in Carácas to arbitrate the territorial dispute between Venezuela and Colombia.[49] In the same year, Honduras asked Spain to oversee the demobilization of the Nicaraguan contras in Honduras.[50] (In a turnabout, Carlos Andrés Pérez, president of Venezuela, offered to mediate between the Spanish government and ETA.[51]

Reflecting these realities, the Socialist government has adopted a policy toward Latin America that (1) supports the Latin American cause vis-à-vis the United States; (2) encourages initiatives in favor of peace and democracy *that have the backing of Latin America*; and (3) stimulates Europe's political support for these initiatives and the European Community's economic cooperation with them.[52]

Spain's role in Latin America has increasingly taken on a European dimension. Since its admission to the EC in 1986, Spain increasingly sees itself as the bridge between the community and Latin America, furnishing through the EC resources that Spain alone cannot provide. As we have seen, the stated objective of the Summit Meetings of the Iberoamerican Community of Nations is to give its members a common voice in the international arena. Spain is the major European voice in the Iberoamerican Community of Nations (one that Portugal might resent but is not sufficiently strong to oppose effectively). Spain, then, sees itself as the vital member common to both communities. In a speech given in October 1991 before the Permanent Council of the Organization of American States, Juan Carlos stressed the links that exit between Spain and Latin America but also highlighted Spain's role in bringing the European Community and the Iberoamerican Community of Nations together: "Spain has gone beyond the path of mere words with Latin America. Spain now aids its former colonies not only through the Treaties of Friendship and Cooperation but also from its position within the European Community ... where it has contributed to changing the attitude, in certain cases decisively, of its fellow members toward Latin America."[53]

Spain's relationship with the United States has improved considerably since the referendum on NATO in 1986, whose terms guaranteed Spain a more favorable position with NATO but especially with the United States. Although Spain could never be the equal of the U.S. colossus, given the latter's size, wealth, and resources, it is today less unequal than it had been since the agreements made in 1953 (subsequently renewed and then turned into treaty) that exchanged money for bases. Many Spaniards believe that the agreements compromised Spanish sovereignty, and even more are convinced that the money that flowed into Spain after 1953 underwrote twenty more years of Francoist repression.

In 1982, in the waning days of the UCD governments, Spain and the United States signed a bilateral treaty that seemed to ignore Spain's new democratic status. Under the terms of the treaty, money would still be exchanged for bases (as in Franco's day), and though Spain was able to exercise more control than before over military forces on its own soil, the presence of those forces remained as it had been since 1953. When the Socialists came into power in 1982, it was understood that fundamental changes in the Hispano-American relationship would have to take place, particularly the assumption that the United States somehow had a *right* to maintain its military presence in Spain. As noted earlier, treaties negotiated after 1986 called for a reduction in the U.S. presence and the removal of certain forces from the peninsula. But most important of all, the new agreement renounced any kind of economic or military aid as a condition for the use of the bases, putting Spain and the United States on more equal footing. "For the first time in the history of Spain-U.S. relations this use is legitimized by the existence of mutual security interests."[54]

In understanding the relationship between the United States and Spain, it cannot be forgotten that the average Spaniard has never felt gratitude toward the United States. U.S. forces did not liberate Spain from oppression as they did Italy and Germany in World War II, and Spain did not share in the largesse of the Marshall Plan. When the Americans did arrive in 1953, they were associated not with democracy but with authoritarianism. The absence of democratic institutions in Spain did not prevent the United States from dealing with Franco and thereby legitimizing his regime internationally. These memories of what many Spaniards consider U.S. complicity with Franco are fading, but a low-grade anti-Americanism lingers.

European Spain

For Spain, democracy was identified with Europe, and Spain's renewed democracy has been its passport to the continent. Without democracy, Spain would have had to live along the periphery of the pan-European entity now coming into being. With democracy, Spain has become a vital force within that entity and an exemplar to those nation-states east of the Oder-Neisse that are now struggling to achieve what Spain has already accomplished and hoping for acceptance into the European family, just as Spain had.

> To ignore Spain is to ignore a country that allows us better to comprehend the most important problems of the contemporary world: the crisis of democracies, the establishment and consolidation of democracy, the problems of multilingual and multinational societies, the processes of change in the Catholic Church and the secularization of society, changes in value systems, generational conflicts, demographic transformations, the transition from an agrarian to an industrial society.[55]

Adam Przeworski wrote in 1991:

> Since 1976, in only fifteen years Spain has succeeded in irreversibly consolidating democratic institutions, allowing peaceful alternation in power; in modernizing its economy and making it internationally competitive; in imposing civilian control over the military; in solving complicated national questions; in extending citizenship rights, and in inducing cultural changes that made it part of the European community of nations. And this is what everyone in Eastern Europe expects to happen. Eastern Europeans deeply believe that if it had not been for "the system," they would have been like Spain. And now this system is gone. They will thus reenter Europe. They will become a part of the West.[56]

Beyond its unique, but passive* role as a model for both peaceful transition from dictatorship to democracy and successful modernization, how has Spain's role changed in post–Cold War Europe? Probably, it is very little changed except for its membership in the European organizations that are the lure for Eastern Europe and perhaps even Russia. Spain was not a significant player in the Cold War (even though U.S. bases on its territory would have been enemy targets should the war have turned from cold to hot); as a consequence, the end of the Cold War did not change the essential circumstances of Spain's place in the world. Its identity and strength today are defined within the European collective. Apart from its special interests in Africa and Latin America (and even the latter has a growing European dimension), Spain's interests are Europe's interests, and Europe's interests are Spain's. As Europe adapts to the post–Cold War reality, so, too, will Spain adapt but as a part of the greater European entity.

Spain does have its preoccupations, however. It fears competition from the Eastern European countries for EC resources, foreign investments, and trading opportunities. It is also concerned that there might develop a new economic and political axis linking east and west across Northern Europe, marginalizing Spain's position on the continent—particularly if the European Community opens its ranks to former Soviet bloc nations. And the PSOE is troubled that the left-of-center parties in Southern Europe would lose political emphasis in the Socialist International, the worldwide social democratic movement, should the Eastern European parties come aboard.[57]

---

*One says *passive* because now that the Eastern European nations are undergoing their own political and economic transformations, they are not turning to Spanish experts as their mentors.

But these concerns about contingencies in no way weaken Spain's strong, secure, and proud commitment to the new Europe that is coming into being.

FINAL MUSINGS

With the ruinous Spanish-American War at the turn of the twentieth century, Spain fell into international ignominy. In the decades that followed, domestic calamity took Spain even lower—into military rule, the lethal democratic experiment of the Second Republic, the armageddon of the Civil War, and finally, forty years of dictatorship. True enough, there were positive aspects to the authoritarian regime, but it remained a dictatorship none the less.

Then, with the death of the autocrat, a miracle seemed to have occurred. The dictator's carefully groomed successor rejected his oligarchic inheritance and chose, instead, to lead his country toward democracy. Encrusted layers of self-destructive political and social behavior were cast off, as were the institutions of repression that had allegedly been created to contain such behavior. Gradually, a new Spain began to emerge, perhaps not the "iridescent gem" that Ortega y Gasset had envisioned years earlier from within the wreckage of his country but a resplendent example to others and a source of deserved pride to itself. As it prepares to enter the twenty-first century, Spain is closer to greatness than at any time since the end of its Golden Age.

NOTES

1. José Luis Gutiérrez and Amando de Miguel, *La ambición del César* (Madrid: Ediciones Temas de Hoy, 1989), p. 13. The translation is mine.

2. With 38.6 percent of the vote, the PSOE won 159 seats in the Congress, a plurality 17 seats short of an absolute majority. With 34.8 percent of the vote, the PP won 141 seats. The IU won 18 seats, the CiU 17, and the PNV 5. All other parties won a total of 10 seats. *Facts on File: World News Digest with Cumulative Index*, vol. 53, no. 2741 (June 10, 1993), p. 431.

3. *El Pais*, International Edition, December 21, 1992.

4. Federico G. Gil and Joseph S. Tulchin, eds., *Spain's Entry into NATO, Conflicting Practical and Strategic Perspectives* (Boulder and London: Lynne Rienner Publishers, 1980), p. 71.

5. *Britannica World Data* (Chicago: Encyclopedia Britannica).

6. *Statistical Yearbook/UNESCO* (Paris: UNESCO).

7. International Bank for Reconstruction and Development, *The World Bank Atlas* (Washington, D.C.: World Bank).

8. *World Development Report* (New York: Oxford University Press).

9. Organization for Economic Co-operation and Development, *More Economic Indicators: Historical Statistics* (Paris: Organization for Economic Co-operation and Development).

10. *New York Times*, November 17, 1992, sec. D, p. 1.

11. Ibid., February 13, 1989, sec. D, p. 12.

12. Ibid., January 27, 1990, sec. A, p. 7.

13. Ibid.

14. European Commission, Spanish Finance Ministry, in ibid., November 17, 1992, sec. D, p. 1.

15. "Spain Survey," *The Economist*, April 25, 1992, p. 6.

16. *New York Times*, September 17, 1990, sec. D, p. 4.

17. *Facts on File: World News Digest with Cumulative Index*, vol. 52 (December 1992), p. 994.

18. *New York Times*, November 17, 1992, sec. D, p. 17.

19. *Wall Street Journal*, March 17, 1993, sec. A, p. 10.

20. *New York Times*, November 17, 1992, sec. D, p. 1.

21. Ibid., p. 17.

22. *Facts on File: World News Digest with Cumulative Index*, vol. 50 (December 1990), p. 983.

23. *Facts on File:World News Digest with Cumulative Index*, vol. 51 (August 1991), p. 581.

24. *Facts on File: World News Digest with Cumulative Index*, vol. 51 (May 1991), pp. 366–367.

25. *El Pais*, International Edition, October 5, 1992, pp. 1, 23, 24.

26. *New York Times*, February 13, 1989, sec. D, p. 12.

27. Ibid., September 17, 1990, sec. D, p. 4.

28. *Facts on File: World News Digest with Cumulative Index*, vol. 52 (November 1992), p. 898.

29. *El Pais*, International Edition, October 26, 1992.

30. Ibid., June 15, 1987.

31. E. Ramón Arango, *Spain: From Repression to Renewal* (Boulder: Westview Press, 1985), p. 223.

32. *El Pais*, International Edition, April 20, 1987.

33. Ibid., April 20, 1987.

34. Ibid., October 26, 1992.

35. *Keesing's Record of World Events*, vol. 34 (February 1983), p. 35,729.

36. *El Pais*, October 26, 1992.

37. Ibid., International Edition, December 7, 1992.

38. Ibid., October 26, 1992.

39. *The Rueter European Report*, July 14, 1993.

40. José Ramón Montero, "Revisiting Democratic Success: Legitimacy and the Meanings of Democracy in Spain," in Richard Gunther, ed., *Politics, Society, and Democracy: The Case of Spain* (Boulder: Westview Press, 1993), p. 143. The chapters that make up this affectionate but academically solid Festschrift honoring Juan J. Linz are of particular interest to the student of Spanish politics because of the

wealth of unpublished material that was made available to the authors, not only by Linz but also by other scholars.

41. Ibid., p. 145.

42. Ibid., p. 146.

43. Ibid., p. 151.

44. Carlos A. Zaldiver, "Conclusion: Spain in Quest of Autonomy and Security—The Policies of the Socialist Governments, 1982–1990," in Kenneth Maxwell, ed., *Spanish Foreign and Defense Policy* (Boulder: Westview Press, 1991), p. 212.

45. *New York Times,* July 5, 1990, p. 4.

46. *El Pais,* International Edition, July 20, 1992, p. 1.

47. Ibid., October 12, 1987, pp. 1, 3.

48. Ibid., February 1, 1988, pp. 1, 2, 3, 14.

49. Ibid., April 3, 1989, p. 6.

50. Ibid., September 11, 1989, p. 11.

51. Ibid., June 12, 1989, pp. 1, 17.

52. Zaldiver, "Conclusion: Spain in Quest of Autonomy and Security," p. 207.

53. *El Pais,* International Edition, October 14, 1991, p. 11.

54. Zaldiver, "Conclusion: Spain in Quest of Autonomy and Security," p. 195.

55. Manuel Gómez-Reino, Francisco A. Orizo and Darío Vila Carro, "Spain: A Recurrent Theme for Juan Linz," in Gunther, ed., *Politics, Society, and Democracy: The Case of Spain*, p. 11.

56. Adam Przeworski, *Democracy and the Market: Political and Economic Reforms in Eastern Europe and Latin America* (Cambridge: Cambridge University Press, 1991), p. 8.

57. *New York Times,* January 27, 1990, p. 7.

Bibliography

Anderson, Charles W. *The Political Economy of Modern Spain*. Madison: University of Wisconsin Press, 1970.

Arango, E. Ramón. *Spain: From Repression to Renewal*. Boulder: Westview Press, 1985.

_____. *The Spanish Political System: Franco's Legacy*. Boulder: Westview Press, 1978.

Balloten, Burnett. *The Grand Camouflage*. London: Pall Mall Press, 1968.

_____. *The Spanish Civil War: Revolution and Counterrevolution*. Chapel Hill: University of North Carolina Press, 1991.

Bonine-Blanc, Andrea. *Spain's Transition to Democracy*. Boulder: Westview Press, 1987.

Borkenau, Franz. *The Spanish Cockpit*. London: Faber and Faber, 1937.

Brenan, Gerald. *The Fall of Spain*. New York: Pellegrini & Cudahy, 1951.

_____. *The Spanish Labyrinth*. Cambridge: Cambridge University Press, 1944.

Carr, Raymond. *Modern Spain, 1875–1980*. New York: Oxford University Press, 1980.

_____. *The Republic and the Civil War*. London: Macmillan, 1971.

_____. *Spain 1808–1975*, 2d ed. London: Oxford University Press, 1966.

Carr, Raymond, and Juan Pablo Fusi. *Spain: Dictatorship to Democracy*. London: George Allen and Unwin, 1979.

Castro, Américo. *The Structure of Spanish History*. Princeton: Princeton University Press, 1954.

Cebrián, Juan Luis. *The Press and Main Street*. Ann Arbor: University of Michigan Press, 1989.

Clark, Robert P., and Michael H. Haltzel, eds. *Spain in the 1980s*. Cambridge, Mass.: Ballinger Publishing, 1987.

Coates, Ken, ed. *ENDpapers Twelve, Spain and NATO*. Nottingham, U.K.: Russell Press, 1986.

Collins, Roger. *The Basques*. New York: Basil Blackwell, 1987.

Coverdale, John. *The Political Transformation of Spain After Franco*. New York: Praeger, 1979.

Crozier, Brian. *Franco: A Biographical History*. London: Eyre & Spottiswoods, 1967.

de Esteban, Jorge, and Luis Lopéz Guerra. *La crisis del estado Franquista*. Barcelona: Editorial Labor, 1977.

319

_____. *El régimen constitutional Español*, 2 vols. Barcelona: Editorial Labor, 1982.

de la Souchère, Elena. *An Explanation of Spain*. New York: Vintage Books, 1964.

de Madariaga, Salvador. *Spain: A Modern History*. New York: Praeger, 1958.

Donaghy, Peter J. and Michael T. Newton. *Spain: A Guide to Political and Economic Institutions*. Cambridge: Cambridge University Press, 1987.

Fisher, B. W., and H. Bowen-Jones. *Spain: An Introductory Geography*. New York: Praeger, 1958.

Fusi, J. P. *Franco: A Biography*. London and Sydney: Unwin Hyman, 1987.

Gallo, Max. *Spain Under Franco*. New York: E. P. Dutton, 1974.

Gallop, Roger. *A Book of the Basques*. Reno: University of Nevada Press, 1970.

García San Miguel, Luis. *Teoría de la transición*. Madrid: Editora Nacional, 1981.

Gil, Federico, G. and Joseph S. Tulchin, eds. *Spain's Entry into NATO*. Boulder: Lynne Rienner Publishers, 1988.

Gillespie, Richard. *The Spanish Socialist Party*. Oxford: Clarendon Press, 1989.

Gunther, Richard. *Public Policy in a No-Party State*. Berkeley: University of California Press, 1980.

Gunther, Richard, Giacomo Sani, and Goldie Shabad. *Spain After Franco*. Berkeley: University of California Press, 1986.

Gunther, Richard, ed. *Politics, Society, and Democracy: The Case of Spain*. Boulder: Westview Press, 1993.

Gutierrez, José Luis, and Amando de Miguel. *La Ambición del César*. Madrid: Ediciones Temas de Hoy, 1989.

Harrison, Joseph. *An Economic History of Spain*. New York: Holmes and Meier, 1978.

Herber, Marianne. *The Making of the Basque Nation*. Cambridge: Cambridge University Press, 1989.

Herr, Richard, and John H. R. Potts, eds. *Iberian Identity*. Berkeley: Institute of International Studies, University of California–Berkeley, 1989.

Hills, George. *Franco: The Man and His Nation*. London: Robert Hale, 1967.

Hubert, Henri. *The Greatness and Decline of the Celts*. London: Kegan Paul, French, Trubner and Co., 1934.

Irizarry, Carmen. *The Thirty Thousand: Modern Spain and Protestantism*. New York: Harcourt, Brace & World, 1966.

Jackson, Gabriel. *The Spanish Republic and the Civil War, 1931–1939*. Princeton: Princeton University Press, 1965.

Kamen, Henry. *Inquisition and Society in Spain*. London: Weidenfeld and Nicolson, 1985.

Kaplan, Lawrence S., Robert W. Clawson, and Raimondo Luraghi. *NATO and the Mediterranean*. Wilmington, Del.: Scholarly Resources, 1985.

Lancaster, Thomas D. *Policy Stability and Democratic Change: Energy in Spain's Transition*. University Park: Pennsylvania State University Press, 1989.

Lancaster, Thomas D., and Gary Prevost, eds. *Politics and Change in Spain*. New York: Praeger, 1985.

Lane-Poole, Stanley. *The Story of the Moors in Spain*. Baltimore: Black Classic Press, 1990.

Lannon, Frances, and Paul Preston, eds. *Elites and Power in Twentieth-Century Spain.* Oxford: Clarendon Press, 1990.

Lieberman, Sima. *The Contemporary Spanish Economy: A Historical Perspective.* London: George Allen and Unwin, 1982.

Malefakis, Edward E. *Agrarian Reform and Peasant Revolution in Spain: Origins of the Civil War.* New Haven: Yale University Press, 1970.

Maravall, José María. *Dictatorship and Political Dissent: Workers and Students in Franco's Spain.* New York: St. Martin's Press, 1979.

_____. *The Transition to Democracy in Spain.* New York: St. Martin's Press, 1982.

Marías, Julián. *Understanding Spain.* Ann Arbor: University of Michigan Press, 1990.

Mariéjol, Jean Hippolyte. *The Spain of Ferdinand and Isabella.* New Brunswick, N.J.: Rutgers University Press, 1961.

Martínez, Rafael Bañón, and Thomas M. Barker, eds. *Armed Forces and Society in Spain Past and Present.* New York: Columbia University Press, 1988.

Maxwell, Kenneth, ed. *The Press and the Rebirth of Iberian Democracy.* Westport, Conn.: Greenwood Press, 1983.

_____. *Spanish Foreign and Defense Policy.* Boulder: Westview Press, 1991.

McDonagh, Gary W., ed. *Conflict in Catalonia.* Gainesville: University of Florida Press, 1986.

O'Donnell, Guillermo, Philippe C. Schmitter, and Laurence Whitehead, eds. *Transitions from Authoritarian Rule: Comparative Perspectives.* Baltimore: Johns Hopkins University Press, 1986.

_____. *Transitions from Authoritarian Rule: Latin America.* Baltimore: Johns Hopkins University Press, 1986.

_____. *Transitions from Authoritarian Rule: Southern Europe.* Baltimore: Johns Hopkins University Press, 1986.

_____. *Transitions from Authoritarian Rule: Tentative Conclusions about Uncertain Democracies.* Baltimore: Johns Hopkins University Press, 1986.

Orwell, George. *Homage to Catalonia.* New York: Harcourt Brace and World, 1952.

Payne, Stanley G. *Basque Nationalism.* Reno: University of Nevada Press, 1975.

_____. *Falange.* Stanford: Stanford University Press, 1961.

_____. *The Franco Regime, 1936–1975.* Madison: University of Wisconsin Press, 1987.

_____. *Franco's Spain.* New York: Crowell, 1967.

_____. *A History of Spain and Portugal,* 2 vols. Madison: University of Wisconsin Press, 1973.

_____. *Politics and the Military in Modern Spain.* Stanford: Stanford University Press, 1976.

_____. *Spain's First Democracy: The Second Republic, 1931–1936.* Madison: University of Wisconsin Press, 1993.

_____. *Spanish Catholicism.* Madison: University of Wisconsin Press, 1984.

_____. *The Spanish Revolution.* New York: W. W. Norton, 1970.

Payne, Stanley G., ed. *Politics and Society in Twentieth-Century Spain.* New York: New Viewpoints, 1976.

_____. *The Politics of Democratic Spain*. Chicago: Chicago Council on Foreign Relations, 1986.

Pérez-Díaz, Victor M. *The Return of Civil Society*. Cambridge, Mass.: Harvard University Press, 1993.

Preston, Paul. *The Coming of the Spanish Civil War*. London: Macmillan, 1978.

_____. *Franco, A Biography*. London: Harper Collins Publishers, 1993.

_____. *The Triumph of Democracy in Spain*. New York: Methuen & Co., 1986.

Pritchett, V. S. *The Spanish Temper*. New York: Knopf, 1954.

Rial, James H. *Revolution from Above*. Fairfax, Va.: George Mason University Press, 1986.

Salisbury, William T., and James D. Theberge, eds. *Spain in the 1970s: Economics, Social Structure, Foreign Policy*. New York: Praeger, 1976.

Share, Donald. *The Making of Spanish Democracy*. New York: Praeger, 1986.

Shub, Joyce Lasky, and Raymond Carr, eds. *Spain, Studies in Political Security*. New York: Praeger, 1985.

Tamames, Ramón. *Estructura económica de España*. Madrid: Guadiana de Publicaciones, 1976.

_____. *Introducción a la constitución española*. Madrid: Alianza Editorial, 1980.

_____. *La república, la era de Franco*. Madrid: Alianza Editorial, 1973.

_____. *The Spanish Economy: An Introduction*. New York: St. Martin's Press, 1986.

Thomas, Hugh. *The Spanish Civil War*. New York: Harper & Row, 1963.

Tovias, Alfred. *Foreign Economic Relations of the European Community: The Impact of Spain and Portugal*. Boulder: Lynne Rienner Publishers, 1990.

Trythall, J.W.O. *El Caudillo: A Political Biography of Franco*. New York: McGraw-Hill, 1970.

Vicens Vives, Jaime. *Approaches to the History of Spain*, trans. and ed. Joan Connelly Ullmann. Berkeley: University of California Press, 1967.

_____. *An Economic History of Spain*. Princeton: Princeton University Press, 1969.

Wright, Alison. *The Spanish Economy, 1956–1976*. London: Macmillan, 1977.

About the Book
and Author

Since the death of Franco in 1975, Spain has passed from repression through renewal to democracy, restored for the first time since 1936. Having survived the threat to its very existence in 1981, democratic Spain—now a member of the European Union and the North Atlantic Treaty Organization—seems as secure as any of its European neighbors. The accession to power in 1982 of the first socialist government in Spanish history marked the smooth transition from right to left that many, including Arango, believe was the crucial rite of passage to stable democracy. *Spain: Democracy Regained* is a greatly expanded and revised version of *Spain: From Repression to Renewal.* Aside from his presentation of historical and geographical background and of the Franco years, the author has rewritten the remainder of his study, utilizing a wide array of new information and interpretation. Arango explores the function of the military, reinterprets the role of the king in the transition and in the 1981 crisis, and provides a thorough analysis of political parties. He reexamines the state of the economy under the socialist government and reassesses Spain's most intractable problem—ETA violence—and its greatest strength—the exuberant Spanish culture that was given international exposure in 1992 at the World's Fair in Seville and at the Olympic Games in Barcelona. Woven throughout are Arango's fresh insights into Spanish society and politics during the socialist decade.

E. Ramón Arango is a professor of political science at Louisiana State University, Baton Rouge.

Index